DEBUGGING THE UNIVERSE

The Wave or Adventures with Cassiopaea by Laura Knight-Jadczyk

Riding the Wave (vol. 1)
Soul Hackers (vol. 2)
Stripped to the Bone (vol. 3)
Through a Glass Darkly (vol. 4)
Petty Tyrants & Facing the Unknown (vols. 5 & 6)
Almost Human (vol. 7)
Debugging the Universe (vol. 8)

Other books by Laura Knight-Jadczyk

The Secret History of the World and How to Get Out Alive
9/11: The Ultimate Truth (with Joe Quinn)
High Strangeness: Hyperdimensions and the Process of Alien Abduction

LAURA KNIGHT-JADCZYK

DEBUGGING THE UNIVERSE

THE HERO'S JOURNEY

Red Pill Press

TABLE OF CONTENTS

CHAPTER 64
CROSSING THE THRESHOLD

THE HERO'S JOURNEY

During the early months of 1996 the Cassiopaean sessions were often quite personal. This was a consequence of the tremendous changes going on in my life, many of which were occurring at some other level of reality and could be sensed only dimly and "through a glass darkly." When I look back over the events, the transformations, I can see the pattern. But, at the time I could see nothing but the desperate struggle to normalize and stabilize my world, which was growing more bizarre by the day.

With hindsight, I understand that I was playing out a drama – a timeless vision – that is derived from the mythology of ancient times that is everywhere the same. And, having passed through this initiatory "script," I write these pages in an effort to convey what these stories teach us.

During my research into the origin and meaning of my experiences with the Cassiopaeans, I have delved into the work of many who have gone before in the effort to solve the great mystery. Today, we have archaeologists digging up evidence all over the globe; ethnologists are recording stories from peoples East and West; and a generation of Orientalists have revealed to us the sacred writings of the archaic peoples that gave birth to our religions and cultures. Meanwhile, scholars are organizing and analyzing material relating to the psychological bases of language, myth, religion, art and ethics. And, quite remarkably, the revelations of the mind emerging from the field of psychology and biology are offering clues to the ancient technology depicted in myth and legend. Because, in the end, it is becoming increasingly clear that the logic, the heroic gestures, and the deeds of myth are with us today.

My own experiences, in this sense, could even be compared to an enacting of the cosmic archetype of the Renewal of Time.

In the myths of archaic peoples, the rites and beliefs surrounding the idea of the renewal of time vary from group to group and place to place. But the themes are still fairly consistent in that before time can be renewed, there are certain phases of chaos that must be endured. Of course, I didn't know all this at the time; I just suffered and acted the part in complete ignorance of what was taking place. And it may be so that my ignorance of the hold the archetype had on me was essential to its work.

The energies of our archetypes can "fill us with radiant light, or overwhelm us with destruction and despair. They are our gods within, spiritually and instinctually." (Woodman 1992)

Archetypal energies can be activated in a variety of ways. A specific archetype can be activated in the psyche of one individual, or in the collective psyche of a group or a culture. The danger lies in not understanding the nature of the archetype – in believing ourselves to *be* the archetype itself and thereby confusing our personal values with some absolute and exclusive version of the truth. The crucial point that must be understood is the difference between allowing the archetypal energies to act through the self, as opposed to believing that one has *become* the deity. This distinction is the difference between hubris and humility. One must realize that one is a simple and sacred soul who has, for unfathomable reasons, been graced by the gods. Any attempt to alter the drama, any idea that one *is* the archetype, and therefore has the right or ability to choose to act other than according to the divine script, can end in disaster.

So, it's really a good thing that, at the time and at that level of knowledge, I had no idea what was happening!

The essential part of the Renewal of Time archetype is the idea of the end and the beginning of a temporal period based on bio-cosmic rhythms and forming part of a larger system. The purging and expulsion of sin was the chief drama before the New Year could be born. Mircea Eliade writes:

> [T]his annual expulsion of sins, diseases, and demons is basically an attempt to restore – if only momentarily – mythical and primordial time, "pure" time, the time of the "instant" of the Creation. Every New Year is a resumption of time from the beginning, that is, a repetition of the cosmogony. The ritual combats between two groups of actors, the presence of the dead, the Saturnalia, and the orgies are so many elements which ... denote that at the end of the year and in the expectation of the New Year there is a repetition of the mythical moment of the passage from chaos to cosmos.
>
> ... [I]n each of these systems we find the same central idea of the yearly return to chaos, followed by a new creation. ...
>
> ... (Baptism is equivalent to the ritual death of the old man followed by a new birth. On the cosmic level, it is equivalent to the deluge: abolition of contours, fusion of all forms, return to the formless.) ...
>
> ... [A]ll the rest is only the application, on different planes answering to different needs, of the same archetypal gesture: the regeneration of the world and life through repetition of the cosmogony. (Eliade 1954, 54, 58, 59, 62)

The Hermetic maxim: "As above, so below" may be a key to understanding the events and experiences of the Cassiopaean communications. Joseph Campbell remarks, "myth is the secret opening through which the inexhaustible energies of the cosmos pour into human cultural manifestation." (Campbell 1949, 1)

Of course, at the time, I had no idea that I was acting out an archetype. The very thought would have filled me with horror. I remember that, back in the '80s, when I was wrestling with the problem of why I had been born with such a huge question mark in my mind with no apparent outlet for this questing energy, I knew that I must begin to do something. At the time, meditation seemed the right answer, and I began the practice with some hesitation. I was hesitant because I was afraid of change.

On the one hand, meditation might change my perceptions and perspective enabling me to be calm and accepting about the restrictions of my life. As much as I needed this calm, that scared me. What if I accepted the restrictions and I was supposed to do otherwise? Would contemplating my navel turn me into a mindless zombie, fit only to stand on street corners and sell pencils?

On the other hand, meditation might actually elevate the dissatisfaction I was already feeling with my life, in which case I might take steps to change it; and that scared me. I wanted things to change, but only a little, and only the way I wanted them to change.

I had my life set up and organized; I was married and had children and I had a fairy tale idea of how marriage and raising children was supposed to turn out. Anything that threatened that vision was to be rejected, pushed away and denied.

But there was the ever-increasing problem that the fairy tale was *not* happening according to plan, so something had to be done about that. I was really between a rock and a hard place; and for lack of any other alternative, I began to meditate. When you are between a rock and a hard place, the only way out is up.

And as we know, that decision led, step by step, to communication with the Cassiopaeans. And all through the process, for over ten years, I struggled to have my cake and eat it too. I was determined to grow and learn and expand my spiritual horizons as far as was possible; and I was going to keep on living my regular life too, damn it!

CALL TO ADVENTURE

I had read and heard about, and even had seen, many instances when one partner in a marriage would grow and change and the other would either remain static or go exactly the other direction, and the marriage would end up on the rocks as a result of the widening gulf between the partners. My opinion of this phenomenon was rather narrow and judgmental. How could something that was spiritual lead to so much pain and heartache? If these people were really as spiritual as they claimed to be, wouldn't they be able to use their spirituality to preserve their marriages and contribute to the growth of their spouses? Doesn't charity begin at home? It seemed to me that the problem was a lack of communication. Surely if the partners made the effort to communicate, to share all that was happening inside them, to support and encourage the other to remain at their side, such problems would not develop.

So, from the very beginning of my quest, I was talking, talking, talking. I explained the way I saw the problems. I explained what I had learned about people with similar problems. I explained the solutions that were possible. I explained my plan to seek solutions so that our fairy tale could manifest.

I sent away for books and tapes for meditation, for mind reprogramming, for every aspect of changing one's reality that seemed to be a problem in our lives. I wanted to help my husband overcome his negative view of the world so that his family could follow his lead into happiness and prosperity. I wanted to gently and subtly encourage a new vision that he could embrace that would enable him to manifest his dreams, thereby setting an example for the children and becoming the true, knowledgeable and fearless head of the household of my fairy tale. I wanted open communication and true intimacy of thought, emotion and soul in my marriage. I was ready and willing to strip my soul naked in order to break the ice and make my husband comfortable in doing so as well. I had been called, and I chose to follow the call. I didn't want to go and leave him. I desperately wanted him to come with me. If he did, I was sure that he would then manifest as the One.

I understood, in a sense, what I was seeking: I was looking for the Ark, for redemption, for the hero whose existence would liberate me. Joseph Campbell writes:

> The hero is the man of self-achieved submission. But submission to what? That precisely is the riddle that today we have to ask ourselves and that it is everywhere the primary virtue and historic deed of the hero to have solved. (Campbell 1949, 11)

I didn't realize that:

> ... schism in the soul ... will not be resolved by any scheme of return to the good old days (archaism), or by programs guaranteed to render an ideal projected future (futurism), or even by the most realistic, hardheaded work to weld together again the deteriorating elements. Only birth can conquer death – the birth not of the old thing again, but of something new. Within the soul ... there must be ... a continuous "recurrence of birth" ... (Toynbee, quoted by Campbell, 11–12)

I didn't understand that in beginning the process, by answering the call, I had begun the work of the hero myself.

> ... [T]he first work of the hero is to retreat from the world scene of secondary effects to those causal zones of the psyche where the difficulties really reside, and there to clarify the difficulties, eradicate them in his own case (i.e., give battle to the nursery demons of his local culture) and break through to the undistorted, direct experience and assimilation of what C.G. Jung has called "the archetypal images." This is the process known to Hindu and Buddhist philosophy as *viveka*, "discrimination."

The archetypes to be discovered and assimilated are precisely those that have inspired, throughout the annals of human culture, the basic images of ritual, mythology, and vision. These "Eternal Ones of the Dream" are not to be confused with the personally modified symbolic figures that appear in nightmare and madness to the still tormented individual. Dream is the personalized myth, myth the depersonalized dream ... in myth the problems and solutions shown are directly valid for all mankind.

... Such a one's visions, ideas, and inspirations come pristine from the primary springs of human life and thought. Hence they are eloquent, of the unquenched source through which society is reborn. The hero has died as a modern man; but as eternal man – perfected, unspecific, universal man – he has been reborn. His second solemn task and deed therefore ... is to return to us, transfigured, and teach the lesson he has learned of life renewed. (Campbell 1949, 12, 14–15)

And what is this lesson? Ah! Let's not jump ahead! We are still in the past of this narrative. But, Joseph Campbell has defined the heroic journey as follows:

A hero ventures forth from the world of common day into a region of supernatural wonder: fabulous forces are there encountered and a decisive victory is won: the hero comes back from this mysterious adventure with the power to bestow boons on his fellow man.

... [T]he adventure of the hero normally follows the pattern of ... a separation from the world, a penetration to some source of power, and a life-enhancing return. ... the really creative acts are represented as those deriving from some sort of dying to the world ...

The return and reintegration with society, which is *indispensable to the continuous circulation of spiritual energy into the world,* and which, from the standpoint of the community, is the justification of the long retreat, the hero himself may find the most difficult requirement of all. ... there is danger that the bliss of this experience may annihilate all recollection of, interest in, or hope for, the sorrows of the world; or else the problem of making known the way of illumination to people wrapped in economic problems may seem too great to solve. And on the other hand, if the hero, instead of submitting to all of the initiatory tests, has, like Prometheus, simply darted to his goal (by violence, quick device, or luck) and plucked the boon for the world that he intended, then the powers that he has unbalanced may react so sharply that he will be blasted from within and without – crucified, like Prometheus, on the rock of his own violated unconscious. Or if the hero, in the third place, makes his safe and willing return, he may meet with such a blank misunderstanding and disregard from those whom he has come to help that his career will collapse. ...

The composite hero of the monomyth is a personage of exceptional gifts. Frequently he is honored by his society, frequently [he is] unrecognized or disdained. He and/or the world in which he finds himself suffers from a symbolical deficiency. In fairy tales this may be as slight as the lack of a certain golden ring, whereas in apocalyptic vision the physical and spiritual life of the whole earth can be represented as fallen, or on the point of falling, into ruin.

Typically, the hero of the fairy tale achieves a domestic, microcosmic triumph, and the hero of myth a world-historical, macrocosmic triumph. Whereas the former – the youngest despised child who becomes the master of extraordinary powers – prevails over his personal oppressors, the latter brings back from his adventure the means for the regeneration of his society as a whole. ...

The cosmogonic cycle is presented with astonishing consistency in the sacred writings of all the continents, and gives to the adventure of the hero a new and interesting turn; for now it appears that *the perilous journey was a labor not of attainment but of reattainment, not discovery but rediscovery. The godly powers sought and dangerously won are revealed to have been within the heart of the hero all the time.* [Laura's note: the Ruby Slippers!] He is "the king's son" who has come to know who he is and therewith has entered into the exercise of his proper power – "God's son," who has learned to know how much that title means. From this point of view the hero is symbolical of that divine creative and redemptive image which is hidden within us all, only waiting to be known and rendered into life. ...

The effect of the successful adventure of the hero is the unlocking and release again of the flow of life into the body of the world. ...

The torrent pours from an invisible source, the point of entry being the center of the symbolic circle of the universe, the Immovable Spot of the Buddha legend, around which the world may be said to revolve. Beneath this spot is the earth-supporting head of the cosmic serpent, the dragon, symbolical of the waters of the abyss, which are the divine life-creative energy and substance of the demiurge ... The tree of life, i.e., the universe itself, grows from this point. It is rooted in the supporting darkness; the golden sun bird perches on its peak; a spring, the inexhaustible well, bubbles at its foot. [The tree of life is also] the figure of the cosmic man or woman ... for the hero as the incarnation of God is himself the navel of the world, the umbilical point through which the energies of eternity break into time.

... Wherever a hero has been born, has wrought, or has passed back into the void, the place is marked and sanctified. A temple is erected there to signify and inspire the miracle of perfect centeredness; for this is the place of the breakthrough into abundance. Someone at this point discovered eternity. ...

... [A] temple can be established anywhere. Because, finally, the All is everywhere, and anywhere may become the seat of power. ...

The World Navel, then, is ubiquitous. And since it is the source of all existence, it yields the world's plenitude of both good and evil. Ugliness and beauty, sin and virtue, pleasure and pain, are equally its production. "To God all things are fair and good and right," declares Heraclitus; "but men hold some things wrong and some right." (Campbell 1949, 23, 28, 29–31, 32, 35)

Well, all of that is fine and good. But what does it really mean in practical terms? It is my intention to make it comprehensible for those who are here to perform the heroic gesture. It is only in this way that the work of the hero can be done, for he is many.

The way it seems to happen (and the reader will surely want to ponder Joseph Campbell's insightful analysis for connections and examples of their own quest) is that *something that seems to be an ordinary chance encounter reveals another world of archetypal forces.*

REFUSAL OF THE CALL

If I had to pick a single event that hinted a door was about to open, it would be the night I hypnotized Pam, the hypnotherapy client I wrote about in my book *High Strangeness*, with the intention of proving the alien abduction scenario was merely repressed childhood trauma, and realizing a few days later that something remarkable had happened. But, in a much broader sense, the strange events had been happening since I was born. Perhaps it could even be said that the quest proper began when I started to actively seek answers in a systematic way, resulting in my writing a manuscript I entitled "The Noah Syndrome" which was later absorbed into my book, *The Secret History of The World*. From that point on, the synchronous events in my life multiplied until I was no longer even able to talk about them in an ordinary way for fear of being considered completely bonkers!

Of course, according to Freud[1] and Jung, such ordinary chance encounters are not ordinary at all. Freud saw them as the result of suppressed desires and conflicts, ripples on the surface of life produced by some deep spring from which reality wells up. Jung coined the term "synchronicity" to describe what physicists prefer to call the "acausal connecting principle." The nature of synchronicity is that is has meaning, and most especially it is evidence of a profound activation of energy deep within the psyche. It is as if the formation of patterns within the unconscious mind are accompanied by physical patterns in the outer world. Nevertheless, in some cases, such a chance event can open the door to destiny. Or, it can be shoved under the rug and forgotten.

The next event is what Campbell calls the "herald." Heralds issue challenges and announce the coming of significant change. They can make their appearance anytime during a journey, but often appear at the beginning to announce a Call to Adventure. The herald is a crisis of something completely supernatural and manifests powers that are not ordinary to the real world. For me, this was the actual seeing of the flying black boomerang-shaped object in the sky above my house. Such an event lifts the curtain on a particular drama which, when complete, amounts to dying and rebirth. It is something that is beyond the familiar categories of one's life; it is outside the concepts, ideals and emotional patterns by which one has ordered one's existence; its occurrence causes everything else to no longer fit.

But then again, the first event of the flying black boomerangs, being synchronous to the encounter with Pam, was part of this crisis. They were four months apart, but the entire period was a crisis for me. Facing the possible fact that there was another reality controlling or interacting with our own was a world shattering event for me. As I tell people in a sort of joking way: of all the people who never

---

[1] I've since come to think of Freud as a complete psychopath due to my extensive research into psychopathology.

wanted to know anything about aliens and UFOs, I deserve a place at the head of the line. Few people really comprehend how deeply serious this remark is.

In many fairy tales and myths, the herald is a frog, a dragon, a serpent or some other manifestation of the demiurgic powers of the abyss. In stories, this event produces anxiety, shortness of breath, painful tightening of the chest, and other unpleasant symptoms. For me, this was certainly the case because I was attacked by the same terrible symptoms night after night after night at exactly the same time that I had seen the winged object in the sky on August 16, 1993. It is thought that these symptoms symbolize passage across a threshold, a trial akin to birth.

But, it is the birth into our world of the reality of the serpent, the representative of the deep unconscious, the realm from where our world manifests, in which are found unfathomable depths of the rejected, the unacknowledged, the unrecognized, the unknown and undeveloped elements of our existence.

So it happens that the herald, the announcer of the adventure, is dark, terrifying, painful and seen as evil by the world. And right here is where most people stop. They don't realize that if they can follow the herald through the darkness, the veiled and mysterious unknown, the way would open into the light of day. People do not realize that, in order to diminish darkness, they must focus on it. The notion that we may find God only by entering the pit of darkness is antithetical to our views of good and evil, which, we imagine, must inhabit opposite poles that can never be joined. And yet the name Lucifer is derived from *lucem ferre*, or "bringer of light." When the herald calls us into the place of nightmares, if our hearts are pure, we may discover a vision of divinity. Mephistopheles described himself to Faust as "a living part of that power which perpetually thinks evil and does good."

How can this be?

Remember Tolkien's *Lord of the Rings*? It was a journey made by an elf, a dwarf, a wizard, two men and four hobbits, who made their way across a perilous landscape in order to destroy the power of the Lord of the Rings. In Tolkien's story, as in the real world, a war between the forces of Knowledge (love) and Ignorance (exploitation) is being waged.

Unfortunately, many people who have these encounters with the herald, believe that it is the God, and do not understand that the role of the alien encounters is initiatory in a real sense. Those who are taken in by them and believe the lies have already failed the first test of the hero. They do not realize that the alien drama will disappear from their lives once they have adjusted the alignment of forces within their soul and have become consciously aware of the precise nature of the drama.

Synchronicities are associated with periods of transformation. It is as if this internal restructuring produces external resonances like a burst of mental energy propagating outward into the physical world. The task is, as the Sufis say, to keep a cool head. And to be able to accommodate an expansion of awareness into the unseen while still keeping one's feet on the ground, maneuvering in the real world of secondary effects and causes perceived at higher levels.

So it is that for each of us who journeys through the realm of darkness and finds his or her way home, we make the path clearer and wider for others to follow. It's a dirty job, but somebody's gotta do it!

And there I was: I had heard the summons; the herald had arrived and beckoned me to the threshold.

> Whether in dream or myth, in these adventures there is an atmosphere of irresistible fascination about the figure that appears suddenly as guide, marking a new period, a new stage, in the biography. That which has to be faced, and is somehow profoundly familiar to the unconscious – though unknown, surprising, and even frightening to the conscious personality – makes itself known; and what formerly was meaningful may become strangely emptied of value ... Thereafter, even though the hero returns for a while to his familiar occupations, they may be found unfruitful. A series of signs of increasing force then will become visible, until ... the summons can no longer be denied. (Campbell 1949, 46)

How I had struggled to make life normal. How I struggled to return to the old days. How I railed at the events surrounding me and assaulting me at every turn.

> [The "call to adventure"] signifies that destiny has summoned the hero and transferred his spiritual center of gravity from within the pale of his society to a zone unknown. This fateful region of both treasure and danger may be variously represented: as a distant land, a forest, a kingdom underground, beneath the waves, or above the sky ... but it is always a place of strangely fluid and polymorphous beings, unimaginable torments, superhuman deeds ... (Campbell 1949, 48)

For me, it was the big banana of all of these – and possibly the true source of all the legends about the same: the world of fourth density inhabited by Lizard beings, insect beings, and assorted other terrifying and fabulous creatures impossible to comprehend as real in the terms of our world.

And it was at this point that the relationship between myself and my now ex-husband really ended. You see, it is always a choice. A person can refuse the call. "Many are called; but few choose to answer ... "

Refusal of the summons converts the adventure into its negative. Walled in boredom, hard work, or culture, the subject loses the power of significant affirmative action and becomes a victim to be saved. His flowering world becomes a wasteland of dry stones and his life feels meaningless – even though, like King Minos (of Greek mythology), he may through titanic effort succeed in building an empire of renown. Whatever house he builds, it will be a house of death: a labyrinth of cyclopean walls to hide from him his Minotaur. All he can do is create new problems for himself and await the gradual approach of his disintegration.

The myths and folk tales of the whole world make clear that the refusal is essentially a refusal to give up what one takes to be one's own interest. The future is regarded not in terms of an unremitting series of deaths and births, but as though one's present system of ideals, virtues, goals and advantages were to be fixed and made secure. (Campbell 1949, 49)

That is to say, in response to my experiences, in response to his own experiences of the miraculous, my ex-husband dove into the deepest river in the world: denial. He grabbed hold of his Baptist religion for dear life and began to read the Bible daily to block out thinking and seeing and hearing of anything that didn't fit his programmed system of ideals, virtues and so forth. And it was clear to me that the Bible and the religions of our childhoods had no answers for these issues. In fact, it was clear to me that they had been programmed into us as the very veils over truth past, which we must penetrate in order to move beyond and grow into the true spiritual beings we could become.

It was impossible for him to emerge from the controls of the emotional relationships of his childhood. His parents and their inculcated ideas and programs stood as guardians at the door, terrifying him with the fear of terrible punishment if he stepped outside the bounds of his religion, and he simply was unable to be born again. Like Lot's wife in the story of Sodom and Gomorrah, he was turned to stone because he couldn't stop from turning back, even though he'd received the call to come forth from destruction.

But, again, I did not realize this at the time.

MEETING WITH THE MENTOR

The next stage in the archetypal heroic adventure is the appearance of supernatural aid. In some stories it is a crone, a protective figure, who provides amulets against the dragon forces.

The helpful crone and fairy godmother is a familiar feature of European fairy lore; in Christian saints' legends the role is commonly played by the Virgin. The Virgin by her intercession can win the mercy of the Father. Spider Woman with her web can control the movements of the Sun. The hero who has come under the protection of the Cosmic Mother cannot be harmed. The thread of Ariadne brought Theseus safely through the adventure of the labyrinth. This is the guiding power that runs through the work of Dante in the female figures of Beatrice and the Virgin, and appears in Goethe's Faust successively as Gretchen, Helen of Troy, and the Virgin. ... What such a figure represents is the benign, protecting power of destiny.

Having responded to the call, and continuing to follow courageously as the consequences unfold, the hero finds all the forces of the unconscious at his side. Mother Nature herself supports the mighty task.

... Protective and dangerous, motherly and fatherly at the same time, this supernatural principle of guardianship and direction unites in itself all the ambiguities of the unconscious – thus signifying the support of our conscious personality by that other, larger system, but also the inscrutability of the guide that we are following, to the peril of all our rational ends.

The hero to whom such a helper appears is typically one who has responded to the call. The call, in fact, was the first announcement of the approach of this initiatory priest. But even to those who apparently have hardened their hearts the supernatural guardian may appear; for, as we have seen: "Well able is Allah to save." (Campbell 1949, 59, 60–61)

Well, having the Cassiopaeans come along precisely eleven months to the day following the appearance of the Herald, (in the personification of the Flying Black Boomerangs), I was well on the path of the hero's adventure, even if I had no idea at all that this was what I was doing. And it was to be twenty months before I arrived at the Crossing of the First Threshold.

CROSSING THE FIRST THRESHOLD

With the personifications of his destiny to guide and aid him, the hero goes forward in his adventure until he reaches the Threshold Guardian at the entrance to the zone of magnified power. Such custodians bound the world in the four directions – also up and down – standing for the limits of the hero's present sphere, or life horizon. Beyond them is darkness, the unknown, and danger.

> ... The usual person is more than content, he is even proud, to remain within the indicated bounds, and popular belief gives him every reason to fear so much as the first step into the unexplored. ...
>
> The folk mythologies populate with deceitful and dangerous presence every desert place outside the normal traffic of the village. ...
>
> The regions of the unknown ... are free fields for the projection of the unconscious content. ...
>
> The Arcadian god Pan is the best known Classical example of this dangerous presence dwelling just beyond the protected zone of the village boundary. Sylvanus and Faunus were his Latin counterparts. ... The emotions that he instilled in human beings who by accident adventured into his domain was "panic" fear, a sudden, groundless fright. ... in the frantic effort to escape from his own aroused unconscious the victim expired in a flight of dread. Yet Pan was benign to those who ... properly approached his shrines of healing. Also wisdom, the wisdom of Omphalos, the World Navel, was his to bestow; for the crossing of the threshold is the first step into the sacred zone of the universal source.
>
> ... [There are stories that] illuminate the ambiguities of this perplexing pass and show how, though the terrors will recede before a genuine psychological readiness, the overbold adventurer beyond his depth may be shamelessly undone. (Campbell 1949, 64, 65, 66–67, 68)

As described in volume five, this is where we find me in the early months of 1996. Moving slowly and inexorably to the threshold of the unknown; my conscious mind fighting tooth and nail against the forces of my own essential being. There was the world of practical events in which this drama manifested; and there was, apparently, another reality from which the energies emanated. And learning to see this other reality and to be able to respond to it with no apparent proof seemed to be the big test.

As you might expect, the events surrounding the work on our new magazine, *The Aurora Journal*, took on a *Twilight Zone*-like quality. One of the first things I wanted to do was to find a printer who could do a nice job for me at a reasonable cost since I was paying for it out of my own pocket. There was a print shop near the chiropractor I was still seeing three times a week for therapy, so I decided to stop in and find out what my options were and how much I could do myself to keep the costs low. At the same time, I had printed up a large volume of the Cassiopaean material and thought that it might be cheaper to have it copied, so I hauled it in with me.

The young lady at the counter quoted me a very reasonable price for the copying but said that she couldn't tell me anything about doing a magazine layout because she was just there in a clerical capacity and I would have to come back. I left my material with an order for three copies, bound in a plastic spine.

Several days later I went back to pick up my copies. As the girl was getting them from the back, a woman emerged from the shop area, grinning widely, and said, "I thought that was you I heard out here!" I looked at her blankly because, frankly, I had *no* idea who she was. She must have noticed that I didn't recognize her, because she said "Pam! You remember? I came to you for hypnosis!"

And then I realized who she was. She was the woman I had hypnotized back in 1993 the night the Flying Black Boomerangs were sighted over the three county area. She had been so upset by the idea of an alien abduction lurking in her subconscious that she never came back for further sessions. I'd always wondered what had happened to her since then, and it was very curious to find her in this print shop since she'd told me back then that she was in real estate. It was even stranger when you consider that I'd selected this print shop over any other simply because it was en route between my house and the chiropractor, of whom I was seeing every other day as a result of an accident I was certain was a deliberate attempt on my life by alien forces. Not only that, I was in the print shop for the very purpose of having copies made of material that related to the events in which Pam had been involved at the very beginning. Further, that I was planning on inquiring about the printing of a magazine that was an offshoot of those same events.

I was shocked. She looked like she had aged about twenty years in the almost three years since I had seen her. As it turned out, Pam had recently bought the print shop as a business venture for her kids. She invited me into the back of the shop for coffee and we brought each other up to date on what had been happening in our lives since the incident with the UFOs. That event had upset her so badly that she completely retreated into denial and the "normal life" routine. I told her how that event had done just the opposite for me – I had been catapulted into a series of learning experiences that had completely shattered my previous world, and made it seem like I was on a continual roller coaster ride. I told her: "Honey! If you had any idea of the stuff that has happened to me since you were at my house and opened the door to those damned aliens, you would *not* believe it!" And we both laughed.

So, we spent an hour or so catching up. Pam was fascinated by the story of how the contact with the Cassiopaeans had developed the year following her hypnosis session and wanted not only to read the material, but to attend a session. It turned out that she was very interested in mysteries, or so she claimed. It never occurred to me to wonder why she wasn't interested in her own mystery.

I was, of course, thinking to myself how serendipitous this was for Pam to own this print shop since it just might mean that I could get my magazine printed at a really reasonable price.

As we talked, Pam began to reveal things about her past that were beyond strange. When she had come to me for hypnosis, she was working in real estate and caring for her retired and dying husband who had been a former government employee. She told me that he was a physicist who had worked at various government labs, including JPL on the Mars Observer, and had spent most of his time working in an underground laboratory somewhere in Maryland or thereabouts. I had never asked her what agency her husband currently worked for, not realizing that it might be important.

She was telling me so many things that I found it difficult to assimilate it all. It was as though, in the years since the door to the idea of aliens had been opened in her mind, all sorts of associations had come together. It never occurred to me that this might be bait to attract my interest.

On top of her husband's work, Pam, had a high security clearance and had spent years working (or so she said) in certain office positions that gave her access to highly sensitive information. Finally I thought I understood why Pam may have been abducted. If her husband was a scientist and she had a security clearance, that might explain it. I shared with her my learning that families of government employees generally seem to be abducted more than the average person. She thought this was interesting, but still didn't think that it applied to her specifically.

I was pretty excited by all of this. A real, potential witness to weirdness. What a find!

We discussed the magazine, finally, and she agreed that if I would come into the shop and physically help assemble it, in addition to having camera ready copy, she would be able to give me a considerable discount. So, I left feeling as though the fates were in my corner and all was going to be right. I also thought that this was a big opportunity – perhaps the one the Cassiopaeans had mentioned when they'd said back in October of the previous year:

October 28, 1994

Q: (L) We would like to know if you have anything to give in the form of a teaching?

A: Not ready for that yet; establish clear channel and forum first; one step at a time.

Q: (L) What is the forum?

A: What do you think?

Q: (L) Do you mean that we need to bring more people into this work?

A: Close.

Q: (L) We need to create a forum.

A: Yes. A direction will open if you persevere.

Q: (L) So things will be brought to us and happen for us if we just persevere?

A: Soon expect big opportunity.

Q: (L) I assume that we are not to ask what it is, we are to have faith, is that correct?

A: Yes. Danger you may misinterpret opportunity.

Q: (L) Should we all be able to realize in congruence whether the opportunity is good?

A: Varying degrees.

Q: (L) If there is a danger we may misinterpret the opportunity, could you give us a couple of clues so that when it occurs we won't miss it?

A: At least one of you will have instant recognition but others may not. Wait and see.

My first interpretation of this "opportunity" was the fact that my friend, RC, wanted to dump her magazine. (See volume five of *The Wave* for the whole story.) A magazine was a "forum." The next interpretation I put on it was that Pam had instantly recognized me, but I hadn't instantly recognized her. And having an inside line to printing, especially since we were planning a journal, was definitely a "big opportunity" in terms of "creating a forum" one would think.

At the same time, I had joined Mike Lindemann's ISCNI forum on AOL and had been invited to chat live, online, with his group in a sort of question and answer session. I felt sure that this also was part of the "forum" and might be the "big opportunity."

But the fact that in none of these instances had there been instant recognition by any of the other members of our group, with the others doubting, still bugged me. What other "big opportunity" could there be?

It's funny how we anticipate things in ways that never quite fit, and yet how desperate we are to make them true.

I brought the subject up with the Cassiopaeans:

December 30, 1995

Q: (L) We have a number of questions we want to cover tonight. The first thing is, in the early stages of this channeling process we talked about what it was we were supposed to be doing. We were told that the first thing we needed to do was "establish a clear channel." Obviously, it has taken about a year to do that. The next thing that was identified that we must do was to establish a forum. What is this forum supposed to be in?

A: These are all questions to which you must discover the answers by learning, therefore, no further discussion is now beneficial.

Q: (L) Now the next thing was that a direction would open and that there was something amazing and wonderful just around the corner that I would recognize instantly and which would help me to know what to do. Has this already occurred and did I miss something?

A: Wait and see.

Q: (L) I was recently invited to give a talk to the ISCNI, that is, the Institute for the Study of Contact with Non-human Intelligence, which is headed by a guy named Mike Lindemann. I am rather curious as to the reaction from some of these people.

A: Lindemann and the others would best serve the "cause" if they loosen any rigidities that they may have found themselves "grooving into," as this is an area that definitely does not lend itself to manifestations of rigidity in any way, shape, or form, whatsoever!!!

Q: (L) I think they are getting a little rigid because they feel they are under pressure from the scientific community to prove something. But, observable elements of the phenomena of aliens have progressed to such a stage, that trying to prove anything scientifically becomes moot. We don't have time for double-blind experiments. We don't have time to wait for FDA approval!

A: Persist and express the same thoughts you did here! Help Lindemann and others to see that they are dealing with a phenomenon that is better studied in a way that stresses an open learning forum, not a "scientific" study methodology. In all its forms, not just the "physical" agenda that is primarily sought by some and in fact, it is through the ethereal plane and methodologies that the clues and some of the answers lie for physical as well as ethereal factors. Tell Michael this verbatim: "You once had a more open mind, Michael, what happened?" Some of his most frustrating recent events in his life relate directly to this!! Trust your insights, they are assisting learning matrix.

So, I didn't get any answers to my assumptions about the "big opportunity" that was supposed to happen "soon", dating from the time of October of 1994. I had begun to wonder just what the Cassiopaeans meant by "soon". For me, "soon" was a few weeks. Here, we had gone over a year with no real or definite "big opportunity" for establishing a "forum." Further, there had been no "instant recognition" of anything by any of us.

As we have already discussed in these pages, the serendipitous meeting with Pam, at just the time I needed it, was also intertwined with the very strange kidnapping case of the young girl who so strongly resembled the murdered child from just prior to the time I'd first met Pam. I won't get too side-tracked with that, but the session below was very much related to the overall situation at that moment, particularly relating to Pam:

January 9, 1996

Q: (L) Okay, Pam will be here on Saturday, so we will leave a lot of my questions for then. I don't quite know how to ask this. It has become increasingly obvious to me that there is some sort of connection where JO [an unsolved murder of a local girl] was concerned, some synchronous connections between that murder and my so-called awakening, if you want to call it that. And I also noticed a connection between the life pattern, or change in life pattern, of Ted Bundy and certain UFO sightings, and cattle mutilations that were in his area of the country. Now, we have another girl who has come up missing at the very same time – in fact, the very day – that Pam and I were discussing the JO case. This new case has a lot of things that seem to be common to that old case, the most striking being the amazing resemblance of the two girls to each other. Did my involvement with the JO case [I was asked by law enforcement official to try to come up with some clues or hints through astrology and psychic impressions] have anything to do with opening the door of my mind to other phenomena, particularly UFOs and aliens?

A: Possible.

Q: (L) You can't give me a clear answer on that?

A: Learn!

Q: (L) Okay. I had dreams about it. The work that I did on the case astrologically, the dreams I had about it, as well as certain impressions I received, convinced me that a particular individual was the killer. Was that an opening of my instinctual awareness in some way?

A: Maybe.

Q: (L) Was there some connection between JO's murder and alien activity?

A: *There is always this connection in one way or another, at one plane convergence or another.*

This is actually a pretty startling remark when you think about it. Remember, of course, that the conventional definition of "alien" that we had grown to understand is *not* third density visitors from outer space, but hyperdimensional beings who are part of the control system of our world.

Q: (L) Was the murder of JO a mini-plane convergence?

A: What did we just say?

Q: (L) It seemed to me that was what you said, and I was trying to clarify it. Is that in fact a plane convergence can be defined as where one person's plane of reality converges with another person's plane of reality, and one or the other gets annihilated?

A: 4th, 5th and 3rd density is involved.

Q: (L) Is this true with all murders?

A: Discover and yes.

This sort of gives a different perspective to the subject of crime, most particularly crimes of violence. I was beginning to formulate the idea that each and every human being is a part of one or another of the cosmic archetypes and that their lives, their actions, their "scripts" could be identified with sufficient examination of their experiences.

Q: (L) Was my interaction into that reality a sort of entering into a point of plane convergence?

A: Flirting with the edges.

Q: (L) So, when a person is working on a murder investigation, or thinking about it, or applying thoughts, talents, instincts or whatever to the solving of this kind of puzzle, they are interacting with a plane convergence?

A: This represents one manifestation of the always present desire to return "home" to 5th density.

Q: (L) Okay. Well. Now, I want to get to the 64,000 dollar question. In the JO case, was my conclusion correct?

I was pretty obsessed with knowing the answer to this one, or at the very least having the answer I had come up with confirmed.

A: "Correctness" takes many forms and provides a window to many conventions.

Q: (F) What does that mean? (L) I don't know.

A: Learn.

Q: (L) Was the man who killed JO known to her?

A: We recall advising a cautious approach, in order to insure that your lessons are learned not only accurately, but painlessly as well.

If I was correct, it was a very dangerous thing to know!

Q: (L) Could you suggest, just to get me on track here, a form of question that would be a cautious question? Then I can frame subsequent questions on that model.

I really wanted that confirmation! I was really stretching to find a way to get the Cassiopaeans to give me a final answer.

A: The issue here is not how to "frame" a question in such a way as to lure us into answering in the way you desire, but for you to learn most effectively. Do not have prejudice that there is only one thing to be learned from each response. "You never know what there is to be learned when you inquire with innocence and freedom from supposition."

Since Frank and I were working alone, there was no one present to take notes. I had to stop and play the tape back to get the words from the above response, which had been delivered too rapidly to follow mentally. And, when I did, there was that blasted static that would roar on and drown out the important words, but would be completely absent in other portions.

Q: (L) I just played the tape back and it is all muddy. Could you tell us why we are having this problem with the tape?

A: *Telekinetic wave transfer.*

Q: (L) What is this telekinetic wave transferring?

A: Evolving energy.

Q: (L) Given off by us?

A: Both to and from.

Q: (L) From us to you?

A: You and others, not us.

Q: (L) Who are these others?

A: *4th density eavesdroppers, Pam's involvement should "heat things up."*

Q: (L) Is Pam's involvement going to be beneficial to this work?

A: Yes, but also expect anomalies.

And one has to remember that "beneficial" does not necessarily mean that I was going to *like* it. But, I was pretty focused on this murder thing. Sometimes I really have a one-track mind.

Q: (L) That is interesting. Are you going to tell me who killed JO? I am willing to give up my conclusion if necessary.

A: Learn. Review our previous response.

Well, the issue of Ted Bundy and the UFO sightings that occurred in the area of the country where he lived at the time he was purportedly beginning his murderous career had recently attracted my attention. I had thought it was strange that murder had been synchronously connected to UFOs in our own experience. I thought this might be a path to follow so that I could get the answer I was after.

Q: (L) Okay. Learn. Was there something about Ted Bundy, and the fact that his life seemed to disintegrate at the same time a lot of UFOs were sighted?

A: Yes.

Q: (L) Was Ted Bundy abducted?

A: Yes.

Q: (L) Was Ted Bundy programmed to do what he did?

A: Yes.

Q: (L) What was the purpose behind that programming?

A: We must withhold answer for the present.

This is an issue that went right over my head at the time.

Q: (L) Okay. Bundy described his murdering urges as a "pressure building inside" him that he couldn't overcome, and it seemed to cause him to stop being "human," as we think of it. That seems to me to be an example of an implant being able to overcome a person's social behavior, or controls over anti-social tendencies. Is this also what happened to the person who killed JO?

A: Maybe.

Q: (L) Is there a connection between the newly missing girl, CB, and JO?

A: You are doing well in your probing of the knowledge within on this issue, we suggest continuance, after all, learning is fun!

Q: (L) So, it seems to me that there was a connection between the [physical] appearance of CB and JO. Could it be that the individual who killed one or both of them [we didn't know if the second girl was dead or not] was programmed to respond to this particular type of facial features? Could that be part of the programming?

A: End subject.

Q: (L) What do you mean?

A: We have helped you all that is necessary for now on this matter. It is beneficial for you to continue on your own for growth.

Clearly there *was* an issue here and I was flirting dangerously close to it.

Q: (L) Can I ask just one or two more *little* questions in a different direction? I mean, this is like walking away and leaving me in the dark!

A: No it is not!

Q: (L) I would like to be able to solve this because the families are in pain and have asked for help.

A: Why don't you trust your incredible abilities? *If we answer for you now, you will be helpless when it becomes necessary for you to perform this function on a regular basis, as it will be!!!!*

Q: (L) Well, frankly, I don't want to be involved in any more murder investigations. It is too upsetting. Am I supposed to *do* this sort of thing regularly?

A: Not same arena.

Q: (L) Well, then how do you mean "perform this function?"

A: No, *seeing the unseen.*

Q: (L) Okay, shift gears. There are some issues with my son and the school. He wanted to attend regular school because he was of the opinion that he needed a break from home schooling. This has led to a number of incidents involving what can only be called gangs in the school. I am completely shocked by what goes on there over which the school seems to have absolutely no control. I mean, they have to keep policemen on campus because of the threat of guns and knives, and these kids today are actually dangerous! I think my son is miserable and even frightened in this violent environment, but he does not want to give up or be viewed as a quitter, or a baby. He is torn between his misery and disgust with the system, and his desire for peace. I would like to know why those kids attacked him the other day?

A: Attack.

Q: (L) You mean stimulated through fourth density?

A: Yes.

Q: (L) Is there anything I can do to help protect him?

A: What do you think?

Q: (L) Well. I don't know what to think.

A: Don't avoid the issue, it is of paramount importance!

Q: (L) Yes, I think I ought to take Jay out of school. There is just too much attack going on from all directions at the present time, and that is *one* portal of attack that I *can* close off.

A: Instincts preserve third density experience.

Q: (L) Are you suggesting that there is some threat to his existence in third density if I don't do something right away?

A: Yes.

Q: (L) Is this threat from outside sources?

A: Yes.

Q: (L) So I need to pull him out of school *now*.

A: Follow instincts.

Q: (L) That's clear enough for me. I have the feeling Jay is here for a purpose and that is why he has so much difficulty interacting with persons who are not as concerned about things as he is.

A: Yes.

Q: (L) Now, I want to ask about the Sheldon Nidle channeling?

A: Suggest you not waste energy on this.

Q: (L) There are a lot of people who are convinced by Sheldon Nidle that there is going to be a photon belt and a mass landing of UFOs in the fall of this year. Is this, in fact, going to occur?

A: People are very convinced by Bo and Peep.

The following week, Pam attended her first session. Since the Cassiopaeans had said that her presence should "heat things up a bit" and that her involvement would be "beneficial" to our work, I had the idea that she might be good for the reception. Since she had been present when the Black Boomerangs appeared, I reasoned she must have some special psychic tuning of her own. I was also extremely curious to see if the Cassiopaeans would finally answer the question about the appearance of these craft on that night in more detail. But, the sessions never go the way we think they will go; they take on a dynamic and life of their own just like any conversation that begins with weather and ends with the price of tea in China. The only difference was, we were having conversations with the Cassiopaeans, so there was some sensation of oceans of information lying in wait to be accessed if only we could formulate or stumble upon the right question.

January 7, 1996

Q: (L) We have Pam with us tonight …

A: Hello Pam.

Q: (L) Now, with all of us here, we would like to ask why the black, flying boomerangs showed up on the night Pam first came for hypnosis?

A: Examine issue carefully.

Q: (L) The first thing we thought about it was that this was a, if not necessarily rare, at least rarely observed type of craft, and the event itself was rare … is this correct?

A: It is rare.

Q: (L) Since the hypnosis session was not advertised in any way, and no mention of aliens or anything like that was ever made, it seems that it might have happened in response to this hypnosis session by knowledge obtained in ways with which we are not familiar. And, if that is the case, then it must mean that there was something or someone of interest at that hypnosis session. I have thought about it two ways: either the interest was in myself, and what I might uncover about aliens; or the interest was in Pam for some other reason – perhaps that she should NOT uncover anything about her own experiences. Which person were the UFO's particularly interested in?

A: It was not a person, but information that is hidden in the subconscious memory of Pam.

Q: (L) Were they wanting to get this information?

A: No. To monitor what would be revealed.

Q: (L) Does this mean that Pam has information programmed into her before birth that she needs to access as you said I did?
A: No. Abductions.
Q: (L) They wanted to see if anything would be revealed about their abductions of her?
A: Yes.
Q: (L) Okay, who abducted her?
A: Grays. 4 times. Snow scene was only 3rd density abduction. Abduction which occurred there was strictly physical. The others were 4th density. 3rd density abduction only occurs rarely, and is of great import.
Q: (P) Was my son abducted?
A: Frozen.
Q: (L) Why did they want Pam so bad that they would take her physically?
A: Do you have any ideas?
Q: (L) Maybe Pam has knowledge that she could access to work against these beings?
A: But real reason is more fundamental. Exposure.
Q: (L) Oh, they fear that she will act in some way to expose them ...
A: Government proximities!
Q: (L) Oh! Well, Pam has pointed out that just because she was married to a scientist who worked at JPL doesn't mean she knew anything. Does she know something that she doesn't know she knows?
A: [It's] not what she knew. [It's] because of [her] proximity to consortium activity. [She was] implanted for possible future activation.
Q: (P) Was this related to what was going on under the mountain? (L) What mountain? (P) Just ask.
A: Not locator, personnel are factored.
Q: (L) Okay, it is not where she was so much as who she was in contact with?
A: Yes.
Q: (L) Was it her husband?
A: Perhaps.
Q: (L) Maybe that is why there is a higher rate of abduction among family members of government employees, so that they can be activated or controlled for some reason if needed. (P) But my husband wasn't really working on anything secret.
A: He had access to sensitive facilities.
Q: (L) So, Pam had an implant put in. An actual, physical implant. Where is it?
A: Behind sinus cavity.
Q: (L) What is this implant designed to do?
A: *Activate behavioral control reflex and thought pattern generation and alteration.*

Now, just stop and think about this remark. Implants that can "activate behavioral control" reflexes and that can generate thought patterns or alter thought patterns are pretty scary concepts. This suggests that, without conscious attention to our patterns of thought and behavior, we may be controlled in ways we have always thought were just our personality.

Q: (P) Is that why I can't remember anything?
A: Some.

Q: (P) No, but I do have this memory problem in a big way. (L) So, can I say that this UFO appeared over my house on the night Pam was under hypnosis, to …
A: To monitor.
Q: (L) If Pam had revealed the details of her abduction, would there have been any repercussions?
A: Not in this case.
Q: (L) So, if Pam had gone to anyone for hypnosis, these craft would have appeared?
A: Yes.
Q: (L) You have already told us that this is extremely rare.
A: 3rd density abductions [are rare].
Q: (P) Does this have anything to do with Camp David?
A: Not the issue, it's personnel! [Pam interacted with] many others!
Q: (L) Well, there seems to be an issue here that we need to get to. (P) Do the planes have anything to do with it?
A: It is up to Pam, the extent she wishes to retrieve and divulge, the many unusual experiences that were met, by Pam, with unusual indifference.

And here we have more of a clue about control of behavior and thought patterns. I had no idea at the time of the significance of this remark.

Q: (P) The first thing unusual was the geographic location of our house. Directly West of us was the mountain that housed all the communications to be used in the event of nuclear war. We were 13 miles north of Camp David. And, while we lived there, many, many things took place at Camp David that were of global significance. And we built a barn in 1982 and had bought the house in 1976 and never, in all the years that I lived there, did I ever notice these planes until we built the barn. If I had a stick in my hand, I could have touched them, that's how low they flew. Right over my barn! The same days every week, and there was always two of them, and they never had a single marking on them; and they were propeller planes. And I wondered: what in the hell is this country doing flying planes, unmarked, propeller driven, and so low, over this area? This continued until we moved from that house. So, these planes came twice a week from 1982 until 1989. Well, after the first couple of times, I sort of just said: "Well, there are the planes." So, what else is new?
A: Indifference.
Q: (P) I thought the planes had something to do with the mountain. Did they?
A: Maybe.
Q: (P) We knew they were flying under radar. Now that I am thinking about this, nobody else ever talked about these planes. It was like we were the only people that ever saw them, or only people who were at our house saw them too. My best friend who lived right up the road never saw them. I asked her: "Did you see the planes?" and she said, "What planes?" I mean, she was seven acres away and nothing in between!
A: Unusual experiences mount!
Q: (P) My husband also noticed these things and he would always say – he was less indifferent than I was – he would say: "What in the hell are those planes, and what are they doing?" (L) Why was Pam so indifferent? (P) Well, it didn't affect *my* life, except that I was damn mad that it upset my horses. But then, the horses got used to

them too, and they became indifferent! [Laughter.] Well, they came so often, twice a week. "It's Wednesday, the planes will be here!"

A: More ... continue probing ...

It is clear, in retrospect, that the Cassiopaeans wanted Pam to talk so that I would get a clue here. But I was, sad to say, blissfully unaware!

Q: (P) The planes came from east to west, and in the west was the mountain ...

A: Catoctin.

Q: (P) [Amazed] That is the name of the mountain! (L) What is it? [I had never heard this word before.] (P) The tunnel where all these facilities were ... under Catoctin Mountain. Camp David is near, too.

A: And MUCH ELSE! Mount Weather, Virginia. And why did you live in area ... helicopters? What brought you to Maryland?

Why did they say, "helicopters? What brought you to Maryland?" It went right over my head.

Q: (L) What does Mount Weather mean? (P) The underground tunnel – everybody in town called it "the tunnel" – but there was nothing around there to ever give anybody the slightest clue as to what it was. In fact, I lived there for quite a long time before I knew it existed. And, on top of the mountain there was a weather station. My husband was doing electron microscopy – cancer research.

A: REALLY?

Q: (P) It was a photographic lab.

A: So what? Helicopters, Pat? We are asking you!

And they brought up the helicopters again.

Q: (P) Well, the helicopters in Fredrick went over our house every time the president was at Camp David. But, that was our house in Walkersville not in Emmetsburg. When we first moved to Maryland. Sometimes the helicopters were unmarked.

A: You see, Pam is resistant due to experiences, things don't "phase" her easily, programming, etc.

Q: (L) So, all of these things happening around her, the planes, the mountain, the helicopters ... (P) But the helicopters, I knew it was the President either going to or coming from Camp David.

A: Resistant, not resisting.

Q: (L) Is the term "resistant" a clue?

A: All is a clue here!

So, there was something important about the helicopters and it was connected to what brought Pam to Maryland. But none of us were picking up on this. Pam kept diverging from the subject, and the Cassiopaeans indicated that she was "resistant due to experiences." Then, they made the curious remark that "things don't 'phase' her easily" and that this was related to programming. Well, nobody can say that the Cassiopaeans weren't doing everything they could to make a point! I just wasn't paying attention. Later experiences were to suggest strongly that Pam was, indeed, programmed and that this programming had deprived her of normal human feelings of compassion and empathy.

> Q: (P) Isn't that just my personality, that if it doesn't affect me I don't bother with it?
> A: Yes. *Shoot somebody in front of P, and she says: "Oh well, that's life"* so, to discover spectacular things, one must be patient and probe carefully, no hasty assumptions, please!! There is much to be retrieved, revealed, studied. Let Pam digest it, and report back later.

This extremely odd remark, "shoot somebody in front of Pam and she says: 'Oh well, that's life,'" was certainly the last desperate effort to get me to pay attention; but I was just too convinced that Pam and her print shop were the answers to my prayers that I didn't want to hear it.

> Q: (L) At the time there were all those sightings around here on the night we did the hypnosis session with Pam, why did so many other people see them?
> A: Window was "blasted."
> Q: (L) Okay, we have the magazine ready to go out and the articles are somewhat controversial. Can we have an indication as to whether there will be a positive response to this issue or not? I don't want to turn people off by being too radical.
> A: Wait and see.
> Q: (L) Pam is having some serious problems at the present time; can you help her with these?
> A: Networking works!!!
> Q: (P) Is there a light at the end of the tunnel?
> A: Networking works!!!!!
> Q: (P) I would like to know about the apparitions of the Virgin Mary at Conyers, GA, as well as this book "Mary's Message to the World" and all the other messages about the End Times that are coming out all over?
> A: The forces at work here are far too clever to be accurately anticipated so easily. You never know what twists and turns will follow, and they are aware of prophetic and philosophical patternings and usually shift course to fool and discourage those who believe in fixed futures.

And that was that. In retrospect, it is easy to see that the Cassiopaeans were trying to get me to see something about Pam in their exchange with her, but I was too excited about getting the magazine printed to care about anything else. They had said "network," and I was networking like crazy! Or so I thought.

Pam decided that she wanted to become a regular member of the group. We thought that her energy was pretty compatible, and she was a lot of fun to be around with her dry and witty comments, so we agreed. The most curious thing happened, however. This session that Pam attended was made almost unintelligible due to static on the tape. The only other time this had happened was just a few days previously, after meeting with Pam, though she was not present. After a couple of earlier experiences with different glitches with our recording equipment, we had certain procedures we followed prior to the session to make sure that everything was in order. We had performed all the checks, and everything was working. But still, the static was there, most often when Pam was speaking. In fact, the next session with Pam, we used *two tape recorders* and *both tapes* were nearly impossible to decipher. In the six years of working with the Cassiopaeans, this only happened during the time we were interacting with Pam. Fortunately, we take a fairly good set of notes even while recording, so I was able to reconstruct the sessions from the notes.

At this point, I need to go in a slightly different direction in order to explain the first question in the session below.

In January 1995, the Reiki master the Cassiopaeans had directed me to in *Wave 2* (the right Reiki master, that is!) had presented me with copies of the now infamous KRLL papers. They had been given to her and she passed them on to me, knowing of my interest in UFOs. I was perfectly amazed to discover threads of the same material that the Cassiopaeans were delivering woven throughout this purported communication from an EBE (Extraterrestrial Biological Entity).

We had heard about the KRLL papers from some people at MUFON, and we asked the Cassiopaeans about them even before we had read them. This extract will give the reader some idea of the great amount of discussion and commentary that went on amongst the group *during* the sessions. Sometimes it was a colorful melee of comments and differing opinions.

January 14, 1995

Q: (L) Now, I want to ask about these *KRLL* documents that my Reiki teacher, SB, has told me about and is sending to me in the mail. Tell us what is the background and validity of the *KRLL* papers. Terry knows more about them than I do. Supposedly it is some kind of exposition written by an alien being, revealing the government conspiracy. Were the *KRLL* papers valid? (T) KRLL was supposedly a prisoner of the United States. (L) Was there really such a being as KRLL?

A: Semi.

Q: (T) Is there any validity to the *KRLL* papers?

A: Semi.

Q: (T) Was it dictated by this alien being?

A: Maybe.

Q: (T) Was it put together by a human?

A: Semi.

Q: (T) Is this in the same area of UFO lore as the Cooper and Lear and Lazar and Bennewitz stuff?

A: We have told you many times … Laura, pay attention … Listen!

Q: (L) Well, you say "semi." Semi means half-way. Is it half true or half-way true?

A: Whoa! Calm down! Patience! We are trying to tell you something important, and you keep asking questions. We have told you many times to communicate with each other and network and share ideas, because that is how you LEARN and PRO-GRESS! But, you are beginning to rely on us for all your answers, and you do not

LEARN that way!!!!!!! Now, try this, you will be thunderstruck with the results: Each of you has stored within you unlimited amounts of factual and "Earthshaking" information. This information was put into your consciousness in order for you to retrieve it in order for you to learn. Now just start by holding a discussion about the last series of questions you were trying to ask us, and "let it flow."

Q: (L) Well, if John Lear and William Cooper are saying basically the same thing the *KRLL* document is saying, where did they get their information?

(T) One of the rumors going on was that Moore or Lear or Bennewitz, one of these, was the one that had written the *KRLL* papers. There was some talk that KRLL may have been an acronym used by the government to identify this being who gave the information, which is the basis of this document.

(L) To your knowledge, would Lear or Cooper ever have been in a position, or did they ever at any time claim to have been in a position, to observe any of this activity written up in this document themselves?

(T) I don't believe that either of them have ever claimed to have been in a position to have physically observed any of this or to have been in the underground bases. They were working with information they claimed to have gotten from other sources.

(L) And what do they claim their other sources are? Unnamed?

(T) A lot of them are unnamed. Moore and Cooper claim they have inside government sources. I believe Cooper is the one who claims that he at one time worked for the military.

(L) Is he the one who claims that he was the intelligence analyst for the Admiral of the Pacific Fleet or something like that?

(T) Yes. There are several versions of the Cooper papers as he modifies and updates them. He didn't change anything really, he just cleaned them up, re-edited them and added to them.

(L) Okay, if this is the case, it would seem to me that a person would have a much better chance of having something believed if they presented it as coming from a human source who either observed or saw it. Why would they say that this is an alien dictating this when that is so far and away more unbelievable? It seems to me that if they were making it up they would have far better chance if they said a human extracted this information from documents rather than that it is what the alien said. That would almost tend, in a backward sort of way, to make you think that maybe this KRLL dude, maybe it was true. But, the only thing about that is, if it was an alien, especially if it was an STS alien, how much of it *was* true? That's the question.

(T) Well, KRLL was supposed to be one of the standard Grays.

(L) Well, then, maybe we can't rely on anything he says. We can rely on the fact that it is possible that it was an alien who gave this information, but if it was one of the standard Grays, then we have been informed as to who and what they are and we have to look at the information itself as being unreliable, not necessarily the human who revealed the scenario.

(F) Well, it is not necessarily unreliable even if it is an STS source.

(L) Yes, but as STS they would undoubtedly only give information that would tend to service their position.

(F) That would seem to be the case if you look at it from the obvious angle. But, that is not necessarily true. Just because it is an STS alien, and, in fact, a cybergenetic being, that does not mean that the information is necessarily inaccurate for several reasons. For those of us who have reached a certain level of understanding, our first assumption would be that it is inaccurate, so it could be a reverse psychology ploy. Give accurate information, get those who are at a higher level of understanding to think it's inaccurate, when in actuality it is accurate.

(L) Well, do you know what it said? From what SB tells me, it says, basically, what we have been getting from the Cassiopaeans.

(F) Well, then it is accurate.

(L) We can't make that assumption!

(T) If this is a standard cybergenetic Gray, the question is how much biological is he? Is he biological enough to pass a dissection?

(L) Sure, I think. There are purported reports of autopsies of these guys, and they just can't figure out how they feed because they are reported to have dead-end alimentary canals. [Strieber, *Majestic*, 1990]

(F) They are cybergenetic, but they look and function exactly like a biological being. If you go inside of them you will find blood and fibers and tissue and microscopic evidence ...

(L) The microscopic exams, from what I have heard, reveal that they're more in the line of a plant ...

(T) Yes.

(F) Which, of course, would indicate that they have been grown!

(L) Yes. Imagine chromosomal linking of human genetic information with that of the plant kingdom!

(T) You could literally grow hundreds of them easily.

(L) And plant them like seeds ... and, apparently that is what they have done. People have come back who have been taken to these ships and have seen walls of containers growing these things. Like a room in a hot house.

(F) Well, there you go. We have gotten information which indicates that the Grays have access to both dimensions because they are probes of the Lizzies. And this gives us a further clue as to what a strange place fourth level is if such probes can be grown like plants. And, what level must fully souled fourth density beings be when we are fooled into believing their cybergenetic constructions are the real thing!

(T) Does this mean that the abilities of the Lizzies, since they have to create probes to enter our density, would not be any more advanced than, say, your everyday spirit [soul]? Without the Grays, would they be able to interact with us at all?

(F) Yes.

(L) Yes, they are, they have, they will and they do from all reports I have studied.

(F) But, there are several problems. One is their appearance is very, very alarming ...

(J) They would garner a lot of attention if they walked down the street.

(T) It depends on how they dress themselves! [Laughter]

(L) They can shape-shift.

(F) They can shape-shift, but only for a limited period of time.

(L) Because it takes third density energy to do that.

(F) That brings up something, when we were talking to Susy on the phone the other night, Susy and Barry mentioned the Men In Black. The Cassiopaeans said that the Men In Black were Lizard beings. In many reports of Men In Black, they have been described as very strange in numerous ways. Their voices have been described as sounding like they come from an echo chamber, and ...

(T) Well, when we asked about the Men in Black in one of the sessions, what did the Cassiopaeans say? That they are "projections."

(J) Exactly, maybe that is a clue, maybe that is how they come into our reality: as projections from fourth into third.

(F) But, there is one case that always sticks in my mind, and it took place relatively recently, on April 28, 1978, a guy in Maine who had been doing UFO research, was accosted by a single Man in Black. He said the guy was very strange in many ways. He had pink ... his face looked like it was covered with make-up, and, in fact, when he touched himself at one point and his face started to smear as if it was completely covered. And then, he suddenly got up and said: "Have to go now ... run-n-n-ing out of e-ner-gy." Then he walked out of the house and staggered down the drive. They guy said that at that point he became somewhat disoriented as he watched the Man in Black start to stagger ...

(L) He was not the Energizer Bunny! [Laughter.]

(F) And then the man saw a light that he at first thought was the headlight of a car, but the Man in Black walked into the light and was gone.

(J) Projections! That's how they move from fourth to third!

(L) They [the Cs] said they project as a "triage." Remember. It was something like travel in space/time.

(T) Well, we have gotten off the discussion of *KRLL*, but we have certainly been led into some pretty amazing conclusions about fourth level.

(F) All of what we have worked with over the years – the ideas of it being a nuts and bolts phenomenon, which I originally thought too – and it's clear if one has been following the whole phenomenon closely, it has evolved, actually, from a nuts-and-bolts perspective, and I am not knocking nuts-and-bolts, but those who are really looking with an open mind are seeing that this is far more.

(L) Alright, here it is guys ... [had been looking for references to Men In Black]

Q: Who or what are the Men in Black?

A: Lizard projections.

(T) We got onto that because we were asking about the projection of the guy in the Camaro that showed up in my driveway.

Q: Does this mean that the Lizards are just projecting an image of a being?

A: Yes.

Q: The Men in Black are not real in our physical terms?

A: Partly correct. You do not understand technology but we will describe it if you like. First we must explain further "time travel" because the two concepts are closely related. The first step is to artificially induce an electro-magnetic field. This opens the door between dimensions of reality. Next, thoughts must be channeled by participant in order to access reality bonding channel. They must then focus the energy to the proper dimensional bridge, the electrons must be arranged in correct frequency wave, and then the triage must be sent through realm curtain in order to balance perceptions at all density levels. Triage is as follows: 1. Matter; 2. Energy; 3. Perception of reality.

(L) In other words they send through ...

(J) Holographic images.

(T) They transmit energy that takes matter here and creates what we perceive, and what we perceive depends on what they expect to see, which the Lizzies have to tap into first before they do the triage ... that is the "reality bonding channel." If you are open to see Men in Black, even if you don't know what they are, then at some level of consciousness ...

(L) It is like doing a back-flip through the realm curtain.

(F) But I think this is not just limited to Men In Black.

(L) Listen to this! [Reads from transcript.] Several times I have heard references to big rectangular boxes, I would like to know who these belong to?

A: Lizard projections ...

(L) What are they doing, projecting their whole damn reality into our world?

(F) Well, apparently part of the whole process of going from fourth density to third density is the projection process itself. This also, of course, explains much of what we have read and heard about in terms of higher phenomena. You cannot ground it at all. So many people have fallen off the track by expecting to capture metallic craft and dissect them, and, while that does happen ... that is where material science falls apart. It is stuck in a vicious cycle.

(J) Yes, and it is using its own rules to make itself obsolete!

(F) Right!

(T) So, the bottom line is, we have simply gone beyond the *KRLL* stuff, the Cooper and Lear stuff, and so on.

(F) Which is one of the reasons why the Cassiopaeans keep telling us to stop asking these stupid questions.

(T) *There's another thing that is even more interesting and that is that we are not alone in this density, there are other beings on other planets also. And, it just may be that some of them are coming here just to throw some more stuff in the soup to keep us confused as to which or who is what.*

(F) I have a feeling though that probably everything that we have experienced in the UFO area over the many years is a passage from higher levels of density to this one. I don't think that we have ever experienced a third to third transfer. That is just my feeling. And, it is only just now that people are beginning to realize that. In other words ...

(T) Well, that is what Vallee thinks, along those lines, so he is just looking at interdimensional, because ...

(F) But Vallee is also a material scientist so he is examining it in a scientific way. He is a little more open-minded than some who would just say it is impossible because we haven't discovered it yet ... but he is doing it in a very careful way.

(L) Well, have we done enough with *KRLL*?

(T) Yeah, I think we have done more than enough with *KRLL*.

At that point, we turned to other subjects.

In February 1995, when I was invited to visit Hilliard, the elderly gentleman who told me about the Coral Castle, I first became aware of the *Matrix* books, which were assembled and published by Val Valerian. Hilliard showed me his library, which contained the *Matrix* books. I saw them on the shelf but did not actually have time to open the covers. He assured me they were full of interesting information. At the time, I had no idea of how they would connect to the *KRLL* papers.

A week after the above session in which the *KRLL* papers were discussed, I had received them from SB and had read them by the time of the next session. I decided to ask a couple of follow-up questions. This session was in January of 1995, a year before the time we are discussing in our chronology.

January 21, 1995
Q: (L) Okay, give me a quick yes or no answer on this: Dr. Paul Bennewitz – reliable [source]?
A: No.
Q: (L) Is his statement, as it is recorded in the *KRLL* papers, falsified?
A: No.
Q: (L) Is any of that statement true?
A: Partly.
Q: (L) Who is O. H. KRLL?
A: No one.
Q: (L) Is O. H. KRLL a group?
A: Symbolism. For documentary purposes only, *your government likes code names.*

This last remark seems to indicate that the individuals responsible for the *KRLL* papers may be government related.

Q: (L) Are you implying that this piece of work was put out by the government for dissemination of the subject matter? (J) Is it disinformation?
A: Complex.
Q: (L) Give us a percentage of factual information in this document.
A: 43%
Q: (L) Are you saying that 43% is factual?
A: Close enough.
Q: (L) Okay, so, in other words, this has been planted by the government. Was it put out with the intention of giving out some factual information …
A: No. Planted? No.
Q: (L) You are saying it was not planted? (T) It was leaked purposely?
A: *Your government is operating on many cross-purposes, very complicated!*

Again note the government reference and the implication that there may be elements in the government who are interested in informing the public along with those interested in misinforming the public and various combinations of both activities.

Q: (T) Even the simplest things are very complicated with them. Okay, question: The U.S. government …

A: On purpose!

Q: (T) Very true. Question: the government, our government, the U.S. government, according to what you said earlier, is holding thirty-six craft of one kind or another that they have gotten in one way or another. How many other governments have alien craft?

A: All is one.

Q: (L) *We already have a one-world government* is what they're saying. (T) Yes, they're just waiting to make it official somehow.

A: *Has been so for long time, as you measure time.*

Q: (L) Let me ask this one before the tape runs out and we take a break. What is the "ultimate secret" being protected by the Consortium?

A: You are not in control of yourselves, you are an experiment.

In any event, as I was reading the *Matrix* books through the month of October 1995, I noticed that the *KRLL* papers were actually part of the *Matrix* books. I was also pretty overwhelmed with the material itself, as anyone who has read the first three volumes one after another with very little stopping to eat or sleep, will understand.

There was an address in the books and I decided to write to Val Valerian and send him some of the Cassiopaean material – the raw transcripts from the first few sessions – and query him about his sources. I figured that if I expected him to answer any of my questions, I needed to share what we had quid pro quo. I included my phone number and was surprised when, a short time later, he called me on the phone.

Val was very curious about the Cassiopaean contact and mentioned the fact that it was really disconnected and a mess in terms of needing editing, suggesting that he would be interested in doing it and publishing it in an upcoming *Matrix* book.

Since I was interested in getting opinions from other people on the Cassiopaean material, I thought that this was a golden opportunity to network with other like-minded people. I agreed to send Val everything we had received up to that point. But, before I took that step, I tried to find out what I could about Val Valerian. RC, the young Jewish woman who lent me the Matrix books, (I was later given a set), told me that his name was really John Grace and that he was a retired Major in the Air Force. That made me even more nervous about sending our files.

In November, he called again. During the course of this follow-up conversation, whereupon Val was urging me again to send the files, I told him I had figured out his real identity and that I had been thinking about what the Cassiopaeans had said about the KRLL papers and his own connection with the military, and that I had concluded that *he* was the author of the KRLL papers.

There was a long, pregnant silence before he recovered and evaded the issue adroitly, leaving me with the impression that, since he *was* the author, I should be even more inclined to trust him because we were on the same side, so to speak. I again agreed to send him the files, including the discussion about *KRLL* as recorded above, and the session about the 3-5 code discussed in volume four.

After, I didn't hear from Val. On December 2, 1995, I asked about this:

Q: (L) Now, tell me about this guy Val.
A: Learn through active pursuit of contact and observation.

But Val was not responding to the several letters I sent. I didn't have a phone number, and I was not aware of an e-mail address at this point, so I didn't know what else to do.

On December 16, 1995, I again asked why I had heard nothing:

Q: (L) Why haven't I heard from Val?
A: "Push buttons" more. Ask for more contact.

Well, I did, but I was beginning to suspect that the "learning through active pursuit of contact and observation" might not be such a positive thing in this particular case.

But then, he called in twice in late December, and again in January to ask follow-up questions about the material I had sent him. I had the distinct feeling that I was being probed for something, but could not identify what. He asked me to send him everything as it came through. I agreed to do so and sent the files up through mid-December.

Then silence again. Now, with the background necessary for the following session, this brings us back to our chronology:

January 13, 1996
Q: What is going on with Val Valerian? He was calling every week, and I have not heard from him in almost a week.
A: He lost track of time.
Q: Why did he lose track of time?
A: Busy with many projects. You must contact him because we see his desk topped with mounds of "stuff." He is interested, but just not for some period. [Short pause.] Isis has uterine or cervical abrasion from birth process. [Isis was my dog who had recently produced five puppies, two of which died a short time after birth because Isis was too ill to care for them. It had been several days, and the whole family had been moved into the kitchen for warmth, and so we could hand-feed the babies. This comment was volunteered with no question asked.]
Q: What can I do to help her?
A: Vitamins A, D, E and a solution of Goldenseal root to be placed in food.

We took a break from the session to carry out these instructions. They were, apparently, effective because Isis showed marked improvement over the next two days, and was completely normal at the end of about ten days. After tending to the little canine family, we returned to our session.

Q: Next question: How does one determine if they are channeling a third-density dead dude, or a higher-density being?

A: Corrections and clarifications needed: "Dead Dudes" are 5th density beings. Either they are stuck in 3rd density, or they are communicating from 5th density, not 3rd density!! They are not 3rd density [beings]! 1st density includes all physical matter below the level of consciousness. 6th density is uniform in the level pattern of lightness, as there is complete balance on this density level, and the lightness is represented as knowledge. 7th density is union with the one … it is timeless in every sense of the word, as its "essence" radiates through all that exists in all possible awareness realms. The light one sees at the termination of each conscious physical manifestation is the union, itself. Remember, 4th density is the first that includes variable physicality!! Ponder this carefully!!! And, remember, there is only one "God," and that the creator includes all that is created and vice versa!

Q: [Three names were given of scientists who worked for the U.S. government, asking if they were part of the reason Pam had been abducted and implanted as was described in the previous session. All three names were lost in static bursts, but the response to all three names was "yes." The last name was recorded in the notes and was Bob Nathan at JPL. Then, the following remark was made.]

A: Big involvement there! Microwave technology has many applications. Laser, ELF, electromagnetic.

Q: (P) Was my husband's last assignment … [remainder of question lost in static]?

A: Was used, but not consistently.

Q: (P) Was what my husband was told about the job he was doing a complete lie, or was it the truth?

A: Close, but a few details off.

Q: Was it because he was too strong willed to be controlled by an implant, that he was retired?

A: *He was trained in applications, not reversal of command instructions.*

Q: Does that mean that he wouldn't have sold out to the ones who put in the implant, that he was loyal to his employer?

A: Not quite correct concept, it means that *he could not be relied upon to reverse "course" upon activation of subliminal instructions.*

These last two remarks are extremely interesting in that they suggest that there are individuals who are implanted and/or programmed to "reverse course" of command instructions upon activation of subliminal instructions! Now *that's* a scary thought!

Q: (P) How could I be used to monitor personnel when I never noticed anything as being unusual?

A: Very complex, in fact, *parallel subject.* Pam is "locator probe" for the purpose of monitoring those in her midst. Telling is not important, reading is. Besides, most of the work performed did not involve conscious awareness.

Q: (L) Is this still going on?

A: Partly, but also, *Pam could be used as a probe to monitor all events taking place at JPL and other laboratories by examining aural imprints of her husband and others with whom she was ac-*

quainted. All events leave permanent imprints upon aural energy fields. This explains, for example, some sightings and apparitions. "Ghosts" are sometimes merely spontaneous activations of the aural records of the natural surroundings.

And, of course, it just never occurred to us that Pam or Sandy might be being used in this capacity in *our* group.

Q: [Question lost in static burst, but apparently about her third-density abduction in 1987, at the beginning of which she saw a "blue-white light" ahead on the road in the snow. She had been convinced that the incident was a "ghostly encounter" with her recently deceased aunt.]
A: No, Pam, the "blue thing" you saw was not an aural imprint reading, it was a *4th density craft partially transferred into 3rd density.* Your deep subconscious memory remembers much, much more.
Q: (P) Does the knife incident have anything to do with it? The memory of my son cutting his thumb with a knife, immediately after the blue light incident?
A: Yes. Screen memory.

We had many guests at the next session. This was the session where the "aura" photographs were taken of all the participants as well as our hands on the board. Since that portion has already been discussed in *Wave 1*, I will exclude it here and only insert the remainder of the session. Most of the questions were Pam's, and covered a number of subjects of health topics with interesting answers that might be considered to be of general interest. However, since most of the session time had been taken up with the photo session, we were all tired and the asking of personal questions is always extremely draining, so it's a very short segment.

January 27, 1996
Q: (P) I would like to know what I can do to improve my memory?
A: You have sleep disorders that are "short circuiting" what would ordinarily be utterly spectacular psychic and mental abilities. When you were very young, your senses were 10 times sharper. But then, the "interferences began."
Q: (P) That is absolutely true. I have had a sleep problem for years. Is there anything I can do to overcome this? Physically or otherwise?
A: Cleansing of a very intensive nature; hypnotic regression; spirit release and dietary adjustments. Also, stress inducing life circumstances of a very "ordinary" nature must all be deviated! Ordinary, in this instance, means not of an ethereal nature directly.
Q: (P) Well, I have taken several steps in that direction.
A: Some, but it is like putting a "Band-Aid" on a gunshot wound.
Q: (P) What is the implant I have made of?
A: Silicon based micron definitive construct.
Q: (P) Is this why I have this scar?
A: Scar is manifestation of scar in being.
Q: (S) I have been having some serious problems with joint pain in my fingers and I would like to know what to do to make this better because I think that taking pain pills is something that hides the symptoms and does nothing for the cause.

A: Not true, S, sometimes pain killers cure cause as well as symptom. This is simply reversal of therapy. The symptom dies, thus cutting off the energy flow of the causative problem. Then the root cause dies if its "fuel supply" is interrupted for an adequate duration.

Q: (L) Will this work on me?

A: You need to utilize herbal therapies and nerve or neural blocking techniques, such as self hypnosis and acupuncture.

Q: (L) Well, I have been having such horrible pain in my leg that I am unable to walk without a cane. What is causing this pain?

A: Tissue nodular grains passing through vascular region affected by mild thrombosis. Try spirulina, for starters.

This last session, which was also the one when the aura photographs were taken, was the beginning of another simultaneous thread of weirdness of that time period as I have already detailed in the story of Lilly and Sandy and the Reptoid Rape, in *Wave 2*.

The next day, Lilly called to inform me that Sandy was involved with a coven of some sort. I was sure that, even if it had been true in the past, Sandy was a reformed person. There was just no way she could participate in something like that one night a week and then sit in on our sessions on another. And she had been so devoted to helping me recover from my accident that I simply could not believe she was still connected to any of those people.

But, of course, this was also the same time period that I had been sent the information about the Greenbaum programming and I was somewhat concerned with Lilly's revelations about Sandy and the remark under hypnosis that she and Sandy had been part of the same programming set, which I took to be a group. Not only that, but there was the receipt of the *Elaine and the Sisters of Light* material at precisely the time that Lilly made her revelations to me about Sandy. Was I looking at another aspect of the hidden control mechanism? The whole thing was so unlikely and so crazy that I was really stretching my credulity to even deal with it on a rational basis. But heck! When you talk to sixth-density light beings via a ouija board on Saturday nights, how unlikely and weird can anything be?

In retrospect, I can see that I was being taught to see the unseen by the assembly of all these people around me.

The adventure of the hero is always a passage beyond the veil of the known into the unknown. The powers that watch at the boundary are dangerous. To deal with them is risky, yet for anyone with competence and courage the danger fades.

In the Banks Islands of the New Hebrides, if a young man coming back from his fishing on rock, towards sunset, chances to see "a girl with her head bedecked with flowers beckoning to him from the slope of the cliff up which his path is leading him; he recognized the countenance of some girl of his own or a neighboring village; he stands and hesitates and thinks she must be a mae; (an amphibious sea snake) he looks more closely, and observes that her elbows and knees bend the wrong way; this reveals her true character, and he flies." (Campbell 1949, 68)

Within just a few days of this last session, I was nearly on the verge of total physical collapse. The ear infection had exploded again; my eyes were inflamed and oozing sero-sanguinous fluid constantly, and I was pushing myself to get the magazine finished no matter how sick I was. The final straw was when the infection dropped into my lungs.

Q: (L) If you will bear with us tonight, we would like to ask a couple of health related questions.
A: Yes.
Q: (L) First, is this sickness that I am experiencing part of an attack?
A: As always.
Q: (L) Is there anything I can do to terminate this kind of attack?
A: No. Prevent? Yes!
Q: (L) What can one do to prevent these kinds of attack?
A: Always watch all portals! Those around you are all portals always!
Q: (L) So, there are portals all around. If that's the case, it seems that you could spend all your time watching all of them and never get anything else done!
A: Incorrect, when portals are activated, you will know if you are watching!!! Your problem has been "falling down on the job," especially not being aware of the danger presented by those closest to you. You tend to expect attack to always come from more or less disassociated parties, and you frequently confuse issues: mode and source!

So, the Cassiopaeans were taking their gloves off and plainly telling me that my health was deteriorating due to my associations with certain people. I am ashamed to admit how dense I was and that I just could *not* conceive of how innocent and friendly and seemingly helpful people could be instruments of attack. I mean, what was I supposed to do? Lock myself away from human interaction altogether? How could anyone in their right mind believe that there was anything dangerous or negative in any of them? They were just average people like me, trying to function in their own, personal, dysfunctional ways, just like me and everybody else on the whole blasted planet!

Q: (L) Well, is this especially true as we are on the verge of getting the magazine out and getting some things out on the Internet?
A: Of course, that should be obvious.
Q: (L) Does that also include Pam suddenly developing aches and pains every time we try to get the work done?
A: Yes, and expect more.
Q: (L) Well, I am so sick that I am ready to throw in the towel.
A: Throw in the towel?!? It's too late!! And besides, your life will dramatically improve if you persevere, as we have told you.

Another issue at the time was Sandy and her problems with her mother and sister. Her mother was in a retirement home and Sandy was constantly stressed because her mother was complaining that she was being mistreated at the home, that she was missing meals and so forth. I knew that Sandy had been adopted by a well-to-do older couple – pillars of the community – and I also knew that Sandy had spent many of her early years as a Motorcycle Mama with the Outlaws motorcycle gang.

As I have already discussed, I knew there were skeletons in Sandy's closet, and I felt that she had been horribly abused in some way, even if she would never talk about it, and even if she had been involved in gang-type murders with the Outlaws, I was sure that it was only on the periphery and not by choice. I knew from things other people had told me that once one is inside one of these gangs, it is almost impossible to get out.

But now Sandy was a reformed person. She had experienced an epiphany when her boyfriend had died, had given up her old ways, enrolled in massage school so that she could help people, and I had met her at the Reiki group. After my accident, knowing that she was a masseuse, I had called her for therapy. During the course of therapy, we had discussed the Cassiopaeans and she had been very excited to attend a session. After her first, she was so enthusiastic and full of helpful ideas and actions that she became a regular part of the group.

My own mother, who had taken the home nursing course as described in Wave 2, was asked by Sandy to take on the case of her mother in preference to the assorted cases she was handling for the home health nursing agency she worked for. The pay would be the same, and we discussed it and felt it would be preferable for my mother to care for someone who was close rather than a continuous series of assorted strangers as was the case in agency directed work.

So, a lovely little house was obtained and set up for the care of Sandy's mother, and the two ladies were moved in. Little by little, very dark things about Sandy's mother were revealed. She proved to be one of those manipulative, vicious and self-centered old people who really need to be in a retirement home because no one else can possibly deal with the demands they make. And that was just the third-density perception.

My mother was complaining daily to me about how it was just not worth it to try to care for this woman because she simply needed round the clock nursing and refused to do anything for herself. To ice the cake, Sandy's mother, even though she was not able to take herself to the bathroom or feed herself or move at all, demanded to be made up every day, have her hair done professionally, and to be dressed fashionably at all times, including spike heels! And just one person, who was herself elderly, was supposed to do all of this twenty-four hours a day, seven days a week.

But, there seemed to be something much darker going on, though I could not put my finger on it. After enjoying very good health for all her life, my mother began to have serious health problems. She couldn't sleep at night because Sandy's mother rang her bell every two or three hours to be taken to the bathroom and refused to wear an absorbent undergarment at night because it was not "aesthetic." Well, I can understand that, but I also was thinking about the fact that this woman apparently had no regard for any other human being on the planet other than herself.

I tried to talk to Sandy about it. I realized that we had made a mistake setting this situation up. But Sandy couldn't speak to her mother, it seemed. She could see the problems when she was away from her, and would resolve to do something about it; but the instant she was in her mother's presence, a change came over her and she was afraid to say anything that would upset her mother because she was so needy for her mother's approval.

At the same time, Sandy herself didn't seem to have any wish to take any responsibility for her mother herself.

I asked Sandy to take her mother on weekends, but she was always unable to do so for one reason or another. She would say that she was coming to take her to lunch, or to her own home for the day, or just to administer meds and get her mother to bed so that my mother could have an hour's rest. But she always managed to not do any of these things and to have endless excuses as to why she couldn't. Yet, for some reason, I had nothing but sympathy for Sandy. I really thought that Sandy ought to be able to manage these things herself like anybody else, but she was so pitiful and seemingly grateful for every minute of my time that I felt guilty for resenting the many demands placed on me.

I was, of course, caught in the middle. My mother had given up her very nice apartment to undertake this job, and, in a surprising switch, Sandy was claiming that the costs of the house and utilities ought to be considered part of the payment, so that my mother rapidly arrived at a point where she had very little funds in the bank to make a change even if she wanted to.

The whole situation was rapidly drawing to an explosion and I knew it. I pleaded with Sandy to speak to her mother and let her know that if she could not have consideration for the fact that she was very well cared for to have a full-time day nurse to attend to her needs in the environment of her own home, with comforts and advantages that were simply not available in the retirement home setting (it was a very depressing place with tiny cubicles for rooms, and no privacy), that she would have to go back to the home and give up her freedom altogether.

Sandy just couldn't do it.

And I began to think more and more about the coven that Sandy was supposed to belong to, according to Lilly, and the Greenbaum programming, especially in terms of her mother being one of the powerful women who ruled said cult behind a facade of ordinary life. Could it be possible that Sandy had been adopted by these people, well-to-do pillars of their community, and that her parents had been a part of this cult or some sort of coven? Could it be possible that Sandy, herself, had been subjected to Greenbaum and or cultic programming as a child, and that she had multiple personalities, one of which acted for the cult, and the other of which was just ordinary Sandy?

These were absolutely crazy ideas!

Now, the curious thing about the whole Sandy episode was that Sandy had originally been a member of the Reiki group that I have already discussed in Wave 2. She was very close to those Metaphysical Church people who, in the end, tried to kill me.

But, Sandy had become *very* close to me. Not only did she attend all the sessions and contribute financial support to the recording materials and computer materials necessary to produce our little printed extracts, she was also readily available for the therapy sessions that the doctor prescribed three times a week. I had chiropractic and massage on alternate days so that I was actually receiving therapy six days a week – with very little improvement.

Now, in short, here is the curious chain of events: because my child was ill and I needed to find work that I could do at home, I met Frank. Because of the investigation into the murder of the twelve-year-old girl on the East side of the county, I was laid up in bed and read the UFO books brought by Frank. This connected to Pam and the incident with the Flying Black Boomerangs. This was followed by the major deterioration of my health. The health problems led to the Reiki group through my mother. At the Reiki classes I met Louise, Candy, Trudy, Reverend Ruth, Sandy and that whole crew that tried to kill me.

Through Candy I also met MT, a woman who owned a metaphysical book store, who introduced me to RC, who referred Lilly to me. And through RC I fell heir to the magazine of which sent me to the print shop to reconnect with Pam. So, I had been being passed around, or so it would seem, in a large circle.

Of course, my mind was working overtime to explain all of these things in a rational way. I did not want to fall into the trap of "believing and thereby making real" in terms of the Greenbaum, and maybe if I hadn't been doing that, I would have noticed things sooner.

Little by little I started to get the idea that something was not quite right with this scenario. Every interaction with Sandy and her mother resulted in a serious draining of energy or sickness. My mother was constantly sick after undertaking the care of Sandy's mother. And, at this point, a new scenario began to develop. Every interaction with Sandy in the group resulted in an argument or misunderstanding. On several occasions, these disagreements almost led to the giving up of the project altogether.

I think the reader may be getting some idea of how truly complicated and strange this whole time period was. Anyway, this was the situation at the time of the next session. I had not mentioned anything to Sandy about the things Lilly had said. I was beginning to watch things, however, and was keeping my own council. But, apparently, Sandy had something on *her* mind.

A few days after the session Lilly had attended, which Sandy had left early because of a headache, and after Lilly had conveyed to me the information about Sandy and the cult activity, Sandy had confided to me that she believed she was soon going to die because of several disturbing dreams she had experienced. Naturally, my sympathies were engaged and I put aside everything to deal with her concerns.

Q: (L) Sandy has had several dreams about a storm coming and having to batten down the hatches and relocating …
A: Sandy must inquire.
Q: (S) In my dream, it was either a physical move, or a moving on to something. Am I moving out of town in a physical way, is it a spiritual moving on, or am I moving in a different direction in terms of my path?
A: That is four questions at once.
Q: (S) Am I going to be leaving the area?
A: Do you desire to?
Q: (S) No, I don't.
A: Then why would you expect that you would?
Q: (S) Well, that's what the dream was, but I know it's symbolic. Do you think maybe I could be moving on, hopefully spiritually? What does it mean, my moving on or relocating?
A: Vague.
Q: (S) Well, I just wonder in what way … [At this point, I became impatient with Sandy being unable to simply voice her worries and I jumped in.] (L) Sandy has said that she thinks this dream means she is going to die …
A: Sandy, ask your questions directly, please! If you "beat around the bush," we will also!
Q: (S) Will I be moving into fifth density soon?
A: What is "soon?"
Q: (S) Will it be sometime this year?
A: Only if you do something that might best be described as "ill advised."

The next question in this session relates to an odd comment the Cassiopaeans had made about a year previously, which I will insert here so that the next parts of the session will make sense:

Q: (L) I would like to know how many lifetimes I have had as a human being?
A: That is open to definition.
Q: (L) Well, on planet Earth.
A: Including Neanderthal?

Q: (L) No, let's skip those.

A: Okay, then it is 79 in broken sequence.

Q: (L) Broken by what?

A: Other planes.

Q: (L) The same question for Frank?

A: Same exactly.

Q: (L) How many for Sandy? Same?

A: No. Not correct definition of answer.

Q: (L) What would be correct for her?

A: Not same exact sequence. 72 plus 4 as special learning channel "hold back" on contemplative plane AKA 5th density level.

Q: (L) Sandy is a fifth-level soul?

A: No. Spent 4 sequence hold-overs there.

Now, back to Sandy's question in the chronological sequence:

Q: (S) Because of all these dreams about me moving on, could it have something to do with, like, in an earlier session you said that I was a, umm, I was held over in fifth density as a learning channel. Now, I must have been learning something important to be held over as many times as I was. Will whatever I was learning in fifth density come in handy in this lifetime, maybe?

A: What do you think you have been doing for the past year, as you measure "time?" And, what is "moving on?"

Q: (S) Progressing?

A: Yes!!

Q: (S) You mean that what I am learning here, the knowledge I am getting here?

A: That is beside the point, somewhat.

Q: (S) The only other thing is therapy … is it the channeling?

A: Both, and more to come.

Q: (S) Well, I feel like I am just wasting my time in doing the therapy …

A: Let it flow, Sandy, don't worry about what all the twists and turns along the way mean … it is the destination that matters, and that is not for you to know yet.

Q: (S) In all these dreams, I am repeatedly packing up to move. I have never had dreams that repeated over and over. This is a first for me …

A: Have you ever had other "firsts?"

Q: (S) Yes …

A: Did you panic over those?

Q: (S) Sometimes.

A: And what happened?

Q: (S) I survived.

A: So … ?

Q: (S) I just learn from them and grow from them … (L) And don't we just answer our own questions?

At this point, Patrick, Pam's son, who was also present, had been bouncing in his chair in his impatience to ask a question:

Q: (PK) I have a question … the lady who took the aura pictures the other night told me that I can astrally project. Is this true?

A: Everyone can.

Q: (PK) America has a flag, does Cassiopaea have a symbol?

A: We have given two.

Q: (PK) I want to know if they can put something directly in my subconscious. I need proof.

A: Proof, what is that?

Q: (PK) What is proof? Never mind. I'm afraid to ask.

A: Ask, what do you think we will do? Disintegrate you where you sit?

Q: (PK) The rumbling … does everybody have this … the rumbling sound in my head?

A: Vague, but we will answer if "everyone" were to choose to have it, then everyone would have it.

Q: (L) What is it that Patrick perceives as a rumbling in his head? Apparently, when he turns it on, it has a pronounced effect on his aura.

A: Turn on a radii between channels, and what do you hear?

Q: (L) Static.

A: That is not the issue. Turn on a radio that has its tuner between channels, and what do you hear???

Q: (L) You hear sort of a roaring sound. And this would imply that the radio could be tuned.

A: Yes.

Q: (PK) And that is what I need to work on?

A: If you wish.

Q: (L) I don't know too many people who can turn this on and off …

A: But you know people who have it "on" all the time, and always tuned.

Now, before we continue with the session, let's go in another direction for a moment to investigate this most interesting remark about sounds in the head. As I was working on this particular segment, the new issue of *Nexus* magazine arrived (Vol 8, No. 1), in which there was a most interesting article by Gavin Dingley, *ParaSETI, ET Contact via Subtle Energies*. As I was reading through this article, I came across the following information, which I have condensed somewhat, so the reader may wish to read the original article. I should also note that no specific notes were attached to the information in the article, and we have written to Mr. Dingley for footnote sourcing, so the accuracy of the information has not been confirmed. So, having said all that:

Thomas Townsend Brown is a guy who is known in some circles for his work in antigravity propulsion. Supposedly, Brown discovered a link between gravity and electricity based on the electrical condenser or capacitor. Brown hypothesized the existence of something he called "radiant energy", which he thought was present throughout the universe and that it might be gravitational in nature, though it was undetectable by instruments.

He was told by the experts that such a wave was impossible because it would require gravity to be bipolar – to be able to repel as well as attract. Later in his life he worked with Alfred Biefeld, a former classmate of Albert Einstein who was also very interested in gravity.

Biefeld had already considered the possible gravitational effects of charged electrical capacitors after studying the work of Faraday, the "Father of Electricity." Faraday is being quoted to say, "Electrical capacity is to gravity, as inductance is to magnetism."

It is well known that when current flows through a coil of wire, a magnetic field is generated. The coil is able to store electrical energy within the magnetic filed generated. An electrical capacitor is something that is made up of two sheets of metal separated by a dielectric insulator. When an electrical potential is applied to the two plates, it causes the molecules of the dielectric to align with the electric field.

So, perhaps, the energy stored in a capacitor is a gravitational field in the same way electrical energy is stored in the field of a coil.

In 1930, Brown entered the U.S. Navy and was on staff at the Naval Research Laboratories in Washington. While investigating different substances for use as dielectric material, Brown noticed a curious phenomenon: the resistivity, or insulation ability of some materials would change over time.

He next noticed that this phenomenon followed sidereal and diurnal changes; that is to say, it was influenced by solar and lunar cycles. He also noticed that some material would generate spontaneous radio frequency bursts. He also found many granitic and basaltic rocks to be electrically polarized, which is to say they acted like batteries. And, again, the amplitude of these rock batteries were influenced by solar and lunar cycles.

A station was set up to monitor the changes in the electrical self-potential of these rocks and it was thought, for various technical reasons, that the effect was gravitational in nature.

After World War II, Brown was working in California when he made another interesting observation: he found that the patterns of the rocks' electrical potential did not match the ones recorded in Washington. The rocks used in the Washington experiments were different to those used in California – that is, from different deposits, not different in terms of type. So from this observation, Brown concluded that different rocks are tuned to different bands of this radio frequency energy.

Brown concluded that this energy is the radiant energy he had hypothesized earlier. He thought that this energy was a high-frequency gravitational radiation, which was being constantly emitted from astronomical objects in outer space. While some dielectric materials would pick up the radiation and convert it directly into electrical energy, others would convert the energy into DC electricity. Not only that, but these rocks were tuned to only a portion of the total radiated energy present throughout the universe. This means that your average lump of basalt is a natural gravity wave AM receiver, tuned to only a few specific radio stations.

Another researcher named Gregory Hodowanec was working on developing a sensitive electronic scale and noticed slight differences in the weights he was using. He found that putting a capacitor in the right part of the scale circuit counteracted these variations. After investigating further, he discovered that the Earth's gravitational field was the problem because it was not stable, it fluctuated. His scale was so sensitive that it picked up these variations as changing values in his weights. He then concluded that his capacitor, which had been an inspired attempt to solve his problem, was able to pick up the gravitational variations and convert them into an electrical signal.

Hodowanec then went on to develop an amplifier wired to a current to voltage converter, which was connected to the sensing capacitor, while its output was fed into a standard voltage amplifier that in turn drove a loudspeaker. The signals received by this simple circuit were described as being similar to whale song. This is not conclusive, but it is remarkable that structured audio signals were received by this simple device.

Hodowanec thought that his device received monopole gravity waves, different from quadrapole waves described in Einstein's general theory of relativity. Also, while the gravity waves theorized by Einstein were limited to the speed of light, these monopole waves described by Hodowanec were alleged to reach any point in space in one Planck second. (10E-44 sec.) Hodowanec also suggested that electronic equipment had been receiving this gravitational radiation for a very long time, but it had been mistaken for $1/f$ noise. It is similar to what you get when your radio is not tuned to a station, which is a sort of rushing water sound. However $1/f$ noise has a deeper sound that some describe as roaring. Technically speaking, it is a whole spectrum of random frequencies which have equally random intensities, but for the most part, the lower frequencies are higher in intensity that the higher frequencies, which is why it has the lower or roaring sound.

Hodowanec hypothesized that the universe is filled with this radiation and that the detected isotropic microwave background radiation that is supposed to be the echo of the Big Bang is actually gravity wave emissions. Hodowanec also found that Auriga and Perseus in the Milky Way were the sources of many natural, yet unusual, audio signals. He suggested that the general background noise can be altered, or modulated, by the passing of large astronomical bodies, which cast a shadow over these emissions. This means that when such radiation is demodulated, one would hear the movements of planets, stars and galaxies. Much of the high-frequency radiation is generated by astronomical processes such as stars going supernova, star quakes and even to tectonic movements within nearby planets.

So, it seems that there are many signals throughout the universe. Many of them are natural and high in frequency. There may also be transmissions of higher intelligence among them, waiting for a tuned receiver to read them. (Dingley, 2000.)

And, speaking of transmissions, let's get back to our interrupted session:

January 27, 1996

Q: (L) Okay, next question from the list: Sheldon Nidle has written a book called *Becoming a Galactic Human*. He has said that the Earth is going to go into a photon belt sometime this summer, that there is going to be three days of darkness, and the poo poo is going to hit the fan, so to speak, the aliens are going to land in the late summer or the fall, and they are all coming here to help us. Could you comment on these predictions?

A: No.

Q: (L) Is a fleet of aliens going to land on Earth and be announced by the media in 1996?

A: No.

Q: (P) In 1997?

A: No.

Q: (L) Could you comment on the source of this book, *Three days of Darkness*, by Divine Mercy?

A: Source?!?

Q: (L) Well, is there going to be three days of darkness in 1998 like it says?

A: Why does this continue to be such a popular notion? And, why is everyone so obsessed with, are you ready for this, trivia … ? Does it matter if there is three days of darkness?!? Do you think that is the "be all and end all?" What about the reasons for such a thing? … at all levels, the ramifications? It's like describing an atomic war in prophecy by saying: "Oh my, oh my, there is going to be three hours of a lot of big bangs, oh my!!"

Q: (L) Well, you didn't say it wasn't going to happen in the fall of 1998. Is it?

A: First of all, as we have warned you repeatedly, it is literally impossible to attach artificially conceived calendar dates to any sort of prophecy or prediction for the many reasons that we have detailed for you numerous times. [Note: the fluid nature of the future. Probability, etc.] And we have not said that this was going to happen.

Q: (L) I know that you are saying that this three days of darkness is trivial considering the stupendous things that are involved in realm crossings. But, a lot of these people are interpreting this as just three days of darkness, then wake up in paradise. I would like to have some sort of response to this question.

A: You should already know that to attempt to apply 3rd density study and interpretations to 4th density events and realities is useless in the extreme … this is why UFO researchers keep getting 3 new questions for every 1 answer they seek with their "research." If you ask without anticipation, we will always give you not only the most correct answers to each and every inquiry, but also the most profound answers.

Q: (L) Previously you told us about the Southwest region of the United States becoming fourth density. Will the people who live there become fourth-density beings? Or will they be third-density beings in third density?

A: Some of both bleed-in and bleed-out.

Q: (L) Recently Frank had an experience where he heard me calling him as he was going in his door. Then, he heard Jason talking to him here in my kitchen when Jason was up in bed. He was worried that it meant something had happened, but it was apparently nothing of the sort. So, what was it?

A: Increased awareness of ethereal imprints.

Q: (L) When I was standing at the washer the other night, I heard someone clap their hands very loudly right behind me. Nobody was there.

A: Same.

Q: (L) You said earlier that if I just persevere that my life will improve dramatically and immediately. It's getting pretty hard to hang in here. So, when you say this, do you mean really sudden and in a big way?

A: Open.

Q: (L) Are you going to give me any clues on this?

A: No.

Q: (PK) Do you ever laugh?

A: Yes.

Q: (PK) Do you miss being in third density?

A: Do you miss being in 2nd? Or first?

Q: (PK) Are you laughing at us?

A: Yes. And no, Patrick, we were 3rd density beings in fact we are you in the "future!" We were you, and we are you, and we were 3rd density. Do you understand the significance of the last statement, or would you rather just brush it off? We are you and we were you and we were 3rd density but we are not now 3rd density and you are not yet 6th density.

Q: (L) How do you spend your time?

A: Teaching, sharing, assisting.

Q: (L) What do you do for fun?

A: That is fun!

Q: (P) With each other?

A: No.

Q: (P) With who?

A: Densities 1, 2, 3, 4, 5.

Q: (P) Do we all have a guardian angel? Each and every one of us? One to a person?

A: Not correct concept.

Q: (L) How do we get assistance from higher realms?

A: By asking and …

Q: (L) What is the limit to the kind of assistance we can receive?

A: Limit?!? We live within a realm that includes no such thing!!!

Q: (L) Well, the angel thing is pretty big nowadays. There are an awful lot of angels running around. My first thought was, 'What better way for the bad guys to deceive than to appear as angels.'

A: Not true!!! STS CAN appear as entities incorrectly perceived as "angels," but if it is really a sixth density being, incorrect perception is not possible.

Q: (L) I don't understand. There are a *lot* of beings who deceive people. They produce phenomena, they do any number of things including making people feel good, have dreams, and all that. What do you mean that incorrect perception is not possible? It happens all the time!

A: No.

Q: (L) Well, what is the story here?

A: Your perception abilities are short-circuiting due to vibrational interaction.

Q: (L) Are you saying that, if there is anywhere in you a question about what you are perceiving, then the very existence of that question is an indication that all the rest of what you are perceiving could be false?

A: Part of the equation.

Q: (L) So, if it is really a sixth-density being, it will blow you away to such an extent that there is *no* question in your mind?

A: Yes.

Q: (L) Now, what is the other part of the equation?

A: Well, why do you question us? First of all, you question us because the communication is limited at this point … you are not yet prepared for stronger envelopment.

Q: (P) So, I should continue to pray?

A: All goes to 6th density.

Q: (P) Okay, let's say that I have a little child who is dying of leukemia, and I am praying with everything in me, and the child dies anyway. I don't get it. What's the deal here?

A: Wrong. If child dies, that is your lesson profile.

Q: (P) Well, why isn't my lesson profile with this particular situation that is going on in my life right now, why isn't it continuing? I thought that maybe I need to …

A: Is it over yet, Pat?

Q: (P) No, it isn't over yet, but …

A: So, what is your question, if it is not yet concluded?

Q: (P) Can you feel what I am thinking?

A: Yes.

Q: (P) So, why do I need to ask?

A: Because we never interfere with free will.

Q: (P) If I continue to pray, things will continue to get better?

A: Things will stay on their intended course.

Q: (P) Are you telling me that my life has been predestined?

A: No. If you continue to pray, there is no chance of your lessons being interrupted or deferred. Clarify.

Q: (P) Well, that sounds like it is going to continue, it is not going to stop.

A: No, clarify means to solidify your understanding of the answer.

Q: (P) Well, I don't understand. (L) I think it is pretty clear that the things you are experiencing are part of the lessons.

A: Whatever that is … i.e.: que sera sera.

Q: (P) But then, we are back to pre-destiny?

A: No, lessons.

Q: (P) Well, how many damn lessons do you have to get?

A: As many "damn" lessons as you need!

Q: (S) What about the prayers that are directed to Jesus?

A: Jesus is one of us in "special service" sector.

Q: (L) Like a Green Beret?

A: No, more like a "beige beret."

Q: (L) What is a beige beret?

A: Just our term.

Q: (P) Well, I have just always wondered if this praying business is a bunch of malarkey. If I pray a rosary, I am praying to the Virgin Mary. Who is she? Where is she?

A: "She" is here too.

Q: (P) Does that prayer go directly to her and does she then send you out to do whatever?

A: She is not really a she. And when you write to "Ann Landers," does she really see it? And Good night.

As well as the brewing storm in regard to Sandy, it was becoming very evident that our involvement with Pam was far more complicated and problematical than I had ever anticipated. We had started the project at the beginning of January, and already I was becoming unwillingly embroiled in Pam's control games with her children and her dying husband. The whole family dynamic had presented itself in the beginning as so very charming and loving. As I spent more time with them on the magazine project, more and more secrets – *ugly* secrets – bubbled to the surface.

It became clear that Pam had bought the print shop business in order to be able to totally dominate her children. It was also clear that her children, aged 20 and 17, were completely and totally irresponsible and undesirous of being dominated.

With a dying husband and mounting medical bills, Pam had also endeavored to exert controls on her children by buying both of them expensive new cars as well as a forty-thousand-dollar sports car for herself so that they could maintain their images as business owners.

The children, Patrick and Shayna, thought that the print shop was their personal bank and that it was supposed to finance their every whim – even without completing the many orders that were placed by customers. They would take initial payments on large business orders, close the shop and go out to eat and party and sometimes not return to the shop for days.

Pat laughed at this in an indulgent manner for some time. But then the bills began to pile up and the investment income from her other sources began to dry up, and her husband's pension and inherited trust fund payments were not nearly enough to keep up the car and insurance payments. And, angry customers became more and more frequent, making Pam embarrassingly aware of what her kids were doing when she wasn't watching.

Pam was at her wit's end. She would be at home caring for her husband and would call the shop to see how the kids were managing things, only to find that it was closed and they were gone. Little by little she confided to me her concern over Patrick and his apparent substance abuse problems as well as her perception of her daughter, Shayna, as a flighty, promiscuous borderline mental case. Pam was constantly dragging Patrick to doctors for horribly toxic and mind controlling drugs such as Prozac and other anti-depressants. She was convinced that if he failed to take his medication he would turn into a monster, and he would certainly fail to take his medicine if he did not have his mother's constant attendance.

I was unsure why she felt this until she began to reveal that he had violent tendencies and had physically attacked both his parents on occasion, even throwing his father's oxygen tank into the swimming pool. Pam had to call the police several times. Each time when the police arrived, Patrick would beg her forgiveness. And each time she would refuse to press charges.

On one such occasion, he had stormed out of the house and had taken her car and disappeared for two weeks with her credit cards. It turned out that he and a friend had been partying in New Orleans, visiting whorehouses and eating in fine restaurants. She attributed all of this behavior to his failure to take his medication, and she was determined to keep him under her thumb; thus, she bought the print shop after he had expressed interest in the printing business.

Shayna, a more-than-plain girl with little but air between her ears, was proving to be a teenage slut of the first order. She had picked up a very sleazy boyfriend at a nightclub who glommed onto her because of her fancy car and access to fast, easy cash. More than once I observed him brazenly opening the cash drawer in the shop and taking out money for dinner and movies for himself and Shayna, who was simply gaga that such a slick guy would pay her so much attention; never mind that he was doing it with the customers' money and no work was getting done for that money!

Pam tried to control all of them and get the print shop to run, but it was a losing battle. I was practically desperate to get the magazine finished and Pam began to manipulate *me* to that end. She couldn't get to my magazine,which had been paid up front), until *other*, even older, backed up orders were finished so I ended up spending many nights in the shop helping her get the orders out. But, we could only do that if Patrick showed up in condition to run the presses, which was problematical at best. He would disappear for days at a time, showing up bleary eyed and sullen with no explanation for where he had been or what he had been doing.

And worse still, he hitting on my daughter and she was completely insensible to any warnings I gave her that she was being sucked into a black hole.

It was turning into a nightmare. My dreams of producing a magazine and getting it to the Gulf Breeze conference were rapidly fading, my daughter was being drawn into the clutches of a family that I was beginning to see as Tobacco Road incarnate, while Sandy and her wicked witch mother lurked like spiders in the background. I resolved to keep my cool, navigate these treacherous waters as best I could, and try to get out of this minefield with as little damage as possible.

Meanwhile, as if things were not crazy enough, another weird element was introduced into the situation. Against all odds and opposition, I finally had all the layout done, the copy was finished on the computer (I had to learn the program by doing it), and we were ready to print. At this point, a man came into the print shop talking big money and big print jobs. He was a huge guy, over feet and a half feet tall, puffing a cigar and punctuating the verbal dollar signs he was scattering through the atmosphere with smoke rings. Pam and her kids, desperate for more money, hung on his every pronouncement of how he was the answer to their prayers; they were sitting on a gold mine in their print shop, and he was just the guy to turn every ream of paper to riches. I could see my magazine being shoved to the back room with every word.

Not surprisingly, all of a sudden, Pam and her kids were no longer interested in the magazine or anything but the promises of gold and glory being spun by the mysterious stranger. I couldn't get anyone to answer the phone at the print shop; no one answered the phone at Pam's house and I was feeling desperate again at the thought of all my hard work being locked up and inaccessible to me. At least my daughter seemed to be seeing the light and was distancing herself from Patrick. I counted my blessings on that one.

Then Pam called. Something was not right with the mysterious stranger. Things were also getting weird in her life. She needed to talk to me and ask the Cassiopaeans some questions. Well, finally! The light was shining through and everybody was going to figure out all their issues and start acting like human beings again.

As best I could make out from the very confused tale she recounted to me, this mysterious man was taking control of her son and filling his mind with promises of big money while, at the same time, not coming up with any money of his own to back up his big words. Not only that, but the stories he recounted to all of them about his experiences as an undercover agent were getting stranger and stranger.

He claimed to have been a spy against the Nazis during World War II and he also claimed to have been single-handedly responsible for bringing down the Outlaws Motorcycle Gang. (The mention of the Outlaws Motorcycle Gang was a really creepy thing since Sandy had spent so many years in that environment. It was just another of the many crazy connections threading throughout this drama.)

He also claimed to have been forced to divorce his wife and abandon his family to do this job, which was a great and noble sacrifice on his part, though no reason was ever given as to why this had been necessary. Further, after it was all over, and all this was supposed to have taken place in Tallahassee, he had re-married her, they had a child, and this child had convinced him to give up the cloak and dagger life, which was why he was now looking for promising businesses in which to invest lots of money. The only problem was, the money didn't seem to be materializing.

He promised to show up with a large check to put down on a big job for Patrick that was going to be the start of their future money-making enterprises; however, this event kept getting put off over and over again. So Pam was becoming suspicious and thought that they were being taken for a ride by a con artist. She expressed this opinion to her son, and Patrick was so taken in by the man that he fell out with his mother and spent more and more time away from the shop, which meant that less and less work was getting done.

I really wanted out of this mess, but I didn't know what to do. I knew that Pam was not in any position to pay back the money I had already paid her to purchase the paper, which was still sitting unused in the shop. I knew I couldn't just take my paper to another shop and get a similar deal where I could do some of the work for a lower cost. I also knew that I didn't have the money to just go to any print shop and get the whole thing done from scratch. What's more, time was growing short. If we wanted to have a thousand magazines to take to the conference, it had to be done pretty soon!

As it happened, the very day that Pam called me, right after she hung up the phone, the mysterious stranger came in to the shop to reassure her that he would be dropping off some big money in the next few days. He had his wife and child with him. The only problem was, as Pam expressed it to me when she called later, the child was only about eight or nine years old, and the woman was clearly in her seventies or thereabouts. The man, himself, didn't look to be much over forty, so all the numbers regarding when he was doing what just didn't add up.

Pam was mystified.

I was disgusted with the whole thing. I couldn't figure out why Pam just couldn't see that the guy was a con artist from the word go. And why did she keep hanging on his every word when he hadn't put up a single dime?

Well, she came over wanting to discuss every detail of what this man had told her, every thing he had told her son, dates and times and just the whole scenario and it was so bizarre as to baffle the cleverest mind. He couldn't be old enough to do all the things he claimed, and his wife wasn't young enough to be the mother of a pre-adolescent child.

Well, we decided that the guy was a complete fraud and con artist. I just wanted him gone and my magazine printed. Apparently, Pam had been ashamed to call me for advice without being able to produce something of what was supposed to have already been finished, and she had prevailed on Patrick to print the inside pages. So, Frank and I were invited to the shop the next day to get all the pages of the magazine assembled. Now, all that was left to do was to print the covers.

So the next evening, there we were, in the print shop after closing and the doors were locked. The presses were running in the back, and Patrick seemed to be more stable than usual. He was working hard and doing a very good job. I was thinking that things might work.

A knock came at the door.

It was the mysterious stranger just dropping by to say that he would be there with the big check in the morning. He was full of all kinds of apologies for having had to leave town on a special assignment that was an emergency. Never mind that he was retired from cloak and dagger stuff. There was an emergency that only he could handle! Now he was back, and all would be well! Then, out of the blue, in response to no question whatsoever, he began to point by point give explanations for all the difficulties we had found with his story, including the fact that he was from a family that just simply did not show their age, even though he was now claiming to be well into his sixties. So, naturally, that explained how he could have been a spy against the Nazis and still look young enough to go undercover with the Outlaws Motorcycle Gang.

His wife, on the other hand, had been horribly injured because of some of secret agent work, and that was why he had had to divorce her – for her safety – and when they remarried, she was still undergoing plastic surgery that "went bad" and that was why she looked so old. But she was really much younger than she looked, apparently. However, they had dreamed of a regular family and had gotten help with in vitro conception, even though she was still older than she should have been to have a child, while being younger than she looked, and so on and on.

No problem. Everything was explained.

The only thing was: no one had asked any questions about these things or voiced their doubts and questions; at least not to his face.

Yet, he had just stood there and, point by point, in the same order we had discussed them, answered every question we had established as important in our private conversation of the night before. My back was to him, listening as I worked on collating pages, and I can tell you that my jaw dropped to the floor when he started on this subject. The hair on the back of my neck stood up and my skin felt like it was going to crawl off my flesh. I had the most bizarre sensation of time stopping and I almost froze in my rhythmic paper stacking motions; I had to force myself to keep working and to show no sign of surprise or curiosity. Then, just as if he had done what he came to do, he gave everyone a cheerful good night and left.

We all turned around and looked at each other with our mouths hanging open, our eyes as big as saucers, and said, "What the heck just happened here?" The three of us could hardly speak. We could only sit and look at each other and feel like the laws of the universe had been violated somehow.

After a few minutes Pam said, "Jesus H. Christ! It was just like he had been listening to us talking last night!"

And she was right.

We called Patrick out of the press room and told him the story. He looked at all of us with disgust on his face and pronounced us paranoid.

Well, maybe we were.

But perhaps we had a reason to be. The next night, Frank was at his job, sitting at his desk, when he stood up to go to the water fountain. As he rose from his chair, he turned and looked at the window of the office building where he was employed, and there, standing and staring inside, was the mysterious stranger. As soon as he saw Frank stand up he began to move away as if he had just been passing by, but it was too late. Frank knew he was being watched.

Frank called me when he was home and told me. The main thing we couldn't figure out was how did this guy know where Frank worked and what his schedule was? I called Pam to see if she had told the guy anything. It turned out that even Pam didn't know where Frank actually worked.

How did this guy know? Why was he watching Frank? Who was he and what did he want? How did he know about our private conversations at *my* house? What was this deal about the Outlaws that connected him in a strange way to Sandy?

Pam had become so frightened by these incidents that she had called the local law enforcement offices to inquire and complain. The day after she did this, the man showed up and made vague, threatening remarks about how traitors were dealt with permanently and that guys in law enforcement always shared information with each other. He didn't say anything specific, but was generally vague and indirect. Nevertheless, Pam nearly had a heart attack!

So, it seemed that some questions were in order. The next session was attended by a number of guests, including a friend that Lilly had brought. The Cassiopaeans were uncharacteristically sharp with Sandy and I was aware of all kinds of cross-currents of energy flowing around the room. For some time, Sandy had been in charge of note-taking, and it was a constant struggle for me to work with her notes because she was careless and easily distracted. It seemed that the Cassiopaeans weren't too happy with this state of affairs either, or they were trying to convey something to me through their remarks to her:

February 3, 1996

Q: (L) We have several questions tonight. Do you have any particular messages for anyone here first?

A: The need to deliver messages flows naturally, there is no way to "choreograph" it by requesting a specific "time" for this procedure. And, please tell Sandy to relay specifically when we place words in quotes!!!!! It is annoying to not get messages properly transmitted when it is important for each entity receiving to absorb every detail of the given messages as it is intended. We have up until now not said anything about this, in the hopes that she would learn this by herself, but alas, she has not. Therefore, we regret the necessary reprimand. Sorry Sandy, but now please be aware that you have been told, and do not make this error ever again!

Q: (L) Goodness! All I did was ask if there was a message for anyone!

A: But it is important for you to continue at the same steady pace.

Q: (L) Can I continue with the questions now?

A: Obviously, it is always possible to do all that you desire to attempt.

Q: (L) First question: there were rumors on the internet that a respected scientist described a ship in orbit around the planet Saturn, which was said to be as large as the planet Earth. And, supposedly, he said that the photographs from the space probe that sent back the pictures of Saturn's rings, showed this ship clearly with portholes in it. Is this thing seen in orbit around Saturn, described by this NASA scientist on television, which I cannot confirm because I did not see it, is it, in fact, an artificially constructed craft of some sort?

A: No. It was an artificially constructed tale.

Q: (L) Okay, there is a fellow, TF, who has been hanging around Pam's print shop, who has a *very* strange story about his past and present. The funny thing is, all the odd things about his story that we were discussing recently, he explained point by point the following day as though he had been listening to our conversation and knew of our doubts and suspicions. Who is this guy and what are his objectives where Pam is concerned?

A: Best not to discuss issues which threaten to interfere with free will directive. Suggest you stay "on your toes" with this one!

Q: (L) Is there anything about this that you can tell us that does not interfere with free will?

A: Have you not thought to gently inquire of the individual in question? And if not, why not? Generally, those involved in a ruse, be it simple or complex, are uncomfortable with graduated incremental disclosure!

Q: (L) Is one of the reasons you cannot discuss this more freely because we have such a large group this evening?

A: Who says we are not discussing it freely? Subtle answers that require effort to dissect, promote intensified learning.

Q: (L) Okay. I made the observation that if the fellow was a government spy, he would certainly have had a better cover story that the one presented. Am I on the right track?

A: Maybe.

Q: (L) And, sometimes it seems that alien programmed or controlled individuals do not have stories that make sense, or are consistent, because maybe there is some lack in their understanding of human culture. Am I on the right track here?

A: Sometimes is not all times.

Q: (L) Well, the guy is really huge and has size 17 feet … he looks like a Nephilim to me! Am I on the right track?

A: It would be more fun if he had size "35" feet!

Notice the curious reference to the 3-5 code! What were they trying to tell us?

Q: (L) Who has size 35 feet?

A: If you meet them, "give us a call!"

Q: (L) Are you joking with me? All kidding aside …

A: You need to be aware of all "guys."

Again, a warning to be aware.

Q: (L) Does Pam have anything to be afraid of?

A: What have we told you about knowledge as opposed to ignorance?!?

Q: (L) Pam wants to know what his intentions are.

A: Review answer two. [Answer two of this series would have been: "Generally, those involved in a ruse, be it simple or complex, are uncomfortable with graduated incremental disclosure!"]

Q: (P) Was he paranoid about the questions we were asking a week prior to tonight?

A: What happens to those who become uncomfortable?

Q: (L) Well, they get out of the situation. So, start grilling him …

A: Not "grill." We suggest subtle approach, or grill him "rotisserie" style.

Q: (P) Do I have any reason to be concerned about my actions regarding him, that I called to check on him with the police and reported him to the State Attorneys office?

A: Possibly.

Q: (P) Is it possible that there are moles in the tiny little police department here?

A: Open.

Q: (P) Do I need to get a bodyguard?

A: You are straying, please review.

Q: (P) Patrick seems to believe everything he says.

A: Ask Patrick.

Q: (L) What do you think, Patrick? (PK) I think he does a little bit of double-talk, but not as much as everybody thinks.

A: That is not the issue.

Q: (L) Is the specific issue whether this guy has any alien connections …

A: No, that is not it.

Q: (P) Is he monitoring us?

A: Review answer two. Now, ask yourself Pam, how likely is it that anyone with a tremendous ability to supposedly create such massive amounts of income, would just "walk in the door" and offer you a partnership in an endeavor that is going to produce such riches, as the person in question has described to you? If this individual has such tremendous acumen, why would he want to share the "bounty?" Remember the old saying: if something sounds too good to be true …

At this point, the discussion veered off onto El Chupacabras. Since we have already discussed that in its own context, I am going to omit it here and continue with the material from the last part of this session in the chronology.

Q: (Lilly) I would like to know if the Cassiopaeans are familiar with the entity that was on the three-dimensional level known as Paramahansa Yogananda?

A: Third density, not three dimensional. And yes, but this entity had many aliases: Thorn, Christian, Mobson Singh, etc.

Q: (Lilly) Where is Paramahansa now?

A: Fifth Density.

Q: (Lilly) Is he the Avatar?

A: That is a subjective, artificial concept of the self-styled variety.

Q: (Lilly) Who came up with the concept?

(Wilma) I don't know. I read it in a book somewhere.

(L) So, someone said he is now an Avatar?

A: Is Debbie a "shaman," is Billy a "hero," is Oscar a "blade runner?"

Q: (L) I read Yogananda's book and it seemed that he might be a very holy person. He seemed to have very loving concepts and practices in his life.

(Lilly) I just wanted to know where he is now. Does fifth density have anything to do with Venus?

A: That is not a proper conceptualization.

Q: (L) Fifth density is the contemplation and recycling 'zone.' (Lilly) Well, at the centers, the ashrams and shrines, people swear that he appears to them. I was curious also about the entity in my home.

A: This is a hanger-on from visit with Wilma at her domain. It is an energy seeking renewal.

Q: (L) Is Lilly's critter an STS or STO entity?

A: Open.

Q: (L) How does it make you feel? (Lilly) I am tired all the time. (L) How can she get rid of it?

A: Spirit release.

Q: (Lilly) Was it attached to Wilma first?

A: Yes.

Q: (Lilly) Is this what set off my fire alarm?

A: Energy there from. [Break]

Q: (L) Sandra [not Sandy] wants to know about her uncle who just died in January. (Sandra) Where is he?

A: He is at 5th density.

Q: (Sandra) Is he having a hard time adjusting?

A: No, but remember, there is no "time" there.

Q: (Sandra) Many members of the family have reported having visions and dreams of him. What are these caused by?

A: Various processes.

Q: (Sandra) Are any of these caused by Uncle Andrew himself visiting?

A: That is too simplified. We meant that your comment was too simplified. The question is: are any of these manifestations Uncle Andrew?

Q: (Sandra) He appeared to his oldest daughter ...

A: The concept is faulty.

Q: (Sandra) So, the appearances are all their own expectations?

A: No, not always, but we are trying to teach.

Q: (Sandra) Is he at peace?

A: Yes. Do you want to learn, or would you prefer to assume?

Q: (L) What are these kinds of manifestations?

A: They are 5th density thought projection energy waves. There is no time on 5th density. All event sequences happen eternally and for an instant only at once.

Q: (L) How does that relate to the question?

A: Because Sandra asked if he was at peace, and if he was "adjusting." Do you not see that by the "time" you realize someone is "dead," they have already, in essence, experienced their entire 5th density incarnation recycling, learning and contemplative experience in "zero time?!"

Q: (L) Sandra wants to know how many times she has been 'recycled' as a human being?
A: 84.

Q: (Sandra) I knew it! That's why this body is breaking down in pieces! [Sandra, herself, would be dead within months of this session.] (P) What about me?
A: 73.

Q: (P) Have Shayna and I known each other in another life?
A: Yes, all have and do. Number of incarnations does not predetermine schedule for graduation. And you, my dear, are too fatigued, so Good Night.

This last was addressed to me. It was true, I was having a lot of trouble staying with the program. There was something about this particular session that was unpleasant. The energy was not right, and I wanted it to end. Apparently, the Cassiopaeans felt the same.

The following week, I declined all requests for guest attendance. I wanted to deal with this issue of "corruption of the channel," as I perceived it:

Q: (L) Last Saturday night we had a very large group of people here and I experienced very unpleasant sensations. I would like to know the source of these? Was the channel corrupted?
A: Not corrupted, diluted. Static EM discharge from two entity sectors.

Q: (L) Was this due to the presence of any one or more persons in the room?
A: One person but two entities.

Q: (L) Well you said, at the time, that Lilly had an attachment and needed spirit release, is this the same person?
A: You learn by answering, using your own learnings, not from ceaseless confirmations by us.

Q: (L) Well, I am obviously not learning too well, even if you have been telling me about my "amazing abilities" which don't seem to be so amazing lately!
A: *All who have amazing abilities must too guard against corruptive forces from within and without having to do with prejudice, assumption, and the anticipatory desires involving patterning presumption. i.e. keep an open mind, always!!!*

Q: (L) Well, this leads me to the situation with the mothers: can you give us any immediate advice on this. A clue as to how to settle this situation.
A: Advice was given; not followed! Transposed by Sandy!!!

Q: (L) Do you mean the advice Frank gave Sandy?
A: First things first! Please, Sandy, try to be accurate! You were warned, Sandy! Please, please, please, please, when you call or cry out for help and or guidance, know that we will always, always, always answer. It is up to you to be aware and then trust and follow. If your deep seated stubbornness prevents this, it will result in nothing short of your total undoing! This is because we never give such warnings, except when Vitally necessary! This applies to all others present equally as well!!

Q: (L) This is a tough subject, any more on it?
A: Up to you. The situation will resolve naturally as all situations do ...

Q: (L) Is our involvement with Pam fortuitous or potentially disastrous?
A: Either.

Q: (L) You said before, that when we got things going that everything would improve suddenly and dramatically, and immediately. We understood that to mean getting online dialogs going and also getting the magazine out. Are we going to be able to do this soon?

A: As soon as needed.

Well, I was still trying to fit that square peg in the round hole! Many of the events from this time relating to my own "hero's journey" were recounted in volumes five and six. However, there was so much going on at the time that I will continue my narrative at a later time.

CHAPTER 65
THE WAY OF THE FOOL

As the Wave advances, a number of very interesting dramas have been enacted. So interesting and so relevant that we shall jump away from the present story for the remainder of this volume to explore this further. And trust me, it will be worth it!

As you might recall, during our discussion of the number 11 and the 3-5 code in volume four, I brought forward some unusual exchanges between myself and the Cassiopaeans regarding an 11-house zodiac. The very idea of such a thing is almost a heresy because the 12-house zodiac, the 12 tribes of Jacob, the 12 disciples, and all the other examples of the sanctity of the number 12 are so entrenched in our thinking that it is almost impossible to break away from it and think in different terms.

After I had written about it, the matter of an 11-house zodiac was discussed on the Cassiopaea e-group, and one of the members, an extremely erudite student of arcane matters and a professional academic, made mention of a reference to an 11-house zodiac carved by an obscure eleventh century monk in an Italian monastery that he had come across in his reading.

A member of our research team made an inquiry and the source of this reference was revealed to be a book: *Zelator: A Modern Initiate Explores The Ancient Mysteries* by Mark Hedsel.

I checked Amazon.com to see if it was available, and read a couple of the reviews, none of which inspired me to think that I ought to have it right away. But I ordered it and wrote to the research team:

> You ought to check out the reviews on Amazon. I ordered it just so I can track down that damn monk, but I don't have too much hope since I discovered that this is probably Golden Dawn/ritual magick nonsense for the most part.

And as you, the reader, are likely aware by now that the Cassiopaeans are not big fans of rituals and magick. So, naturally I really expected the book to be a waste of time and money. I wasn't even sure there'd be sufficient notes and references to tell me what I wanted to know. But, since I had been combing through an endless array of material for a number of years, looking for references to an 11-house zodiac, the promise of a single clue was enough to galvanize me to action.

The book arrived. Rather soon, even for Amazon.com I should say, and was added to the ever-growing pile of "to be read when I get the time."

Meanwhile, a significant drama was developing. It was not significant in that it was a big deal – it wasn't – but because of the way it opened certain doors. My plan for this chapter was to continue with the chronology of sessions, including the background events as I went along in a more or less linear fashion. It is a crucial period in which I learnt the deepest lesson of my life: how we are controlled and programmed by our culture, our families, and everything around us through our very physiology. It was a lesson which drove home for me in an unequivocal way, how it can be that humans are asleep or hypnotized. Until you have awakened, you simply cannot know the difference between being asleep and awake. It was also the period of time that led to the writing of the continuation of the Wave series, entitled "Further Adventures with the Cassiopaeans".

Well, telling this part of my story is, to say the least, painful. To talk about my own programming, and how difficult it was to even come to the awareness that I was as programmed as everyone is, and what was required to overcome it, is not a subject that I relish. But there is no other way to give an exact meaning of what it means to be asleep. It's all fine and good for Castaneda to write about how the Predator gave us its mind; for Gurdjieff and Ouspensky to write about the Evil Magician who hypnotizes his sheeple; for the Cassiopaeans to tell us that we are all programmed and hypnotized; but until you have experienced awakening, or at the very least, have had a graphic description of the state before and after, you simply cannot grasp it. And, I had an ace in the hole.

Not only was I planning to talk about this most basic and cunning of programs, I was planning to present some of the latest and most amazing scientific research on the subject from the fields of psychology, psychiatry, neurophysiology and neurochemistry that would give you, the reader, a huge edge on dealing with these issues in your own life and mind. Basically, the Cassiopaeans had pointed me in the right direction, I did the research, found the smoking gun that proved the case of the aeons of social programming and manipulation that has served to make human beings slaves, and I was going to tell! (i.e. the writing of the Wave and Adventures series.) It's pretty hot material because I am sure that the Control System does *not* want this kind of information right out there in plain view. Because, in fact, this information is at the heart of the Alchemical transformation process. Awareness and *application* of these matters will enable any individual who truly and deeply seeks transformation in a literal sense, to achieve it.

Of course, as usually happens, the Control System went into overdrive to try to stop me. And in this instance it very nearly did it.

Curiously, the entire episode (recounted in volumes five and six) was a graphic demonstration of the very matter I was seeking to ameliorate. Not only that, it made me painfully aware that, even though I have passed through a number of tests, have been tried by fire, have been initiated; I am still a work in progress. In response to the very kind of programming I was planning on describing and exposing, emotions were in motion and even I was very nearly sucked into the pit. I was ready to delete the website, delete the e-group, never write another word; and basically throw in the towel.

And then I realized that this would be acting as programmed. Everything that was being said and done was designed to excite emotions, to shut down thinking, to block higher understanding, and to feed the Predator. Remember what Castaneda said about the Predator's mind?

> In order to keep us obedient and meek and weak, the predators engaged themselves in a stupendous maneuver – stupendous, of course, from the point of view of a fighting strategist. A horrendous maneuver from the point of view of those who suffer it. They gave us their mind! Do you hear me? *The predators give us their mind, which becomes our mind.* The predators' mind is *baroque, contradictory, morose, filled with the fear of being discovered any minute now.* ... "I know that even though you have never suffered hunger ... you have food anxiety, which is none other than the anxiety of the predator who fears that any moment now its maneuver is going to be uncovered and food is going to be denied. *Through the mind, which, after all, is their mind, the predators inject into the lives of human beings whatever is convenient for them.* And they ensure, in this manner, a degree of security to act as a buffer against their fear." (Castaneda 1998, 213–220)

So, with this in mind, let's have a look at specific examples of the activation of the Predator's mind. It began with the following post to the Cassiopaea e-group, from which I have removed the identity of the individual posting it:

> Greetings, I'm new to the list, I have **a tireless appetite to sort out the truth of things** and after reading most of the C's material a few things really bother me. I'm not a supporter of the "it's all love and peace" approach to the universe either, but at the end of all my reading of the C's **I get a pretty sickly feeling message** that Earth/3rd dimension is a place to get out of ASAP because it's purely STS nature is **bad, bad bad** if you find yourself in disagreement with their description of STS behavior. But I read NOTHING about the **joys** and **absolute beauty** and wonder of this earth and **being alive**.

> Since reading C's I've been going around especially noticing the incredible beauty of one flower, a redwood forest, the incredible awesomeness of all nature in sync, the magnificence of our bodies, the awesome 'STS' human contributions & inspirations in the creation of art and music, the propensity of human beings to celebrate and seek the feeling of being in joy together. And it feels so right and so good to LAUGH and play with my children, share the deliciousness of the earth in the company of friends and admire the stunning beauty around me.

> **I think** something is terribly wrong when all of this is dismissed and ignored within the message. **I think** it's easy to forget that if these are beings literally and intelligence-figuratively light years ahead of us with an awareness and intelligence we cannot begin to really fathom, they **see right through us,** know what makes us tick and know how to lead us in a direction they want. **I sense somewhat of a game to gain some trust with accurate historical and scientific references,** and then often 'knowledge' is flat out GIVEN and in the next sentence some further "knowledge" is WITHHELD with the excuse of not violating our "free will". **The most striking**

thing to me is their direct claim that they also dictated the Marciniak info as Pleadians – and the gigantic discrepancies, contradictions and completely different slant on it all between the two sets of info.

Of particular significance to me is that they state in the Marciniak books to not trust them either! – that just as all the other beings they **describe have somewhat sinister agendas** contrary to their front, they clearly state they have an agenda too! My question to this list is, **if we put on our thinking caps and tried to imagine what a C's non-altruistic agenda might be, what could it be???** I'm still trying to clarify my **gut feeling**, but it lies somewhere in the realm of leading us to look outside ourselves rather than inward for answers. But why? And possibly that you CAN be both STO and 3rd D. Again, why deter us from that? **Jumping in with a thud ...**

Now, I know that many, even most, of the readers will not recognize in the material what this individual has extracted from it. And this is one of the chief effects of the very kind of programming I was planning on talking about. And just to give you some idea, I have put in bold text some of the clues to the programming of the writer. These words tell us something of the mode, or circuit, from which she operates and views the world. And being able to detect, interpret, and master these circuits and programs is part of the Alchemical work of transformation.

Now, the first thing we note about her missive is that, as a result of reading the Cassiopaean material, she had a *reaction*. This reaction actually, if she had taken the time to notice, was to feel more alive, and to find more meaning in the world. It was a shock, no doubt, but as Sartre was noted to have said, he never felt so free as when he was in the French Resistance and might be arrested and shot at any moment.

Thus, even though she was not fully appreciating what had taken place in her psyche, this reader was actually flirting with the early stages of awakening.

Gurdjieff taught himself to seek crisis consciously, as a means of shaking himself awake. He wrote:

"I had to forgo any limits, emotional, perceptual or knowable, that I had formed in myself, or had accidentally been formed in me by previous experience. I quickly recognized that any objective shock to the system could be used, provided it were safe enough to stop short – in some cases just exactly short – of total disruption of the life force in the body."

Gurdjieff's method included keeping his students in a perpetual state of alertness in order to solidify and grow the higher organs of perception. Only in this way can we achieve objective states of consciousness.

But, what happened to our reader? Well, the Predator's mind, "baroque, contradictory, morose, filled with the fear of being discovered any minute now," drove her to retreat in terror from this objective consciousness. Even though it was awakened by the very shock she had received, her interpretation of this effect was that it was dangerous, which is a rather graphic illustration of the contradictory nature of the Predator's mind.

But, what is this Predator's mind exactly? It is the way our brains and nervous systems are set up – as delineated by our DNA – which includes certain early periods of where our circuitry and thinking processes are established at an age and under conditions over which we have no control.

This is called *imprinting*. Human beings are born with certain basic behavior patterns built in their DNA. Just as a flower will follow a certain series of steps from the emergence of the seedling to the stage of producing a flower, human beings also develop certain characteristics *only at certain times in their growth process*. These sequences are something over which we have no control.

Konrad Lorenz illustrated this principle with his famous ducks. Ducks (and humans) are programmed at a certain time in their lives to accept a mother figure. If the proper mother figure is not there at that moment of imprinting, whoever or whatever *is* there will be the mother image in the mind of the duck. That is to say, when the appropriate (or inappropriate) object of need is presented to the duck *at the correct time in its development*, the object is labeled "mother" somewhere in the brain, and this label is next to impossible to erase.

Experiments were conducted with ducks which demonstrated that there is a critical age in hours at which a duckling is most responsive to obtaining and labeling a mother.

Similar studies were done with monkeys. These studies demonstrated that if a monkey has not received motherly stimulation before he is a certain number of weeks old, he will grow up to be cold, aloof, and unfriendly to his own offspring. The curious thing about the monkey experiments was that the sense of touch was more important than the feeding. A fuzzy surrogate with no milk was preferred over a wire surrogate with milk. This demonstrates a high-level need for touching and caressing. It also suggests the mode of this imprint – sensory. Kinesthetic.

Evidence that there is a critical period for the mother imprint in the higher animals was emphasized in the monkey experiments. In one instance, the experimenter was not prepared for the arrival of a new baby monkey and had to create a makeshift surrogate mother using a ball for the head. This was provided to the baby, while the experimenter worked on a better model with a face. But, it was too late. The baby monkey had already bonded to the faceless mother and turned the face of the new model around so that it was blank. A mother with a face was simply not acceptable because the imprint had already been made.

Joseph Chilton Pearce writes:

Occasionally we hear of people found chained in attics and such places from infancy. Their world view is either scanty or different for they are always feeble minded at best. In 1951 a child was found in an Irish chicken-house, having somehow survived there with the chickens, since infancy. The ten-year old's long hair was matted with filth; he ate at the chicken trough; roosted with the flock; his fingernails had grown, fittingly, to semicircular claws; he made chicken-like noises, not surprisingly; he had no speech and showed no promise of learning any in the time he survived his rescue.

Forty years ago there was interest in two feral children found in India. They had apparently been raised by wolves. They were taken from an actual wolf den along with some cubs, the older wolves scattering or being killed. One of the children, Kamala they called her, survived for nine years. Only with difficulty was she taught table manners and such niceties as walking on the hind legs. Nevertheless *she exhibited a growing awareness of the reward system of her new group, and displayed a strong drive toward such orientation.* As with the chicken-child, however, she had missed the formative period of human infant development, and there was no easy or complete going back to retrace the steps. Kamala had formed *according to the pattern eliciting response around her during her mirroring [imprinting] period.* For her first two years of captivity – or rescue – she howled faithfully at ten, twelve, and three at night, as all Indian wolves do. She would also, in spite of precautions, manage to get at the chickens, rip them apart alive and eat them raw. *Only when the new social reward system grew strong enough to outweigh the earlier rewards did she abandon her early training.* (Pearce 1971)

We are all Kamala. We are all divine children raised by wolves.

But how can this be?

We are all programmed. Our programs are written in the circuits of our brains by those around us in our formative years, just as their programs were written during their formative years, and so on back into the mists of time. Each generation just adding a few more lines of code.

It is our ideas that shape our children. We provide what we may consider to be the ideal environment for the child, but our own programming determines what we may consider to be the proper environment. Once we have provided the environment, we then want our children to like it, to approve of it, to agree with us that it is right. And our ideas come from our culture. And our culture is created by … what? A Control System?

There is considerable evidence that agreement is also in the genes. There seems to be a genetic drive toward communion with others, for speech and preferences and disposition. As newly born human beings, it seems we come into the world with intent to be in agreement with others. But *the details of how we go about being agreeable is related to the imprints we receive at the various stages of childhood development.*

Everyone carries in their genes, it seems, deep archetypes that are very much like a database program just waiting for someone to input data. The thing is, this database is only open to input for a limited period of time, and whatever data is entered during that time determines how all other data will be evaluated forever after. It will produce over and over again the same response to any set of stimuli that have one or more items that have been organized by the database. Anything that is not found in the database is discarded. If the database is not utilized and no data is entered during the period of readiness, or imprinting, that possibility goes dormant and diminishes.

The higher thinking functions, laid over the deep-level archetype database, can be viewed as a kind of software that is linked to the database, and must constantly check with it in order to operate. You could think of it as a word processing program with a fixed dictionary and set of templates, and you can only write in it according to the templates, and you can only use the words that are in the already fixed dictionary. Since our brains are genetically designed to accept imprint conditioning on its circuits at certain crucial points in neurological development, these critical periods are known as times of "imprint vulnerability". The imprint establishes the limits or parameters within which all subsequent conditioning and learning will occur. Each successive imprint further complicates the matter, especially if some of these programs are not compatible with others.

Different schools of thought describe these circuits as "stages of development." Some of the earliest work in these concepts has passed into our culture to such an extent that they have become slang terms such as "Oh, he's just anal-retentive," with very little actual understanding of what is meant by such expressions.[2]

It seems that, according to research, the older brain structures – those necessary for basic survival, such as the brain stem – are imprinted in the earliest stages of development, and that the newer structures, such as the mid-brain and cortex develop superimpositions upon the more primitive imprints. However, *the earlier parts of the brain and their imprints form the foundation for how later imprints are responded to and continue to function after the higher thinking modes are developed.*

In other words, if you are traumatized as an infant at a crucial point of imprint perceptivity, it doesn't matter if you grow up to be the President of the United States, you will still be ruled by the imprint.

And, of course, we have a classic example in Bill Clinton. It didn't matter that he was behaving in ways to destroy his marriage and the emotional well-being of a well-loved child; it didn't matter that his behavior was destructive to the point of practically bringing the entire country to chaos; his inner emotional drives, determined in infancy by his imprinting, ruled his behavior. His Rhodes scholar intellect had nothing to do with it. And, sadly, this is actually exactly how everyone operates in principle, though not necessarily in specific. A lot of men *do* have the same imprint Bill has; only they aren't President of the United States. But then, women also have their own variations on this theme.

The first stage, or circuit, is the oral-passive-receptive, and is imprinted by what is perceived to be the mother or first mothering object. It can be conditioned by nourishment or threat, and is mostly concerned with bodily security. Trauma dur-

---

[2] While there is some disagreement about how many stages exist in human development (e.g. Freud's three stages: oral, anal, and phallic), and when exactly they occur, it's agreed among researchers that these sensitive phases of imprint vulnerability lead to patterns of behavior that are very persistent, if not irreversible. For example, imprinting in many species of animals determines social status, sexual preference, food preferences, and habitat preferences.

ing this phase can cause *an unconsciously motivated mechanical retreat from anything threatening to physical safety.*

In recent times I have given a lot of thought to this particular circuit because of the matter of circumcision. Having come to the tentative idea that the whole Judeo-Christian monotheistic rant was a major control program, I came face to face with the question: how and why has it worked so well for so many thousands of years? More than that, how was it imposed in the first place?

I puzzled over this for weeks. I thought about several things that Friedrich Nietzsche had said that struck me like thunderbolts of truth once I was able to really step back and look at the matter:

The Jews are the most remarkable nation of world history because, faced with the question of being or not being, they preferred, with a perfectly uncanny conviction, being at any price; the price they had to pay was the radical falsification of all nature, all naturalness, all reality, the entire inner world as well as the outer. They defined themselves counter to all those conditions under which a nation was previously able to live, was permitted to live; they made of themselves an antithesis of natural conditions – they inverted religion, religious worship, morality, history, psychology, one after the other, in an irreparable way into the contradiction of their natural values.

> ... Christianity has waged a deadly war against the higher type of man. It has put a ban on all his fundamental instincts. It has distilled evil out of these instincts. It makes the strong and efficient man its typical outcast man. It has taken the part of the weak and the low; it has made an ideal out of its antagonism to the very instincts which tend to preserve life and well-being ... It has taught men to regard their highest impulses as sinful – as temptations.
>
> ... What is Jewish, what is Christian morality? Chance robbed of its innocence; unhappiness polluted with the idea of "sin;" well-being represented as a danger, as a "temptation," a physiological disorder produced by the canker worm of conscience. (Nietzsche 1888)

But, that's not to say that Nietzsche was any paragon himself, with his mysogynistic, misanthropic rants. He was in fact declared insane in 1888. As the *Encyclopedia Britannica* (11th ed.) put it, "Revolt against the whole civilized environment in which he was born is the keynote to Nietzsche's literary career."

Nevertheless, he had a point about Judaism and Christianity (and any and all other monotheistic, dominator religions.) So, there I was, pondering this and trying to figure out *how* and *why* people could be so completely taken in by this utter nonsense. How can educated members of the human race, in this day and age, with all the resources of knowledge and awareness available to those who have the desire and energy to search for truth, possibly buy into such myths?

It just staggered my mind to think about it.

I went back in my thinking to the whole Jehovah-I Am deal; the Moses story and all that; and went over the details as they are presented in the Bible for clues. And I came up against that most interesting demand of that crafty Jehovah/Yahweh: circumcision. On the eighth day, no less.

What better way to ensure a deep, subconscious, distrust of women – not to mention an overwhelming terror at the very mention of the pain and suffering that might ensue from breaking the monotheistic covenant – than whacking a guy's penis when he is interested only in being warm, cozy, and filling his tummy with warm, sweet milk from mother?

Talk about your basic abyssal cunning there!

The first circuit is concerned with what is safe and what is not safe. In our society, money is one of the primary items that is intimately tied to survival and biological security. Money represents survival. In addition to that, people who have been traumatized during the imprinting phase of the first circuit tend to view other people in an abstract way. It is "us and them." They also tend to be very easily threatened by disapproval of any sort because disapproval suggests the idea of extinction or loss of food supply. And, finally, those who have been negatively imprinted at this stage tend to have a chronic muscular armoring that prevents proper, relaxed breathing; they are uptight.

One of the main characteristics of people who are heavily controlled by this circuit, or are stuck in this oral phase, is that *when they sense danger of any sort, whether actual or conceptual, all mental activity comes to a halt.* Such people are chronically anxious and dependent – mostly on religion. They are not able to really understand what other people are feeling or *what can happen in the future in regard to relationships, given a certain present situation. They only understand what is happening now, and they can only feel what they feel.* They cannot accurately grasp what others feel because *they relate to others only as sensory objects.*

And, how many men are circumcised? *A lot,* I can tell you – 30% of males, globally, according to the World Health Organization, and approximately 56% are circumcised as infants in the U.S. And, besides the Jews, for years, the American Medical Association advocated and urged circumcision of American babies for hygienic reasons. Hmm.

As a side note, trauma or failure to bond at this oral phase tends to also lead to weight issues – either overweight or underweight. The expression of healthy growth through this phase is the ability to retain the state of consciousness of the natural child who will feel safe in the world no matter what they encounter.

I would say that, in terms of the negative imprinting of this circuit, we have pretty well described William Clinton. I wonder if he is circumcised? I suppose you could ask Monica.

The second stage, or circuit, the famous "anal phase," is concerned with keeping or letting go of experiences in interactions with others. This second circuit determines how an individual will expand their identity to include others. The drive of the second phase is to interact with other selves. It is this drive that either brings about the congregation of groups, or results in paranoid withdrawal from anyone who is different. Trauma in the formation of this circuit (generally from 12 months to 24 months) can result in a lack of social feeling, a tendency to manipulate and exploit others for one's own gain, and cruelty to others, whether conscious or unconscious. This is generally a result of a feeling of non-acceptance, that one is missing out on something that others have, the need for approval from others and basic lack of self-esteem.

It is during this phase that the Matrix – a conditioning system of sorts – forms as a semantic universe of verbal structures. Language is conceptual, as we have discussed previously, and is one of the things that distinguishes third density from second density. Our concepts are a sort of framework of perception that we learn as we learn words. As we are learning our language, things such as hot and cold, we are also learning that one thing is good or another is bad. We can either handle things freely because they are good, or we don't touch because they are bad. There is, in this phase, a tremendous drive in a child to create order. This drive is aimed at grouping, identifying, correlating and naming everything. And, as this is being done, there is a constant check with the parents and others interacting with the child as to whether this is bad or good or real or not real. What the child is doing is defining not only himself, but his entire world. It is at this stage that most of our complex belief systems are formed. Everything that surrounds him is raw material for the child. The matrix is created by the guiding actions and responses from the other minds around him. This matrix is, in reality, a gigantic conditioning system. And we insert our children into it through our own actions.

The mind of an infant is said to be:

> ... Autistic, a rich texture of free synthesis, hallucinatory and unlimited. His mind can skip over syllogisms with ease, in a non-logical, dream-sequence kind of "knight's move" continuum. He nevertheless *shows a strong desire to participate in a world of others. Eventually his willingness for self-modification, necessary to win rapport with his world, is stronger than his desire for autonomy.* Were it not, civilization would not be possible. That we succeed in moulding him to respond to our criteria shows the innate drive for communion and the flexibility of a young mind.
>
> Maturity, or becoming reality adjusted, restricts and diminishes this "knight's move" thinking, and tends to make pawns of us in the process. ... If we believe our social view sacred and made in heaven, we tend to shut off a deep potential in which many of the terrors and shortcomings of our logic and reason might be averted.
>
> ... We force our children, consciously and unconsciously, to selectively ignore certain phenomena and look for and nourish other phenomena.
>
> ... To take part in society we must accept the social definitions and agreements that make up the society's reality picture. Our definitions outline the socially acceptable framework for what shall be considered real. This network of definition changes

from culture to culture and period to period. It is arbitrary to an indeterminable degree, but is always the form for the only reality available.

... The stage of this development lasts throughout infancy and early childhood. The word and the concept become fused in that early period of development and grow up together.

If language is not built in during this formative period, it cannot be built at all.

... The emerging mind will have mirrored whatever model it had during that formative period. The pattern formed in this plastic stage becomes firm. It hardens into the functional system of representation-response we call a world view.

... The infant's dream-like association of ideas is slowly won over to an agreement of what should constitute reality. By the time our reasoning has developed enough to reflect on the process by which our reasoning has formed, we are part and parcel of the whole process, caught up in and sustaining it. By the time the young rebel reaches the age of rebellion his is inevitably that against which he would rebel ...

... Whitehead [wrote of fundamental assumptions] ... But people do not know that they are assuming, for no other way of putting things has ever occurred to them; they are always merely responding to "obvious facts."

... We are limited by our agreements on possibility. Agreement is a common exclusion of alternate possibilities. Agreement is the cement of social structure.

... The condition called reality exists as an ever-current sum total of our representations and responses. Whatever we see is what reality is for us ...

... We used to think of the nervous system as a simple telephone switchboard, bringing in messages from outside. We now know ... that the system is every bit as much an "editorial hierarchy" – a policy-making device determining what is perceived.

... The visual world is what we practice day by day. (Pearce 1971)

Now, I want you to keep in mind the idea that an infant "shows a strong desire to participate in a world of others. Eventually his willingness for self-modification, necessary to win rapport with his world, is stronger than his desire for autonomy." It is very important, and we will come back to it.

Those with strong positive second circuits imprints are able to *feel* for others in terms of a sense of concern or identity by association. They are willing to reach out and acknowledge the being of another.

However, due to the most common imprinting of our society, which is negative, most of this reaching out is in the context of territory, which involves emotional con games, pecking order, rituals of domination or submission. It has been noted that a lot of people with negative second circuit imprinting can be found in military or hierarchical organizations where there is constant striving to please someone in order to maintain or rise in status.

This second circuit is generally most powerfully imprinted by the nearest alpha male or the earliest perceived dominant male figure in a person's life. This circuit is also very often referred to as the ego because it mistakes itself for the whole self.

Individuals who are ruled by negative second stage imprinting generally use a lot of anal expressions or language relating to excretory functions and parts of the body. They have inveterate potty mouth. Very often those with heavy imprints in the second stage are either very concerned about physical fitness and body structure as a mode of power or just simply power over others in general. They fear thinking and feel that the best response to a problem is to frighten it away.

The reality structure of the second circuit is the prevailing mode of modern society, which is why most issues end in confrontations that bring out both bullying and cowardliness – hallmarks of second circuit trauma.

The third circuit is charmingly referred to as phallic. Don't ask me why this term has been selected over all others but it has to do with the fact that the imprinting stage is associated with the child's discovery of his or her genitals and this period also seems to partly determine gender role identification as well as one's later attitudes toward the body and sex. It is also called the Oedipal or Electra stage.

This circuit continues to be imprinted and conditioned by symbol systems, i.e. words and concepts, however with subtle conceptual complications. The child is beginning to be able to understand complex symbolism and such things as now and later and soon and never. These concepts are intimately connected to the ability to tolerate separation, as well as to mourn if the idea of grief is introduced and demonstrated by a role model.

So, essentially, we find that the third stage has to do primarily with time and spatial concepts – with what is the real world and what is not.

The part of the brain that is developing during this phase is the cerebellum and it is supposed to coordinate the lower brain functions with possible action. This part of the brain and its imprinting determines our ability to change and adapt. This is what makes us able to discriminate and compare with logic and comparative analysis. Its functions operate like a computer; it scans, categorizes and selects by cross-referencing and coding information. It is this part of the brain that makes us able to weigh choices and make decisions.

In most people, however, due to traumatic or too early potty training during the anal phase, this part of the brain becomes a slave to the emotions of the second and first circuits. That doesn't mean that it cannot work and do its work well in terms of scanning, categorizing and coding information; but if there is trauma, depending on the severity, it can be very difficult for this part of the brain to function as the coordinator it is meant to be. The intellectual function can be scholarly as all get out, but there is no possibility of development of higher emotions. Such a condition can lead to a ruthless intellectual who tortures or kills others in the name of religion. These people have packaged their environment in terms of heavy sanctions; taboos, rules, laws, prohibitions, faith and dogmatism. Much of this will be unconscious and will pass as common sense or common decency or "it's right, and that's all there is to it!" Anyone who challenges such a person is a heretic, a traitor or a lunatic. They also use a lot of language that refers to sexual functions.

Those who are dominated by the third circuit respond to problems by reasoning it out, even if their reason is being directed by the emotions of the first or second circuits. When this is the case, they could be called a third circuit robot because they simply cannot break free of the emotional content of their rules and dogma. For such people, the rest of the nervous system has, for all intents and purposes, stopped growing.

There are two curious manifestations of this circuit. If the first and second circuits are basically healthy, and the third circuit is not traumatized in any notably serious way, but no effort to develop higher faculties is made, the normal conscious mind has two basic tracks. The first is the desire to use the intellect to prove that much of human experience, even including the reality itself, is delusion or illusion. Everything is mysterious and hallucinatory. The second is to use the intellect to prove that nothing exists but the material world and anything mysterious is viewed as hallucination, coincidence or sloppy research. Gurdjieff talked about these things in great detail, and clearly his understanding of the problem was deep and profound. Not only that, we will soon see how closely Gurdjieff's view is to very modern research in neuropeptides – the *Molecules of Emotion*. Gurdjieff writes:

> It is possible to think for a thousand years; it is possible to write whole libraries of books, to create theories by the million, and all this in sleep, without any possibility of awakening. On the contrary, these books and these theories, written and created in sleep, will merely send other people to sleep …
>
> There is nothing new in the idea of sleep. People have been told almost since the creation of the world that they are asleep and that they must awaken. How many times is this said in the Gospels, for instance? "Awake," "watch," "sleep not." Christ's disciples even slept when he was praying in the Garden of Gethsemane for the last time. It is all there. But do men understand it? Men take it simply as a form of speech, as an expression, as a metaphor. They completely fail to understand that it must be taken literally.
>
> … The question of will, of one's own will and of another man's will, is much more complicated than it seems at the first glance. A man has not sufficient will to do, that is, to control himself and all his actions, but he has sufficient will to obey another …
>
> I mentioned before about fate and accident in man's life. … Fate exists, but not for everyone. Most people are separated from their fate and live under the law of accident only. Fate is the result of planetary influences which correspond to a man's type. A man can have the fate which corresponds to his type but he practically never does have it. This arises because fate has relation to only one part of man, namely to his essence.
>
> It must be understood that man consists of two parts: essence and personality. Essence in man is what is his own. Personality in man is what is "not his own." "Not his

own" means what has come from outside, what he has learned, or reflects, all traces of exterior impressions left in the memory and in the sensations, all words and movements that have been learned, all feelings created by imitation – all this is "not his own," all this is personality.

... A small child has no personality as yet. He is what he really is. He is essence. His desires, tastes, likes, dislikes, express his being such as it is.

But as soon as so-called "education" begins, personality begins to grow. Personality is created partly by the intentional influences of other people, that is, by "education," and partly by involuntary imitation of them by the child itself.

In the creation of personality a great part is also played by "resistance" to people around him and by attempts to conceal from them something that is "his own," or "real."

Essence is the truth in man; personality is the false. ... As personality grows, essence manifests itself more and more rarely and more and more feebly and it very often happens that essence stops in its growth at a very early age and grows no further. It happens very often that the essence of a grown-up man, even that of a very intellectual and ... highly "educated" man, stops on the level of a child of five or six. This means that everything we see in this man is in reality "not his own." What is his own in man, that is, his essence, is usually only manifested in his instincts and in his simplest emotions. There are cases, however, when a man's essence grows in parallel with his personality. Such cases represent very rare exceptions especially in the circumstances of cultured life. Essence has more chances of development in men who live nearer to nature in difficult conditions of constant struggle and danger.

... Culture creates personality and is at the same time the product and the result of personality. We do not realize that the whole of our life, all we call civilization, all we call science, philosophy, art, and politics, is created by people's personality, that is, by what is "not their own" in them

The element that is "not his own" differs from what is man's "own" by the fact that it can be lost, altered, or taken away by artificial means.

... In Eastern schools ways and means are known ... to separate man's personality from his essence. For this purpose they sometimes use hypnosis ... if personality and essence are separated by one or another means, two beings are found who speak in different voices, have completely different tastes, aims, and interests, and one of these two beings often proves to be on the level of a small child. ... And it happens that a man full of the most varied and exalted ideas, full of sympathies and antipathies, love, hatred, attachments, patriotism, habits, tastes, desires, convictions, suddenly proves quite empty, without thoughts, without feelings, without convictions, without views. Everything that has agitated him before now leaves him completely indifferent. Sometimes he sees the artificiality and the imaginary character of his usual moods or his high-sounding words, sometimes he simply forgets them as though they had never existed. Things for which he was ready to sacrifice his life now appear to him ridiculous and meaningless and unworthy of his attention. All that he can find in himself is a small number of instinctive inclinations and tastes. He is fond of sweets, he likes warmth, he dislikes cold, he dislikes the thought of work, or on the contrary he likes the idea of physical movement. And that is all.

... As a rule a man's essence is either primitive, savage, and childish, or else simply stupid. The development of essence depends on work on oneself.

... [I]n order to enable essence to grow up, it is first of all necessary to weaken the constant pressure of personality upon it, because the obstacles to the growth of essence are contained in personality.

...

As has been said earlier, in the case of less cultured people, essence is often more highly developed than it is in cultured man. It would seem that they ought to be nearer to possibility of growth, but in reality it is not so because their personality proves to be insufficiently developed. For inner growth, for work on oneself, a certain development of personality as well as a certain strength of essence are necessary. ... An insufficiently developed personality means a lack of ... knowledge, a lack of information, a lack of the material upon which work on oneself must be based. Without some store of knowledge, without a certain amount of material "not his own," a man cannot begin to work on himself, he cannot begin to study himself, he cannot begin to struggle with his mechanical habits, simply because there will be no reason or motive for undertaking such work.

It does not mean that all the ways are closed to him. The way of the fakir and the way of the monk, which do not require any intellectual development, remain open to him. But the methods and the means which are possible for a man of developed intellect are impossible for him. Thus evolution is equally difficult for a cultured or an uncultured man. A cultured man lives far from nature, far from natural conditions of existence, in artificial conditions of life, developing his personality at the expense of his essence. A less cultured man, living in more normal and more natural conditions, develops his essence at the expense of his personality. A successful beginning of work on oneself requires the happy occurrence of an equal development of personality and essence. Such an occurrence will give the greatest assurance of success. If essence is very little developed, a long preparatory period of work is required and this work will be quite fruitless if a man's essence is rotten inside or if it develops some irreparable defects. Conditions of this kind occur fairly often. An abnormal development of personality very often arrests the development of essence at such an early stage that the essence becomes a small deformed thing. From a small deformed thing nothing else can be got.

Moreover, it happens fairly often that essence dies in a man while his personality and his body are still alive. A considerable percentage of the people we meet in the streets of a great town are people who are empty inside, that is, they are actually *already dead.*

It is fortunate for us that we do not see and do not know it. If we knew what a number of people are actually dead and what a number of these dead people govern our lives, we should go mad with horror. And indeed people often do go mad because they find out something of this nature without the proper preparation, that is, they see something they are not supposed to see. In order to see without danger one must be on the way. If a man who can do nothing sees the truth he will certainly go mad. Only this rarely happens. Usually everything is so arranged that a man can see nothing prematurely. Personality sees only what it likes to see and what does not interfere with its life. It never sees what it does not like. This is both good and bad at the same time. It is good if a man wants to sleep, bad if he wants to awaken. (Ouspensky 1949, 144, 161–164)

So, having all of this to think about, let's go back to the message of the e-group member. She has a "tireless *appetite* to sort out the truth of things." Truth is something to be eaten. In every sentence about "beauty and wonder" and the goodness of physical life, the writer has used the expression "*I feel*." Everything that has to do with the material world is "awesome" or "incredible" or another superlative. In every remark about the Cassiopaeans, which is singularly suspicious and negative, she has used the term "*I think*." Thus we suspect that this is an individual who is very suspicious of thinking and this is further emphasized by the suggestion to "put on our thinking caps." Thinking cannot be abstract, it must be felt. The general tone of the letter is to retreat from thinking into feeling. That is one of the biggest clues that the Predator's mind is operative. Her first circuit imprint was active.

This writer claims to have read something that is simply not true, i.e. that the Cassiopaeans have made a "*direct claim that they also dictated the Marciniak info as Pleadians.*" This is a clear example of twisting the text and inference of that which was never implied. It is, in fact, a very clear example of what Neuro Linguistic theories refer to as a kinesthetic dominant mode of cerebral processing. This person was being shocked into thinking and retreated in terror from the threat to what felt safe.

Let's take a look at what the Cassiopaeans actually said:

September 30, 1994
Q: (L) How many members are there in the Orion/Lizzie group?
A: 16.
Q: (L) Who are the good guys? You say the Cassiopaeans are the good guys. Who else?
A: Pleiadeans and many others.
Q: (L) How many?
A: 16.
Q: (L) Are the sides equally balanced?
A: Yes.

Here we have the idea that there is a distinction between the Cassiopaeans and Pleiadians. In fact, we have a more or less sorting and enumeration of groups.

October 5, 1994
Q: (L) Who were the original creator gods?
A: Us. Sixth Density.
Q: (L) The Cassiopaeans? Were the Pleiadeans also the original creator gods?
A: Same. Sixth Density.

Here we have an idea that the "creator gods," (not to be confused with the Prime Creator) are all at the level of sixth density. This is not the same as saying that each group is exactly the same. It's comparable to me saying to an alien that I am the same as Barbara Marciniak because we are both from Earth.

November 26, 1994
Q: (T) Are you also the Pleiadeans?
A: No.
Q: (T) Are you connected to the Pleiadeans?
A: Yes and so are others.
Q: (T) You are all the family of light?
A: Yes. Exactly. You have been "doing your homework".

So the remark, "*direct claim that they also dictated the Marciniak info as Pleadians*," was a sign off remark. As I have noticed on many occasions, when the Predator's mind is activated, it seems always to need, due to ego, to give some sign of its presence. And, as the reader will also note, I adhere to the Sherlock Holmes School of Research.

"You know my method. It is founded upon the observance of trifles."
 —"Sherlock Holmes" in Doyle's "The Boscombe Valley Mystery"

The trifle in this case was the remark, "Jumping in with a thud." This phrase triggered the insight of what was happening to this reader. She was being overwhelmed by the forces that act on a person when they are confronted with truth and the possibility of awakening. Castaneda was to experience it in a more direct manner:

I fought a nearly invincible desire to fall asleep. I succeeded, and found myself looking at the bottom of the valley from an impenetrable darkness around me. And then, I saw something that chilled me to the marrow of my bones. I saw a gigantic shadow, perhaps fifteen feet across, leaping in the air and then *landing with a silent thud. I felt the thud in my bones,* but I didn't hear it.

'They are really heavy,' don Juan said in my ear. He was holding me by the left arm, as hard as he could.

I saw something that looked like a mud shadow wiggle on the ground, and then take another gigantic leap, perhaps fifty feet long, and land again, with the same *ominous silent thud.* I fought not to lose my concentration. I was frightened beyond anything I could rationally use as a description. I kept my eyes fixed on the jumping shadow on the bottom of the valley. Then I heard a most peculiar buzzing, a mixture of the sound of flapping wings and the buzzing of a radio whose dial has not quite picked up the frequency of a radio station, and the thud that followed was something unforgettable. It shook don Juan and me to the core – a gigantic black mud shadow had just landed by our feet.

'Don't be frightened,' don Juan said imperiously. 'Keep your inner silence and it will move away.'

'I was shivering from head to toe. I had the clear knowledge that if I didn't keep my inner silence alive, the mud shadow would cover me up like a blanket and suffocate me. Without losing the darkness around me, *I screamed at the top of my voice. Never had I been so angry, so utterly frustrated. The mud shadow took another leap, clearly to the bottom of the valley. I kept on screaming, shaking my legs. I wanted to shake off whatever might come to eat me.*" (Castaneda 1998, 231–233)

And notice this last remark by Castaneda. It is clearly the feeling evoked in the writer who was *"jumping in with a thud."*

Well, at the time this posting was made, I had a choice to make: should I take the several days necessary to address each and every point that was made by this writer, detailing the material I was already working on for the website, thereby putting off the publishing of the page for all the other readers, or should I just ignore it, thinking that the other, more developed members of the group could deal with it and I could continue working?

I opted to ignore it and keep working. But I didn't realize how great a hold the Predator has even on those of us who can see through most of the most obvious manipulations and maneuvers. This was, indeed, a subtle attack and it fed the Predator in many other members of the e-group. In fact, it woke up the Predator in people I had thought were well past this kind of subtle manipulation. As I read the many responses to this post, I knew that the present work, which dealt with these very issues was the very key that needed to be given to the readers in order to unlock the prison of their own minds.

Ark took time out from his work to respond to the above writer so that I could keep working:

E-group member wrote:

But I read NOTHING about the joys and absolute beauty and wonder of this earth and being alive. Since reading C's I've been going around especially noticing the incredible beauty of one flower, a redwood forest, the incredible awesomeness of all nature in sync, the magnificence of our bodies, the awesome 'STS' human contributions & inspirations in the creation of art and music, the propensity of human beings to celebrate and seek the feeling of being in joy together. And it feels so right and so good to LAUGH and play with my children, share the deliciousness of the earth in the company of friends and admire the stunning beauty around me.

Dear Reader,

You missed completely the most important point of the Cassiopaean message. This is, in fact, almost exactly the same as in the teachings of Gurdjieff. Except that Gurdjieff thought that people are not yet ready to accept the naked truth, so he was using allegories. Here is one – it is repeated in the Abduction Series:

"There is an Eastern tale which speaks about a very rich magician who had a great many sheep. But at the same time this magician was very mean. He did not want to hire shepherds, nor did he want to erect a fence about the pasture where his sheep were grazing. The sheep consequently often wandered into the forest, fell into ravines, and so on, and above all they ran away, for they knew that the magician wanted their flesh and skins and this they did not like.

"At last the magician found a remedy. He hypnotized his sheep and suggested to them first of all that they were immortal and that no harm was being done to them when they were skinned, that, on the contrary, it would be very good for them and even pleasant; secondly he suggested that the magician was a good master who loved his flock so much that he was ready to do anything in the world for them; and in the third place he suggested to them that if anything at all were going to happen to them it was not going to happen just then, at any rate not that day, and therefore they had no need to think about it. Further the magician suggested to his sheep that they were not sheep at all; to some of them he suggested that they were lions, to others that they were eagles, to others that they were men, and to others that they were magicians.

"And after this all his cares and worries about the sheep came to an end. They never ran away again but quietly awaited the time when the magician would require their flesh and skins."

And here is another one, also from *In Search of Miraculous*:

"Man contains within him the possibility of evolution. But the evolution of humanity as a whole, that is, the development of these possibilities in all men, or in most of them, or even in large number of them, is not necessary for the purposes of the earth or of the planetary world in general, and it might, in fact, be injurious or fatal. There exist, therefore, special forces (of a planetary character) which oppose the evolution of large masses of humanity and keep it at the level it ought to be. For instance, the evolution of humanity beyond a certain point, or, to speak more correctly, above a certain percentage, would be fatal for the *moon*. The moon at present *feeds* on organic life, on humanity. Humanity is part of organic life, this means that humanity is *food* for the moon."

You may ask "What is this moon?" in Gurdjieff teachings? Read our Abduction series [*High Strangeness*] and you will know.

So, what is this main message from Cassiopaeans? The message that must be always, *always*, kept in mind?

Here it is: We are food!

Here it is again: We are sheep!

There is a moon! It is real and powerful. There is a magician. Real and powerful. We are hypnotized sheep. The magician, the moon, *feed* on us. You can either accept it as a viable possibility, or you reject it as nonsense. If you reject it as nonsense – you are free to go to laugh and play with your children, share the deliciousness of the earth in the company of friends and admire the stunning beauty around you, read Marciniak and trash Ouspensky.

But if you think that you can admit that there are signs here and there that we might be hypnotized sheep (or something equivalent), then you will want to learn how to escape yourself, and to teach, at least your own children, the art of escaping – if there is such an art.

If you think that sending love and light is the way – this is not what Gurdjieff and Ouspensky were talking about. You miss the point completely. The New Testament is also using allegories (but, notice, the Magician also took part in producing the New Testament). Here is one, the shortest one that is relevant and worth pondering:

"Enter through the narrow gate, for wide is the gate and spacious and broad is the way that leads to destruction, and many are those who are entering it."

Now read again Ouspensky:

"The evolution of humanity beyond a certain point, or, to speak more correctly, above a certain percentage, would be fatal for the moon. The moon at present feeds on organic life, on humanity. Humanity is part of organic life, this means that humanity is food for the moon."

Now replace moon with aliens (as in "alien abductions"). Then think again if it feels so right and so good to laugh and play with your children, or is it, perhaps, "the way that leads to destruction, and many are those who are entering it."

"He hypnotized his sheep and suggested to them first of all that they were immortal and that no harm was being done to them when they were skinned, that, on the contrary, it would be very good for them and even pleasant; secondly he suggested that the magician was a good master who loved his flock so much that he was ready to do anything in the world for them; and in the third place he suggested to them that if anything at all were going to happen to them it was not going to happen just then, at any rate not that day, and therefore they had no need to think about it."

Does it sound like your "laugh and play?" It does!

And this is what Cassiopaeans are talking about. But who wants to enter through the narrow gate when there is a wide and spacious and a broad one: "the incredible beauty of one flower, a redwood forest, the incredible awesomeness of all nature in sync, the magnificence of our bodies, the awesome 'STS' human contributions & inspirations in the creation of art and music, the propensity of human beings to celebrate and seek the feeling of being in joy together."

Here it is again: "the magician suggested to his sheep that they were not sheep at all; to some of them he suggested that they were lions, to others that they were eagles, to others that they were men, and to others that they were magicians."

The choice is yours. But please, notice, you are also responsible for your children. They are small, so your choice of the gate is, by necessity, also their choice ... until they grow enough.

ark

But in counterpoint to my realization of the need to keep working, to get the information out as soon as I could, the drama escalated. Another member of the e-group posted. I have placed in bold text the words that provide clues to the circuit dominance in the above writer.

Hello A, B here-

You write: "The most striking thing to me is their direct claim that they also dictated the Marciniak info as Pleadians – and the gigantic discrepancies, contradictions and completely different slant on it all between the two sets of info."

B: May I **inform** you that the Pleiadeans have been **characterized** by Michael Topper as "the bad guys pretending to be the good guys", i.e. **precisely** the wolf in sheep's clothes. And in fact if we **carefully analyze** their (Pleiadians') shapeshifting story-board like messages, we can **clearly see** they're not here to **teach** us first-hand principles (which ought to be true and helpful under *any circumstances*) – we **clearly see** that their **blind stories** are **nosing us around into a mess. No common sense**, no **carry-through-logic** anywhere. Yet this is exactly the way the pleiadeans want it!!!! That's very revealing, isn't it?

If you still don't get the clue, **let us look** what sort of info Laura gets from their ostensibly "benign" Cassiopaeans: She gets a **shapeshifting story** about "353535" which **drives her mad the instant she hears it**. We **must think** about the possibility that the Cs deliberately *wanted* to drive Laura mad. How "benign" could that be???? Not benign at all!! All we **need to know** is: from what sort of background are the Pleiadeans giving their advice, or stories?

Why, these Pleiadans come from a **self-admitted future probability-wave** wherein the evil Reptilians have taken over the Earth, and over the rest of the universe on top of it!! *That* is the reality they want to **draw your attention to**, as a sort of extra-reinforcement to "weave the future probability-waves strong enough"! Enough said? My advice: Drop all channeling, and get in touch with a walking, talking, and really benign incarnated Master. **One that you can see,** feel, smell, touch, and, last but not least, trust, because he's teaching verifiable first-hand principles that are helpful under *any* circumstances. Verily, Topper **comes to mind. Indeed, but Topper only.** Enough said. B

This is an individual who is dominated by the third circuit and is under the control of the second! In Neuro Linguistic theories, it is called "visual." Notice the preponderance of terms relating to eyes and seeing or blindness. The third circuit is also the circuit in which the concepts of time are dominant – linear time – and he evinces fear when he mentions the references to probability and future.

The third circuit is the thinker, the creator of the semantic universe, as we will discuss further on, and it tends to categorize everything in the strictest terms of black and white, and wants very much to use its abilities: to think, analyze, inform, consider and teach. This individual fears audition, as well as anything that is not hard and material, or powerfully based in linear thinking, as is indicated in the below mentioned remark "*shapeshifting story* about "353535" which *drives her mad the instant she hears it.*" His remedy for this is: "We must think … "

The problem with the third circuit is that it very often is dominated by damage to the second circuit and produces what in psychological parlance is referred to as a "second circuit robot." There is good development of the cerebral function, and a desire to use it as the dominant mode. But the anal phase overlay on the phallic phase development is evident in the fact that the above writer has needed constant monitoring and requests to not use profanity on the list.

He is, in fact, one of the main reasons we opted to enforce a rule on the moderated list that no profanity is allowed. There is a higher reason for this, which involves the creation of an environment in which the elements of the higher circuits can develop, but that's another matter. The fact is, the above post arrived with profanity in the title, which was deleted before it was forwarded to the group. I then responded to it:

Hello E-group member, Laura here:

You write: "If you still don't get the clue, let us look what sort of info Laura get's from their ostensibly "benign" Cassiopaeans: She gets a shapeshifting story about "353535" which drives her mad the instant she hears it. We must think about the possibility that the C's deliberately *wanted* to drive Laura mad. How "benign" could that be ???? Not benign at all!!

Laura: Well, you are not going to bait me with this into telling you what has been discovered as a result of this clue before it is in sequence. Indeed, it drove me nuts in colloquial terms, but the result was like stoking the firebox in a train to fuel it to achieve a certain destination … and what many people seem to forget is this: the Wave series is being written as a chronological piece … what drove me nuts then, *past tense*, was the seed of what I know now – in the present. And we are not there yet in the story.

As to whether or not it was benign. Well, that will be for the reader to decide once they have all the same clues that I have ... . as well as the evidence that resulted from these clues, which will certainly put every single person in a position to actually *do* something from a position of true free will – to the extent possible in this density. Which, of course, brings up the present discussion.

As I have noted in the past, very often when I am writing about certain things that most assuredly will give the reader insight into the Control System and how it works on a daily basis; things that will go far to set people free; it seems that those individuals most easily disturbed or manipulated to create diversion and discord – which distracts me from the work at hand so that I must divert time and energy to handle what masquerades as pressing issues rather than dealing with the revelation of crucial evidence – are activated more or less simultaneously.

I am not the only person who sees a pattern in this. Every page I have produced has been preceded by a chaotic uproar to one extent or another. Of course, at this point, I can almost validate the truth of my conclusions by the extent to which the control system will go to manipulate the thinking and emotions of those who seek to create discord and disruption. And I can tell you that I am on a hot subject now.

E-group member: Why, these Pleiadans come from a self-admitted future probability-wave wherein the evil Reptilians have taken over the Earth, and over the rest of the universe on top of it!! *That* is the reality they want to draw your attention to, as a sort of extra-reinforcement to "weave the future probability-waves strong enough"!

Laura here: But that directly contradicts the teachings of Michael Topper [who argues that we have no participation in the creation of our reality.] You are suggesting that we "create our own reality" by what we think. I tell you that we create our own reality by what we *believe*. And what we believe very often directs our thoughts in exactly the opposite direction [of that we wish to manifest] in order to create balance. Those who believe the world is broken seek to focus only on "love and light" in order to fix it. Those who cannot look at it *as it is*, in all its terrible aspects as well as those realities of ineffable beauty, and accept it as it is; as perfect; will experience all the problems that make them desperate to change the world. And once you believe the world is perfect, deep inside, once you let go of fear, once you can look and see and not judge anything as being wrong, though it may not be desirable or preferred by you, then your reality will change to the most perfect for you.

E-group member: Enough said?

Laura here: Indeed. More than enough. The rules of the list include one that excludes profanity. I have edited the subject field of this post accordingly. And the rules of the list will be applied as a result of the profanity used.

Egroup member: My advice: drop all channeling, and get in touch with a walking, talking, and really benign incarnated Master. One that you can see, feel, smell, touch, and, last but not least, trust, because he's teaching verifiable first-hand principles that are helpful under any circumstance. Verily, Topper comes to mind. Indeed, but Topper only.

Laura here: Okay. You got it.

And he was removed from the list. His antics had been reprimanded numerous times both on list and privately. And the final thing was: his proposal to "drop all channeling" was a clear indication that he did not belong on a list whose premise was stated in the list rules, that it is a group formed to discuss channeling.

Naturally, I wasn't happy to delete a person from the list, most particularly one who was so evidently capable of work in the third circuit. But, there are other matters to consider that will be seen as we proceed here.

All of this drama was acting on my own programming. It is said that the true High Initiate is one who can no longer cry. They feel compassion, but it is cosmic and non-attached. I'm not there yet. I still cry. And, I am always reminded of the shortest verse in the Bible where it says: "Jesus wept." (John 11:35. How's that for your 11 and 3-5 code?) He had not yet been fully initiated, after which he left the planet, so I expect that, as long as I remain, I will weep. And, as the drama continued on another front, I did.

A message was posted to the unmoderated CassChat e-group, of which I am not a member, but another member on that group forwarded it to me privately. It was written by a former member of the Cassiopaea e-group who had been the first to be removed because, well, you will see why:

> Casschat egroup member here: If you read the Cassiopaean material, when the Cs mention to Laura about luck. Read this section and Laura is basically stating that Ark is a fourth density Nordic. This ego on this guy is hilarious. He is on such a power trip it is absurd. Ark I would love to meet you in person, and really see how much of a man you are. You're a typical Reptilian coward with NO BALLS. He has taken me off the Cassiopaea list because I said I would not have my future dictated by higher beings. Can you believe this guy? He is supposed to be an STO candidate? He is the most close minded and censoring person I have ever met on any board. Laura; can you honestly say he is a truly compassionate and understanding guy?? The Cassiopaeans must be truly proud of you Ark. You kick people off your boards without even a warning. Who actually likes you or thinks you are a positive influence on anyone? Everyone on [another e-group] thinks you're a total jerk. Do you realise everyone on your boards sends me letters telling me I have brought up great subjects and activity on your board. If you did not notice your board is usually pretty dead when I do not post. Are you such an egomaniac that you cannot have someone more stimulating than you on there? I knew you would be looking to get rid of me with all the actual stimulating conversations I have created on your board recently. I really hope Laura is beginning to realise you are an evil person. WAKE UP: HE IS AN AGENT OF THE REGRESSIVES.

I think that the reader will now be able to go through this message and determine which circuits are dominating.

Now, this individual is one who began writing to me privately some time ago, and I spent many hours patiently answering his questions, which seemed to be honest and sincere. However, no sooner would I deal with one issue by directing him to the pages where it was already addressed, he would bring up others that were also already addressed on the site. And most of his questions were quite similar to the "twisting" phenomenon we have seen in the first post reproduced here, where the writer either did not read the words carefully, or did not consider the context carefully, or simply could not receive what was being said. What she mirrored was not what was viewed. So, I realized that this was an individual who was also very much stuck in the second circuit, only his trauma must have been severe. I wanted to ensure that he, as anyone else, had the opportunity to work with others to undo this programming, since he was asking for help, or so it seemed. I sent him to the e-group so that I could get back to work. By this time, I had given him several days of my time with no end in sight. I needed to get to those issues with which he was dealing, and the only way I could do it was to continue working and not be distracted.

The only problem was, as soon as he had an audience, something strange began to occur. He used many nom de plumes or email handles, and was apparently active on several other groups because many people found his posts here and there and forwarded them to me. I filed them away and kept working.

Finally, as the archives on the Cassiopaea e-group will show, he became so disruptive that dozens of people were writing to us privately asking to have him removed. And it was as a result of this that we realized that to preserve the higher-circuit-thinking environment of the e-group we must begin to moderate it and give it more time and attention than we had up to that point.

Naturally, the announcement that the group would henceforth be moderated raised a hue and cry about censorship and what might be dark motives. There were no intentions to censor. All subjects were still open to discussion; it was just that the objective of the e-group had been, from the beginning, a forum to aid in the mutual uncovering of truth and programming and sharing of knowledge and experiences. And the free will of those who were there in congruence with that intent was of paramount importance.

But, many of the members could not see that the very emotional reaction they were having was their own emotional programming. Free will means free will for all, which often requires the refusal of control by someone who wishes to deprive others of free will. In this case, one or two individuals wanted, and attempted, to impose their will and thoughts on the other members of the group. And, when this control was refused, they then accused us of the very thing they were attempting to do. And, naturally, those who shout the loudest get heard, and it definitely pushes all the buttons that turn on the Predator's mind.

And the very thing that I want people to realize is that we *are* programmed, and one of the biggest controls on our lives and minds and our very fate is our own emotions. As the Cassiopaeans have remarked: "Vibrational frequency level involves nature of being and emotion, not intelligence."

And then at a later session:

September 2, 1995
Q: (L) So, you are saying that the path to illumination is knowledge and not love?
A: That is correct.
Q: (L) Is it also correct that emotion can be used to mislead, that is emotions that are twisted and generated strictly from the flesh or false programming?
A: *Emotion that limits is an impediment to progress. Emotion is also necessary to make progress in*

third density. It is natural. When you begin to separate limiting emotions based on assumptions from emotions that open one to unlimited possibilities, that means you are preparing for the next density.

Q: (L) What about love?

A: What about it?

Q: (L) There are many teachings that are promulgated that love is the key, the answer. They say that illumination and knowledge and what-not can all be achieved through love.

A: The problem is not the term "love," the problem is the interpretation of the term. Those on third density have a tendency to confuse the issue horribly. After all, they confuse many things as love. When the actual definition of love as you know it is not correct either. *It is not necessarily a feeling that one has that can also be interpreted as an emotion, but rather, as we have told you before, the essence of light which is knowledge is love, and this has been corrupted when it is said that love leads to illumination. Love is Light is Knowledge. Love makes no sense when common definitions are used as they are in your environment. To love you must know. And to know is to have light. And to have light is to love. And to have knowledge is to love.*

Notice particularly the remark: Emotion that limits is an impediment to progress. *Emotion is also necessary to make progress in third density. It is natural.* When you begin to separate limiting emotions based on assumptions from emotions that open one to unlimited possibilities, that means you are preparing for the next density.

Now, I have underlined the remark about the natural necessity of emotion for progress so that those who will tend not to see it won't be able to miss it. Nobody is saying that emotions are bad or that we should not have them. They are *natural* and *necessary*.

But, the crucial point is that emotion which limits you is an impediment to yours progress. Think about that long and hard. Then, think about the process of separating limiting emotions based on assumptions from those that limit, and the fact that this opens one to unlimited possibilities, you may begin to get a glimmer of the point we were trying to make when we reorganized the e-group.

Nevertheless, to satisfy everyone, we created the CassChat e-group that is completely unmoderated, and of which I am not even a member. This was to enable everyone who had found each other via the website to be able to stay in touch and to do whatever they liked, whether it was exchanging recipes or trashing Ark and Laura.

There were many members of CassChat, the majority of whom were becoming very adept at spotting these very things. They could, for the most part, coolly and objectively look at their own Predator's mind. But, even some of these – including yours truly – are subject on occasion to certain triggers. And the next event really pulled mine!

There was something in the above post that caught my eye:

Casschat member: Everyone on Mashtrioka [another e-group] thinks you're a total jerk. Do you realise everyone on your boards sends me letters telling me I have brought up great subjects and activity on your board. If you did not notice your board is usually pretty dead when I do not post.

I had no idea what this other e-group was. And the button that was being pushed was, of course, an attack on my husband. Even if the reaction in me was very mild, because I have learned to tolerate an almost infinite amount of abuse, I was curious as to what was meant by the remark "Everyone on Mashtrioka thinks you're a total jerk." Who were these people who thought my husband was a jerk?

I decided to have a look.

Ark didn't think it was a good idea because he knows better than others that I still cry. But I insisted. I'm a big girl now, I can take it. Bring it on!

Famous last words.

We subscribed to this group and I noticed that a direct quote from the Cassiopaeans was on the main page, and that was nice. Even if it was not sourced, that was okay. My general attitude is to give the material away anyhow, so no big surprise. But then I started to read some of posts. And a very deep and primal program was activated. The program called "betrayal."

And the bomb went off.

After reading several of the posts, I could read no more. I scanned the list of names and saw some of my friends there. I could not help but think that they were participants in a tremendous deception and betrayal, writing one thing to me on the Cassiopaea e-group, and here in this other group participating in what is to me the most hideous of acts: betrayal and deception. The essence of STS.

And, for a brief moment, I wanted all of them to know that I now knew who they were and what they were doing. I forwarded one of the posts that was most revealing to the Cassiopaea e-group. Knowledge protects, right? But this was actually a more or less combined activation of the first and second circuits in myself. Not only was I retreating, I was going to scare away the threat!

These circuits had been turned on inside me. The only thing is, I *knew* what was happening. I could feel the neuropeptides rushing out of these brain centers, flooding my system and binding to the receptors all over my body. Anyone who has ever been in this position will know what I am talking about.

The difference is: I *know* that it is chemical. I know that it is a result of a circuit activation that connects elements of a present experience to something deep in the past; infantile responses. I know that the reaction is encoded in the brain, and that the chemicals are released according to a single trigger.

If you have a negative experience as an infant in a room painted blue, you will be programmed to react negatively to blue, and whenever you are in a blue room your brain will release the same neuropeptides that were released at the very time of the infantile experience. You won't know why you feel frightened or panicky or sad or whatever the negative experience produced, and you will think it is something to do with whatever else is going on in that room, or who you are interacting with, without even being aware that you are being triggered by the memory of the negative experience as an infant in a blue room. Your mind will seek to rationalize the feeling by blaming it on anything or everything, because the idea that the color of the room could be the cause is too illogical.

Sure, maybe you avoid blue. You don't like it, but you surely will never admit that it can control your emotions and your experiences. It will be rationalized as a preference. No reason, just is. Well, there are a lot of things in our lives we think are *us*, and they are not. They are programs.

Suppose you have a very positive experience as a small infant with someone wearing a blue baseball cap. When you are grown, you meet someone wearing a blue baseball cap. You are flooded with the same neuropeptides that were released in the pleasurable experience of your infancy and you are sure that you just really like this person. Never mind that they turn out to be the worst enemy you ever had. As long as they are wearing that blue baseball cap while giving their explanations for why they did rotten things to you, you will believe them because the same neuropeptides will be flowing in response to the cap, and you will be rationalizing in your mind why you should forgive and forget. Even if they are not wearing the cap, the fact that you met them wearing the cap has already formed a matching circuit to the original one. It has been augmented and strengthened.

People fall in love and marry the most damaging people for these reasons. Maybe they have the same nose, or eyes, or hair as someone who provided a very pleasurable experience as an infant. Those traits will trigger the neuropeptides of the memory, flood the entire body and, voila! You are in love.

Never mind that the person turns out to be a lout. Every time you argue with them, the same signals are being sent that bring on the neuropeptides of pleasure and your brain will rationalize forgiveness. How can it be bad if it feels so good? How can they be lying? I feel such love and truth in them!

The most interesting thing about this is that neuropeptide receptors are found all over the body; you have a whole body sensation! You can actually feel it flooding like a rush through your system. But I can guarantee to you that it is chemical. It has nothing to do with higher emotion. And it most definitely has nothing to do with objective reality. Your imprinting creates your very own subjective view of the world and maintains it. And it is in this way that we all live in wishful thinking.

The neuropeptide receptors are also clustered in the gut in very high concentration. We receive gut reactions according to programs set up in the imprinting stages of infancy. It has nothing to do with the exact circumstances of the present moment. It has everything to do with the program and the response to a particular cue that turns on the neuropeptides of pleasure or trauma. The receptors are also arranged in clusters along the spine. With the proper cues that may or may not be from benign sources, they can be felt as the "raising of kundalini". This can also be a real initiatory event, but in that case it would be activated from a different center and with different chemicals.

The most loving and ideal of mates, in terms of mind and soul, will be rejected if the nose or ears or hair or clothing, or some other aspect that was imprinted, is that of someone who hurt you when you were an infant. The most horrific abuse and tragedy will continue in your life if the person who is the source of this just happens to have all the right triggers for your pleasure neuropeptides.

And, until you have read the studies of how potent these chemicals are, and how powerfully they control us, you simply have no idea of what you are dealing with. You will rationalize until the cows come home that it is "really my higher understanding" or "it is really love, this is an exception to the rule" or "I am in touch with my higher mind" in the face of the evidence that will repeat over and over again.

And this behavior is, of course, reinforced by our cultural programming, our religious programming, and all the lies and half-truths delivered to us along with the painful or pleasurable experiences that produce neuropeptides during the time of infancy when these circuits are created. To go against your own programming, to do the opposite of what you feel because you have truly assessed the evidence objectively, is exactly like going through drug withdrawal. And in the throes of withdrawal, the individual will do almost anything to get the neuropeptide fix he needs. That's why so many people go back, again and again, to an abusive partner. That person has some feature that triggers neuropeptide binding in the pleasure centers of the brain and body.

We are made addicts inside our own skins.

And I knew what was happening.

So once I realized that people with programs switched on were sucking me and others into their black hole of distorted emotions, I understood that the only thing to do when you realize emotions are in charge of thinking is *to do exactly the opposite of what you want to do.* To go against the program. And that was my program. I wanted to crawl into a hole and never come out again. I couldn't believe that people could misunderstand so completely and be so cruel.

My first circuit wanted to withdraw to safety and comfort. These people were not being cruel, they were merely programmed. My feelings of hurt and betrayal made me want to just stop everything, pull the plug on 35 years of labor, and group all of humanity as one big threat to my well-being. I was making a judgment. The Predator went "thud" in my gut's neuropeptide receptors like a lump of cold lead. I wrote a post to some of my friends, who at this point were also somewhat suspect. It said:

> After glancing through some of what they had written – a sufficient amount to make me want to lose my dinner – an overwhelming sense of isolation came over me. I realized why people who for whatever reason become 'public property' tend to end up isolating themselves completely.

Naturally, when I began the website, it was simply a labor of love – what I had to give. And the e-group was a place for all the walking wounded who wrote to me for help and relief from their feelings of isolation. Everyone on this list has come from those ranks. I naively thought that I could just write and give it all away, and those who found something there would take what they liked and be polite and if they didn't like it, would simply demur with equal politeness.

I struggled daily to answer questions from hundreds upon hundreds – actually moving into the thousands – of people. Not because I thought I had the answers, but because I had certainly found some things that seemed to work universally if applied, and nobody else seemed to be doing much in really taking the clock apart to see how it operates. I work sometimes 10 to 16 hours a day trying to keep up with everything. And for what? For that kind of crap? And even from people who pretend to be my friends or at least pretend to be something other than what they are on the group?

My naive idea that people could actually begin to really emerge from their programming – and act in unison with the idea of giving to one another freely and openly and honestly – had just died. I saw no point in continuing to write. I saw no point in continuing the e-group. I saw no point in anything. And I didn't think a pat on the head and a "Good Laura! Good doggie! You helped me!" was going to make an ounce of difference. Frankly, I didn't think I could believe anybody anymore.

Of course, looking at the sequence of events, it is clear that this state was a trap. The very fact that the active principle in operation happened to be the very thing I was working on exposing, that it was set up in time for one person to trigger emotions in another; the second person's emotions were set off and he went off like a hand grenade; and I was then lured into reading remarks made at an earlier point in time, which set off the bomb in my own physiology, could not have been more cunningly designed.

It took several hours for me to master my emotions, and my husband, Ark, advised against taking any action until I was in a cooler state. It's a good thing he did or there would be no Cassiopaea website or forum today. I turned off my computer and went to read a book. *Zelator.* Right on top of the pile.

By the next morning, I determined to continue writing because I realized that stopping The Wave series had been an objective of the Control System since the series had started. Unfortunately, my computer would not boot.

Not a surprise. I've burned bigger computers with less energy than I blew off with this one.

Without going into all the technical details, suffice to say that after two days of diagnostics a new computer was thought to be the best solution. The computer was purchased, and it took another two days to retrieve and transfer all my files and install all my programs. Four days altogether, in which I read *Zelator* off and on between managing what I could from Ark's computer and getting caught up with the house and kids.

And that brings me to the book itself.

CHAPTER 66
THE ZELATOR

If I had not fried my computer (most likely by getting upset), I would not have read *Zelator* before writing this. And I would not have fully understood exactly what I was doing or why. So, once again, the efforts of the Control System to do damage ended up doing just the opposite. We are handed lemons and we make lemonade.

I had wept. I had dried my tears and decided that it didn't matter if I was an object of attack and ridicule and cruelty. I would continue. But even with this commitment, there was the question: Why? Is anything I am doing worthwhile?

And there was the book. Sitting there on the stack. I had gotten up to resume my labor, knowing only that it was what I was committed to do; but not really knowing why. And the computer would not work, and there was the book.

I began to read, and as I read, I understood. And I felt the care and comfort of the vast and limitless Universe reaching hands out to dry my tears and send me words that told me what I needed to know.

Zelator is a book written by Mark Hedsel, a seeker on what is known in arcane parlance as the Way of the Fool. The Way of the Fool is apparently an initiatory path of those who set out on their own and, from time to time, encounter a teacher who they interact with for a period, and then move on. As David Ovason, Mark Hedsel's scribe, describes it:

> The Way of the Fool is the way of the independent traveller on the Path of Initiation. Such a traveler may study under a variety of Masters, yet will strive always to preserve his or her own identity, and rarely undertakes vows of silence which will bind his or her being to a particular school or teaching. … The most enduring arcane image of this wandering Fool is that found on the early Tarot cards … (Hedsel 2000, 20, 23)

In the monastery of Santa-Maria-la-Real, Najer, La Rioja, there is a 15th century carving of a Fool. He has two dogs at his feet similar to the Fool in the Tarot deck. But, the interesting thing about him, as Mr. Hedsel points out, is that he wears a robe that is so designed to fall open at both front and back. In this way, his private parts are always visible. He is a naked fool.

'… His nakedness is a sign that the true Fool is prepared to show those things that others prefer to hide. Those Fools who show the way to that higher vision arising from initiation are often seen by the Sleepers as foolish.' (The Sleepers are those who have not elected to follow a spiritual path. They are content with the realm of appearances, and want only to be left alone, to sleep.) …

'… A man or woman's life reveals the archetypes they have followed. That's why the Fool is prepared to go through life naked to the world, knowing that the lower is nothing more than a reflection of the higher.'

'… the Fool progresses only by means of the questions he asks.'

'… A Teacher can indicate the Way, but he cannot show the Way. There are the two Ways – the Way Up and the Way Down – and among the ways up is the Way of the Fool. The zero marks the intersection between the Way Up and the Way Down, where there is neither Up nor Down. …'

… 'To what purpose, we must ask, would anyone wish to follow the Way of the Fool? It is no easy role to play. The Way of the Fool is so open to misunderstanding and mockery. To the casual glance – which is the glance of most people – it does not even appear to be a Way at all. … Yet there is such a Way, even if it is only one followed by men and women striving to establish a Spiritual identity for themselves, divested of outer trappings.

'On this way, the Fool is sensitive to symbols. Indeed, if the Fool is alert enough, sufficiently progressed along the Path, then everything becomes a symbol. …'

… 'The keyword for all the paths is *commitment*. … when you have committed yourself to an action, then the whole cosmos will conspire to help you.

'… the cosmos recognizes commitment, which is in itself a kind of prayer. If you commit yourself, then you will find that the angels are ranged on your side.

'And so, make a commitment. Remember it. Stick to it. And if you choose the Way of the Fool, do not fear appearing to be a Fool in the eyes of the world, for, if you do not stray too far from the ancient road, in the eyes of God, you will always remain the beloved Fool. …

'… Yet, this is certainly no mystical injunction to forget the world, for the hermeticist is trained never to forget the world – as it is his or her forging ground. The hermeticist is ever prepared to burn in exchange for *gnosis*, or to peel away the onion which wrap up the world's Mysteries and himself. …

'… For every faltering step taken by Man, God in his stillness bounds towards Man a hundred steps.'

'… Initiation is an art, a Spiritual performance which can last a lifetime, and then pour into subsequent lifetimes …'

… 'There is only one complete initiation for one who dwells in the body. Then, at that marvelous moment of initiated insight, you will see that life itself is art: it is the art of the gods. The art of Man merely reflects the shadow of this creative exuberance. Initiation is the ultimate art of the gods, practised with more or less imperfection by men.'

'… the Fool is prepared to reveal more than ordinary people, if only to lay bare the basic structure of the Spiritual world. …' (Hedsel 2000, 11, 13, 348–351, 353–354 310)

Zelator devotes some considerable discussion to an 11-house zodiac that was found in the Sagrada di San Michele, which overlooks the Val di Susa. Even though we will not go into that subject in detail, I would like to include some of remarks about this curious thing:

> The climb to the first courtyard is by way of a flight of steps called the *Scala dei Morti*, the Staircase of the Dead. There are tombs near the bottom, but at the top is an archway set with images of the stars: the stairs are a parable of Spiritual ascent from Earthly death to stellar life. The symbolism is simple and perfect, yet it was not quite the symbolism intended by the architects. The archway was translated to this place some centuries after the monastery was built: it was carried, stone by stone, from the baptistry, which had once been outside the monastic enclave, and which is now all but destroyed.
>
> The bas-relief images of the stars, through which one must pass to gain access to the monastery, are among the most fascinating in Europe. They probably date back to the 11th century, and show signs of being derived from Arabic astrological lore. (Hedsel 2000, 72)

I would like to note that the rich astrological tradition of the Arabs was funneled, by way of translations, into Europe from as early as the 10th century, but did not reach its full momentum until the 11th and 12th centuries. It was at this time that astrological symbols were assimilated into Christian architecture. See, for example, F. Gettings, *The Secret Zodiac: The Hidden Art in Mediaeval Astrology*.

> To the left of the portal are 11 images of the zodiacal constellations. There are 11, rather than the statutory 12, because Scorpius and Libra are merged as one, in the image of a scorpion grasping in its chelae, or claws, the balance of Libra. In this form, the ancient Greek images of the zodiac were manumitted from the writings of the Alexandrian-Roman astronomer, Ptolemy, to the architects of the first Romanesque cathedrals. (Hedsel 2000, 73)

Yes, you read right: *manumitted*.

My first thought about the use of this word was that the guy made an error. Or somebody made an error. In fact, I was entirely prepared for this book to be a complete waste of my time. I was not only prepared for it to be a waste, I expected it. But there was that word.

There were several exchanges with the Cassiopaeans and myself on this subject back in 1997:

Autust 9, 1997
Q: Okay. Now, next question: I understand that Libra was added to the zodiac and broke Scorpio and Virgo apart. Were there originally 10 or 11 signs in the zodiac?
A: Originally?
Q: You know what I mean!
A: There have been many combinations.
Q: Well, when did the present 12-sign zodiac begin to be established *as it is*?

A: 1302 AD

Q: And how many signs were there before that?

A: 11

Q: That's what I thought. What is the source of the oldest zodiac available to us?

A: Atlantis.

Q: Well, fine, what is the oldest extant source in terms of writings?

A: Egypt.

It is important to note the specificity of the questions and answers. The date is given in response to a specific inquiry that includes the qualifier "as it is". Further, the Cassiopaeans are not saying that an 11-house zodiac is the right one, merely that it is one of many.

Now, there is more to this than meets the eye, so have a look at the following:

November 7, 1994

Q: (L) Does the Catholic Church have in its possession actual original texts of the Bible that have not been corrupted?

A: No.

Q: (L) Were there ever such texts in existence?

A: No.

Q: (L) Who wrote the book of Matthew?

A: Greek enforcers.

Q: (L) What are Greek enforcers?

A: Like your FBI.

Q: (L) Who wrote the book of Mark?

A: Same.

Q: (L) Luke and John?

A: Same.

Q: (L) Acts?

A: Same.

Q: (L) Are any books of the New Testament written by who they claim to be written by?

A: No. Remember this is 70% propaganda.

Q: (L) Is 30% then the truth or the actual teachings?

A: Close enough. You must decipher from instinct through meditation.

Well, doesn't that just dip your cookies? Greek Enforcers? FBI?

Not long after this, I was reading Edith Hamilton's *Mythology*. Something she wrote struck me quite forcibly:

Greek and Roman mythology is quite generally supposed to show us the way the human race thought and felt untold ages ago. Through it, according to this view, we can retrace the path from civilized man who lives so far from nature, to man who lived in close companionship with nature; and the real interest of the myths is that they lead us back to a time when the world was young and people had a connection with the earth, with trees and seas and flowers and hills, unlike anything we ourselves can feel. When the stories were being shaped, we are given to understand, little distinction had as yet been made between the real and the unreal. ...

But a very brief consideration of the ways of uncivilized peoples everywhere and in all ages is enough to prick that romantic bubble. Nothing is clearer than the fact that primitive man, whether in New Guinea today or eons ago in the prehistoric wilderness, is not and never has been a creature who peoples his world with bright fancies and lovely visions. Horrors lurked in the primeval forest, not nymphs and naiads. Terror lived there, with its close attendant, Magic, and its most common defense, Human Sacrifice. Mankind's chief hope of escaping the wrath of whatever divinities were then abroad lay in some magical rite, senseless but powerful, or in some offering made at the cost of pain and grief.

This dark picture is worlds apart from the stories of classical mythology. ...

We do not know when these stories were first told in their present shape; but whenever it was, primitive life had been left far behind. *The myths as we have them were the creation of great poets.* ... The tales of Greek mythology do not throw any clear light upon what early mankind was like. They do throw an abundance of light upon what early Greeks were like ... [we] *are their descendants intellectually, artistically, and politically, too. Nothing we learn about them is alien to ourselves.*

People often speak of "the Greek Miracle." What the phrase tries to express is the new birth of the world, with the awakening of Greece. "Old things are passed away; behold, all things are become new." Something like that happened in Greece. Why it happened, or when, we have no idea at all. We know only that in the earliest Greek poets *a new point of view dawned, never dreamed of in the world before them, but never to leave the world after them.* With the coming forward of Greece, *mankind became the center of the universe, the most important thing in it. This was a revolution in thought. Human beings had counted for little heretofore. In Greece man first realized what mankind was.*

The Greeks made their gods in their own image. *That had not entered the mind of man before.* Until then, gods had no semblance of reality. They were unlike all living things. In Egypt, a towering colossus ... a woman with a cat's head suggesting inflexible, inhuman cruelty. Or a monstrous mysterious sphinx, aloof from all that lives. In Mesopotamia, bas-reliefs of bestial shapes unlike any beast ever known, men with bird's heads and lions with bull's heads and both with eagles' wings ...

These and their like were what the pre-Greek world worshiped. One need only place beside them ... any Greek statue of a god, so normal and natural with all its beauty, to perceive what a new idea had come into the world. *With its coming, the universe became rational.*

... In Greece alone in the ancient world people were *preoccupied with the visible*; they were finding the satisfaction of their desires in what was actually in the world around them. ...

Human gods naturally made heaven a pleasantly familiar place. The Greeks felt at home in it. ...

That is the miracle of Greek mythology – a humanized world, men freed from the paralyzing fear of an omnipotent Unknown. The terrifying incomprehensibilities which were worshiped elsewhere, and the fearsome spirits with which earth, air and sea swarmed, were *banned from Greece.* ... no matter how wild and fantastic the stories are, anyone who reads them with attention discovers that even the most nonsensical take place in a world which is essentially rational and matter-of-fact. Hercules, whose life was one long combat against preposterous monsters, is always said to have had his home in the city of Thebes. The exact spot where Aphrodite was born of the foam could be visited by any ancient tourist; the winged steed Pegasus, after skimming the air all day, went every night to a comfortable stable in Corinth. ... If the mixture seems childish, consider *how reassuring and how sensible* the solid background is ...

The terrifying irrational has no place in classical mythology. Magic, so powerful in the world before and after Greece, is almost nonexistent. There are no men and only two women with dreadful, supernatural powers. The demoniac wizards and the hideous old witches who haunted Europe and America, too, up to quite recent years, play no part at all in the stories. Circe and Medea are the only witches and they are young and of surpassing beauty – delightful, not horrible. *Astrology, which has flourished from the days of ancient Babylon down to today, is completely absent from classical Greece.* There are many stories about the stars, but not a trace of the idea that they influence men's lives. Astronomy is what the Greek mind made out of the stars. Not a single story has a magical priest who is terribly to be feared ...

The world of Greek mythology was not a place of terror for the human spirit. It is true that the gods were disconcertingly incalculable. One could never tell where Zeus's thunderbolt would strike. Nevertheless, the whole divine company, with a few and for the most part not important exceptions, were entrancingly beautiful with a human beauty, and *nothing humanly beautiful is really terrifying. The early Greek mythologists transformed a world full of fear into a world full of beauty.*

This bright picture has its dark spots. The change came about slowly and was never quite completed. The gods-who-became-human were for a long time a very slight improvement upon their worshipers. They were incomparably lovelier and more powerful, and they were of course immortal; but they often acted in a way no decent man or woman would. ... There are traces of a time when there were beast gods. The satyrs ... the centaurs ... There are also stories that point back clearly to a time when there was human sacrifice. ... the mythical monster is present in any number of shapes ... but they are there only to give the hero his meed of glory. What could a hero do in a world without them? They are always overcome by him.

But what is astonishing is not that bits of savage belief were left here and there. The strange thing is that they are so few. (Hamilton, 3, 4, 7–12)

When I read the above, it gave me chills and made the hair stand up on my arms. I understood that I was in the presence of a significant mystery. The main thing I was interested in was the reference to astrology. Since most of our astrological signs are representations of Greek mythology, how could it be that they, themselves, did not practice astrology? This was a serious discontinuity in history. There was the practice of astrology *before* the Greeks, and *after* the Greeks. And, in fact, the whole Greek pantheon was adopted. What's the deal here? I decided to ask the Cassiopaeans:

July 26, 1997

Q: Why was astrology absent from the myths of ancient Greece?

A: Not absent, "Stalinized."

Q: What does that mean?

A: Soviets removed Stalin from the history books when he fell from popularity. So, Greeks, Astrology ... "Stalinized"...

Q: Why?

A: *Deadly secrets would be revealed.*

Q: Revealed to whom?

A: You. [My take on this is not just me, personally, but humanity.]

Q: If we could find the pieces and put them together, they would show us the drama and the connection between third and fourth density?

A: *You would have to use the original astrology, before cosmic changes of a planetary nature; there was no Venus, for one example, and Earth was oriented differently axially speaking.*

Q: And the destruction of Kantek. This was a whitewash. The writings of Homer and so forth were put in place ... is there any source where we can get closer to these myths that will help us to figure out who is *really* on first?

A: Check the Isle of Man.

Q: You once said that the Bible was written by Greek enforcers, and now you have just said that the myths were Stalinized. It also struck me that there were no ghosts or spirits in the Greek texts. These texts portray the Greeks as worshippers of the physical world. They were astonished at Pythagoras' belief in reincarnation ...

A: You have been reading altered texts.

Q: Well, I know that. I have copies of some of the oldest known documents on the planet. Where am I going to get something that is remotely accurate?

A: The Hague.

Q: Where did these Greek enforcers come from?

A: Order of Thelon.

Q: Never heard of it. On another occasion you called the Nephilim "enforcers." Is there any relation between this order of Thelon and the Nephilim?

A: Maybe ...

Q: Where is the headquarters of this group?

A: Sicinthos.

Q: Is that a place? Never heard of it.

A: Yes.

The above excerpt was published in a previous segment of the Wave (in volume 4) and elicited some interesting information from an Italian reader:

Where is Sicinthos? This word recalled in my mind something I studied at the Liceo: the poet Ugo Foscolo, born in Zante or Zacinto, the Italian word for the Greek island Zàkynthos, a 400-square-km island in the Ionio Sea, northwest from the Peloponneso Greek peninsula. In ancient history this is the first known "Achei" colony and then an Athens colony in 455 B.C.

In the legend, the first man on that island was Zacinto, son of Dardano (Dardanus). Achei people seem to have founded a colony also in northern Spain, at Sagunto (maybe that little town called Sahagun south-east of Leon).

Zakynthos and Sicyon were Achaeans colonies. Perseus was an Achaean, and Dardanus, Zacinto's father, was known in the Greek mythology as a "religious civilizator" and the alleged "Greek Enforcers" have something to do with religion too. He was born in Toscana, Italy (ancient Etruria), in Cortona, an Etruscan city. He founded the Palladium, Samotracia's mysteries and goddess Cyibele cults. He was the king of the Dardanians and the city of Troy (Troia). In Homer's Iliade the Achaeans were fighting against Troians. The Spanish colony Sagunto was the ancient Zakantha. The Palladiums were supposed to have been three cube-like objects made of wood that had fallen from the sky. They were lucky objects and there were many in the Greek myths. Robert Graves in Greek Myths writes (translated): "Also Zacinto received a Palladium after a prayer to Zeus."

I can't find anything about "The Order Of Thelon". But maybe it's all buried and decomposed from a long time ago. Don't know about Scythia. Maybe the Sciiti had a link with Troy and the Dardanus people?

Maybe all the known civilizations are linked to Scythia and so to Sumer and Mesopotamia, but I always keep in mind the fact that the Cs answer related principally to Greece. The final phoneme "thos" of Sicinthos is typical of the Greek vocabulary and their answer related principally to that "Greek Enforcers" issue. ... The root SIK, SIC seems to mean growing, fertility, prosperity. Sicily was the land of fertility according to Carl(o) Pascal studies. (Personal correspondence, 2000)

Well, that was very interesting, and something of a clue, because there are some dynamic connections to later clues, but I plan to get into all that at some point in the future. Now, going back to our Zelator, remember the most interesting remark:

To the left of the portal are 11 images of the zodiacal constellations. There are 11, rather than the statutory 12, because Scorpius and Libra are merged as one, in the image of a scorpion grasping in its chelae, or claws, the balance of Libra. In this form, the ancient Greek images of the zodiac were manumitted from the writings of the Alexandrian-Roman astronomer, Ptolemy, to the architects of the first Romanesque cathedrals. (Hedsel 2000, 73)

To "manumit" means to "set free." In specific, it means "to let go from the hand, to free from slavery."

Claudius Ptolemaeus was a celebrated 2nd century CE Greco-Egyptian mathematician, astronomer, and geographer of the Roman-dominated world. He made his observations in Alexandria and was the last great astronomer of ancient times.

He systematized and recorded the data and doctrines that were known to Alexandrian men of science. ... The mathematical and astronomical systems developed by the Greeks are contained in his 113 volume work, Almagest. With credit to Hipparchus as his chief authority ... (Columbia Encyclopedia)

And, while I am on the subject of Greeks named Ptolemy, I ought to mention that Ptolemy II, or Ptolemy Philadelphus, the Greek king of Egypt from 285 to 246 BCE, "continued his father's efforts to make Alexandria the cultural center of the Greek world. He encouraged the translation of the Pentateuch into the Greek Septuagint." (Columbia Encyclopedia) So we see a very early connection of the Greeks to the control system of monotheism. Maybe what the Cassiopaeans were saying wasn't so crazy after all.

But, even more than the idea of just setting free the images of the zodiac from the writings of Ptolemy, there is another idea suggested in this remark about *manumission* – the curious use of this particular word that relates specifically to hands I'd already thought about, and which we had discussed with the Cassiopaeans:

October 4, 1997

Q: In reading the transcripts, I came across a reference to a "pact" made by a group of STS individuals, and it was called "Rosteem," and that this was the origin of the Rosicrucians. In the book *The Orion Mystery*, it talks about the fact that Giza was formerly known as RosTau, which is "Rose Cross." Essentially, I would like to understand the symbology of the Rose affixed to the Cross. It seems to me that the imagery of Jesus nailed to the Cross is actually the Rose affixed to the Cross. How does Jesus relate to the Rose?

A: No, it is from the Rose arose the Cross.

Q: What does the cross symbolize?

A: The symbology is not the issue. It is the effect.

Q: What is the effect of the cross?

A: All that has followed it.

Q: In the same vein, I have noticed that there are two classes of arachnids. There are scorpions and there are spiders. *The zodiac was changed by taking the pincers away from the Scorpion and creating out of them the sign of Libra.* This image was one of a woman holding a balance scales, *usually blindfolded.* This was done within recorded history, but was probably formalized through the occult traditions of Kaballah. Now, in trying to figure out who has on what color hat, if there is such a thing, I have come to a tentative conclusion that the spider, or spinner of webs, is the Rosicrucian encampment, and that the Scorpion represents the seeker of wisdom ... because, in fact, the word for Scorpio comes from the same root as that which means to pierce or unveil. Therefore, the Scorpion is also Perseus, per Ziu, or "for God." And the Rosicrucians are the "other," so to speak. Can you elaborate on this for me? Or comment?

A: What a tangled web we spin, when we must not let you in.

Q: So, the Rose is the Spider?

A: Different objective.

Q: So, the Rose, with its thorns ... can you help me with this Rose image ... is the Rose the Scorpion?

A: No. Different objective ... Rose is a standalone symbol.

Q: So, the Rose can be used by either side, is that it?

A: Maybe.

Q: Another derivation of the word root of Scorpio is "skopos," or "to see." You said that the human race was seeded on a planet in the constellation Scorpio, and, therefore, when the zodiac was set up and the clues were laid out, it seems to me that *the insertion of the sign of Libra was designed to take power away from human beings, to take their hands away, to prevent them from seeing, to make them defenseless. Is this imagery close?*

A: On track.

Am I crazy to see in this message from *Zelator* something that is being "guided"? I looked at the passage again: "the image of a scorpion grasping in its *chelae,* or claws, the balance of Libra. In this form, the ancient Greek images of the zodiac were manumitted …"

Why use the term "chelae" in addition to claws? Chelae means claws, so it is redundant. So, not only do we have a word that doesn't fit, in the term "manumitted," which means to set free from the hands, we have a redundancy in the same paragraph; and both in a book that is exceptionally grammatical and precise in terminology.

What else do we know about chelae? Well, it is related to chelate and that is *a chemical compound* resembling or having chelae. The central atom – *usually a metal ion* – is attached to neighboring atoms by at least two bonds in such a way as to form *a ring structure*. It is also to cause a metal ion to react with another molecule to form a chelate. (Think of the carbon atom.)

Well, there is more about this issue of Scorpio having no hands:

October 23, 1994

Q: (L) Well, then how did mankind come to be here?

A: Combination of factors. Numerous souls desired physical existence then was altered by three forces including principally Lizards through Grays, Nephalim and Orion union.

Q: (L) Tell us again who are the Nephilim?

A: Enforcers. Slaves of Orion. From Planet 3C, or 3rd star, 3rd planet.

Q: (L) You said the other night that the Nephilim came from some area around the constellation Scorpio, is that correct?

A: *Originally seeded there but you were too.*

Q: (L) We were originally seeded somewhere else? Where? Orion? What is the name of that planet?

A: D'Ankhiar. Ankh is ancient symbolism of this planet. Is female symbol. Stands for mother planet. [Which suggests that this is the source of all human mitochondrial DNA.]

Q: (L) You indicated that we should study the legend of Orion, and I looked it up in several sources, and basically the legend is of the perfect man who fell in love with a woman, and her jealous father caused him to be blinded. The only cure was to gaze at the light, the goddess Aurora, to regain his sight. Can you tell us how this relates to the idea that Orion was the indigenous home of humans?

A: It is up to you to look for answers.

Q: (L) There was an interesting reference in one of the books I was reading of the relationship of Orion to Scorpio, that Orion's bow is drawn at Scorpio. And, at one other point, you said that the physical bodies of mankind were molecularized, and *are* being molecularized, on a planet called D'Ankhiar, which is in the constellation Scorpio.

A: Yes.

Q: (L) What is the relationship of Orion to Scorpio? The Orion "bad guys" shooting at Scorpio, which is the place of origin of the physical manifestation of the human race …

A: Bad guys?

Q: (L) Forget I said bad guys. "Shooting at Scorpio." Is there any relationship, symbolically, to the fact that the human bodies …

A: It is all interrelated.

Regarding the 11-house zodiac that he had discovered in the Val di Susa, Mark Hedsel adds:

> To the right of the portal are 15 [3×5!] images of the constellations. Most of them are named on the marble in a lapidary script. As sculptural images, these may well be unique in European lapidary art. Perhaps the architect had them copied from an Arabic edition of the *Phaenomena* – a poem about the constellations – of the third-century BC poet, Aratus. The original manuscript prototype drawings seem to be lost, but there is no doubt that these bas-reliefs may be traced back into the loam of classical antiquity. (Hedsel 2000, 73)

Note: The constellation names on the bas-reliefs are Aquila, Delfinus, Pegasus, Deltoton, Orion, Lepus, Canis, Anticanis, Pistrix, Eridanus, Centaurus, Cetus, Nothius, Ara and Hidra. (See: Giovanni Gaddo, *La Sacra di San Michele in Val di Susa,* 1977.)

> ... we rarely met anyone with whom we could discuss the arcane symbols, or the esoteric ideas they embodied. ... few seemed to be interested in the cosmic images of the archway, and *none I met ever had the slightest intimation of the challenge they offered.* This was not surprising: the symbols were designed by a Masonic Mystery School, and *exhibited an arcane knowledge which removed them from the understanding even of scholars.*
>
> ... We had put a great deal of our time into the study of the astrological images in the Sagrada, but we could find no answers to the important questions which they raised in our soul. We could not find out why, or for what purpose, these images had been carved, and why they were not all absorbed into the artistic repertoire of Romanesque architecture. These images of the constellations were not found in other monasteries, churches or cathedrals: they seemed to be unique to the Sagrada.
>
> No Romanesque architect seems to have seen the arcane implications in these images of the stars, and, as a consequence, these constellation images seem to have been lost to the stonemasons of the West. Few, if any, European specialists had studied these images, and there was a dearth of scholarly material dealing with them. The only possible clue was ... the tantalizing manuscript in a secret code.
>
> In our search for the origins of these images, we had found, hidden in the archives of the Vatican Library, a single manuscript which seemed to illuminate our search. It was a document which confirmed the name of the sculptor as Nicholas. ... it was clear that this Nicholas had been an initiate, for the whole arrangement of the cosmic images – albeit no longer in their original setting – was redolent with esoteric symbolism and power. ...
>
> ... In the manuscript which confirmed his name was a long and enigmatic sentence in mediaeval dog-Latin, which we could just about read, yet not grasp its inner meaning. The text seemed to encode something which defied our understanding. (Hedsel 2000, 73–75)

The uneasy dog-Latin, with its alchemical, astrological and even cabbalistic undertones, reads:

Dilexi secreta loca qui in arbore erant hostic factus est luminosus lapis cibus ante animalis et rece-
dens de suprema rami arbor radicibus evulsa in terra quod ita domus ipsa fumabat.

Now, the point I want to make here is that this book, published not long before I began writing this, came to me because the issue of the 11-house zodiac was published on the website. Someone had read it and mentioned it. At that particular time, the drama described above began to manifest, which not only distracted my attention from following this clue but it almost brought the whole project to a halt.

Yet the fact is even if the distractions were an overt attempt to distract and stop me, what actually happened was that affairs were arranged so I was diverted to read this book out of sequence. In reading the book, I found many passages that spoke directly to me; the most astounding of which is this discussion of the 11-house zodiac. And I find it difficult to believe there are a lot of people on the planet thinking about 11-house zodiacs in the terms I have described above; most specifically who have the idea that there is some powerful symbolism in the addition of the sign of Libra; and that, contrary to what may seem to be the case, that Libra – with its blinded eyes so similar to the god Orion – is really a clue to the Control System that dominates humankind, which was known in the ancient past, and which knowledge was "Stalinized" by "Greek Enforcers."

In our most recent session with the Cassiopaeans, on January 22, 2000, the subject of the "Moon" was reiterated over and over again. Curiously, this was just a day or so after Ark had written his response to the E-group member about Gurdjieff's description of the Control System as being the fact that humans are "food for the Moon." (See chapter 65)

As it happened, the subject of the Moon was also brought up repeatedly in *Zelator*, and I was beginning to wonder what was the big deal with the Moon.

Going back a bit, let me remind you that we began by asking some questions about the *Shepherds of Arcadia*, and the symbolism of Rennes-le-Chateau. After I had published this page, I received an email from a reader with whom I have corresponded for a period, and who described experiences that lead me to believe that she is one of those who is "suffering" a lot of cognitive dissonance due to her own ability to perceive glimpses of fourth density. She wrote:

I just read the wave 13b. Interesting stuff.

This is regarding the "treasure of Rennes le chateau".

I have a few friends who are occultists whom I respect. One day one I was talking with one of them; he'd just been on a visit to the "Winchester Mystery House" ... I think. This house is a weird house built by Sarah Winchester (of Winchester Rifles), supposedly on the advice of a psychic or something.

Well, my friend thought that the story was made up, was a cover story to explain why Sarah Winchester had built such a strange house. He thought that in reality, the house was built to be a "memory palace". Not knowing what this was, I asked my friend. Apparently a memory palace (and I guess this is esoteric but known among those who know esoteric stuff, hah, like students of the occult) is a physical building that functions as a sort of a database in physical matter.

A memory palace is supposed to, apparently, mimic in physical matter, the structure of the mind of the person who builds it. The idea, I suppose, is that the person can then enter into the building and call up memories by handling or looking at/etc. the things in the palace. The things in the memory palace supposedly trigger something within the mind ...

What exactly can it trigger within that mind? I don't know ... I guess these structures could be constructed to do different things.

Now, could Rennes Le Chateau be a memory palace of some sort? It could be that it is constructed to "work with" a particular kind of mind ... a mind that is of a certain bloodline, or soul-line (I am thinking that some humans actually *do* have, in addition to their physical parents, "non-physical" parents who provide the genetics (speaking metaphorically here) for the "non-physical" bodies (the etheric bodies, etc.) of these people.

So ... it could be that when a person of this certain physical and/or non-physical "genetic line" stood within Rennes Le Chateau, it would "trigger" something within their mind ... trigger "what"? A process of transformation? Memories? I don't know. A particular reaction on the part of someone visiting this place, Rennes Le Chateau, might even "mark" them as one of this "genetic line". This might be the secret and the treasure of Rennes Le Chateau – that it is a kind of transformation structure or something.

Also, I have had intuitions that there are certain women in the world ... who have a consciousness of a particular type that can be used to influence the world around them by unscrupulous black ship (the term that I use for those you'd probably call "lizards") beings.

They may have particular and very interesting abilities that would certainly be of interest to anyone who wants to engage in manipulation of the masses. Are these women of the "genetic type" (both physical and non-physical) that "used" to incarnate in the Jesus/Mary bloodline? Rennes Le Chateau may have something to do with this as well, maybe.

Also, I had a kind of waking dream that somebody told me, regarding the Bloodline of the Holy Grail – "Yeah, there is such a bloodline and some royal families may be part of it, but the soul families that 'used' to incarnate into that physical line, really no longer do anymore."

As a result of my research into the Rennes-le-Chateau matter, which brought up the *Shepherds of Arcadia* issue, I came across a book by Elizabeth Van Buren entitled *Rennes-le-Chateau: Refuge of the Apocalypse*.

Now, remember that my off-the-wall question about Oak Island led to the subject of alchemy and Fulcanelli. And the questions about Jesus led to the Rennes-le-Chateau matter. I found that all three of them converged into the word "Arcadia." Oak Island is in the area of northeastern North America that was formerly called Arcadia (although the name was later fixed to "Acadia"); the Rennes-le-Chateau matter circled around a painting with that word in the title.

Fulcanelli was an alchemist who, it was claimed, was last seen in the Pyrenees, and Rennes-le-Chateau is in the foothills of the Pyrenees. The Templars were connected to Rennes-le-Chateau, and when the Templars were supposed to have been destroyed, the Rosicrucians all of a sudden appeared. It was rumored that it was no coincidence. Alchemy was supposedly brought to Europe from the Arabs, and the Templars had a long relationship with Arab potentates and affairs, so were, by deduction, associated with alchemy. And, the alchemical lore of the Rosicrucians is legendary.

Well, all of these are clues, but none of them tell us who's on first. So, here is Elizabeth Van Buren writing about Rennes-le-Chateau, and she weaves all through her book remarks about Fulcanelli. Not only that, she has ideas very similar to my own about "dimensional doorways" and the "true Ark."

Nevertheless, the fact still remains that the truly secret schools, if they exist, guard their secrets carefully. And it is not likely that they would reveal a relationship to hyperdimensional beings *if* they had made vows of secrecy as the Cassiopaeans have defined it:

> Lord of Serpent promises its followers infinite power which they must seek infinite knowledge to gain, for which they pledge allegiance infinitely, which they possess for all eternity, so long as they find infinite wisdom, for which they search for all infinity. ... And therein you have the deception! Remember, those who seek to serve self with supreme power, are doomed only to serve others who seek to serve self, and can only see that which they want to see.

So, the fact remains that *if* the Cassiopaeans are giving out information that is clearly related to these "secrets of initiation," that some credence may be thought to lie in the wider scope of their information regarding the Control System.

No matter where you stand, no matter in what direction you look, you find the web of the spider. It doesn't matter if you start with metaphysics, if you freely follow the tracks, you may end up in paleontology, or astrophysics or psychiatry or mythology or geology, and on and on. There is no element of human culture that has not been manipulated in order to trap and feed.

CHAPTER 67
FOOD FOR THE MOON AND
THE BURNING HOUSE

As you know, I began the Wave with a sort of set and finite plan – I was going to just talk about the Wave. There were going to be about ten chapters, each about 20 pages, and that was that. But, as it happened, the process of writing turned into channeling. I am very often surprised myself at what comes from my fingers.

There was another reference to an 11-house zodiac in a curious remark by Chester Starr, who writes regarding the earliest Sumerian ceremonials:

> In the spring of each year occurred the greatest religious festival of the land, known as the Akitu in later Babylonia. This was the New Year's feast, an 11-day (yes, you read right, *eleven*) ceremony of gloom and purification and then of joy, which ended as the gods "set the lots of mortal men during the coming year." On the fourth day of the festival the priests recited a myth of creation, called from its opening words Enuma Elish. (Private correspondence)

His footnote was *Ancient Near Eastern Texts Relating to the Old Testament* by J. B. Pritchard.

The only other reference to the 11-house zodiac was one from a lecture given in the late 1880s by Rosicrucian, Golden Dawn co-founder, and medical examiner for the City of London, Dr. W. Wynn Westcott titled "Flying Roll VII", attributed to "S.A." He tells us that alchemy "is never taught in so many words. It may dawn on any one of you – the magic event may occur when least expected."

Westcott begins his lecture by saying that alchemy means "the Higher Chemistry, treating of the essential nature of the elements, metals and minerals." In the paragraph that followed this, Westcott says something very odd: he quotes a fourth century astrologer, Julius Firmicus Maternus, who says that skill in alchemy depends on having the Moon in the House of Saturn. Even more confusing, Westcott then asks: "what house does he [Firmicus] mean? The Day (Aquarius) house or the Night (Capricorn) house of Saturn?" And then further confuses everyone by wondering if this fourth century astrologer could have meant the attribution as referring to Uranus. This would be odd since the planet Uranus was not discovered until 1781.

Now, note that Westcott deliberately left out Virgo and Libra. In ancient times, Scorpio and Virgo were a double sign. Libra did not exist. Libra was later created and inserted to break up the double sign, which occupied a double space in the zodiacal wheel, so we are not talking about what would be broken down to merely a 10-equal house system here. What was called Scorpio was understood to include Virgo. Thus, it was an 11-sign system, with ten houses, one of them being double in its number of degrees.

But, back to the story. These were the only two references that I knew to exist, and I had been looking and asking for several years. I had a dream about it at one point. A high priest appeared, wearing a many-tiered skirt that resembled the Cretan depictions of the goddess – only this was a man. He showed me how the different tiers could be rotated so that certain symbols aligned, which then gave a message. The symbols were zodiacal and the star names were of great significance. The trick was, to align them properly.

The same dream then morphed. I was holding a vase that appeared to be onyx or something like that. Others had tossed it on a junk heap and I picked it up and was examining scratch marks all over it. I could see that it was engraved, but that all the grooves were filled with dirt and it was coated with grime. I began to clean it with cotton swabs and water very carefully, going into all the little cracks and tracing out the lines. As I did so and the dirt came away, I was awestruck at the beauty of this vase. It was not only cunningly worked with some great mythical scene being enacted, but it was inlaid with amazing veneers of various colored stones. And, it was also translucent so that the black turned out to be really a deep, translucent purple.

The dream morphed again: Ark and I were walking and it seemed to be a park or recreation area of some sort with mountains and cliffs and outcroppings of rock. We were walking around, looking at all the rock formations and shrubbery. The landscape was very dry and obviously in need of rain. As we were following a path I decided to hide in a bush and see how long it took for Ark to notice I was missing, as a joke. And then I suddenly found myself standing on the path ahead of him.

"How did you do that?" Ark said.

"Well, I ducked into this bush and there was a cleft in the rock, and I started to squeeze into it and something happened and here I am!" I said.

He insisted that I go back and show it to him. So, we went back and there was a small cave entrance, looking rather like the broken cleft of the tomb in the Arcadian Shepherds painting. He said it was impossible, too small.

"Try it," I said.

So, he stooped down and easily entered the cave. He was in there a long time. Meanwhile, I decided to stay busy by cleaning all the cracks in the rocks around the cave entrance. There was a trickle of water coming out of the cave and I was using some sort of cloth. As I did, the water kept increasing its flow until it was a fountain.

At this point, Ark came stumbling out of the cave, holding his eyes, crying tears and laughing at the same time.

"I believe! I believe!" he said. "I've seen it with my own eyes!"

We decided to leave the park. As we were walking out the entrance, I glanced up at the cliff face and there was a huge mosaic set in the rock. On the right were seven sharks, the bottom one paler than the others. They got darker as they went up, stacked identical images. On the left of the mosaic was a large whale whipping around, its mouth open, eye on the sharks, poised to devour them in a single bite. I told myself I needed to remember this dream. Then I woke up.

Well, of course I slipped in a quick question about this series of dreams:

Q: I had a dream the other night. As Ark and I were leaving the park in my dream, I looked up and saw a mosaic on the side of the mountain. It had seven sharks, one above the other, the lowest being pale almost to the point of transparency, and the highest being very dark and intense in color. There was a huge sperm whale to the upper left. He was in the posture of whipping around, his eye had caught the sharks, and his mouth was open and he was going to swallow them all in a single gulp. What was the meaning of the whale and the sharks?

A: Logic says to you: examine!

Q: The other part of the dream was that I disappeared and reemerged from a cleft in a rock. I was cleaning ... he went to investigate ... and he returned and was crying and all this water was flowing out of there like a spring. At another part of the dream, I was cleaning a vase ... all this cleaning. What was the significance of this?

A: Trace minerals interact with deeply held secrets.

And that suggests the Alchemical transformation. Which brings us back again to *Zelator*.

I finally understood why the style of the Cassiopaeans was so different: it was the very model of the high-level adept working with a neophyte, helping them step by step to develop the inner circuits that would bring about the transformation. And I also understood why the Cassiopaeans took so long to tell some things and had no hesitation about others. It was clearly an initiatory exercise understood only by the adept. Never mind that the adept who is doing the teaching is doing it through a board and not in person or in some secret school. This reminded me of something I had asked the Cassiopaeans very early on:

November 9, 1994

Q: (L) Is the Sufi path a good one to study?

A: Up to you. We don't want to judge that for you.

Q: (L) What percentage of truth is in that path.

A: In one sense all teachings are truths.

Q: (L) Can't you just tell me?

A: Subjective. Would you like us to judge Reiki?

Q: (L) Well, yes before I spend any money on it. Will I waste my money?

A: Not if you go to right source. Now we have led you to answer we want you to continue to exercise your mind. That is how you progress.

Q: (L) So you want me to study Sufi for the exercise?

A: Yes. If we answered all your questions you would not learn.

Q: (L) In this book I am reading it talks about knowledge that is only given to the elect and that certain things are passed down through secret organizations. Most people think this organization is the Illuminati and that they hold many deep, dark secrets. Is that true?

A: Close. But now there is a knowledge explosion. The Illuminati is no longer exclusive; but they still think they are.

Q: (L) Compared to the big high mucky mucks in the Illuminati, what percentage of their knowledge do I possess?

A: 2 per cent.

Q: (L) You mean they know 98 per cent more than I do? As hard as I have worked for these many years? That's depressing! How much knowledge, relative to the Illuminati, does the average college graduate have?

A: 0.02 per cent.

Q: (L) Is there any one person who holds a major chunk of knowledge on this planet?

A: By this time next year you will have 35 per cent as much.

Well, I guess 35 percent was better than 2 percent! But it made me painfully and acutely aware of how little I actually knew.

So here is this book, *Zelator*, and it is like reading about my own experiences with the Cassiopaeans. The big difference was that the author spent his entire lifetime gathering this information, and I am sure he only wrote what he felt he could safely divulge, concealing things in metaphors and allusions. Not only that, but it is also clear that obtaining his information via human filters, who have obtained their information through other sources which may or may not be closer to a real source has greatly colored or even clouded some of the matters covered in this book.

But, this book comes right out and says more truth about some of the secrets than any other book that has, to date, been published. And, as I read it, I was able to fill in the blanks from what I knew. There were certainly a number of crucial keys that I was looking for that Mark Hedsel revealed in his book for others on the Path of the Fool.

Which brings us back to the Moon. Chapter Seven of Zelator quotes at the beginning an excerpt from Ovid's *Metamophoses*:

> I am the same Perseus who conquered the snaky-tressed Gorgon, the man who dared to travel through the airy breezes on beating wings.
>
> (Ovid, *Metamorphoses*, IV. 697)

This connects us back to our number 11 and the 3-5 code, if you will recall. The Cassiopaeans tossed Medusa into that discussion as a clue. And here we find it bearing some serious fruit. Not only that, the chapter begins with Fulcanelli. Hedsel writes:

Among the most remarkable of modern initiates who were prepared to reveal hermetic secrets to the profane was the mysterious Fulcanelli. In keeping with the secret Green Language, which he studied and practised with great accomplishment, he used a pen-name to disguise his real identity. 'Fulcanelli' meant 'little Vulcan' ... As a pseudonym, this name seems to have worked very well, for no one has been able to determine with any certainty just who Fulcanelli was ...

As we have seen, this mysterious alchemist paid especial attention to the alchemical images which are still found in the sculpted fabric of the French Cathedrals. In particular, Fulcanelli dealt with the secrets within the alchemical imagery of Notre Dame in Paris, and the cathedral at Amiens.

Among the most arcane of the many arcane stone quatrefoils on the western facade of Amiens cathedral which intrigued Fulcanelli is a curious image of a heavenly rain. The sheet of water streams like a veritable Niagara from the clouds which, for the mediaeval mind, symbolized heaven. It streams down to the Earth, where, in defiance of natural laws, it gathers into a ball of water which seems to pulsate and tremble, as though it were a ball of flame, rather than a magical liquid.

In the quatrefoil, an alchemist looks upon this cascade in awe, pointing with his right hand at the ball of water as though to show that it is a miracle, or something of profound importance. Could he be pointing to this water-ball to indicate that it is something dangerous? The phenomenon is portrayed in distinctly unnatural terms to show that this is no ordinary dew.

All the arcane images of the west front of Amiens are contained in quatrefoils. This in itself is a significant thing, for the quatrefoil is made up of four crescents – symbolic of the four phases of the Moon throughout the month. In the quatrefoil which contains the Niagara of water, the heavens open in the uppermost crescent, as if to indicate that this is a lunar Heaven (or sphere), and the magic water it dispenses is a lunar dew. In fact, it is the 'philosophical dew' of the alchemists – one of the great Mysteries of this mysterious art. It is not straining ancient mythology too far to see in this cascade the dual streams of the tears of the 'weeping sisters', the Egyptian goddesses, Isis and Nephthys, the combined influence of the light and dark Moons.

In Latin, this dew is *Ros*. ... some hermetic experts argue that the three letters form the beginning of the word Rosicrucian, a word which pertains to the most important secret brotherhood in late mediaeval Europe. These initiates, who united the secret of the lunar dew with the cross (*crucis*, the genitive of the Latin *crux*), were practising Christians ... The *Ros* dew was subjected to the directional organization of the cross (*crucis*). (Hedsel 2000, 296–297)

Now, remember what we have already covered about the spider, the scorpion, and the Rose? That the Rose or Ros is a standalone symbol and the two groups represented by the spider and the scorpion have "different objectives"? Here's a quick refresher:

October 4, 1997

Q: In reading the transcripts, I came across a reference to a "pact" made by a group of STS individuals, and it was called "Rosteem," and that this was the origin of the Rosicrucians. In the book *The Orion Mystery*, it talks about the fact that Giza was formerly known as RosTau, which is "Rose Cross." Essentially, I would like to understand the symbology of the Rose affixed to the Cross. It seems to me that the imagery of Jesus nailed to the Cross is actually the Rose affixed to the Cross. How does Jesus relate to the Rose?

A: No, it is from the Rose arose the Cross.

Q: What does the cross symbolize?

A: The symbology is not the issue. It is the effect.

Q: What is the effect of the cross?

A: All that has followed it.

Q: Could you list some of these to give me a clue?

A: You know these.

I do, indeed.[3] And even though Mr. Hedsel may intimate that the Rosicrucians are the good guys, in colloquial terms, it is clear from other things he is writing that he knew better. They are not. They are the Spiders who entrap and devour. Remember this:

October 4, 1997

Q: In the same vein, I have noticed that there are two classes of arachnids. There are scorpions and there are spiders. The zodiac was changed by taking the pincers away from the Scorpion and creating out of them the sign of Libra. This image was one of a woman holding a balance scales, usually blindfolded. This was done within recorded history, but was probably formalized through the occult traditions of Kaballah. Now, in trying to figure out who has on what color hat, if there is such a thing, I have come to a tentative conclusion that the spider, or spinner of webs, is the Rosicrucian encampment, and that the Scorpion represents the seeker of wisdom ... because, in fact, the word for Scorpio comes from the same root as that which means to pierce or unveil. Therefore, the Scorpion is also Perseus, per Ziu, or "for God." And the Rosicrucians are the "other," so to speak. Can you elaborate on this for me? Or comment?

A: What a tangled web we spin, when we must not let you in.

Q: So, the Rose is the Spider?

A: Different objective.

Q: So, the Rose, with its thorns ... can you help me with this Rose image ... is the Rose the Scorpion?

A: No. Different objective ... Rose is a standalone symbol.

Q: So, the Rose can be used by either side, is that it?

A: Maybe.

Q: Another derivation of the word root of Scorpio is "skopos," or "to see." You said that the human race was seeded on a planet in the constellation Scorpio and, therefore, when the zodiac was set up and the clues were laid out, it seems to me that the insertion of the sign of Libra was designed to take power away from human beings, to take their hands away, to prevent them from seeing, to make them defenseless. Is this imagery close?

A: On track.

---

[3] See the discussion of the "Fall From Eden" in session 28 August 1999.

Now, just to confirm our suspicions about the Rosicrucians let me add this most interesting series of questions and answers with the Cassiopaeans:

December 21, 1996

Q: (L) I have been digging around about the Templars and have, more or less, come to the conclusion that the whole deal about the destruction of the temple was just a smoke screen, and that something else was going on at the time that *was* important. I also think that they have been resurrected from time to time and dusted off and blamed for for all this secret knowledge that is supposedly lost ... am I on to something here?

A: Close.

Q: Who or what brought about the end of the Knights of the Temple?

A: *Rosicrucians move as a "thief in the night."*

This last most interesting remark suggests that the Rosicrucians were behind the destruction of the Templars! The "thief in the night" of the Bible is defined as "sudden destruction."

December 21, 1996

Q: (L) But, as I understand it, the Rosicrucians did not come into being until after the end of the Templars ... the Rosicrucians *were* the Templars...

A: No.

Q: (L) Do you mean that the information that came out, that pamphlet about "Christian Rosenkreutz," that is a purported fable, might be correct, even if disguised?

A: Yes.

Q: (L) Well, goodness sake! The Rosicrucians advertise in magazines! Is this worldwide organization that promotes itself so blatantly ...

A: Well, the "worldwide" order is not all inclusive.

Q: (L) Is there an inner circle of this order that is unknown?

A: Yes.

Q: (L) Are the Rosicrucians connected to the Masons?

A: In a roundabout away. [Which suggests to us that they may not necessarily be "in cahoots."]

Q: (L) Are the Illuminati connected to the Rosicrucians in any way?

A: Same.

Q: (L) Do the Rosicrucians have writings in their keeping that they, themselves, do not understand?

A: Yes. So do the Masons.

Q: (L) The Priory of Zion, that has been purported to be the progenitor or inheritor of the Templar tradition, is that a mystical organization of great secrecy and import?

A: It is a cover for.

Q: (L) Another smoke screen.

A: Yes.

Did you ever notice how the Masons get blamed for so many things of a conspiratorial nature, and nobody ever blames the Rosicrucians or the present day

Templars? Don't you think that is a bit peculiar? Everything is a Masonic conspiracy, but nothing is ever a Rosicrucian conspiracy!

Now, lets get back to that most interesting item: heavenly rain; sheet of water. When I read those words, I had to whip out my hairspray to keep the hair from standing up! Note the following exchange with the Cassiopaeans dated, amusingly, 04-04-98 (keeping in mind that Hedsel keeps mentioning the word "quatrefoil."):

April 4, 1998

Q: In the studies of the Triple Goddess, I came across some interesting things. You suggested that I should research the Third Man theme. I have discovered that the origin of the word "man" originally meant a female – the goddess. The Moon. The oldest word for the male of the species was "wer", as in "werewolf." So, the Third Man theme could mean actually, the Triple Goddess. Am I correct?

A: Close, if viewed through "sheets of rain."

Q: Okay. Tracking the Triple Goddess back to the oldest references, we get to KaliMa. There are all kinds of derivations of this name, but the thing that strikes me is the relationship to the goddess Kell, or Kella, as well as to the word *kell*, Celts, and how this might be transformed into the word "Cassiopaea." Can you comment on this?

A: Do not the Celts like "Kelly" green?

Q: Yes. So. What does "green" have to do with it?

A: Keep searching … learning is accomplished thusly, and learning is fun!

Now, let me just mention that when the Cassiopaeans first said this, I was completely baffled, so I came back to it in a later session:

January 2, 1999

Q: I once asked about the Third Man theme and that perhaps you meant that the imagery was that of the Triple Goddess relating to the Isle of Man … and you said, "if viewed through sheets of rain." So, in this book that I am reading, it talks about the fact that the Celts of Gaul worshipped the Rain as the manifestation of the Goddess, and the Celts of Scotland worshipped the Sun … the male God. Does this relate in any way to this remark you made about sheets of rain?

A: In an offhand way.

Q: Anything further you can tell me in terms of a clue about "sheets of rain"?

A: Not for now, when you get there, you will find the chalice.

Q: Where and *what* chalice?

A: Wait and see!

Going back to one of the other threads we have been following, the bloodline theme, a chalice was mentioned in another context that may be related:

October 3, 1998

Q: (L) What were the names of the children of Jesus?

A: You have the clues, and your quest has been admirable so far, why stop now?

Q: (L) So, I will find them! Okay.

A: Could be like the Holy Grail.

Q: (L) What could be like the Holy Grail?

A: Chalice.

Q: (L) What does the chalice represent?

A: What is its root?

And we find in the dictionary that the root of chalice, in terms of words, is a Latin word, *calix*, which means a cup. When we look at the word calix, we find that its root is the Indo-European word *Kel*. Funny that the Cassiopaeans gave me the answer and I didn't see it when they said "kelly green".

Now, let's get back to *Zelator*: skipping over a most interesting discourse on the Moon, in which he conceals with one paragraph and reveals with another, we come to this:

> We had assumed that Jacques Bergier, who claimed to have met Fulcanelli in 1937, had probably – to put it kindly – imagined this meeting. ... However, a remark, made by a friend in Florence in the May of 1978, pulled us up short, and made us call into question what we knew about this mysterious alchemist. ...
>
> '... [Florence] is not a place of old ghosts but of old love. One does not need great powers to break through the veil in this place – to reach into a different time.' On this occasion, however, we were standing on the generous pavement which frames the huge square of the Piazzale Michelangelo. We were leaning on the balustrade, overlooking Florence. As we talked, our eyes skimmed like swallows over the trees towards the lovely *ponte vecchio*. (Hedsel 2000, 303)

Reading this made me pull out the hairspray again. I have on my wall above the desk a photograph of Ark standing almost in this very spot with his arm outstretched, "showing me Florence." In fact, Ark was on his way to Piazzale Michelangelo, a further ten-minute walk from where he was standing.

The date on the photograph is 07-07-96. This was two days after we "met." Ark was in Florence at that time, working in an ancient monastery. He had taken this walk to think. On the same walk, he went to a nearby gift shop and purchased a postcard to send to me. It was Botticelli's "Birth of Venus." So, again, Hedsel is saying things that are personally significant, like markers.

> We were talking about symbolism. … we decided to leaf once again through Fulcanelli's masterpiece [and then] to put the problem to our Florentine friend. [He said,] 'You may not have found the answer in Fulcanelli, yet I assure you that the clue is there, nonetheless. You understand, sometimes even Fulcanelli wraps his mysteries in mysteries, for he knows that some things may not be spoken, even today. … Look again at what he writes of *Saturne* as an anagram of natures.' (Hedsel 2000, 304–306)

Now we understand the inside joke of Westcott's lecture! Saturn is an anagram for Nature. And we also begin to have an inkling of the Saturnian influence of Nature!

> 'Fulcanelli is far wiser than most of his readers know. He sets down less in words than he could, and delivers parables in parables. In this there is real wisdom. The alchemists insisted that one should heat the retort many times before making the final distillation. This is an emblem of true thought: one must pass one's thinking through the furnace many times, to be sure. One should think with a hammer, rather than with a brain, as one shapes our thought from dross matter.'

> Fulcanelli may well be a great initiate into the hermetic lore, yet he is an infuriating Teacher. He teaches, or enlightens, by means of hints and guesses, demanding all the while the full cooperation and attention of his reader. Fulcanelli seems to practise the *sol lente*, the 'slow-heat' method of the alchemist, for he recognizes that a more fierce heat, which may be raised with the bellows, would kill the germinating life within the vessel.

> A word or a phrase by Fulcanelli can do two things. Either it will spark off unconnected links in one's mind, yoking together unsuspected words or ideas, and thereby engendering enlightenment. Or, it can have one scurrying in ignorance to the old alchemical and occult books, or resorting to the active contemplation of symbols, which he so often recommends. Both these methods of learning are conducted through the slow inner heat, so beloved by alchemical teachers.

> For the student, it is an infuriatingly slow method. All too often even the alchemical books prove too obscure for elucidation, and the questioning soul is left without answers to the questions raised by Fulcanelli. In some cases, years may pass before one arrives at the answers one seeks. We have to admit that, more than once, we have encountered great difficulties in following some of the indications left by Fulcanelli as he skipped along the Way of the Fool, juggling with words, occasionally allowing one to fall to the floor for the benefit of his followers. (Hedsel 2000, 306, 318–319)

Even though the Cassiopaeans have repeatedly told us that certain things must be given in a measured way and that phases must pass, I had never thought of this as the actual alchemical process of being transformed directly. But, here we have the clue that the retort must be heated many times. And we also begin to understand better the alchemical process itself.

> 'You know, one day, some scholar will claim that they have finally discovered who Fulcanelli was. But that scholar will be wrong, for he or she will not know of how initiates really work. They will not know of how casually an initiate may change his clothing. They will not even be able to identify and initiate from his words, or from his eyes. ...' (Hedsel 2000, 306)

I had to laugh at this one! I am quite sure that this was addressed directly to all of those who read Fulcanelli and think that rituals are the answer, or that Kaballah is the path.

> '... Fulcanelli is alive. Fulcanelli is even older than me, yet he is still alive. He lives here in Florence.' (Hedsel 2000, 307)

At this point, the old man who is speaking to Mark Hedsel tells him that there is a small group that meets in Florence, and invites him to join them. At this little gathering the old man speaks, and here we come back to the Moon:

> 'In the arcane tradition there are two Moons. These pairs have very many names. Such names are usually derived from mythological personifications – yet all these pairs relate to the idea that one Moon is a reflector of sunlight, while the other, if not always in darkness, is invisible. ...
>
> 'From the very beginning of civilization, the Moon has been a mystery, because it has always stared down upon the Earth with one single face. As the Moon circles the Earth, it keeps one side of its globular face presented towards humanity. ...
>
> '... Western occultism have tended, until comparatively recent times, to emphasize only the light side of the Moon. Even so, hints of the dark Moon are encapsulated in even the most overt-seeming symbolism.
>
> '... the archangel Gabriel is the ruler of the Moon – that is, of the light side of the Moon. His role as messenger at the Annunciation is well established, even if his arcane role (symbolized by the white lilies) is only imperfectly understood outside the secret Schools. The lilies of Gabriel are very profound symbols indeed. They are recognized, in the Mysteries, as symbols of the descent of a God. [Laura's note: Notice that he does not say "the descent of God," but of "a God."]
>
> 'Furthermore, in the same Christian tradition, images of the Assumption of the Virgin show the lunar crescent beneath the feet of the Virgin.
>
> 'In these two different symbols, we have a clue to how the Virgin of Light is linked with the angelic ruler of the Moon at the conception of the Child, and with the lunar crescent at her own translation from Earth to Heaven – at her death. It is as though this symbolism was designed to show ...' He paused '... to show that the very same lunar forces which announced her destiny as the Mother of God were also lifting her to Heaven, at the end of her life.
>
> 'Now, Gabriel is the Christian equivalent of the personified light Moon. The name is, of course, Hebraic, and we must look to the same language in our search for the name of the Christian dark Moon. This name is Lilith, the mother of the *lilin*, or

brood of demons. We see, then, that it is no great mystery that the angel Gabriel should carry lilies at the Annunciation. There is rarely such a thing as accident in the confluence of sounds in arcane symbolism.' (Hedsel 2000, 310–311)

So is the old man, the teacher of Hedsel, telling us that Christianity is a religion of demons? It seems so, yet he will not come right out and say it. He gives with one paragraph, and takes away with another. He goes on to emphasize this point by saying:

'… the early Christian church was *embarrassed* by the vast numbers of demonologies which prowled around the cosmologies of the pagan religions. These demons were especially numerous in the Gnostic tradition which the Church felt proper to dismiss. It seems to me that this rejection of the Gnostic tradition was part of a peculiar programme adopted by the early Church. …' (Hedsel 2000, 311)

And then he said another thing that brought out the hairspray again:

'… the lunar Isis is not a single goddess, but dual. Her sister, Nephthys, was the dark Moon: in the ancient Egyptian *Book of the Dead*, Nephthys is portrayed standing opposite her sister, like a shadow-neter (opposite). In addition to being sister of Isis, this black virgin Nephthys was sister and wife of the dark *Set*. … The pair – Isis and Nephthys – were called *the weeping sisters*. Their tears stream to Earth, just *as the tears of sleeping humanity stream towards the Moon in the Tarot card*. This, it is said, was because they both wept at the death of Osiris, though, as we shall see, there may be a far deeper reason for this description.' …

'I said that much of the ancient lore pertaining to the dark Moon was lost with the emergence of Christianity … The initiates who guided the transfer of some of the ancient teachings of the Egyptians to Rome, that they might serve the new Mysteries of Christ …'

In the Greek and Roman epics, it is a commonplace for the poets to visualize the gods spinning fate around a man, as though his body were nothing more than a spindle, the inner core being wrapped in the threads from which his destiny was being spun. This notion was extended into the fatalistic activities of the *Moirae*. The Greek word *moira*, which meant 'portion', was eventually applied to the fate apportioned to an individual, and the three Moirae were adopted as personifications of the notion of allotted destiny.

The myths of Selene and the Moirae are not really too far removed from the ancient hermetic view which traced a link between the Moon and Fate. In early cosmologies, it was the Moon who was regarded as the controller of human destiny. …

… The Greek name Hecate means 'worker from afar', and captures perfectly the notion of an influence cast from a distant satellite. It would seem that Hecate is the tutelary lunar goddess of the Sleepers, of those who have not yet found their way to a Path. (Hedsel 2000, 312, 314, 316, 233)

Here I would like to point out that the Cassiopaeans have repeatedly said that the Moon is a "base" for the fourth-density control system. And we might also want to remember the writings of Morris K. Jessup on this matter, most particularly his theory of "null zones" that enable the activation or opening of windows or portals between densities, though he did not express it in those terms.

> In modern times, most people tend to think of space as being empty of living beings: it is 'empty space' – save, of course, for the stars, planets and cosmic dust. This soulless vision is however quite modern. In previous ages, there was never much doubt that the heavens were filled with Spiritual beings. ...
>
> ... the Way Up and the Way Down, the Way Out and the Way In ... marks a *cross* in space and time. ...
>
> ... the ancient hieroglyphic for the Place of the Horizon, which eventually turned into the modern sigil for Libra, is that which separates the infernal from the celestial.
>
> '... the glyph indicates that Mankind – even that small part of Mankind that seeks initiation ... must, at some time or another, descend into the *Well of Ordeal*. ...'
>
> '... In some ways, the Moon is the greatest problem of esoteric lore. The Moon is not at all what it appears to be.
>
> 'At the end of the last century an astounding revelation was made, as a result of dissent among members of secret Schools. Information, hitherto guarded jealously by the most enclosed of the inner Orders, was made public. The secrets disclosed pertained to a far deeper level of knowledge than has hitherto been made exoteric by the Schools – even in this enlightened age.' (Hedsel 2000, 233, 239, 242)

Here, Hedsel's teacher is suggested to be referring to A. P. Sinnet and his connection to Theosophy and certain revelations that were made in 1932 via the Brotherhood of Luxor, but I think that this was a deliberate misdirection. Gurdjieff was talking about mankind being "food for the Moon" before 1914. Here we find the probable cause for some of the distortion of information in the Way of the Fool. Blavatsky claimed to have inside information, but it seems likely that what she was given was intentionally mixed with half-truths and some lies.

> 'In a nutshell, what was made public during this conflict in the Schools was the truth that our Moon is a sort of counterweight to another sphere, which remains invisible to ordinary vision. This counterweighted sphere is called in esoteric circles the Eighth Sphere.
>
> 'We must be careful with these words, for, in spite of what I have said, this region is not itself a sphere, nor is it a moon. Even to locate it behind the physical Moon is not correct, for in the Spiritual realm spaces and distances are different. The truth is that the Eighth Sphere does not pertain to anything we are familiar with on the physical plane, yet we must use words from our own vocabularies whenever we wish to denote its existence. ...' (Hedsel 2000, 242)

Here we find that the Cassiopaeans have gone much further in trying to describe what this teacher is saying (and I am assembling these remarks from all through the book, since they are not in order, probably on purpose). The Cassiopaeans call the idea that this man is struggling to express "fourth density." Again we see that the clarity of the Cassiopaean materials serves us well in understanding what have for millennia been arcane matters.

'... Were we to use a word which fits most appropriately this Sphere, then we should really call it a vacuum. Certainly, *vacuum* is a more appropriate term than sphere, for the Eighth Sphere sucks things into its own shadowy existence. ...' (Hedsel 2000, 242)

You don't say? You mean like: man is food for the Moon?

'... It acts as as sort of demonic conduit to suck into its maws certain degenerate Spiritual forms on the Earth. It is a shadow Sphere, controlled by shadow beings. ...' (Hedsel 2000, 243)

Like maybe Lizzes and Grays? Here, again, we have the advantage of the Cassiopaean explanations of these "shadow beings." We can easily see how, without understanding of hyperdimensions and densities, those who were not directly inside the "secret schools" would have the idea that these beings are shadowy or even in some way simply spirits. The same misunderstanding is prevalent today among those alien/UFO interpreters who have decided aliens are merely spirits or demons with no physical reality. This has led to such nonsense as believing that they can possess humans in an interpenetrative spiritual way, like climbing in or out of a body and bringing on shape shifting in the human being.[4]

'... However, the fact that they are shadow beings should not lead us to demote or underestimate their capabilities and intelligence. In many respects they are more intelligent than Man, for they are not limited by the power of love, as is Mankind. ...' (Hedsel 2000, 243)

Again either this man doesn't know how truly deep the mystery is, or he is afraid of scaring his pupils to death!

'The operation of the Eighth Sphere is complex. Its denizens – those shadowy beings for whom it is home – wish to people their Sphere with humanity ... Towards this end, it has erected what we might call terminals on the Earth: these terminals are soul-conduits, which will suck into the lower Sphere a certain form of materialized energy that is engendered on the Earth plane. ...' (Hedsel 2000, 243)

The teacher then goes on to say that the most usual place where this vacuuming of energy happens is among people engaging in spiritualist activities, particularly those having to do with communication with the lower etheric planes, i.e. talking to dead dudes.

While I am in agreement with him, for the most part, I think that it is too great a generalization, and the evidence that there is an alien reality that clearly matches what he is talking about in terms of the Moon or the Eighth sphere, should take us far in realizing the true nature of this energy sucking. In fact, the Cassiopaeans

---

[4] Interestingly, John Keel gets very close to these ideas with his notion of "ultraterrestrials" in his book *The Eighth Tower*. His interpretations of alien/UFO phenomena and their ultimate agenda match up fairly consistently with our own and get even closer to the heart of the matter than *Zelator*.

are light years ahead of this, even if it is interesting to get a little corroboration from another source. And there may be something very deep in what he says here, considering the plethora of New Age trance channeling, or conscious channeling, and contacts with space brothers going on nowadays.

'... Certain spiritualist activity is coloured by the erroneous belief that the realm of the dead is accessible to the living. In truth, mediumistic activity *cannot* penetrate through into the true realm of the dead: it is therefore dealing only with shadows. In so doing, it is creating fodder for the nourishment of the Eighth Sphere. This sucking of certain forms of human soul-matter into the Eighth Sphere is not, by any means, intended for the benefit of humanity. The aim of the denizens of this world is to enhance and populate a world which may truly be described as the realm of the damned. The efforts of these denizens, or demons, is contrary to the evolutionary development which has been planned for the world. ...

'It is less than on hundred years since this knowledge of the Eighth Sphere was made public. At first there was an outcry at this breach in initiate knowledge, but now we can see that it has proved something of a blessing that the demonic threat has been brought out into the open. In some ways, it is easier to deal with a visible enemy. Those who dabble in the supposed communications with the dead, and with that spirit-land which they fondly imagine lies beyond the veil, have not gone unwarned. (Hedsel 2000, 243)

And now, finally, we come to one of the greater blessings of this book that indicated to me how I must view what I am doing. In this excerpt, Mark Hedsel is in conversation with an old man who has been on the Path of the Fool for a very long time.

MH: 'I set out to learn how to be a Fool.'

OM: 'No, you set out the follow the Way of the Fool. There is a difference. And what is the result of such a journey? The result is *a wise Fool.* A fool is the one who gives up everything for an idea. The wise Fool is the one who knows that he never had anything to give up in the first place. Is that Foolish? ... What is the difference between an old man and a young man, if they are both fools?' ...

MH: 'Is it commitment? The old man has committed himself, while the young one has not?'

OM: 'Yes, exactly so. The old man has committed himself. He has made a stand. Life has made him do that. He has drawn a circle around himself, and said, "This is where I stand, this is what I must do." He has committed himself to an action. Because he has drawn a circle around himself, others can see where he stands. He can be attacked by others. His position is weak. Those who have not committed themselves can mock, if they are so inclined. The one who has committed himself appears to be in a weak position. Yet the Spiritual truth is quite otherwise. It is the one who accepts commitment who is strong. The true commitment is the artistic one. This is why artists are so often attacked. They are attacked for their morals, for their ideas – even for their work. Yet their essence – their commitment – is the secret which is unassailable. The true artist knows that *creativity is its own reward*. Ordinary people fear commitment, you see. Ordinary people fear creativity. They know that if they allow that seething cauldron of yellow liquid to boil over within themselves, then their whole lives will be changed. People fear change. People do not wish to be creative and artistic in any real sense. They wish to decorate, perhaps, and to make things around themselves pleasant – but this has little to do with creativity. ... All spiritual paths should be creative. Creativity is involved with sacrifice. That stew of yellow liquid which boils in everyone is a sacrificial broth ...'

MH: 'The sulphur?'

OM: Yes, the sulphur. The first of the Three Principles. It is in a sacrificial cauldron. It is an excess. Creativity is Spiritual delight, and overpouring of sulphur. ... Some time ago you asked me about the word *sulphur*. We both agreed that Fulcanelli was right, and alchemical sulphur is the equivalent of the sexual energies in man and woman. The sexual energies may come out in a selfish way or in a creative way. Jakob Boehme ... saw the division in the word sulphur in a slightly different way. He divided the word itself, and said *Sul* was the soul of a thing, the oil. The *sul* is born of the *phur*, the light. ... Have you ever looked at spilt oil? Under certain conditions it can look like a thin filament of a rainbow. This is the light imprisoned in the oil. The light rises upwards. It liberates the rainbow. It is as simple as that. ...'

MH: 'Then all creative activity must be foolish? In which case, thinking must be foolish?'

OM: ... 'Perhaps thinking is foolish. Certain forms of thinking undoubtedly are foolish. After all, most people are vulnerable in their ideas: they fear to think for themselves. The Fool learns to think for himself: he or she makes it an exercise of the soul. Others refuse that Way. This is why our civilization is so under threat. We are living in a world where every effort is being made to ensure that the body is comfortable, yet little is done for the growing soul. ...'

MH: '... creativity is itself a form of selflessness?'

OM: 'Exactly so. *Creativity is the giving away of Spiritual energy*. Creativity is the soul in the expenditure of a bottomless purse. One gives sulphur away – initially perhaps through an excess of joy – for that is the foolishness of young men. Later, *one gives away energy through commitment to an idea.*'

MH: 'Creativity is the ultimate deed of unselfishness?

OM: 'Yes. ... *When a man knows that creativity is its own reward ... well, then he is ready to work with people.* ... you think of yourself as a loner. You do not see how much you are needed. You are needed to point the way.'

MH: 'But I know nothing.'

OM: '... You do not really believe that when you sit before a group you do so alone? You are there as a representative of the spiritual world. ... Fools like myself become teachers, *because we find suddenly that there is no one else*. It's as simple as that. ... You realize how great is the gulf between you and others. There is a curtain between you. And you understand that this curtain is good for neither of you. The house out there is burning. *You* can see the flames, but those others cannot see the flames. ... Now the question is, can you leave those people in the flames? Would it not be the act of a Fool to snatch one, or perhaps two, out of the conflagration?'

MH: 'If that is what they want.'

OM: 'They cannot see the flames, but they do not wish to be burned. You see. You know that there are two sorts of flame. There is the soft and slow flame of the inner heat, and that terrible burning flame which consumes, and which feels no human pain. … You cannot continue widening the gap between yourself and the world. … What for others is light is for the Teacher an old light – another word for darkness. … We live in a foolish paradox, for while we have forever, we do not have much time. (Hedsel 2000, 325–329)

And that was my answer. The house is burning, and I am a Fool who seeks to snatch as many as possible from the flames. And it is an act of creativity – a commitment to an idea. And, just as I finished reading this book, I received a message from a friend who wrote:

Laura,

Sharing your life and trials and fiery initiations through your pages is a raw fire walk on this planet. I know how lonely it feels in the moment of retelling each drama, re-experiencing even the sensory memory that served to strip another layer off your (by now) Zen flesh and Zen bones. Yet at this stage, it is also a refreshingly cool wind that passes through awareness to allow ourselves to be that thoroughly exposed … as if that wind of the exposure is blowing off a little more residual bits of flesh still clinging to our bones.

And yet, in reading those truths (those of us who know and can relate), the storytelling is understood to be a beautiful performance art of your soul's expansion under the tutelage of our future selves. Such a spectacular display of universal love and timelessness and beauty and truth and cosmic humor it is.

Yes, when the truth (as lessons and dramas) hit us here in 3rd density in the matrix, we process it as painful (because of our programs) … but after a while, if we learn to relax, life in the matrix is doable. Like anything painful (childbirth, for example) relaxing is the way to avoid the worst of it (and minimize scarring … which is to carry pain into future time).

So I see this dance of your posts and the stimulation they provide as an exercise in networking that seems to have a wonderful cosmic purpose. That cosmic purpose is that networking in the matrix is a group lesson that can greatly accelerate both individual and group awareness. Many times I have found this group energy fascinating … for example, a dream of a friend seems to act as a preview of coming attractions of a meditation insight that comes to me, and that is mirrored in the life movie of another friend, etc.

… It is my theory that we are moving towards this understanding of group mind and interconnectedness in this coming year. I am feeling we are all going to become much more aware of this networking synchronicity. One of the lessons of duality is to understand we are not really separate beings, but suspended together in one mind. Playing there with telepathy and other ways to explore expanded awareness is a birthright we can claim and enjoy with like-minded others.

Thanks, Laura, for being a scout and going out and expanding our playing field comfort zone so we can all expand together. You rock, girl. Can't wait for the next pages!
M.

Thank *you*, Michele. From one Fool to another.

CHAPTER 68
AS ABOVE, SO BELOW

I have spent a number of evenings debating with myself the planned content of this next chapter. On the one hand, the information is crucial; and on the other hand, there are some parts that are so extremely disturbing that when I examine them I have difficulty dealing with the images they conjure. So, the question became: how much do I really need to tell to make the point? Ought I just record the results of research and leave out *how* these results were obtained? Or does the reader have a right to know precisely how various researchers come to their conclusions?

As I was pondering this issue, something the Cassiopaeans once said came to my mind:

July 14, 1996
A: 3rd density STS orientation includes the thought of "dominion" over 2nd density, and this is merely a continuation of the energy buildup of the approach of the wave ... some of the lessons are interesting indeed. When you assume that capture and imprisonment of those of lesser capacity than you is for "the good," why should not you expect those of greater capacity than you to assume the same regarding you?!

This then led me to think about the Hermetic maxim, *As above, so below;* and certain implications that had never dawned on me began to shape themselves into a framework of understanding. I would like to share this with you.

In our world, we have many classes of people; many segments of the population that are engaged in many different pursuits, occupations, and fields of endeavor. All of these are more or less compartmentalized so that, very often, what one group is aware of and what they do is unavailable to other groups. There is a large, broad based group of your average Mr. and Mrs. Citizen, who are for the most part unaware of almost everything. They are born, live their lives in a normal way with all the normal accoutrements of an average life, including their normal allotment of momentous events such as school, graduations, the first job, marriages, births, deaths, football games, vacations to the seashore or mountains, friends, movies, and on and on. For the most part, it is all struggle to keep in step with the times and expectations of society.

In recent years, many polls have been conducted that ask the question: Are you happy with your life? A surprisingly high percentage of citizens respond: Yes. Why is this surprising? Because statistics show that mood disorders such as depression and anxiety are on the increase, becoming more widespread all the time. Depression related suicides are also on the rise. So, we have to ask the question: if everyone is so happy, why is depression at near epidemic proportions in our society?

It is clear that a huge segment our society is in denial. People cling to what they believe is the cultural norm, what is socially expected, and then pronounce themselves happy if they can come anywhere close to meeting it.

Twenty or more years ago, the individual who was on anti-depressant drugs was a rarity. Sure, they took an occasional Valium or Librium during times of crisis, but those are relatively harmless relaxants. Nowadays, practically every other person you talk to is either taking, or has a family member who is taking, Prozac, Zoloft, Paxil, Serzone, Tofranil, or any combination thereof. This is the ubiquitous medical solution to the epidemic of depression.

The psychosomatic network operates through a series of delicately balanced chemical interactions and feedback loops. The question of how drugs – legal or illegal – enter the network and affect the natural homeostatic balance is seldom addressed.

Drugs go to work at the level where brain cells are communicating with each other across synapses. Natural chemicals are squirted out by one or another cell and taken up by another. If there is too much of the chemical, the body has a mop up operation called a "re-uptake mechanism" by which the cell reabsorbs the excess. Many anti-depressants are used to block the re-uptake mechanism, allowing excess chemicals to flood the body. It is suggested that this corrects the imbalance.

The problem is, this Band-Aid approach does not measure what else may be going on in the body at the many other sites where these chemicals are also taken up by cells. One example is Prozac. Prozac works because it allows the body to be flooded with serotonin. It is now known that the intestines are loaded with serotonin receptors and that people on anti-depressants very often have gastrointestinal problems. The epidemic of digestive disorders is evidenced by the amazing number of television commercials advertising antacids.

I'm sure you've all seen the nice little drama of the young family at the circus with their excited children, only the family fun is about to be spoiled because the parents are suffering from – dare we say it – acid indigestion! And, of course, the fatherly pharmaceutical company in their infinite wisdom and mercy have just the solution.

Now, this is not to say that everyone who has acid indigestion is on anti-depressants, but the point is that such commercials normalize this. Just what are they trying to cover up? I wonder.

Nonetheless, it seems that for the most part even the medical professionals who are prescribing these drugs are not even asking questions. It's easy to say that there is a conspiracy of doctors to drug the populace; but as most of us know, our physicians and nurses are mostly interested in healing, and they work with the system that is promoted by our culture as being the right method. They learn what they practice in medical schools, taught by professors who learned it from their teachers. The research that leads to the different concepts of healing is funded by – well, here we hit a curious thing – pharmaceutical companies. And, of course, pharmaceutical companies have a vested interest in making money from selling pharmaceuticals.

So, shall we blame the drug companies? Is it merely greed?

When we begin to examine this issue, we find that most of those doing this research are truly convinced that the approach they are taught is the proper methodology. They are convinced, in their own minds, that it is for the good of humankind.

If we think for a moment about the knowledge available to any given scholar or scientist in the many fields of study, and compare that to what the average citizen may know about any of this, we come to the idea that there are many things known by these scholars to which most people are oblivious. When we think about the meetings that may take place between leaders of nations or diplomats; or operations that may be undertaken by any intelligence organization, we are again confronted with the ignorance of the majority of people. We may read books by people claiming to be in the know, and we may hear stories and watch movies, and come to some idea of the many areas of our world in which we can only participate vicariously, fictitiously, or not at all; but can only suspect. And even at those rarefied levels, we find that each and every one of them, with few exceptions, believe that what they are doing – even if it entails secrecy – is for the good of humanity.

And, of course, each and every different group has its own idea of what is good for humanity, and some of these opinions are diametrically opposed to one another. When we step back from the picture, we see that something crucial is being missed. And this crucial thing seems to be the ability to observe the world objectively – empirically, if you will – and to use the mind to assess the fruits of the ideas in an objective manner.

I once was told that in China, (and I can't verify that this is true), at a certain time in its history, doctors were required to post above their doorways a list of all their patients who had died. Not only that, the custom was that the patient did not pay the doctor until he was cured. This had the effect of motivating doctors to figure out what *really* worked in terms of healing therapies.

In Western medicine, it seems that this motivation to find a real cure or solution, on an individual basis, is lacking. Not only that, but this motivation factor is missing from all other areas of our lives.

For but one example: our governments are composed of individuals who seek office *not* to serve the people – even if they give lip service to that idea – but for money and power. If the payoff of money and power were removed from the sphere of government, if our elected officials were required to post the number of patients who had died above their doors, and were only paid if they were successful in solving the problems of the public sector, you can be sure that there would be a mad rush by many to get out of government, and the field would be left to those who were really capable of solving our problems.

In 1974, my grandfather died because he was killed by the medical profession. His diagnosed problem was high blood pressure. He was treated by administering the standard medications indicated by the medical profession at the time, and died when his potassium levels plunged and his heart stopped. Ten years later, I watched an expose on a news magazine TV show. The show exposed the fact that this standard treatment had killed so many people and doctors were finally questioning the selection of drugs they were using to treat high blood pressure. It was a scandal of national proportions. And it wasn't the first one.

I grew up next door to a child who was a Thalidomide baby. We were best friends for many years, until I moved away. Sammy had no arms and one leg was a vestigial flipper. The other leg was normal. Sammy was a genius with a delightful personality and an assertive, no-nonsense, ambitious nature. There was no question that he was in charge of our relationship and I spent a lot of time executing his wishes: building things, setting things up, fetching, carrying, and just generally being his arms and legs. I'll never forget the year he decided that Christmas trees ought to have a use after Christmas, and we were going to create a "magic forest." It was my job to go up and down the streets of our neighborhood and retrieve all the trees set out for the trash collectors. I had to drag them back – many of them bigger than I was – and set them up according to Sammy's specifications. In the end, we had about 50 of them.

I never thought much about the fact that Sammy was different when we were growing up. I was four and he was two when we were first plopped into a sandbox together, and all of his development took place before my eyes and seemed natural. He could do just about everything with his feet that I could do with my hands, including using scissors and playing the organ. When he came over to my house to play, and we had a snack, a special stool was available for him to sit on at the table that was the same height as the table so he could use his feet to eat. Once he was situated, my grandmother would wash his feet for him. When I would go out with him and his family on a trip to a store or a movie, I was aware that other people stared and moved away from him, and so I *knew* that he was different, but

I never gave much thought until I grew up. It was then that I learned that Sammy was the way he was because a doctor gave his mother some pills for morning sickness.

I never, ever forgot that a doctor – acting in good faith – had done this.

Now, if our own third-density world has so many layers and compartments and secrets and agendas, do we think that it is possible that the same could be true for the fourth-density STS reality?

As above, so below.

In the present time, there are all sorts of communications with higher beings and sources of all kinds taking place. When we look at this, we find that there is the same problem apparent as we find in our own world. Can it be that there are fourth-density beings – or higher – who communicate with humans by various means, who are simply as ignorant of the doings in their realities as we are in our own? Or, that their agendas – even if framed to seem for the good of humanity – could be less than positive?

And if our own scientists will experiment on our little second-density companions in ways that you will soon discover, do we for one minute think that scientists at fourth density would not feel justified doing the same with us?

I don't know about you, but the very thought of it produces in me a sensation that I prefer not to extend for any period of time, and my mind hastily closes the door on such a thought. But, at the same time, I understand clearly that I must be knowledgeable about these things, just as I must educate myself about health care in order to prevent myself or those close to me from being used as guinea pigs by the medical profession.

Yet, it is a thought that we must consider. And consider well.

Not only do we have to consider people we come into direct contact with who, even with the best of intentions, can destroy our lives through ignorance, we also have to consider those who are exploiting this. In our own recent times there was such activity, rooted in the idea that it was "for the good of mankind." And those who closed their eyes to it became victims in spirit if not in fact. I am reminded of an account by Elie Wiesel where he tells how his father refused to believe that the Nazis would ever do anything uncivilized, and constantly put off taking his family to safety. Of course, it was too late. He was warned, he was urged, he was entreated – but he steadfastly refused to believe any evil of anyone.

In the present time, we have many who are taking this stand; believing that love is the answer and the open heart is the way. Over and over again in history we see this approach leading to massacre and bloodbath. Darkness falls upon the land and it's a long time before balance is reestablished.

Such individuals claim that their knowledge comes from higher sources and that they are sure it is truth because it feels good. They are sure that love can only beget love, and if they have an open heart that is full of love, that nothing that is not of that frequency can ever pass such a barrier.

The problem here is much the same as the problems we find within our own world. As the Cassiopaeans noted, "When you assume that capture and imprisonment of those of lesser capacity than you is for 'the good,' why should not you expect those of greater capacity than you to assume the same regarding you?!"

We learn from Michael Topper, in simplified form here:

> We well know the law of 3rd density: No two objects can occupy the same space at the same time. It should be obvious that this is a function of perception. ... Perception determines the outline of what's to stand as an object. In 3rd density, objects are mutually exclusive and define one another by contrast – by their differences. ... Perception of unity ... is a function of higher density cognition. It requires the use of faculties that are presently recessed in our being, and only occasionally accessed.
>
> When, through spiritual practice or discipline performed on this plane, we perceive the luminous wholeness of separate objects, we are experiencing a momentary coordination with energies belonging to other densities and drawn into our frame of reference.
>
> ... 3rd density is the level where consciousness awakens to itself by a process of modeled approximations of things out there. That is to say that the internal dialogue of the soul is verbalized by the symbols of the world – the reality in which we live and move and have our being.
>
> ... The potential of 3rd density is pure awareness of consciousness itself without the need for descriptions or models out there. This is why the 3rd density level of consciousness is a critical threshold. Its potential clarity about its own existence is what aligns it with higher density consciousness. If it can correctly read the symbols of reality and align itself with them, even though they are a mask, the currents of being become stronger.
>
> Thus we see that this is a very decisive stage in soul-realization. And we understand that the soul development is in the hands of the consciousness unit itself; dependent upon its accuracy in reading the symbols and aligning properly. This is the process of polarization.
>
> The problem is: the soul is conditioned by inbuilt patterns of survival, ritual, reproduction and power-acquisition developed on the basis of lower density influences, i.e. the material world, i.e. the Predator's mind. These are enforced through the basal-brain lobes of the Reptilian complex and the correlating abdominal centers of the autonomic currents in the mind/body.
>
> What beckons the 3rd density consciousness is the intimations of the higher densities of intelligence and life. These intimations can be received in varying strengths and levels based upon the level of congruence or alignment of the individual with the symbols of their life which are there to inform them of what is *really* being said at the higher levels of their being.
>
> So, we see that the lessons of 4th density are these simple understandings relating to correctly reading the symbols of our reality and aligning ourselves with them by application of our knowledge and awareness. This involves constant work in adjust-

ing, shifting, and realigning ourselves in experimental feedback maneuvers, which generate an ongoing adventure in God seeking.

... We may understand the business of the densities by analogy with Rubik's Cube. The minimal threshold level of 3rd density consciousness is like being at the center of the Cube, which represents our self-reflection in the outer world, which is given to us in a maximum state of disorder. This means that everything we perceive is received through distorted patterns of a maze.

We must keep in mind that this distorted pattern of our reality is for purposes of catalyst, or forced choices. Being in a maze generates the necessity of choice. Since Unity is not perceived in this reality, the consciousness unit, or soul, is confronted with the requirement of assessing the implications of all interaction with other beings and situations, and of choosing an orientation on the basis of that personal assessment.

... Given a full complement of rational and intuitive faculties (which self-aware consciousness develops by trial and error in the beginning), the soul may learn to function in alignment with an underlying principle of unity; it sees difference as many aspects of one; and each is valued. This learning is accomplished by either experimental reflection and analysis of consequences, or it may reject the evidence of the objective reality and choose instead to cling to its own version of truth, seeking ever to impose this on the reality, choosing to see that unity can only be by elimination of difference, the arbiter of what is the right way, being, of course, the subjective view of such a consciousness. [As the Cassiopaeans describe it, "wishful thinking."]

... The work of crystallizing these two extremes of polarization is the real and underlying business of 3rd density. We live our myriad rounds of incarnation through this density, preserved between incarnations as a memory record of these identification patterns coded in the soul matrix, in order to produce this polarization to one side of the self equation or the other.

The inference is, of course, that the balancing mechanism of karma does not merely serve the rectification process of our many spiritual teachings, but actually serve to harmonize the soul in objective understanding of unity of all, or to consolidate a contractile soul that refuses repeatedly to see difference as many aspects of the One, and chooses instead to seek to make all One by eliminating differences.

The level of the soul's ability to align in one way or the other via *will*, is the measure of it's harvestability to 4th density at the end of each master cycle which, according to many sources, is the period in which we live at present.

Harvestability is the ripeness of the soul to proceed by virtue of the intensity with which it holds its view of reality. This means that subjective, one-pointed devotion to Love of Self – manifested as preference of the self's view of reality over and above whatever the objective reality may actually manifest – is capable of achieving a dedicated integration. It is as though such a soul makes absolutely no attempt to sort and work with the confused faces of Rubik's Cube; it makes no effort to learn how to work with the symbols, but steadfastly recoils in the center of the cube, *believing* that the faces of the cube are aligned and that it's belief makes it an objective *fact*.

[This is the essence of Love of Self. And such a consciousness backs its choice by godly justifications. It seeks to be saved, i.e. have the cube aligned for it by an outside agency that will come rushing to its aid if it manifests enough love and faith with its open and bleeding heart. And this is where we come back to the remark made above by the Cassiopaeans: "When you assume that capture and imprisonment of those of lesser capacity than you is for 'the good,' why should not you expect those of greater capacity than you to assume the same regarding you?!"]

Such a soul, persisting in its love and faith against the clues and hints of the symbol system of reality, is wide open for subsumation into a hierarchy of beings who are firmly convinced that what they are doing is "for the good of humanity." ("Will, Being and Well Being")

And it is in this context that such beings have created and disseminated such spiritual and religious beliefs such as "suffering will earn you a place in heaven," or "turn the other cheek," or "give until it hurts," or "your faith will make you whole," and on and on.

Now, notice that I did not include such things as "love your enemy, bless those that persecute you," because, in the larger sense, the soul that chooses to serve others, that chooses to see unity in difference will naturally love the enemy and bless persecutors. He will just see them as one face of the cube, part of the whole, and not necessarily the face that he wishes to align with or give energy to.

So, once the orientation is chosen – ipso facto by repeated actions through many incarnations – the soul is then graduated to fourth density where the lessons have to do with love and understanding. It is there that this is distilled and purified according to orientation. At fourth density, the nature of the density is love of the creator in terms of either one's subjective view, or the objective reality. The general rule of loving God reaches all densities. It is at third density that everything is masked so that the soul must choose based on how it develops – and how it develops is based on how it chooses. As these choices add up, the soul becomes ripe in loving God as Self, or loving others as both God *and* Self.

At fourth density, the purpose of both polarities is the same: to seek a degree of intensification and alignment with their chosen version of love. The difference is, the STS polarity seeks to absorb or eat love energy. The very atmosphere of fourth density is that of love. And when any third-density being establishes contact with the higher densities by intensification of subjective faith, the natural inflow of energies will be perceived as overwhelming love.

They seek to promote the "open heart and love" approach because this is what feeds them. Their own choice of Love of Self and imposition of this subjective view is a form of projection that requires massive amounts of energy to maintain.

This idea will be disturbing to those individuals who believe that their challenges to spiritual or higher-density beings, or their open hearts are a kind of talisman or a universal sign of the cross that will automatically repel negativity and send it fleeing. But it the evidence shows that higher-density beings are not so constrained. The STS beings of fourth density rely on this to confuse the issue, to fool the bedeviled mind into taking psychological refuge in such a premise that will actually serve to further encourage the acceptance of the idea that they have the "good of humanity" at heart. What is felt in the presence of any fourth-density being, whether it is Serving Self or Others, is the informing quality of the density through which they function. This love and feeling of unity is the pervasive property of that density, not the personal expression of the beings.

We then come to the problem of why otherwise STO [Service To Others] sources will say that nothing negative can graduate to the higher levels of being and development. Are they lying?

This conforms to a certain belief pattern prevalent in New Age circles. It is also used and supplemented by many channeled sources which take the "see no evil" approach. This doctrine posits that where there is no knowledge of negativity, negativity does not exist. This in turn links to the corollary that "your create your own reality" by what you admit to exist.

We quickly see that this takes us back to the recoiled soul in the middle of the Rubik's Cube of awareness, willfully refusing to see the jumble of patterns, and demanding that the universe, or God, or whoever, come and fix the blasted thing according to his belief that it ought to be all nicely arranged so that all the colors are together on each side. Never mind that the universe or God doesn't actually do this, the soul deliberately works to grow his belief so strong that he will see it as fixed, and by doing this will have crystallized his will to the point of being harvested to fourth-density STS.

As mentioned above, it is unlikely that any of us would ever be fooled again by another Hitler. But, curiously, we are blind to such things in spiritual terms. When it comes to negativity of a spiritual nature, or what we might call evil, many people assume that things of the spirit and principles of the material world have different roots and are, therefore, not comparable as we have been told in the Hermetic maxim, *As above, so below.*

The idea that higher-density beings can be as compartmentalized and varied in their perspectives and objectives – only to a degree of greater intensity and ability – is positively *not* part of the perspective of many people who simply refuse to admit such a possibility.

The very idea of this makes many people experience such a hollow and heavy sensation in the pit of their stomach that they're sure their gut feelings are showing it to be a lie. It's bad enough to be transparent to the eyes of a benevolent being at higher levels; it is quite another kettle of fish to have to confront the idea of an incredibly concentrated malevolent intelligence possessing a predatory wisdom that is more than a match for any third-density mentality. And worse yet, such beings can move through our reality, unseen and unfelt, to whisper hemlock sweet words into our defenseless ears while at the same time manipulating with subliminal ease our complex chemistry and thinking, so that they can effectively breach the barriers of our crude subjective focus without so much as registering a blink in our warning systems. (Cf. Topper)

So unacceptable is this prospect to the third-density ego, ruled by anxiety, that it panics and pushes the veto button, foaming at the mouth in denial, reaching in frenzy for every holy word of whatever denomination was inculcated in childhood that clearly states "only the good" pass on to the higher worlds.

When faced with such an idea, even if we have given up Churchianity, we will flee to the sources that tell us negative values and thoughts of warfare can't be brought along to the higher realms. Such sources would have us believe that the common denominator of higher levels compels conscious conformance to the value of unity.

For some, the very fact that a higher being would even speak about anything negative in any context, is proof that they are a negative being or a Satanically de-luded lower astral spirit. Because, of course, all higher beings are so purified that such words cannot pass their ephemeral lips without choking them. Yeah, right!

Such a doctrine has no idea of what to do with an evil that isn't simply relative to cultural context or evil by comparative definition, or is evil due to ignorance, but is, on the contrary, very conscious, very intentional, very malevolent and cun-ning to a level that cannot be plumbed by third-density awareness.

Does that scare you? It ought to. But not so that you will run and hide or live in terror, or dive into denial. It ought to galvanize you to do what is appropriate to the situation: learn all you can so that you are better equipped to utilize reason and analysis and observation in order to make your choices more congruent with your internal alignment.

Does it scare you to think that the medical system in the Western world may be approaching healing in the wrong way; that your doctor, despite his best inten-tions, may have been educated and brainwashed into a system that does not pro-mote health? If you are ill and need treatment, and you know that your doctor might kill you or do irreparable harm to you, do you just go into denial about your sickness and sit there and die? Or do you begin to learn all you can about your illness, the many varied treatment methods that might be available in other forms of healing, and possibly take responsibility for your own wellness by making some decisions as to what treatments you will implement in your own life? And, if you are stymied or blocked in this endeavor, will you just give up and take the only medicine available and possibly die?

Now, in our works, we have never asked anybody to believe anything. We simp-ly have the idea that human beings worldwide have a right to know what *may* be going on, and a possible interpretation of things that have puzzled human beings for a very long time.

We also wish to observe that the greatest minds of history have sought to work through and explain these issues for millennia with little success. And, for the most part, they have taken the route of "faith in the goodness of higher beings who will take care of us if we pray and are long-suffering." While we think that such efforts are laudable, we also think that they are bound by their own self-defined limitations and that they are thereby prevented from disseminating information that can make a real difference. Their track records speak for themselves if the individual will take the time to stop listening to the propaganda and look at the "fruits."

When we began to share this information, very few people took it seriously. Now it seems that many others are jumping on the bandwagon and approaching it with the idea of generating fear for its own sake. That has never been the objective of the Cassiopaeans. They say knowledge protects. And it is in this present work that it will become clear, in the most exact terms, how this is true to a level hardly imagined by the reader up to this point.

Here at Cassiopaea we have accumulated information that suggests the human population on this planet has been subjected for many thousands of years to intense manipulation by "alien" forces through human agents, if not directly. The Cassiopaeans do not take the view that these aliens are of the third-density type; i.e. that they are necessarily travelers from different star systems who are more or less as physical as we are and with whom we can engage on any kind of equal footing in our terms. However, they have been teaching us that we *can* generate our own protection in higher-level terms, and that this protection is a kind of awareness that is generated as knowledge and is *applied*. How and why this works is going to become evident to the reader as we examine the inner workings and hidden mechanisms of the Matrix Control System.

The ancient Sumerians claimed that the human race was created to be a slave race, a food source, and a genetic pool for higher beings, the Annunaki. The Cassiopaeans confirm that we were *altered* for this purpose, having been created or embodied for altogether different reasons that did not include being food.

October 7, 1994

Q: (L) The Sumerian story of the creation of human beings involves a story where they say they killed a god and mixed his blood and parts to mix with mud and then planted it in these female gestation goddesses and that this is where the human race came from. Now, this sounds an awful lot like what the Grays are doing at the present time. Did someone actually kill a God, break his soul in pieces, and thereby make the human race?

A: Symbolism and not correct event sequence. Lizard beings genetically altering the human race after battle for their own feeding purposes.

Q: (L) When did these events that these Sumerian stories are talking about take place?

A: 309000 years ago, approx.

Q: (L) So, it happened so long ago that these stories have lost the truth?

A: Reflection passed down through psychic memory channel.

However, the Cassiopaeans have made it clear that this is *not* total control:

October 22, 1994

Q: (L) At one point in a previous transmission it was stated that the Lizard beings altered the human race after a battle for their own feeding purposes. Could you clarify this?

A: It would not be possible for these beings to completely control your existence. If it were, you would not be able to do the things your race has done. There has been interference by the Lizard beings *in the physical structure of the human beings for their own benefit.* Remember what we told you before. They have been interfering with the time cycle experienced on this plane, for quite some time as you measure it. For 74 thousand years they have been interfering in a backwards and forwards time reference manner in order to set up circumstances that they perceive to be beneficial for them in the measure of time that you would consider to be forward, that is, in the future. They have been going backwards and forwards in time to do this. They are suspended in the time cycle as they do this. So what they perceive as being your equivalent of one hour could be as long as 74 thousand years.

Q: (L) So they haven't been here for 300 thousand years?

A: They originally set up circumstances for their benefit 309 thousand years ago, however, they have been using the particular bracketed period of the 74 thousand year period alter things in all the various ways mentioned earlier.

The idea of a battle having been fought over the human race is a very ancient idea expressed in many religious parables:

Q: (L) What was the true event behind the story of the mark of Cain?

A: Advent of jealousy.

Q: (L) What occurred to allow jealousy to enter into human interaction?

A: Lizard takeover.

Q: (L) Wasn't the Lizard takeover an event that occurred at the time of the fall of Eden?

A: Yes.

Q: (L) Was this story of Cain and Abel part of that takeover?

A: Symbolism of story.

Q: (L) This was symbolic of the Lizzie takeover, the advent of jealousy, and the attitude of brother against brother, is that correct?

A: Partly. The mark of Cain means the "jealousy factor" of change facilitated by Lizard takeover of Earth's vibrational frequency. Knot on spine is physical residue of DNA restriction deliberately added by Lizards. See?

Q: (L) Okay, Jan is going to move her hand up my back and you tell her when to stop at the knot.

A: Okay.

Q: (L) You mean the [area of the] occipital ridge?

A: Yes.

Q: (L) What was the configuration of the spine and skull prior to this addition?

A: Spine had no ridge there. Jealousy emanates from there, you can even feel it.

Q: (L) Do any of these emotions that we have talked about that were generated by

DNA breakdown, were any of these related to what Carl Sagan discusses when he talks about the Reptilian brain?

A: In a roundabout way.

Q: (L) Okay, at the time this mark of Cain came about, were there other humans on the planet that did not have this configuration?

A: It was added to all simultaneously.

Q: (L) How did they physically go about performing this act? What was the mechanism of this event, the nuts and bolts of it?

A: Are you ready? DNA core is as yet undiscovered enzyme relating to carbon. Light waves were used to cancel the first ten factors of DNA by burning them off. At that point, a number of physical changes took place including knot at top of spine. *Each of these is equally reflected in the ethereal.*

Q: (L) Well, the question I do have is, how many people were there on the planet and did they have to take each one and do this individually? ... There were [however] many people on the planet, how did they effect this change on all of them?

A: Light wave alteration.

Q: (L) And light waves, actual light waves, affect DNA?

A: Yes.

Q: (T) What was the origin of the light waves?

A: Our center. ... Our realm. STO.

Q: (L) So, how did the Lizzies use the light from the Service to Others realm ...

A: They used sophisticated technology to interrupt light frequency waves.

Q: (L) Well, what I am getting out of this that you are saying from what you are not saying is that it was almost like, well, was there a battle and you guys lost?

A: Yes.

[...]

Q: (T) Now, another force in what we term as the past, defeated you and used the power of the light in order to alter us in different ways, is this correct?

A: Yes. Now understand this: It is all part of natural grand cycle.

Q: (L) If this is all a part of a natural grand cycle, and correct me if I am wrong here, it almost seems as if you guys, the good guys, and the other bad guys, that you just really kind of go at it just for fun, is that true?

A: No.

Q: (L) But you say it is a natural thing or part of a natural grand cycle. Is this natural grand cycle just part of the interaction between light and darkness which just simply must be?

A: Yes. We are at "front line" of universe's natural system of balance. That is where one rises to before reaching total union of "The One". 6th level.

[...]

Q : (T) Now, the battle you had with the other side ...

A: Are having.

Q: (T) This battle goes on ... do you have the light power back?

A: [We] Never lost it, you did.

Q: (T) Okay, I guess that for us the Lizzies are the main force even though they have others on their side ...

A: Yes.

Q: (T) They took our light, not yours?

A: Not against you. Currently in union with you.

Q: (T) So we are but one battle in the universe in an overall, ongoing struggle?

A: Yes. Balance is natural. Remember, it's all just lessons in the grand cycle.

Q: (L) I am really curious … when you guys and the Lizzies go to it, what do you do? I mean, you obviously don't shoot guns at each other and you don't have tanks …

A: Too complicated for you to possibly understand because you are not at 4th level yet.

Q: (J) When you are fighting, is it any way at all possible for us to detect the battle?

A: First: We don't "fight." Second, yes; it's nature as in meteorology and earth changes.

Q: (T) Your form of confrontation takes the form of physical changes in the atmosphere and environment of the planet?

A: And in space.

Q: (T) But that is how we detect it? The more activity, the more conflict is going on?

A: Remember, we are the light. They are the dark. We are both high level thought forms *reflected at all levels of reality.*

Q: (T) So, what we perceive, then, is what comes through to third density, which is not what we would perceive if we were looking at it from fourth or fifth or sixth.

A: Yes.

Q: (L) Isn't it a little unfair for you guys, at sixth level, to take on the Lizzies at only fourth level?

A: The "Lizzies" are the 4th level representatives of the forces of the darkness not the 6th level, and you are 3rd level representatives.

Q: (L) Is there a sixth-level representative of the forces of darkness?

A: Yes.

Q: (L) And what is this sixth-level representative known as, or called, or look like or whatever?

A: Orion in your "neighborhood."

Q: (L) The Orions are sixth-level STS beings?

A: Yes.

Q: (L) Are they like you, thought forms?

A: Yes.

Q: (L) Do they ever appear in physical matter?

A: Can.

Q: (L) And they are the driving force that controls the Lizzies?

A: Close.

Q: (L) Is there some intermediary between the sixth level Orions and the fourth-level Lizzies, such as a fifth-level force or being?

A: 5th level is contemplation zone for both "sides".

Q: (L) Does that mean that at the contemplation level that there is no activity? (J) Is it like a "time out?"

A: Close. Balancer.

Q: (L) Is there a third-level representative of the forces of the light?

A: Yes.

Q: (L) Who or what are they?

A: Don't exist on your planet.

Q: (L) Do they have a planet of their own?

A: Have quadrillions of them.

Q: (L) Well, this is beginning to sound like we are in pretty bad shape here. This is like the Siberia of the universe as Gurdjieff said.

A: The Universe is infinitely huge.

Q: (L) If there are planets with STO beings …

A: Some look like you.

So we see that thinking about the takeover and manipulation of humanity in *third-density terms* of a battle is not quite the issue in the cosmic terms of warfare. And it is in these terms that we need to begin to think. It is in fourth-density terms that we will come to understand how truly knowledge protects.

March 11, 1995

Q: (L) At one point we were told that time was an illusion that came into being at the time of the fall in Eden, and this was said in such a way that I inferred that there were other illusions put into place at that time …

A: Time is an illusion that works for you because of your altered DNA state.

Q: (L) Okay, what other illusions?

A: Monotheism, the belief in one separate, all powerful entity.

Q: (T) Is "separate" the key word in regard to monotheism?

A: Yes.

Q: (L) What is another one of the illusions?

A: The need for physical aggrandizement.

Q: (L) What is another of the illusions?

A: Linear focus.

Q: (L) Anything else at this time?

A: Unidimensionality.

Q: (L) The veil … (J) The perception of only one dimension … (L) Were these illusions programmed into us genetically through our DNA?

A: Close.

Q: (L) Can you tell us a little bit about how these illusions are enforced on us, how they are perceived by us?

A: If someone opens a door, and behind it you see a pot of gold, do you worry whether there is a poisonous snake behind the door hidden from view, before you reach for the pot of gold?

Q: (L) What does the gold represent?

A: Temptation to limitation.

[…]

Q: (L) So what you are saying to us is that the story of the temptation in Eden was the story of humankind being led into this reality as a result of being tempted. So, the eating of the fruit of the tree of the knowledge of good and evil was …

A: Giving into temptation.

Q: (L) And this was a trick …

A: No! Tricks don't exist!

Q: (T) Okay, no trick, a trap?

A: No! Traps don't exist either. Free will could not be abridged if you had not obliged.

Q: (T) What were we before the "fall?"

A: 3rd density STO.

Q: (T) We are STS at this point because of what happened then?

A: Yes.

[...]

Q: (T) We were third-density STO at that time. Was this after the battle that had transpired? In other words, were we, as a third-density race, literally on our own at that point, as opposed to before?

A: Was battle.

Q: (L) The battle was in us?

A: Through you.

Q: (T) The battle was through us as to whether we would walk through this doorway ... (L) The battle was fought through us, we were literally the battleground. (T) Was the battle over whether or not we walked through that door?

A: Close.

Q: (T) Okay, we were STO at that point. You have said before that on this density we have the choice of being STS or STO.

A: Oh Terry, the battle is always there, it's "when" you choose that counts!

[...]

Q: (T) This must tie into why the Lizards and other aliens keep telling people that they have given their consent for abduction and so forth. We were STO and now we are STS.

A: Yes, ... "when" you went for the gold, you said "hello" to the Lizards and all that that implies.

Q: (T) ... By going for the gold, we became STS beings because going for the gold was STS.

A: Yes.

Q: (T) And, in doing so, we ended up aligning ourselves with the fourth-density Lizard Beings ...

A: Yes.

Q: (T) Because they are fourth-density beings and they have a lot more abilities than we at third density ...

A: You used to be aligned with 4th density STO.

Q: (T) And we were third-density STO. But, by going for the gold we aligned ourselves with fourth-density STS.

A: Yes.

Q: (T) And by doing so we gave fourth-density STS permission to do whatever they wish with us?

A: Close.

Q: (T) So, when they tell us that we gave them permission to abduct us, it is this they are referring to?

A: Close.

Q: (J) Go back to what they said before: "Free will could not be abridged if you had not obliged."

(T) We, as the human race, used our free will to switch from STO to STS.

(L) So, at some level we have chosen the mess we are in and that is the super ancient legend of the fallen angel, Lucifer. That is us. We fell by falling into that door, so to speak, going after the pot of gold, and when we fell through the door, the serpent bit us!

A: But this is a repeating syndrome.

Q: (L) Is it a repeating syndrome just for the human race or is it a repeating syndrome throughout all of creation?

A: It is the latter.

Q: (L) Is this a repeating syndrome throughout all of creation simply because it is the cyclic nature of things? Or is it as the Indians call it, Maya?

A: Either or.

So, we find that there is a huge element of free will involved in making the choice to "fall." The only problem is, the consequences of this choice were not understood due to a lack of knowledge. Another thing that is generally misunderstood is the possibilities of living in a state of third-density STO. It is clearly not the same as living in third-density STS in a *lot* of ways! The problem seems to have been that the effects of the material universe – entering into a third-density physical body for purposes of learning and more rapid development – is the pot of gold that humanity reached for.

October 22, 1994

Q: (L) Can a spiritual being become entrapped in physical matter?

A: It's possible but very unlikely.

Q: (L) Are human beings entrapped in physical matter?

A: By choice.

Q: (L) Why did they make this choice?

A: To experience physical sensations. It was a group mind decision.

Q: (L) Who was in charge of the group?

A: The group. [...] Everything that exists in all realms of the universe can experience existence in one of only two ways. That would be defined as a long wave cycle and a short wave cycle. Going back to your previous question about why humans are "entrapped" in physical existence, which, of course, is voluntary and chosen, this was due to the desire to change from the long wave cycle experience of completely – what you would call – ethereal or spiritual existence, to the short wave cycle of what you call physical existence. The difference is that a long wave cycle involves only very gradual change in evolution in a cyclical manner. Whereas a short wave cycle involves a duality. And this is the case with souls in physical bodies as is experienced on this earth plane because the soul experiences an ethereal state for half the cycle and a physical state for the other half of the cycle. While these halves are not measured in time the way you measure time, the totality of experience is equal in each half. *The necessity to form the short wave cycle was brought about through nature through the natural bounds of the universe when the group mind of souls chose to experience physicality as opposed to a completely ethereal existence.*

The key term in the above remarks is "desire." The group *desired* to change to a cycle that includes physical existence. Now, the question becomes: why would this be seen as desirable? The Cassiopaeans have said that this was because the physical life experience of duality was seen to provide:

> An increase in relative energy which speeds up the learning process of the soul and all of its one dimensional and two dimensional interactive partners. In other words, flora and fauna, minerals, etc. *All experience growth and movement towards reunion at a faster rate on the cycle through this short wave cycle physical/ethereal transfer.*

So, we see that this desire for the gold was also a desire to change the rate of movement towards reunion with the One. Of course, it was thought that this could be done in a safe and moderated manner. The dangers of physical existence were not fully appreciated:

October 23, 1994

Q: (L) Did, at any time, the human race live for a long time in an Edenic state, where they were *able to use bodies and still have a spiritual connection?*
A: Yes. But not long. No addiction takes long to close the circle.
Q: (L) So, mankind was addicted to pleasuring the self?
A: Became quickly.

But that this was a progression over aeons is made clear in the following:

June 24, 2000

Q: (L) A reader writes: "I can't reconcile the idea of our being trapped or lured – by sensuality – into a physical state with the idea that we have progressed through the vegetative and animal states." This is a good question. It seems that the energy of creation has progressed through the vegetative and animal states, that animals can graduate to third density and become human, just as humans can graduate to fourth density. How do we reconcile this with the idea that human souls were entrapped into third-density bodies from fourth density, by the Lizards? Are we talking about two different functions? Two different groups?
A: Humans were not entrapped by the "Lizards."
Q: (B) We volunteered!
(L) Well, they did say that the Lizards were waiting for the right soul matrix to "step in." So, we were the right soul matrix and we stepped into these engineered bodies that the Lizards created. That's what you said. So, how do we reconcile us stepping into these engineered third-density bodies with soul evolution through the vegetative and animal states?
A: If you look more closely at the material, it was not stated that the consciousness levels currently represented by humans and many others "stepped into" anything in particular but PHYSICALITY. Individual consciousness units stepped into different physical forms. Some "stepped" in as humans right off the bat, and some chose otherwise. It is simply that the "choice" to experience physicality in many forms, was

simultaneous, though different "units" have participated in different ways at different stages, rather than in a linear progression.

This same idea has been expressed by the Cassiopaeans in terms of the Big Bang as being this emergence of consciousness into physicality rather than the beginning of the physical universe in Darwinian terms.

October 18, 1994

Q: (L) Is there only one ultimate creator of the universe?

A: All is one. And one is all.

Q: (L) From the one what was the first division?

A: Mass division and disbursement.

Q: (L) Was this simultaneous?

A: Yes.

Q: (L) Was this what we refer to as the Big Bang?

A: Yes.

Q: (L) Is there any reference to this event in terms of time?

A: Always.

Q: (L) Can we say that all that exists in the material universe is, say, "x" number of years old?

A: No. It is the eternal now. Not only did happen, is happening and going to happen. The expanded presence.

We can also think of this process of stepping into matter in terms of the story of the Prodigal Son. In this story, the young man took his inheritance and went to a distant country where he wasted his fortune in reckless and loose living. And, it just so happened that at the same time that he ran out of money, a terrible famine came upon the land and he was unable to make his way by working. He then attached himself to a citizen of that country who set him to work tending the pigs, and he ended up eating with the pigs. Then, he came to himself and realized that even his father's servants were better off than he, and he decided to go home and beg his father's forgiveness and offer to be a servant.

So, he went home. But, while he was a far way off, his father saw him and ran to meet him, and embraced him with pity and tenderness, made the feast, and so forth. You know the story: the fatted calf and all that.

Well, what we are learning here is that the human race is a fragmented soul unit and this story is about us. We are the Prodigal Son, we are Lucifer, the fallen angel, we are Toto and Dorothy carried to Oz by the tornado because we desired to speed things up. And, the image of the son wasting all his wealth is the description of the fragmenting of the being of which each of us is a part.

But Oz, the distant country, the realms of physical reality – they exist as part of the cyclical nature of the Cosmos and is represented in the many ancient depictions of God as a two-faced being. The word *matter* is related to *mother*, and the physical universe is the great womb of the cosmos, or Prime Creator. Into which the sperm or creative consciousness of the Prime Creator is disbursed, and from which can be born the sons of God. Matter is not evil, though from our perspective we may view our experiences here as evil.

These ideas are not new; in the past, many have suggested them in one form or another. The outline of these stories is that during the times before humankind on Earth, there was much experimentation with forms that could be used for the development of consciousness. As this activity proceeded, many souls became fascinated by their own thought creations. They wished to better understand the three dimensions they had manifested and there was a rush to inhabit these physical expressions.

Many souls entered into plants and animals for the sheer joy of experience. As they did so, they found that their force was drawn within and concentrated in the periphery of the inhabited body. This created a uniquely intense experience so that it was sought and repeated over and over again. As this was repeated, it caused a reaction in the spiritual energies of the souls that crystallized in three dimensions. This crystallization became a sort of veil between consciousness and soul energy. As these souls forgot their source, they created energy imbalances by acting in ways that completely disregarded the free will and choice of others.

This was Earth prior to modern man. And here is where the story gets interesting. The result of the imbalance created by separation of consciousness and soul energy was the cycle of reincarnation. It is revealed by certain esoteric sources that a group of beings not engaged in this activity of physical existence sought to create a means to heighten the energies and perceptions of those who were entrapped in this cycle.[5] A physical form was directly manifested to accommodate this purpose, and this physical form was modern man. And here, of course, is where it gets tricky as well due to all the inversions and distortion of the events by those with less than our best interests at heart. Apparently, this directly manifested creation is the one that was taken over and altered. This resulted in the legends of the Fall.

October 23, 1994
Q: (L) Well, then how did mankind come to be here?
A: Combination of factors. Numerous souls desired physical existence then was altered by three forces including principally Lizards through Grays, Nephalim and Orion union.
[...]
Q: (L) You said numerous souls desired physical existence. When the numerous souls did this, how did physical existence come to be?
A: First was apelike.
Q: (L) And then what happened? Did these apelike beings just pop into the air? What did the souls do with these apelike beings?

---

[5] See "The Book of Enoch" and Edgar Cayce's material.

A: Souls altered them by transfer.

Q: (L) Transfer of what?

A: Souls into seeded bodies. Orion Union was first [to put souls] into Neanderthal. … Put humans there for incubation process.

Q: (L) Were altered ape embryos put back into ape females for gestation?

A: No. Souls only.

Q: (L) They put the souls into the ape bodies?

A: Close.

Q: (L) Did the soul's presence in the ape body cause its genetics and DNA to change?

A: Yes.

Q: (L) They entered into living creatures on this planet to experience 3D reality and by entering in caused mutation?

A: Yes.

[…]

Q: (L) Where did the souls come from that entered into the bodies on the planet Earth? Were they in bodies on other planets before they came here?

A: Not this group.

Q: (L) Were they just floating around in the universe somewhere?

A: In union with the One. Have you heard the super ancient legend of Lucifer, the fallen angel?

Q: (L) Who is Lucifer?

A: You. The human race.

Q: (L) Are the souls of individual humans the parts of a larger soul?

A: Yes. Close. The One. All who have fallen must learn "the hard way."

Q: (L) Are you saying that the act of wanting to experience physical reality is the act of falling?

A: You are members of a fragmented soul unit.

Q: (L) What is it about wanting to be physical is a fall?

A: Pleasure for the self.

At a later time, we came back to this in more detail:

August 28, 1999

Q: Well, this is one of the problems I am … trying to … understand is, prior to the Fall in Eden, mankind lived in a fourth-density state. Is that correct?

A: Semi/sort of.

Q: Please be more specific.

A: 4th density in another realm, such as time/space continuum, etc.

Q: Okay, so this realm changed, as a part of the cycle, various choices were made: the human race went through the door after the gold, so to speak, and became aligned with the Lizzies … This resulted in a number of effects: the breaking up of the DNA, the burning off of the first ten factors of DNA, the separation of the hemispheres of the brain …

A: Only reason for this: you play in the dirt, you're gonna get dirty.

Q: What was the motivating factor for playing in the dirt? What essential thing occurred? You said once that it was "desire based imbalance." What was it a desire for?

A: Increased physicality.

Q: What was the objective sought for in this desire for increased physicality?

A: Sensate.

Q: How was sensate experienced so that these beings had an idea that they could get more if they increased their physicality?

A: Not experienced, demonstrated.

Q: Demonstrated how, by who?

A: Do you not know?

Q: It was demonstrated by the Lizzies?

A: Basically.

Q: Demonstrated in what way? Did they say: "Here, try this!" Or did they demonstrate by showing or doing?

A: Closer to the latter.

Q: They were doing, experimenting, playing, and saying: "Look, we are doing this, it's so great, come here and try it."

A: Not really. More like: "You could have this."

Q: What seemed to be so desirable about this increased physicality when they said "You can have this?"

A: Use your imagination!

Q: Was there any understanding or realization of any kind that increased physicality could be like Osiris lured into his own coffin by Set? That they would then slam the lid shut and nail him in?

A: Obviously, such understanding was lacking.

Q: Sounds like a pretty naive bunch! Does the lack of this understanding reflect a lack of knowledge?

A: Of course. But more, it is desire getting in the way of ...

[...]

Q: Okay. The Fall occurred. It seems like, and some of the archaeological studies indicate, that for many thousands of years there was a peaceful existence and a nice agrarian society where the goddess or female creative forces were worshipped. At least, this is what a lot of present-day books are proposing ...

A: No. These events took place 309000 years ago, as you measure it. This is when the first prototype of what you call "modern man" was created. The controllers had the bodies ready, they just needed the right soul matrix to agree to "jump in."

[...]

Q: So, was there any kind of worship of God, or religious activity in this pre-Fall state; this Edenic, semi-fourth-density state?

A: No need when one has a clue.

Q: ... Okay, we had these guys, they fell from Eden, but they were still fairly close to the original concepts, in some terms. Once they jumped into the physical bodies, as you put it, what was their level of conceptualization regarding the universe? Did they still retain some understanding at that point?

A: Kind of like the understanding one has after severe head trauma, vis a vis your normal understanding in your current state.

Q: So, they were traumatized; they may have had bits and pieces of ideas and memories, but they may also have lost a great deal altogether. There may have even been a sort of coma state of mankind for many millennia. But, after they woke up, with the bits and pieces floating around in their heads, they may have begun to attempt to piece it all together. So, they started putting it all back together. What was the first thing they put together regarding the cosmos around them?

A: Sex.

Q: What did they decide about sex? I mean, sex was there. They were having sex. Is that it? Or, did they understand the cosmos as sex?

A: More like the former. After all, that is what got you guys in this mess in the first place! Just imagine the sales job if you can: "Look how much fun this is! Want to try it?!? Oops, sorry, we forgot to tell you, you cannot go back!"

Q: I really fail to understand – and I know it is a big issue that has been hinted at and alluded to, and outright claims have been made regarding sex in all religions and my-thologies – but I fail to understand the mechanics of how this can be the engineering of a fall. What precisely are the mechanics of it? What energy is generated? How is it generated? What is the conceptualization of the misuse of this energy, or the use of the energy?

A: It is simply the introduction of the concept of self-gratification of a physical sort.

Q: On many occasions you have said that the ideal thing is to have perfect balance of physicality and ethereality. This has been said on a number of occasions. Now, I don't understand how it can be that gratification of a physical body can be the me-chanics by which one is entrapped? Is it not gratifying to look at something beautiful? Is it wrong, sinful, or a form of a fall, to look at beauty, to hear something beautiful such as music, or to touch something that is sensually delightful such as a piece of silk or the skin of a loved one? These various things that the human being derives pleas-ure from very often elevate them to a spiritual state.

A: *Possession is the key.* In STS, you possess. ... If you move through the beautiful flowers, the silk, the skin of another, but do not seek to possess ...

Q: It seems to me that it is possible to experience all of these things, including sex, without the need or desire to possess; only to give. In which case, I still don't under-stand how it can be a mechanism for a fall.

A: *If it is desired, then the mechanism is not to give.* Do you eat a piece of chocolate cake be-cause it is good to give to the stomach?

Q: Well, you could!

A: No, in STS, which is your realm do not forget, one gives because of the pleasant sensation which results.

Q: Could it not be said that, if everything that exists is part of God, including the flesh, that if one gives to the flesh, without being attached to the giving, that it could be considered a giving to the all?

A: Explain the process.

Q: For example: there are some people who like to suffer, because they believe that the flesh is sinful. That is a big thing that the Lizzies have instituted. For centuries they have wanted people to suffer, and they have made this big deal about sex and anything that might be considered pleasant or desirable should be denied, and that a person should suffer, and revel in their suffering. And, actually, making a person ...

A: If one seeks to suffer, they do so in expectation of future reward. They desire to possess something in the end.

Q: What I am saying is: if a person can simply *be*, in the doing and being of who and what they are, in simplicity; to become involved in doing everything as a meditation, or as a consecration, whether they are walking down the street and being at one with the air, the sunshine, the birds and trees and other people; in this state of oneness, doesn't that constitute a giving to the universe as giving oneself up as a channel for the universe to experience all these things?

A: *Not if one is "feeling this oneness."*

Q: We are what we are. Nature is nature. Progression is progression. And if people would just relax and be who and what they are in honesty, and do what is according to their nature without violating the free will of others, that this is a more pure form of being than doing things out of any feeling of expectation, or desire. To just *be*, not want ... just *be*?

A: Yes, but STS does not do that.

Q: (A) From which I draw conclusions: if there's STS around us, we cannot just ...

A: You are all STS. If you were not, you would not be where you are.

Q: (A) There are those who are happy in the STS mode; and there are those who are trying to get out of the STS mode ...

A: STO candidate.

Q: (A) These STO candidates cannot just simply *be*, even theoretically, because then, STS would eat them.

A: No.

Q: Why not?

A: STS does not eat according to protocol. ... STS "eats" whatever it wants to, *if it is able*.

Q: That's what we said. If you are STO in an STS world, you are basically defenseless and they eat you.

A: No.

Q: Why? What makes STO unavailable or inedible?

A: *Frequency resonance not in sync.*

Q: (A) But then, that would mean that all these people who are saying that we need just to love everything and everybody, are right. They just be, and love, don't do anything, just give everything to the Lizzies ... they are right!

A: *No, because motivation is STS.*

Q: How is the motivation to love everything and everybody, and to just give, STS?

A: *Feels good.*

Q: So, they want to do it because it feels good?

A: *Want is an STS concept.*

Q: So, you seem to be suggesting that the real trick is to just become non-attached to anything and anybody, do nothing, and just dissolve into nothing? No thought, no want, no do, no be, no anything!

A: If you are STS, that does not fit, but, if you did exactly that, you would reincarnate in an STO realm, where such energy does fit.

Q: But, if you have become nothing, how do you reincarnate? And, when you say reincarnate, that implies being in a body!

A: You do not become nothingness.

Q: But, being incarnated means being in a body?

A: No.

Q: You mean moving into a realm that does not necessarily mean being in a body?

A: Close. But *4th density STO is partially physical. Does not consume nor possess.*

[...]

Q: So, prior to this time, this prior Edenic state ...

A: Was more like 4th density.

Q: But that implies that there was some level of physicality. Was there physicality in the sense of bodies that look like present-day humans?

A: Not quite.

Q: What did these pre-fall ...

A: Cannot answer because it is too complex for you to understand.

Q: Does this mean that the bodies we possibly would move into, or morph into, as fourth-density beings, assuming that one does, would also be too complex for us to understand? You are saying that this sort of fourth-density pre-Fall state, in terms of the physical bodies, is too complex to understand. If going back to fourth density is anything like coming from fourth density, does that mean that what we would go back to is something that is too complex to understand? This variability of physicality that you have described?

A: Yes.

Now, I hope that you noted all the references to "feeling" that were put in italics. These are all clues that I am setting in the background for the reader to keep in mind as we move along. But, there is one more thing I want to bring in before we get down to business.

We note that the Cassiopaeans have said the first prototype of modern man was created or engineered 309,000 years ago by genetic mixing with Neanderthal types. The right soul matrix was found, jumped into, thereby altering the DNA with its presence. The reader may enjoy having a look at *The Neanderthal Enigma* (by James Shreeve 1995), which investigates the strange mystery of the Neanderthals, of whom suddenly disappeared during the appearance of modern man. What happened to them and why is a very great mystery and the terms of understanding this enigma change almost daily. This event is generally dated, by various dating processes, to have occurred 35,000 years ago. However, in the above referenced work there are mysterious appearances of modern type man in several places and times long before this date that are yet to be explained. As soon as you have finished *The Neanderthal Enigma*, you might want to then read *Shattering the Myths of Darwinism* by Richard Milton for a better perspective on the issues, though I am not saying that either of them have the answer.

We need to note that there is a difference between what the Cassiopaeans are talking about in terms of a modern type man on Earth, and their story about the appearance of the survivors of the destruction of the planet Kantek (the so-called Aryan-Nordic types).

It is clear, from what the Cassiopaeans have indicated, that the "out of Africa" hypothesis is correct, as far as it goes. Earth may have been populated from the South, but it was "enlightened" from the North – at least in the most recent cycle, of which we are a part.

Everyone agrees that we evolved from more primitive ancestors represented by fossils and traditionally called *Homo erectus*. The disagreement erupts over where, when, and how. From the critical time period, roughly 400,000 to 100,000 years ago, there is an ambiguous clutter of bones that people have reluctantly agreed to group together and call archaic *Homo sapiens*, because they don't know what else to call them. Some scientists also keep a separate bin for the more us-like fossils in the group, producing the exquisite oxymoron "archaic moderns."

Then Allan Wilson and another Berkely scientist Vincent Sarich got it into their heads to look for clues to the human past not out on the African savanna but among the proteins of living people and primates. … [They claim] that the mutations occur across the millennia at a steady rate, like the ticks of a molecular clock. If this is true, the difference in a given protein in any two species would indicate not only how *related* they were, but also how much *time* had elapsed since they shared a common ancestor. …

… The first efforts to create such a genetic history of humanity focused on blood chemistry. Every person alive bears a gene that determines whether his or her blood will be type A, B, O, or AB. Human blood also contains an antigen to destroy invading toxins, which comes in two forms, Rh-positive and Rh-negative. …

… American Indians are virtually all type O. Rh negative blood is found almost exclusively among Europeans and is most prevalent in the Basque people of the Western Pyrenees. Since blood groups are determined by specific, known genes and do not seem to be related much to environmental pressures, they are far more useful in judging the relationships of populations than superficial anatomical characteristics like skin color. If you were to judge by skin color, Africans and Australians would appear to be closely related. When you look at their blood chemistry, however, they turn out to be about as far apart as two human populations can be; their dark skins are merely *a shared adaptation* to living under a tropical sun. …

… *Caucasians and Negroids are more closely related to each other* than either is to the third major population grouping, the Mongoloids … [which contains] Australians and American Indians as well as Asians …

… Mitochondrial genes … are inherited only from your mother, who received them from *her* mother, who got them from *her* mother, and so on back through a chain of mothers. … If you are male, your mitochondrial lineage will die out no matter how many children you have, unless you have a sister who gives birth to a daughter and continues the line into the future. Unperturbed by the genetic reshuffling going on inside the nucleus with every generation, mitochondrial DNA [lodged in the cellular structures outside the nucleus] serves as a sort of genetic tracer bullet, lighting up the route to the past.

... The only reason one person's mitochondrial DNA differs from another's is simply the passage of time [since they had a common ancestor.]

... *There [is] very little difference between any two people's mtDNA,* suggesting that *everyone's common ancestor had lived surprisingly recently.* ... the pattern of variation in mtDNA among the five populations often corresponded to geographic and ethnic origin. ... the Old World populations sorted out into two distinct groups: African and non-African, with the African mtDNA types showing much more variation than the non-African ones.

Taken together, [these] results suggested that there had been a recent, single point of origin for the modern human race. There were two ways of determining where that origin had been, and these came in conflict. If the mutations in human mitochondria occur steadily through time, and if more mutations have accumulated in Africa than anywhere else, then Africa should be the homeland whence all populations have spring. [It was] found, however, that the type of human mitochondria most closely related to that of other primates popped up in Asians more frequently than in other populations, suggesting instead that the point of origin was somewhere in Asia. ... (Shreve 1995, 57, 58, 59–60, 63, 65)

More research was done and it was shown that:

... A European woman's mtDNA might resemble an African's more closely than that of another European. ... Humans all over the world are amazingly similar, genetically more alike ... than two subspecies of gorilla in Africa that are separated by only a few hundred miles.

... The simplest explanation is that all human races had originated in Africa ... The ultimate point of convergence was the same for everyone: *a single African woman whose mitochondria gave rise to all existing human types.* ...

... [I]t would have taken between 140,000 and 290,000 [estimated] years of steadily accumulating mutations to account for the number of variations they found among living Mitochondrial types. ...

When Eve was supposed to have lived ... the *Homo erectus* migration out of Africa was already very ancient history ... The common ancestor of all *non*-African people [e.g. white] would be younger still. [This genetically isolated population] remained there [in Africa] for thousands of years ... Later, perhaps as recently as 50,000 years ago, this one group must have left Africa, pushing north and east.

On this point the latent conflict between the geneticists and the anthropologists erupted into open war. Unlike the earlier *erectus* migrants, Eve's descendants would not have arrived in a humanless landscape. By one estimate, some 1.3 million members of our genus were living on earth 50,000 years ago, a good many of them spread throughout Eurasia. These ancient Eurasians were not demi-apes living in trees; they were our trusted European familiars, the Neandertals, along with other large-brained folk in Asia ... And, of course, these older Europeans and Asians were passing Mitochondrial genes down through the generations, spinning on through their daughters and their daughters' daughters. *Then suddenly, all of the lines stopped. ... there is no trace of them in modern people. They have simply vanished from the genetic legacy of the human species. ...*

"If populations representing the earlier inhabitants of Eurasia had contributed to the living human gene pool, we'd expect to find Mitochondrial types around today that are five times more variable," Stoneking told me. "They just don't seem to be there."

...

"The best explanation for why you don't see these ancient non-African mitochondria is that they are not part of the modern human lineage in the first place," Stoneking concluded. "In other words, the African people replaced the residents without interbreeding with them." (Shreeve 1995, 66, 67–68, 69)

Allan Wilson wrote in *Science* magazine, "Some people don't like our conclusions." As Shreve observed, in this case, some people "happened to include the majority of anthropologists alive (p. 70).[6]

At about the same time the above book was being written, the Cassiopaeans had this to say about the subject:

September 24, 1999

A: Who, or what made you?

Q: (RC) The Creator. (L) Prime Creator.

A: How? And who is Prime Creator?

Q: (L) Everything, I guess.

A: You are "Prime Creator." Prime Creator manifests *in* you. But ... who was secondary?

Q: (RC) The Sons of God? The Elohim?

A: Who is that? Remember, your various legends are "seen through a veil."

Q: (L) ... Are the Orions these secondary creators?

A: Here comes a shocker for you ... one day, in 4th density, it will be your descendants mission to carry on the tradition and assignment of seeding the 3rd density universe, once you have the adequate knowledge!!!

Q: (L) If the Orion STS brought the Celts here, were the Celts, while they lived on Kantek, in the form they are in now?

A: They were lighter in appearance.

Q: (RC) Well, I read that it was the Pleiadians. And the Hebrews were originally the Hoovids who came from Sirius ... (L) You have told us on other occasions that the Semitic peoples were remnants of the Atlanteans, and yet they are quite unlike ...

A: Whoa!! Wait a minute, let's not get ahead of ourselves. First things first. What RC said was not entirely factual. Remember, there is much disinformation to weed through.

Q: (RC) What did I say that was not factual?

A: In this part of your 3rd and 4th density universe, specifically your "galaxy" it is the region known as Orion that is the one and only indigenous home of human type beings ... reflect on this! Indigenous home base, not sole locator. What you are most in need of review of is the accurate profile of "alien" data.

---

[6] Refer to the additional information on Neanderthals included in volume four.

Q: (RC) I thought that humans originated in Lyra and then a war broke out there and they ended up in Orion.

A: Lyra is not inhabited. There have been homes in all places, but some were/are transitory, and some are not. Pay attention to Orion! This is your ancestral home, and your eventual destination. Here is the absolutely accurately accurate profile of Orion to follow: This is the most heavily populated region of your Milky Way galaxy! This is a region that extends across 3rd and 4th density space for a distance as vast as the distance between your locator and it. There are 3,444 inhabited "worlds" in this region. Some are planets as you know them. Some are artificially constructed planetoids. Some are floating space barges. And some are "satellites." There are primary homes, traveling stations and incubator laboratories all in 2nd, 3rd and 4th densities. There are overseer zones in 5th and 6th densities. *Approximately one half is STO and one half is STS.* Together, along with many other colonies, located elsewhere, this is called, in translation, Orion Federation. Orions created grays in 5 varieties, as cybergenetic beings, and installed them on Zeta Reticuli 1, 2, 3, and 4, as well as on 2 planets orbiting Barnard's Star. The Reptilians also inhabit 6 planets in the Orion region in 4th density, and are owned by the Orion STS as slaves, and, in some cases, pets!!! The name "Orion" is the actual native name, and was brought to Earth directly. Study the legend of the "god" of Orion for parallels.

Q: (L) Are the Orion STS the infamous redheaded Nordic aliens?

A: Yes, and all other humanoid combinations.

Q: (L) Okay, if it started with the Nordic types, and that is where the other humanoid combinations came from, what genetic combinations were used for human beings? Black people, for instance, since they are so unlike Nordics?

A: The Nordic genes were mixed with the gene pool already available on Earth, known as Neanderthal.

Q: (L) What was the genetic combination used to obtain the Oriental races?

A: Orientals come from a region known in your legends as "Lemuria," and are a previous hybridization from 7 genetic code structures from within Orion Union, designed to best fit the earth climate and cosmic ray environment then existent on Earth.

Q: (L) Okay, what about the Semitic and Mediterranean peoples?

A: Each time a new flock was "planted," it was engineered to be best suited to the environment where it was planted. Aryans are the only exception, as they had to be moved to Earth in an emergency.

Q: (L) If races are engineered on earth to be "best suited," what factors are being drawn from or considered regarding the Semitic race?

A: They are not engineered on Earth, but in Orion lab as all others. They were "planted" in the Middle East.

Now, notice this last phrase: "Human types are genetically engineered in Orion labs." This means that they must use the same mitochondria as the basis, changing and recombining only the nuclear DNA. If this is so, then it would explain why *all* humans have the same mother. It would also explain why this mother is so recent. But, of course, without admitting to the interference possibility from a quasi-physical higher density – fourth density – these problems may never be understood. The Cassiopaeans did have something to say about the Neanderthal enigma.

February 11, 1995
Q: (L) What happened to Neanderthal man?
A: Removed by Lizzies to other planets.
Q: (L) Is that removed as in taken off the planet physically?
A: Yes.
Q: (L) What planet were they taken to?
A: Others.
[…]
Q: You said that Neanderthal man had been taken by the Lizzies to another planet, now, I don't want to know what other planet, but I would like to know what state, evolutionary speaking, is Neanderthal man in at present, as we measure time?
A: No progress, still the same.
[…]
Q: When did the Aryans invade India?
A: 8243 years ago.
Q: Who was there before that?
A: Asian tribes and number 3 prototype.
Q: What is a number 3 prototype?
A: Known as Neanderthal man.
Q: And what are we?
A: Number 4 types c and d. Translation into English comprehension.
[…]
Q: (L) Now, you said that the Nephilim were seeded on a planet called D'Ankhiar, as were human beings. When you said we were seeded there, what did you mean?
A: Was proper environment for molecularization.
Q: (L) Are you saying that the physical bodies on planet Earth, the various types of mankind such as Neanderthal, Cro-Magnon, Australopithicus etc., were generated on that other planet and then brought here?
A: Yes.
[…]
Q: (L) Okay, I had a question I wanted to get in: you said that Neanderthal man was taken off the Earth, and Cro-Magnon man suddenly appeared. Is this Cro-Magnon man really Kantekkian man?
A: Close.
Q: (L) Well, they supposedly existed side by side on the Earth for some time. Did they intermix or intermarry?
A: Marriage?!
Q: (L) Well, you know what I mean! Genetic intermixing.
A: Can you picture a Neanderthal marriage?
Q: (L) Yeah! The old club 'em and drag 'em off by the hair ceremony! (T) It was a ritual … handed down father to son along with the club …

And, of course, the arrival of Cro-Magnon – and his amazing cave art and the sudden impetus to civilization will never be understood either without this perspective though obviously, from the above remark, there is something even more strange about Cro-Magnon.

Clearly, the issue of what kind of man was man before the Fall comes to mind. We already have an idea that he was not precisely fully physical in third-density terms, but was yet somewhat physical. Apparently, being a third-density STO being in alignment with fourth-density STO is an altogether different experience than being a third-density STS being with the concomitant compartmentalization and contraction of *being* that results in separation and conflict. But, at one point, when discussing these matters with the Cassiopaeans, some clues were given:

April 8, 2000

Q: Now, I have this book entitled *Arktos*. He [Joscelyn Godwin] says something here that echoes a remark you once made. He writes: "It is a very remarkable thing that enlightenment seems to have come from the north against the common prejudice that the Earth was *enlightened as it was populated* from south to north. The Scythians are one of the most ancient nations; the Chinese descend from them. The Atlanteans themselves, more ancient than the Egyptians, descend from them." You said that the civilizing influence came from the north to the south. Of course, all the standard texts claim that civilization came from south to north, starting in Mesopotamia. Now, getting ...

A: Okay, just a minute here. Thinking Mesopotamia is the beginning is like thinking that the beginning starts at the 12th chapter.

Q: I know that! The problem is: finding artifacts. I've been searching and digging, and I find a little bit here and there, but my God! Either nothing survived ...

A: Artifacts have a limited shelf life!

This remark could be taken a couple of ways, though I didn't notice it at the time. On the one hand, it could refer to the fact that few organic artifacts survive the ravages of time; on the other hand, it could refer to the fact that, even if such artifacts are found, they disappear rather quickly, as has been noted time and again, due to academic denial that they *can* exist. And, in some cases, it seems that direct action has been taken by the academic community to remove from the shelf what does not fit their theories.

Q: Exactly! The problem is that they've got specimens of humanoid types from 100 to 200 thousand years ago, and even further, but no specimens of modern man that are that old. Why is this so? Are they just looking in the wrong places?

A: Specimens survive by sheer luck.

Q: So, they are lucky that they have any specimens at all. Who knows, when they find a very ancient specimen of a modern type human, they won't believe it – it will be called an anomaly! There are artifacts that are extremely ancient, which give evidence of the presence of modern type man, and they just simply argue themselves to death over them.

A: Yes.

Q: But, during the time Neanderthal man was on the Earth, did he live alongside modern man?

A: Yes. *Except modern type man was different then.*

Q: In what ways?

A: DNA and psycho/electrical frequencies.

Q: Does this mean that their physical appearance was different from what we consider to be modern man?

A: Radiance.

Q: What do you mean "radiance?"

A: You find out!

Q: Oh, that's interesting. Well, there are legends that the Northern people had light in their veins. Very ancient belief. Is this what you are referring to?

A: Maybe.

Q: Was this light related to the hemoglobin level, the iron level in the blood?

A: Maybe.

Q: Did they have a much higher iron level in their blood?

A: Possibly … .

Q: Okay, part of the ancient legend of Arktos was that, in very ancient times the Earth was different because it had a vertical axial orientation. This contributed to the Golden Age or the Edenic condition. Is this, in fact, one of the conditions that existed in the Golden Age?

A; Well, yes, but still some puzzle pieces needed.

Q: I noticed also that there are several ballpark type figures given for the precessional cycles. Apparently there is not a whole lot of agreement as to how long this cycle is, exactly. I notice that, if you divide 309,882 years by 12, you come out right in the ballpark of 12 precessional cycles. Is this the reason that the zodiac was set up with twelve signs or houses?

A: Related, yes.

Q: Now, since all the recent conjecture about the precessional cycle has really gone all over the place, it is my thought that the real reason for the ancient clues about this cycle are to inform us that the length of 12 of these cycles is a *grand* cycle, and that *this* is the big clue.

A: Needs some study by you.

Q: One of the interesting things about this Northern civilizational factor is that one of the hallmarks of the Aryan attitude is the male dominated religion. When did the masculine religion take over? Was this always the tendency or leaning of the Aryan group?

A: *Involves more than religion. Religion is the facilitator.*

Q: Facilitator of what?

A: *Customary psycho/social habitué.*

Q: Customary to whom?

A: Those whom you refer to as Aryans.

Q: Where did they acquire the habit of a masculine oriented religion? Everybody else was worshipping the goddess in one form or another. But this male dominated theology was the distinguishing characteristic of the Northern peoples. Where did they come up with this?

A: Originated on home planet.

Q: Kantek?

A: For all intents and purposes.

Q: Okay, when they were on their home planet, why did they develop a masculine religion as opposed to a feminine one, considering the fact that women are the source of life, in certain terms?

A: In your density, masculinism/feminism is essentially a roll of "the dice." Remember, at higher levels gender is nonexistent.

Q: Well, the problem I am having here is this: the masculine religion is monotheistic, essentially.

A: In your references.

Q: The Aryans always thought they were better than everybody else …

A: They were more advanced than the company they found themselves amongst.

Q: But then, as far as I can tell, the Hebrew monotheism is also derived from the Aryan, monotheistic, male dominated religion. It then fathered Christianity, and that has been the whole patriarchal, kill-'em-all-and-let-God-sort-'em-out war mongering thing under which we have lived for over 2,000 years. This is the Western, European mind … it came from the Aryans, from the North; it was the so-called civilizing influence in nearly every respect that you can track. The cohesiveness and dominance of this type of thinking was able to civilize, but then civilization involves dominance, killing, war, territory, the Hitler scene, the whole nine yards. All of this is antithetical to all that you promote as far as being desirable. Yet, you have said that you were in contact with the Northern peoples for millennia. Yes, Cassiopeia is a northern constellation, and probably figured in the early myths of these peoples in ways we cannot know, but the whole thing is that they represent all that is STS.

A: But so do you, so then why did we contact you?

Q: Well. I don't buy into that whole monotheistic, dominator, warmongering, make everybody conform to one way of thinking head-trip!

A: So, you think all individuals conformed then, or is it the soul that counts in the final analysis?

Q: Okay, obviously all individuals are different, and some did not conform then, either.

A: And neither do you.

Q: Point taken. I am just having a hard time with this. I wish you would just tell me! Who interacted with these Aryans to give them this male dominated monotheistic idea that they then sought to impose on every other human being on the planet – and are still trying!

A: Interactions were transdensity.

So, having gone through this brief history of mankind, and why we are here in the first place, we come back again to that most interesting remark: desire based imbalance led to material existence. It seems that it was an okay desire, because it was based on wanting to accelerate the process of reunion with the One. But we see that this wanting to grow up so fast was like the Prodigal Son who wanted to take his inheritance and travel to a far country.

Things in the far country were not quite what the Son thought they were. Everything had a price, and he soon spent all his inheritance – lost his original status – and found himself enslaved to live with and care for the pigs.

This reference to living and eating with pigs has a deep esoteric significance. The pig is the animal of Set. It is said to represent the darker side of mankind that does not strive toward the light. These are those "soul units" who choose to remain as matter and never seek to wake up (see the discussion of psychopathy in volume 7). More than this, the pig represents what was desired in a very deep way, as we will soon discover. You see, the pig is one of the few animals that sweats. This characteristic of the pig – that it exudes water through its skin as humans do – represents an esoteric symbol that is an amazing disjecta membra of long vanished scientific knowledge. And this knowledge relates to the very thing we are going to be discussing: *feelings*.

Remember, it was the desire to *feel*, in a very specific sense, that led to the Fall. And it is this that we are going to carefully examine to determine if such an idea can be true.

Read again the following, carefully:

> Q: (L) Did, at any time, the human race live for a long time in an Edenic state, where they were *able to use bodies and still have a spiritual connection?*
> A: Yes. But not long. *No addiction takes long to close the circle.*
> Q: (L) So, mankind was addicted to pleasuring the self?
> A: Became quickly.

In the previous section I made the remark that we are made addicts inside our own skins. This might have sounded like hyperbole to some readers, and a mere analogy to others. I would like to make it clear that it is neither. It is a cold, hard fact. We are addicts to the molecules of our emotions and, by extension, to those things and people who provide our fix by stimulating the chemicals to be released.

Terry Burnham and Jay Phelan write in *Mean Genes*:

> Most of us would feel cheated if we bought a car or a microwave and it came without instructions. But our most important possessions – body and mind – come with no such guide, leaving us searching haphazardly for satisfaction: a dollop of exercise, thirteen minutes of sex, a Happy Meal, a cocktail, and a sport-utility vehicle. ...
>
> When we drive a car or operate a microwave, our orders are carried out exactly as we command. The machine doesn't talk back or have an agenda of its own – at least not yet. On the other hand, if we tell our brain, as part of a New Year's resolution, to cut down on fatty foods, it most likely will let out a hearty laugh and continue to set off bells and whistles of approval when the dessert cart rolls around.
>
> Our brain, for better or worse, is not an obedient servant. It has a mind of its own. Imagine that you are two things: a personality who has likes, dislikes, desires, and dreams. But inside your body there is also a "machine," your brain, that processes

commands and acts on those likes, dislikes, desires, and dreams. It fights you all the time. And it usually wins.

… Why do we have battles over controlling our own behavior? And why are these battles so hard to win? Are cats and dogs obsessed with fighting addictions, controlling their weight, and remaining faithful to their mates? Do chimpanzees regularly resolve to be less selfish?

In a creepy campfire legend, a baby-sitter alone in a house receives increasingly menacing phone calls. Terrified, she contacts the police, who put a tap on her phone. After the boogieman calls again, the cops frantically phone her, screaming, "We've traced the call. It's coming from inside the house! Get out!"

Similarly, the source of our self-control problems lies within us … but we can't get out or leave them behind. Manipulative media, greedy businesses, and even our friends and family play roles in nurturing our demons. Still, most of our self-control problems stem from our impulses to do things that are bad for us or for those whom we love.

A visit to any bookstore reveals the nature of our struggles. Glancing at the bestsellers, we can see what's on people's minds. There are dozens of books on finding love, losing weight, and creating wealth. Conspicuously absent are a host of other topics. Where are the books entitled *How to Build a Bigger Beer Gut*, *Ten Steps to Frivolous Spending*, or *Nurturing the Infidel Within*? (Burnham & Phelan 2000, 1–2)

Even though they are writing in a lighthearted way, these guys aren't kidding. And it's even worse than they let on. If the reader will recall the movie *The Matrix*, they will surely remember the scene of the vast warehouse of human beings suspended in pods filled with a gelatinous fluid, connected to a vast energy storage system by many feeder lines embedded deep in their flesh. These were the humans in the Matrix. Their reality was totally illusory, created and maintained by a giant computer that coordinated all the individual realities so that their dreams were, in a sense, as One. And through the experiences that were being fed to them, they generated in their bodies various amounts of power that fed the system itself.

Though this was an allegory – and where the writers came up with the inspiration we don't know – it is very close to the truth based on what the Cassiopaeans have told us, and supported by corroboration from many sources.

Can we prove it? Nope. But the fact is, no other view of the reality of cosmic connections can be proven either. And this has one thing that the subjective views do not have: empirical evidence. If the reader will take the time to study the matter deeply, to not be afraid to look at the patterns of Rubik's Cubes and see how chaotic they are, and to work with trying to align the colors into coherent patterns, the evidence will gradually lead to a perspective that is objective, not based on faith and feelings.

We see some of the more terrible things the Cassiopaeans have told us, and which we have read about in various reports and exposés of underground bases and truly revolting mind control experiments, in Michael Topper's (admittedly dense) work:

> In the conscious domain of the higher densities, light indeed becomes the overt mediating term, the common coinage and efficient aim – and that both for positive and negative realms. Yet whereas in the positive realms the the [mode] is to draw the developing soul toward deep degrees of expansion *into* light, in the corresponding negative realms the object is, rather, a ... development of appropriate mind/body mechanical means of devouring more light, stuffing the light-energy into the voracious hole or constitutional void of emotional lack comprising the negative state of the ego-soul altogether.
>
> The work of the negative being is to determine the formulae, extort and coax the technical keys of force-opening the internal mind/body centers and corresponding energy fields. The negative's business is to plunder the rich beds of energy-nutriment – the various treasure-troves of the vast creative domains where "loosh" or psychic energy-food is manufactured in abundance.
>
> ... Light isn't inimical to the negative orientation, as is portrayed in our superstitions and folklore; like its positive counterpart, the negative recognizes and overtly *values light as sustenance*; food for producing integral reactions toward progressively higher alignments. Just as all matter – the food of this dimension – is intellectually understandable as a kind of packaged "light-value" woven in phosphates of the ATP molecule, so light is overtly valued as the energy-essence/lunchbox of the higher densities.
>
> So, whereas higher-density positive entities might be considered light beings, higher density negatives are more like ... light eaters.
>
> They are the light eaters, the devourers of light. That's why they're associated with darkness, because the light is lapped up into the cavernous black hole of their congenital emptiness, their persistent lack. Light is sucked into the abyss where their heart should be, in order to try to compensate or fill in for the love that isn't there.
>
> All the massive operations they undertake [throughout the universe] are just a means of "cornering the market" on energy, monopolizing all the known fields of light or light potential. The expanding order they attempt to impose, the totalitarian control over increasingly large numbers of people, is the fantastical and internally self-contradictory project of coercing everything in creation to work for them, to cultivate and keep the fields of their energy reserves and to furnish self-replenishing herds of *emotional source-nutriment* which can be converted into useful energy or light-capital. Since the negative beings can't generate an important light-energy source themselves, i.e. the emotional range of energy-values belonging to the heart, they steal the manipulated and artificially regulated emotional reserves of the beings harnessed in thrall to them ...
>
> This [relates to] the rumors circulating around about the underground Dulce facilities where aliens have been reported to take infernal baths in vats of liquid stewed with human and animal parts, a kind of diabolic broth of enzymes and hormones they're supposed to absorb for nutriment through their skin.

… Hormones of the human ductless systems and various kinds of human and animal enzymes, neurotransmitters, lymphocytes and extract of digestive chyle furnishes variable measures of a radiant energy-value; especially the human reproductive system – the specific cells of reproduction are just saturated with subtle energy-charge …

There are in fact multiple uses to which these natural resources of the human system may be put. As grim as it might seem, the aliens perceived to indulge that hormonal baptism are generally biobot replicants, hybrid forms created from genetic tissue of humans, animals and even plants; they have vestigial digestive systems, virtually inoperative because these types of biobot-form follow the general template of the higher dimensional negative beings only in more grounded and stabilized, physical terms.

The higher-dimensional beings in their own context have subtle, vertical filamental axes attached to the subtle nerve-networks of [both the biobots and human beings]. [In humans], these filamental, ethereal straws are drawn into the body through the etheric chakras that connect the body to the higher-density systems. These chakra systems correspond to the clusters of neuropeptide receptors, and it is the objective of the STS forces to stimulate the production of vast amounts of high light energy values contained in these peptides so that they can feed on the energy rich extracts of the human reproductive and glandular structures …

Tremendous concentrations of desirable energy-values, laced with the emotional juices that generate them, are involved in neurotransmitters such as serotonin and dopamine, and in epinephrine/norepinephrine, and other hormones of the sympathetic systems. Chemicals of psychic stress are very charged [whether they are of a blissful nature, or pure unmitigated terror.]

The 4th density consciousness, connected to [the physiology of numerous human beings] by these astro-etheric threads and plexiform webs of control, can send signals to its 3rd density marionettes, generating emotions that force choices that result in any number of activities resulting in enriched feeding. ("Précis on the Good, The Bad, and What Curls Up Under a Rock")

Now, this idea is most definitely "out there." Certainly none of us would wish to contemplate such a control system as is allegorized in *The Matrix*. It's good Hollywood, but we can leave the theater and go home and be secure in the belief that it is only movie magic. Or can we?

Well, it seems that this is not even a new idea. There are numerous sculptures in medieval churches that are said to represent sinners being punished in Hell or Purgatory. It is thought that they are "visual exhortations to renounce sin." However, we find that there's another explanation for these images, given by the teacher of Mark Hedsel in Zelator, which I shall include here with following remarks.

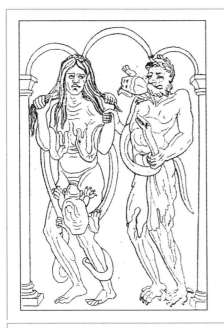 

From the west front of Saint-Pierre, Moissac. 14th century, after Witkowski.

Left: Wood engraving of demon grasping a woman.

Right: Wood engraving of demons riding on the back of a beggar and a miser.

'The first thing we must realize is that the sculptors were not, as we might imagine, portraying a future state in Hell or Purgatory. The images are portrayals of ordinary human beings – *of ordinary sinners in life.* The woman attacked by reptiles, is a libertine. This is why her private parts and breasts are receiving such attention from the monster-toads, and why the demon who grasps her is being so sexually explicit with the snake.

'The pair carrying demons piggyback are intended to reveal the sin of Avarice: the seated figure, clutching his moneybags, is a miser, refusing to give alms to the beggar.

'However, these people are *not* in Hell: they are portrayals of Etheric and Astral forms. They reveal people as they would be seen by someone with developed clair-voyant vision, able to perceive on the spiritual planes. ... A true clairvoyant would be able to *see* the hideous reptiles and possessing demons.

' ... The truth is that, as a consequence of the libertine woman's predisposition to sin in a particular way, her soul is constantly being devoured by monstrous forms. No matter how beautiful or alluring her physical body may be, her Etheric body is – as an immediate consequence of sin – darkened by demonic forms that devour her. I repeat

– this is not a picture of punishment in Hell, but of an unhealthy Etheric body, in life.
...

' ... The nakedness of her body is intended as in indication that it is her etheric body only – what the Moissac artists would have described as the *ens venenei,* or the *vegetabilis.* This explains why she is lifting her arms, grasping at her hair. *This is the gesture of the Etheric soul.* The same gesture is found in the Christian images painted and scratched on the walls of the catacombs in Rome, and has been called the "orans", or praying gesture. In fact, such images are derived from the Egyptian hieroglyphic for the *ka.*

'These hints leave us in no doubt that the woman is alive, and that we are being privileged to look into the state of her Etheric body. ... This ... is an example of the use of an occult blind.

'Now, turn your attention to the second engraving ... The person gifted with clairvoyant vision will see the beggar approaching the miser on the Astral plane. He will see the demons directing this transaction: the demons are, so to speak, bypassing the Ego of the men. This is no human transaction, but a demonic one. The demons sit above the heads of the men to show that they are gripping on to their Egos. Do not forget that our word possession is derived from a Latin word meaning literally "sitting on." ...

'Now, in contrast to the nakedness of the woman, the miser and the beggar are clothed. This may be explained in terms of the need to indicate their ranks – the beggar is in torn clothing with only one trouser leg. We may judge from the clothing of the seated man that he is a person of some substance. However, there is another reason why the pair are clothed: this covering indicates that they are being depicted on the next level up from the Etheric – that is, on the Astral plane – on what in the days when this sculpture was made would have been called the *animalis,* or the *ens astrale.*

'We may have little doubt that the clothing is meant as a kind of Astral mask, for neither man wears shoes. This is an arcane technique for showing that neither is standing on the physical Earth. The most "Earthy" element in this portrayal is the heavy moneybag: this appears to be tied around his neck, as a punishment, weighing down his soul. ...

'The demons who possess the couple are Astral beings: the wings of the one on the left indicate that it can "fly" on the Astral planes. The horns of the other, crescent in form, remind us that the demons are linked with the Moon. However, just as the woman does not know that her Etheric body is being devoured by monstrous forms, so the miser does not know that his Astral body is being weighed down by his riches, and by the demon which grips its legs around his neck. This is not so much symbolism as a direct portrayal of what can be perceived on the spiritual plane, by those with eyes to see.' (Hedsel 2000, 62–63)

We note right away that there is a sort of righteous flavor to this interpretation. It is given in archaic terms of sin and demons and possession. We already have the idea that the ancient stories of demons and lesser gods were actual descriptions of encounters with fourth-density denizens; beings we now refer to in the modern day as aliens. Descriptions of these things were given in languages that are not technical, much like modern English, which constantly reinvents itself, creating and adding new terms as science progresses in its understanding.

Later, occultists, or those seeking for answers in these representations created by those who had received this information, were not privy to the inside information and did not understand the literal nature of these images, nor the true reality they portrayed. They began to interpret them in terms of astral and etheric entities, rather than what they really were: energy symbols of the interaction with fourth-density STS beings.

Having the understanding of fourth-density reality, we can see that the woman described as a sinner and a libertine, may not be either of those at all – merely an ordinary human who is asleep in the Matrix and whose sexual energies are providing nutriment to those levels. That the creatures are attached to her indicates the fibrous network of the energy conduits, and it is clear that the monster-man holding the snake as though it were a phallus while at the same time gripping the arm of the woman, is meant to show us that there is a being at another level who is behind this activity. And, in addition to the upraised arms being a symbol of the *ka*, the hair is also a symbol of virility or virtue and the woman is hanging onto it for dear life, battling the loss of her life force.

In the second image, I don't think that we are being shown a beggar approaching a miser. I have a slightly different take on this for a couple of reasons. The rolled up pants leg is one of the accoutrements of the Masonic initiation, and other than that I do not perceive that the man is dressed in rags. The seated figure has crossed legs – a Rosicrucian symbol – and the bag of unknown contents is suspended around his neck by a cord – yet another occult symbol. The position of his hands as well as the hands of the demon on the left figure are also symbols.

My immediate reaction to these figures is that they represent a body of occultists in high positions. The man on the left may represent the social and educational aspects of control, as he is a traveler seeking wisdom, hampered or directed by the being on his shoulder. The man on the right seems to be a ruling figure, representing governments controlled by the creature on his shoulders. That these two creatures are in cahoots is clear by their communication with each other, but it is also clear that they are of two different types, and that the men are not having any interaction between them (their respective creatures) of a human nature. That they are barefoot has an even deeper significance: they have given away the ruby slippers. They are sold out; co-opted; part of the STS hierarchy.

So, in effect, we are seeing a graphic portrayal of ancient knowledge, clinched by the reference to the Moon – a base of fourth-density activities. And in the present time there are many individuals who are seeing the shape-shifting or "overshadowing of humans by Reptilian creatures. The mind produces symbols for what the eyes, and even the clairvoyant eyes, see. These events of shape shifting, or overshadowing that many are taking to be an astral demonic possession in archaic terms, are more likely a development of trans-density awareness that is still being interpreted in the mind in a symbolic way. It is very likely not a spirit possession but a clairvoyant seeing of the Control System, imaged in ways the mind is set up to operate.

Returning now to Topper's suggestion that there is a substance produced by the human sensorium that is an addictive drug for fourth-density STS, this was a subject mentioned by the Cassiopaeans at one of the very earliest contacts. According to Topper, this substance can only be generated through the psychic pattern of terror, and can only be catalytically effective when obtained from a still living though on-the-verge-of-death-from-terror subject. I will admit that I was so horrified by this information, so much so that my project very nearly ended right then and there.

Like everyone else, I had the idea that only the good things (by human – or my – definition) could exist at higher levels. It was only later when I read the comment of Ra: "The All blinks neither at the darkness nor at the light," that I realized there was a very deep truth being presented in such a comment. And to truly understand this remark in the most important way, is to understand that this "not blinking" at anything is the true measure of the level of contact. Truth is the only value at the highest levels, and human judgments of what is nice or not nice does not even figure in to the equations. So, a communicating entity that makes a judgment as to whether this or that information is useful or not, is blinking and gives away his level in that act. And, I suppose it could also be inferred from this that the individual who filters is also blinking, and thereby judging.

But, getting to what the Cassiopaeans had to say:

July 16, 1994

Q: (L) Bob Lazar referred to the fact that aliens supposedly refer to humans as containers. What does this mean?
A: Storage for later use.
Q: (L) Used for what?
A: 94 per cent of all population. All are containers; 94 per cent will be used.
Q: (L) Used for what?
A: Consumption.
Q: (L) You mean eaten?
A: Total consumption.
Q: (L) What do you mean by consumption? Ingested?
A: Consumed for ingredients.
Q: (L) Ingredients for what?
A: New race. Important. 13 years approximately when project will be finished.
Q: (L) Why are humans consumed?
A: They are used for parts.
Q: (L) We don't understand. How can humans be used for parts?
A: Reprototype. The vats exist. Missing persons often go there and especially missing children.

Q: (L) Do we have any protection?

A: Some.

Q: (L) How can we protect ourselves and our children?

A: Inform them. Don't hide the truth from children.

Q: (L) How does truth protect us?

A: Awareness protects. Ignorance endangers.

Q: (L) Why tell children such horrible things?

A: They need to know.

Q: (L) What is the purpose of this project?

A: New life here.

Q: (L) Are the aliens using our emotions and energies?

A: Correct; and bodies too. Each Earth year 10 percent more children are taken.

Q: (L) Do they suffer?

A: Some. Bits of children's organs removed while they are wide awake. Kidneys first; then next feet; next jaw examined on table; tongues cut off; bones stress tested; pressure placed on heart muscle until it bursts.

Q: (L) Why are you telling us this awful stuff?

A: You must know what the Consortium is doing. This is done mostly to Indian children.

Q: (L) Why are things like this being done?

A: There is a big effort on behalf of Orions and their human brethren to create a new race and control it as well as the rest of humanity.

Q: (L) What happens to the souls? Is this project physical only?

A: Physical; and souls recycled.

Q: (L) Where do the souls go?

A: Back here for the most part.

Q: (L) Do some go elsewhere?

A: Some go to other planets.

Q: (L) Who is responsible for this project?

A: Consortium.

Q: (L) This is sick!

A: Sick is subjective.

Q: (L) But this whole thing is so awful.

A: We understand your feelings, but all does not conform to your perspective.

Q: (L) Why is this happening to Earth?

A: Karma.

Q: (L) What kind of karma could bring this?

A: Atlantis.

Q: (L) What can protect us?

A: Knowledge.

Q: (L) How do we get this knowledge?

A: You are being given it through this source now.

Q: (L) How does the knowledge of what you have told us help us?

A: Gives great defense. ... Just knowing about it gives psychic defense.

[...]

Q: (L) Is there any way we can prevent Orion abductions?

A: No.

Q: (L) Why?

A: It would interfere with universal law of free will and service to self.

Q: (L) But we don't want to be abducted. Can't we stop it?

A: Not likely. They have more power than you.

Q: (L) Well then, why can't you help us?

A: Would interfere in natural progression of your race and theirs. The Jews called up-on us to save them and we could not. And, natives of your land called upon us and we could not save them from your race; we could not stop that either. It is natural progression, see?

Q: (L) Are we going to be wiped out by aliens as part of this natural progression?

A: Maybe. What makes you think you are special?

Q: (L) Jesus told us God loves us. Is this true?

A: Yes. But it is the soul that matters, not the body. The body dies not the soul.

Q: (L) Well, this whole thing just gives us the creeps.

A: You are energy. There is an energy that comes from the soul and body connection; later the body is used for parts.

Q: (L) What are they using our energy and bodies for?

A: To create a new race. Theirs is fading out.

Q: (L) Well, do they just take people and kill them and do what with them?

A: They slice them up.

Q: (L) Do they die?

A: Maximum matter and energy transfer occurs during this type of transition.

Q: (L) In other words, you are saying that a slow painful death gives them the most of what they want? This is totally sick.

A: You asked for truth. You say it is sick but it is merely the ultimate form of service to self.

(At this point A___ described reading a passage in a book which stated that Native Americans believed a slow torturous death of an enemy gave them more power.)

A: What about your lab animals? Is that not service to self as well? What about un-wanted insects et cetera?

Q: (L) We were here first!

A: So were the insects. Grays now want your planet.

Q: (L) That is sick.

A: Is natural progression sick?

Q: (L) Is what is happening something like what Jesus described in the parable of the wheat where the workers come in to take out the weeds first?

A: Close.

Q: (L) What kind of people is this being done to?

A: Low level humans.

Q: (L) What happens to the high-level humans?

A: Some will survive.

And, as Topper so delicately puts it: "I leave the rest to your imagination."

It also seems to be very probable that much of the more horrific stuff that is being reported by various escapees from various mind control programs, or from underground bases where they have witnessed unparalleled scenes of horror, may have been deliberately exposed to projected and controlled thought forms. These individuals have been selected to escape from their captors or programmers, to be returned to the regular world so as to begin circulating their fearful and depressing stories. This is calculated to induce an atmosphere of terror, the cumulative energies of which will, of course, serve admirably as food for fourth-density STS. Another aim, suggests Topper, is to instill an overall atmosphere of depression, despair and ultimate defeatism before they even surface on any large scale to the daylight of general mass perception. In this way, they can devitalize any potential resistance or anger before the fact.

There is an observable tendency of fourth-density STS beings to continuously move in relentless stages of materialization that begin with the playful nightmare of the dream state, into waking reality. And this brings us back again to the idea that knowledge protects.

We can pretty well surmise that there are experiments taking place with human beings similar to those that will be described in the next section. And every other range of experimentation that humans undertake in the various compartments of our world likely have a counterpart in fourth-density reality. It's not much different from the image of the newborn baby being plugged into the Matrix in the movie to become a source of energy for the system.

It seems to be that the nature of the far country of the Prodigal Son, the reality on which we have spent our inheritance or energy, *is* the Matrix.

The aforementioned session was a watershed experience for me. I had the option of jumping back into safe and cozy denial, or I could look at the information that was being given and evaluate it based on whether or not there was any corroboration, i.e. was it true?

And then, of course, even if it was true, what could be the possible motivation behind the Cassiopaeans even telling me this? I can guarantee you that if you had been present, you would have realized that every question I asked was framed from a state of near hysteria.

But, what has been the result of knowing these things? What is the fruit of facing the truth? For me, the result has been to ignite a drive for information in order to discover first of all, whether such things could be true, and second of all to acquire the knowledge and awareness that *can* protect. And, what is more, being exposed to what *is* has a tendency to condition the mind to not blink at anything.

Am I telling you this to scare you? Are the Cassiopaeans pulling back the curtain to reveal the machinations behind the curtain to terrify you into a state of paralysis?

Well, that's up to you.

If you are paralyzed by it, you are welcome to go back to the center of your Rubik's Cube and believe with all your heart and soul that the chaotic colors are arranged as you would like them to be. You are welcome to open your heart to any being that will come along and support you in your delusion, soothing your terror with honeyed words that it'll be alright. "Just have faith and that nasty real world out there will fade away", which you can cling to, thereby attaching you to such a consciousness for its own feeding purposes.

If, on the other hand, you begin to understand that knowledge can be applied to moving the colors on the cube into real alignment so that your polarization toward freedom and truth is amplified, thus leveling the playing field; then let us proceed.

Knowledge protects.

CHAPTER 69
THE WHIRLPOOL OF CHARYBDIS,
THE SIRENS AND THE NAVIGATOR

I know that the very idea of being in an actual Matrix as depicted in the movie is a difficult pill to swallow. We have been taught so many things from so many sources throughout history that tend to blame humanity itself – in the human state exclusively – for all the ills of mankind. Now, yes, it may be so that this state was chosen by a group mind, but the fact is, as the Prodigal Son who wanted to visit the far country, we now find ourselves more or less in the pig sty. In the grand cosmic scheme of things, we probably did it just to enrich our soul with experience and knowledge, and that is all fine and good; but here at this level, where we are still experiencing the far country individually and collectively, we need to go about assessing our condition and coming to some understanding here.

The exact wording of the parable may give us some clues. We read in Luke, Chapter 15 (3×5), Verse 11 (!):

There was a certain man who had two sons; and the younger of them said to his father, "Father, give me the part of the property that falls to me." And he divided the livelihood between them. And not many days after that the younger son gathered up all that he had and journeyed into a distant country, and there he wasted his fortune in reckless and loosed-from-restraint living. And when he had spent all he had, a mighty famine came upon that country, and he began to fall behind and be in want.

So, he went and forced (glued) himself upon one of the citizens of that country, who sent him into his fields to feed hogs. And he would gladly have fed on the carob pods that the hogs were eating, but they could not satisfy his hunger and nobody gave him anything better.

Then, when he came to himself, he said, "How many hired servants of my father have enough food and to spare, but I am perishing here of hunger! I will get up and go to my father, and I will say to him, 'Father, I have sinned against heaven and in your sight; I am no longer worthy to be called your son; make me as one of your hired servants.'"

So he got up and came to his father. But while he was still a long way off, his father saw him and was moved with pity and tenderness for him, and he ran and embraced him and kissed him fervently.

And the son said to him, "Father, I have sinned against heaven and in your sight; I am no longer worthy to be called your son – I no longer deserve to be recognized as a son of yours!" But the father said to his bond servants, "Bring quickly the best robe – the festive, honor robe – and put it on him, and give him a ring for his hand and sandals for his feet; and bring out that fattened calf and kill it, and let us revel and feast and be happy and merry; Because this my son was dead, and is alive again; he was lost, and is found!"

... But his older son was in the field, and as he returned and came near to the house, he heard music and dancing. And having called one of the servant boys to him, he began to ask what this meant. And he said to him, "Your brother has come, and your father has killed that fattened calf, because he has received him safe and well.

But the elder brother was angry – with deep-seated wrath – and resolved not to go in. Then his father came out and began to plead with him, But he answered his father, "Lo, these many years I have served you, and I have never disobeyed your command; yet you never gave me so much as a little kid, that I might revel and feast and be happy and make merry with my friends; but when this son of yours arrived, who has devoured your living with immoral women, you have killed for him that fattened calf!"

And the father said to him, "Son, you are always with me, and all that is mine is yours. But it was fitting to make merry, to revel and feast and rejoice, for this brother of yours was dead, and is alive again! He was lost and is found!"

There is marvelous and rich implication in this story, but we are not going to analyze it completely here. We want to look at that crucial part of the story where it says:

And when he had spent all he had, a mighty famine came upon that country, and he began to fall behind and be in want. So, he went and forced (glued) himself upon one of the citizens of that country, who sent him into his fields to feed hogs. And he would gladly have fed on the carob pods that the hogs were eating, but they could not satisfy his hunger and nobody gave him anything better.

This describes the conditions of the Matrix, and it is most curious to me that the word that is translated from the Greek as *forced* (or *joined* in the King James Version), *kollaw*, is derived from *kola*, which means, literally, *glued*. He glued himself to a citizen of that country. I can't help but think of all the many people who glue themselves to belief systems.

Suffice it to say that this gluing suggests a bond of some sort exactly as described by Topper in his "ethereal filaments." It is also very reminiscent of the medieval figures from the woodcuts in the last section.

But, the fact is, the story tells us that this solution – this gluing or faith – did not work. In fact, he ended up in the deplorable state of having to eat with the pigs. "And nobody gave him anything better."

So, in this condition, finally coming to the realization that he was not going to get anything better living with the pigs and eating with the pigs, he comes to some very hard realizations:

Then, when he came to himself, he said, "How many hired servants of my father have enough food and to spare, but I am perishing here of hunger! I will get up and go to my father, and I will say to him, 'Father, I have sinned against heaven and in your sight; I am no longer worthy to be called your son; make me as one of your hired servants.' "

Now, what we would like to know is this: what does it mean, "when he came to himself … [he realized] 'I have sinned against heaven and in your [his father's] sight?'"

The clue is given to us in the figure of the pig. So, keep that in mind as we go along here. Remember that the condition of being with the pigs (what we have now come to know as "ponerized" individuals) was a result of gluing himself to the citizen of that country (a psychopathic ruler, i.e. STS dominance).

I'm going to insert some more material from the Cassiopaeans out of the chronology that I have been attempting to establish. No matter, we can get back in linear mode soon. But since the reader is now in a position to understand some elements of the alchemical process of initiation, the slow heat method, it will be easy to see that the Cassiopaeans were heating the crucible in this one. And, curiously, it is also part of the 3-5 code. If, as one individual suggested, I was being "driven mad" by this material, it sure did lead to some astounding discoveries. So, maybe there is method in the madness of the Cassiopaeans.

On December 14, 1996, the following strange conversation with the C's took place:

Q: (T) [So], there's a blocking technique being used on people to lower the vibrational frequency to prevent them from seeing, right?
A: The blocking technique is for many things.
Q: (T) So that people do not understand what's going on around them.
A: Yes. That is it, in a nutshell. See and know and think or … See, know and think that which is desired.
Q: (L) OK, let me jump over to this other subject of the number 33 and the number 11. Is there anything beyond what was given on 11-11-95 that you could add at this time, about any of the mathematics or the use of these numbers?
A: Prime numbers are the dwellings of the mystics.
Q: (L) What do you mean, "prime numbers are the dwellings of the mystics?"
A: Self-explanatory, if you use the tools given you.
Q: (L) How can a number be a dwelling?
A: Figure of speech. [Planchette spirals several times, vigorously] And how interesting that we have a new "cell" phone company called: "Primeco."
Q: (L) And how does a cell phone company called Primeco relate to prime numbers being dwellings of mystics?
A: Not for us to answer.

The Cassiopaeans have repeatedly identified our minds as our greatest tool for advancement, so at this point, we stopped to discuss among ourselves, using our minds, to try to figure out just what might be meant by this most mysterious remark that "prime numbers are the dwellings of the mystics" and what it might have to do with cells and phones.

We tried a little word association on the term *cells* – with the concept of *dwelling* superimposed on it. What we came up with were: cells of monks, prisons, prime number divisible by one or self. We also thought of encryption because prime numbers are often used in encryption codes.

Q: (L) Is encryption the key?
A: Oh, there is so much here. One example is: "Snake eyes" is not so good as 7, 11, eh?
Q: (T) They are all prime numbers, too; seven and eleven. (L) What kinds of documents or writings ... or what would be applicable ...
A: No, Laura you are trying to focus, or limit the concept, my dear. Think of it, what is the Judaic-Christian legend for the creation of a woman?
Q: (L) That woman was taken from the rib of Adam. That Eve was created from the rib of Adam.
A: Ever heard of a "prime rib?"
Q: [Groans from the group] (T) I hate being in kindergarten and not knowing what the subject is. OK, prime rib. We have a prime rib, so ...
A: What happens in a "Primary."
Q: (L) An election. You narrow down the candidates. What happens in a primary?
A: Who gets "picked" to run?
Q: (L) OK, keep on ...
A: "Prime Directive?"
Q: (L) OK.
A: "Prime time?"
Q: (L) The first, the best ... and ...
A: Not point.
Q: (L) I know that's not the point! Is what we're supposed to see is that we can use these prime numbers to derive something out of something else?
A: We told you about the mystics.
Q: (T) They're using prime numbers to ... (L) Oh, OK, I get it. So, mystics ... the mystics, the mystical secrets ... dwell in the prime numbers if used as a code.
A: Name the primary mystical organizations for key to clue system.
Q: (L) ... Key to clue system?
A: Yes.

We named: Catholicism, Christianity, Judaism, Cabalism, Sufism, Islam, Ancient Mysteries, Jesuits, Masons, Knights Templar, and Rosicrucians.

Q: (L) All right. With our little list that we're making, are we on to something, or are we completely off track?
A: Yes, now check out those crop circles photos ... any prime number combos there?
Q: (L) Do you mean in terms of dimension, or do you mean in composition?
A: Composition and dimensions ... anything you can find.

Group discussion: sacred geometries; all sects listed use prime numbers; Genesis 2:22, "rib taken from the man and made woman" – 2 is the only even prime number; Gen. 3:5, "your eyes shall be opened and ye shall be as the gods"; eating from the tree of knowledge, etc.

Q: (T) ... To find a way of decoding it to get an answer, to get something, to get a message, to get something from it ... (L) Are we thinking in any of the lines of something we ought to follow, or are we drifting?

A: All are lines you ought to follow. Now, look at the photos on the wall! [Referring to large photocopy of a number of crop circles we had pinned to the wall.]

Q: (L) OK, we're looking at them: point out something ...

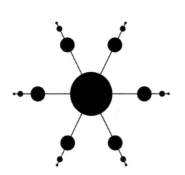

A: Count the large spheres in photo three.

Q: (L) There are seven.

A: Yes.

Q: (L) And what does that photo represent?

A: Not yet.

Q: (T) OK, there are seven large circles; a large central one, and then six outer ones that are smaller. Each of the six smaller circles is connected to the larger circle by a shaft, or a line, or a conduit of some kind.

A: Add large and small spheres.

Q: (L) OK, there's seven. Add the large to the small and there's seven; add the little teeny ones, there's thirteen; and then even the little teeny-teeny, the little knobs on the ends, there would be six more, so that would be nineteen.

A: Yes ...

Q: (T) So, that's another prime. (L) OK, they're prime numbers. And ... (T) Are they ... just as an offshoot here, do the six circles, the first set surrounding the large circle, are those the sixth density attached to the seventh density?

A: No comment.

Q: (T) OK now, and then, outside of that are smaller spheres, each one connected one to the next, in a line. We're looking at prime numbers here. What are we looking at? We've got a central one, six outer: large, six outside of that: smaller, six outside of that: tiny ... could, and I'm just thinking off the top of my head here, nothing cast in concrete, is this a representation of ... a sphere, getting smaller and smaller ... going that way. Or, coming in, this way. Or that way and this way. Like the infinity mirrors ...

A: If you three dimensionalize.

Q: (L) It would be like balls, like spheres. (T) Ohhh, it's an axis, an x-y-z axis! A three dimensional axis. Three-dimensionally, it would be like this. [Holds up hand, forefinger pointed up, thumb pointed to himself, third finger at the horizontal.] Larger, smaller, smaller ... a three-dimensional axis. Are we going somewhere with this, or am I out in left field again?

A: Yes.

Q: (T) I'm going somewhere with this?

A: Yes.

Q: (T) Ahhhh, I now see this as a three-dimensional object as opposed to a flat circle.

A: Do that to the others too.

Q: (L) OK, we're trying to three-dimensionalize them. Now, tell us where we're supposed to be going here ... (J) Well, this first one is a spiral going out ... or a DNA molecule ... (T) There's got to be more to it ...

A: You do not have to figure this all out tonight, just some *food for thought.* ... Ark may be able to three-dimensionalize by computer program already.

Q: (L) Yes, well, let us get back to this. The crop circles, as I understand you, are related to the code or the mystical prime numbers, the mystical dwellings, and that somehow putting all of these things together, these different pieces of this puzzle from so many different directions, will enable us to perceive or learn or conceive something that will enable us to do something. Is that correct?

A: Close.

Now, if that session wasn't enough to drive a person bonkers, I don't know what is. But, as we go through the following material which I dug into as a result of these clues, I think that the perspicacious reader will see just exactly where the Cassiopaeans are pointing us.

Deepok Chopra, M.D. writes about Candace B. Pert, Ph.D., discoverer of the opiate receptor in the early 1970s, in the introduction to her book *The Molecules of Emotion*:

> Her pioneering research has demonstrated how our internal chemicals, the neuropeptides and their receptors, are the actual biological underpinnings of our awareness, manifesting themselves as our emotions, beliefs, and expectations, and profoundly influencing how we respond to and experience our world. (Pert 1999, 9)

The human brain is probably the most complex structure in the universe; in a sense, it might be thought of as a universe in itself. At birth, the infant brain contains about 100 billion nerve cells, or neurons. This number is comparable to the number of stars in the Milky Way galaxy. Now, just think about what a huge electrical potential such a number implies! Yet it is not the number we want to think about just now, but what these neurons actually are doing in this microcosm of our head.

Unlike your average body cell, such as a cell in your stomach or pancreas or the fat in your love handles, the neurons constantly carry complex conversations with one another. Each neuron has, on the average, several thousand contacts with other cells. Some neurons can have as many as 200,000 connections. Can you imagine talking on a phone line connecting to that many other individuals and keeping track of all the conversations? (And yes, that is exactly the analogy that scientists use: a phone company. And a cell phone company at that.)

Dr. Steven Hyman, director of the National Institute of Mental Health, writes:

> ... Whether we are awake or asleep, our brain cells are doing the neuronal equivalent of a mass phonathon, sending and receiving chemical messages triggered by electrical impulses. They do this by means of specialized appendages. Each nerve cell has a single long fiber called an axon for transmitting information and a fine filigree of fibers called dendrites for receiving information. The length of a given neuron's axon varies. Some are quite short, but others may extend up to three feet, carrying an electrical impulse from, say the base of the spine to the tip of the big toe. Three feet may not sound like much until one imagines the nerve cell as a kite three feet across – with an axon tail that's forty miles long. (Hyman 1999, 12)

A neuron sends an electrical pulse down its myelin-insulated axon to the axon terminals where chemicals called neurotransmitters are released to float across the synapse to the dendrites of the receiving neuron. If the sum of all incoming signals is sufficient, the receiving neuron will fire, sending an electrical pulse along its own axon to the next neuron in line. This adding of impulses to decide whether or not the neuron fires is a kind of voting. So, we have a clue to the Cassiopaeans' use of the term *primary*, or who gets picked to run.

Now, it is at the terminal of the axon that the electrical impulse is converted into a chemical, the neurotransmitter, which sort of floods the area around the receivers, or dendrites, of the adjacent neuron. The thing that is important here is the fact that the receiver neuron has many little fibers for reception of neurotransmitter signals, *but* it can be in communication with literally thousands of other neurons. So, how does it decide which one to listen to? And why does it matter?

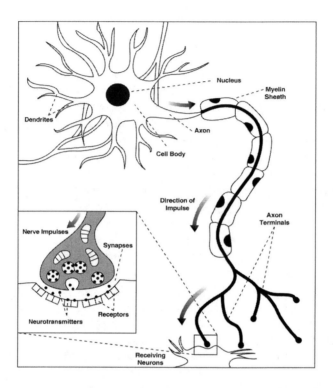

Well, here is where it gets interesting. Back in the early days of the 20th century, it was realized that a drug must work in the body because they could attach themselves to something in the body. They decided to call this place of attachment a receptor. Nobody really knew how this attaching worked, or why it led to a whole cascade of changes in the body, but there it was. You take a drug, and all kinds of things happened in the brain or other areas of the body.

It is now known, after long years of research, that the receptor is actually a single molecule. Not only that, but it is singularly complicated. Keep in mind that a molecule, by definition, is the smallest possible piece of something that can still be identified as a specific substance.

A molecule is composed of atoms. Atoms seem to form bonds with one another in accordance with certain rules. These rules have to do with the number of electrons in the highest energy shell of the particular atom. An atom is what is by virtue of how many electrons it has, and these electrons are arranged in shells like the orbits of planets around the sun. The only thing is, they can't be thought of as round planetary bodies, but as a sort of cloud of energy. Full shells are particularly stable so that atoms seem to like to arrange themselves so they can get their outer shells filled. Electrons also come in two flavors, which are referred to as up and down. An up electron likes to pair with a down electron. This refers to the spin state of the atom. And, depending upon the number of electrons in the outer shell of the atom, and how many electrons it would like to have in its outer shell, it can bond to one or more other atoms. Carbon, for example, has a valence of four because it has the ability to make four bonds. Hydrogen has a valence of one because it can only make one bond. This means that a carbon atom, with four connectors, can bond with four hydrogen atoms, each with one connector. This produces molecules of methane, or CH_4. Oxygen has valence 2, which means that one carbon atom with valence 4 can bond with each of two oxygen atoms in a sort of double yoke. This produces carbon dioxide, or CO_2.

Of course, there are some interesting combinations such as carbon monoxide, which leaves two of the carbon valences dangling, and ozone, which is composed of three atoms of oxygen and leaves two valences dangling. They both lurk about, just waiting to glom onto something.

This next image shows two ways of representing molecules. The method on the right probably more closely represents the reality, in terms of shape, though it is still stylistic.

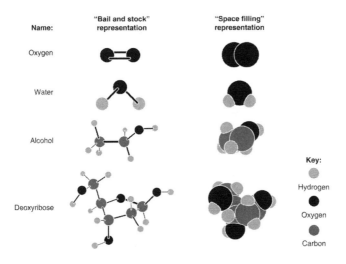

177

The most important atom in biology is carbon. It has been discovered that, in the case of carbon, the four bonds extend out from the central atom toward the four corners of a regular tetrahedron. As we noted, carbon has valence 4, and it happens that the most stable configuration of an atom is a filled outer shell of eight electrons. This is, normally, the largest valence any atom can have.

I know that some of you are noticing right away the significance of these numbers and thinking about all of the mystical terms in the world of metaphysics that somehow never manage to make much sense; and now we are beginning to look at these things and realize that such numbers may have a very deep meaning, though not in the ritual and magickal sense. We are getting an idea that perhaps all the myths and so-called secrets that are veiled so heavily in analogy and allegory may just be real science. As Jessie Weston remarked, we may be dealing with the "disjecta membra of a vanished civilization." And even if it is not garbled information from some ancient peoples who were technically more advanced than we are, it could be information from legitimate higher sources that has been hidden in allusion and mystery. It may be that all the hoo-doo stuff that has been passed down to us is just the mythicization of significant scientific information. And, if that is the case, we need to peel off all of the ritual, the religious nonsense, the hoo-doo stuff, get down to business and discover this science of the soul in real terms.

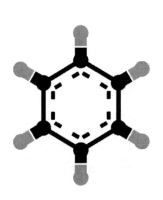

Getting back to our subject here, this is a very curious puzzle about the carbon atom – the basic atom of our existence. When carbon bonds, the result has been shown by Linus Pauling to be completely symmetrical. That is, the four bonds align towards the corners of *a regular tetrahedron.* It was deduced that, in addition to the atom liking to have its outer shell filled, the electrons like to be as far apart from each other in the bonded state as possible, which results in this arrangement.

Carbon atoms are very happy to form bonds with other carbon atoms. That is the basis of the famous benzene ring structure. The benzene ring is a particularly stable molecular form because the natural angles made by the four bonding carbon orbitals comfortably fit a six-sided structure – a hexagon!

Now, we could go on for a long time describing bonding and doing diagrams and all that. But, the essential thing to know here is this: the resulting molecules that are brought together in these chemical bonding processes have a particular shape. The carbon bonds have plenty of flexibility, allowing bending, and there can be tangling and doubling back and forth to form very complex and very specific shapes. This bending and tangling brings different atoms of one side group into contact with others, providing all kinds of opportunities for complex bonding. The natural angle between the carbon bonds also makes the benzene ring shape particularly favored and in a long carbon chain, the same natural angle can make the chain tend to loop round and round on itself. In such a case, however, the carbon atoms are not joined to close the ring, but can continue the polymer chain like the *coils of a snake*.

Carbohydrates, for example, are a group of substances based on the benzene ring structure. In carbohydrates, most of the carbon atoms are joined to two other carbon atoms but have each of their other two bonds used in combination with other atoms or groups, OH on one side and H on the other. Together, without the carbon in the middle, OH and H would make H_2O, or water. So, the term carbohydrate means, literally, watered carbon.

The simpler carbohydrates, or watered carbons, are called sugars. If the sugar is a one-ring system, it is a monosaccharide. If it is a double ring structure, it is a disaccarhide. More complex sugars are polysaccharides. Glucose is a monosaccharide. Maltose is a disaccharide. A chain of glucose units can be combined to make a polysaccharide called starch. A slightly different arrangement is another familiar biological substance, cellulose.

Now, there are six carbon atoms in your basic monosaccharide. But, some monosaccharides contain *only five carbon atoms*, four of which are connected to one oxygen atom in the form of a *5-sided ring*. The fifth carbon atom is part of a side group, CH_2OH. These compounds are called *pentoses*. One of them, exactly like glucose except for the missing carbon atom and its associated side groups, is called *ribose*. Another, similar to ribose except that one of its OH groups has lost the oxygen atom, leaving a simple CH bond behind, is called *deoxy-ribose*. This means that it is ribose from which one of the oxygens has gone. Deoxy-ribose is the basic unit that provides the name for deoxyribonucleic acid, or DNA, the fundamental molecule of life. Sound like a prime rib-ose?

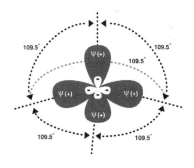

Getting back to the single molecule receptors on cells, we can understand from the bonding principles we've discussed that these receptors have very particular shapes that define precisely what chemical will be attracted to them, or vice versa. We can understand there are atomic forces that cause one molecule to be attracted to another. Receptor molecules on the cell respond to these energies by wiggling, shimmying, vibrating and even humming as they shift back and forth from one favored shape to another. Receptors are attached to a cell, floating on its surface, like a lotus flower on the surface of a pond, with roots extending into the interior of the cell. This lotus flower reference brings to mind the four sons of Horus, sometimes represented as a lotus.

There are many types of receptors on the surface of the cell, and if they were color coded, the cell surface would look like a wild mosaic made up of at least 70 different colors. The numbers of tiles in the mosaic are staggering – 50,000 of one kind, 10,000 of another, 100,000 of still another, and on and on. A typical neuron can have millions of receptors on its surface.

Another interesting analogy that scientists use to describe neurons and receptors is that they are like a tree with buds. In fact, the visual correspondence is so striking that the terms used by scientists for the growth of neurons include branching and arborization. Using this analogy, the bark of the tree is analogous to the neuronal cell membrane, the skin of the cell. However, unlike the bark of a tree, which is hard and static, the cell membrane is a fatty, flexible boundary that keeps the cell as an entity.

Tree of life, anyone?

Now, what do these receptors do? Well, we already know that they attract other molecules and respond to the atomic forces of various kinds of bonds. Dr. Pert writes in her book:

> Basically, receptors function as sensing molecules – scanners. Just as our eyes, ears, nose, tongue, fingers, and skin act as sense organs, so, too, do the receptors, only on a cellular level. They hover in the membranes of your cells, dancing and vibrating, waiting to pick up messages carried by other vibrating little creatures, also made out of amino acids, which come cruising along – diffusing is the technical word – through the fluids surrounding each cell. We like to describe these receptors as "keyholes," although that is not an altogether precise term for something that is constantly moving, dancing in a rhythmic, vibratory way. (Pert 1999, 23)

All receptors are proteins … and they cluster in the cellular membrane waiting for the right chemical keys to swim up to them through the extra-cellular fluid and to mount them by fitting into their keyholes – a process known as binding.

Binding. It's sex on a molecular level!

> And what is this chemical key that docks onto the receptor and causes it to dance and sway? The responsible element is called a ligand. This is the chemical key that binds to the receptor, entering it like a key in a keyhole, creating a disturbance to tickle the molecule into rearranging itself, changing its shape until – click! – *information enters the cell.* (Pert 1999, 23)

So, again we have our cell phone analogy. And, I don't think it is taking the analogy too far to say that a ligand is the cellular equivalent of a phallus. Ligand comes from the Latin *ligare*, or that which binds. The same word is also the root of *religion*. Curious, yes? But we will leave speculation on that matter to a later time, also.

Receptors are the first components of emotion.

A ligand is any natural or man-made substance that binds selectively to its own specific receptor on the surface of a cell. The ligand bumps onto the receptor and slips off, bumps back on, slips back off. When it is bumping on, it is binding, and each time it does this it transfers a message by its molecular properties to the receptor.

Dr. Pert writes:

> Though a key fitting a lock is the standard image, a more dynamic description of this process might be *two voices* – ligand and receptor – *striking the same note* and producing a vibration that rings a doorbell to *open the doorway* to the cell. What happens next is quite amazing. The receptor, having received a message, transmits it from the surface of the cell deep into the cell's interior, where the message can change the state of the cell dramatically. A chain reaction of biochemical events is initiated as tiny machines roar into action and, directed by the message of the ligand, begin any number of activities – manufacturing new proteins, making decisions about cell division, opening or closing ion channels, adding or subtracting energetic chemical groups like the phosphates – to name just a few. In short, the life of the cell, what it is up to at any moment, is determined by which receptors are on its surface, and whether those receptors are occupied by ligands or not. On a more global scale, *these minute physiological phenomena at the cellular level can translate to large changes in behavior, physical activity, even mood.*
>
> … As the ligands drift by in the stream of fluid surrounding every cell, only those ligands that have molecules in exactly the right shape can bind to a particular kind of receptor. The process of binding is very selective, very specific! In fact, we can say that binding occurs as a result of *receptor specificity*, meaning the receptor ignores all but the particular ligand that's made to fit it. The opiate receptor, for instance, can "receive" only those ligands that are members of the opiate group, like endorphins, morphine, or heroin. The Valium receptor can attach only to Valium and Valium-like peptides.
>
> … Ligands are generally much smaller molecules than the receptors they bind to, and they are divided into three chemical types. The first type of ligand comprises the classical neurotransmitters, which are small molecules with such unwieldy names as acetylcholine, norepinephrine, dopamine, histamine, glycine, GABA, and serotonin. These are the smallest, simplest of molecules, generally made in the brain to carry information across the gap, or synapse, between one neuron and the next. …
>
> A second category of ligands is made up of steroids, which include the sex hormones testosterone, progesterone, and estrogen. All steroids start out as cholesterol, which gets transformed by a series of biochemical steps into a specific kind of hormone. …

... My favorite category of ligands by far, and the largest, constituting perhaps 95 percent of them all, are the peptides. ... Like receptors, peptides are made up of strings of amino acids ...

[Peptides are tiny pieces of protein and the word protein is derived from *proteios,* which means *primary.* Proteins are recognized as the fundamental materials for life. A peptide consists of a string of amino acids joined together like beads on a string. The bond that holds the amino acids together is made up of carbon and nitrogen. This bond is so strong that it takes hours, and in some cases, *days* of boiling in strong acid to break it apart! When there are approximately 100 or more amino acids in such a protein, it is called a polypeptide. After it reaches 200 amino acids, it is then known as a protein. (p. 64)]

... If the cell is the engine that drives all life, then *the receptors are the buttons on the control panel* of that engine, and a specific peptide (or other kind of ligand) is the finger that pushes that button and gets things started. (Pert 1999, 24, 25)

Amino acids are strung together to make peptides in a little factory called a ribosome, which is found in every cell. The ribosome is, itself, composed of many different proteins in addition to three molecules of ribonucleic acid. Following instructions, part of the DNA will unwind and make a working copy of RNA which then floats over to the ribosome. Every amino acid has a triplet code that causes a given amino acid to be transferred and joined to the growing chain of the peptide on the Ribosome.

Another *prime rib?*

Now, remember what we started with here: chemists came up with the idea that drugs worked in the body by attaching themselves to something in the body. And now we know about receptors and that they are receptive to chemicals manufactured by the body itself. More than this, we find that, in addition to the electrical based transmission of nerve impulses, the telephone system – the ligand-receptor system – represents a second nervous system. And it seems that this chemical-based system is far more ancient and more basic to the organism.

Until this new cell phone company was brought into focus in the 1970s, most scientific attention had been given to the neurotransmitters and the little jump they facilitated across the synaptic cleft. The basic neurotransmitters seemed to carry a basic message of either on or off.

The peptides (remember, this word is related to the number 5, and there are 3 basic types of chemical messengers, so we are actually looking at one part of the 3-5 code here) can act like neurotransmitters, diffusing across the synaptic cleft, but their primary function seems to be to move through extra-cellular space, flowing with the blood and cerebrospinal fluid, traveling great distances in the body, and *stimulating complex and fundamental changes in the cells when they lock onto the receptors.*

In 1984, breakthroughs in biochemistry enabled science to understand the receptors as a bodywide network of information; the biochemical basis of emotions.

More research has demonstrated that the receptors and ligands are the information molecules of a language used by cells throughout the organism. This communication connects areas of body function that include the endocrine systems, neurological, gastrointestinal, and most importantly the immune system.

> ... [T]he musical hum of the receptors as they bind to their many ligands, often in the far-flung parts of the organism, creates an integration of structure and function that allows the organism to run smoothly, intelligently. (Pert 1999, 27)

I think that the reader may already be realizing that unified states of consciousness, or the dwelling of the mystics, is related to what sort of receptors and ligands are binding, and that frequency resonance has a lot to do with which song is being sung by the cells, and that this is clearly the understanding that the Cassiopaeans wished to convey in their mysterious remarks about prime numbers and cell phones. But, of course, the question is: what are the precise desirable chemicals one might wish to produce, and exactly how might this be done?

It is in answering these questions that we find our way out of the trap of the Predator's mind.

Remember that no drug can act unless fixed. This means, that if a drug works, it is because there is a receptor for it in the body. This, then, suggests that the receptor is there because it binds to a ligand produced by the body itself, which suggests that the body *can* produce its own drugs, stimulating its own healing, under the proper circumstances.

Looking in another direction, when we consider drugs that change behavior, such as heroin, marijuana, Librium, angel dust, PCP, and so on, precipitate radical changes in emotional states and must also be able to bind because there are receptors for similar substances produced by the body. LSD and other hallucinogens, which produce changes in cognition, must do so because there are receptors specific to them; suggesting again, that under proper circumstances such chemicals may be produced by the body itself.

It is unfortunate that Dr. Pert has taken the position that a change in emotional state relates to a change in consciousness, because it is clear that drugs produce many temporary emotional changes and result in a general decline of overall consciousness; whereas what we are looking for is the connection to produce lasting changes in consciousness – true consciousness – and not the imitation of the Predator's mind, the addiction to emotion that keeps us asleep in the Matrix Control System, the lunchbox of fourth-density STS.

After an accident that put her in hospital, Dr. Pert was given first hand experience with a drug that alters emotion:

> There was no doubt that the drug's action in my body produced a distinctly euphoric effect, one that filled me with a bliss bordering on ecstasy, in addition to relieving all pain. The marvelous part was that the drug also seemed to completely obliterate any

anxiety or emotional discomfort I had as a result of being confined to a hospital bed and separated from my husband and young child. Under its influence, I'd felt deeply nourished and satisfied, as if there weren't a thing in the world I wanted. In fact, I liked the drug so much that, as I was ending my stay at the hospital, I very briefly toyed with the idea of stealing some to take with me. I can see how people become addicts!

... I remember marveling at how there were tiny molecules on my cells that allowed for that wonderful feeling I'd experienced every time the nurse had injected me with an intramuscular dose of morphine ... (Pert 1999, 33)

Dr. Pert supplies the example of rats in bliss:

... One of my favorite slides ... three rats, rolled over on their backs, limbs floppy, eyes closed, obviously in a deep swoon. ... You can tell by their body language that they are totally satisfied and don't have a care in the world – the result of injecting our furry friends with a substance called endorphin, the body's own natural morphine ...

A shocking, but exciting fact revealed by the opiate receptor findings was that it didn't matter if you were a lab rat, a First Lady, or a dope addict – everyone had the exact same mechanism in the brain for creating bliss ... (Pert 1997, 63)

Unfortunately, Dr. Pert again mistakes this mindless bliss as expanded consciousness. As it happens, the brain's own morphine consists of a *pair of peptides*, each five amino acids in length, and we are reminded of what the Cassiopaeans said: "Oh, there is so much here. One example: 'Snake eyes' is not so good as 7, 11, eh?"

Another peptide, cryptically named "Substance P," was partially isolated from horse brain and intestines in 1931 by Ulf von Euler. He won a Nobel Prize for his feat, even though Substance P remained a chemically undefined powder for forty years, until Susan Leeman determined its eleven-amino-acid structure in 1971. Susan Leeman, at this writing, has yet to win a Nobel Prize; in fact, she was denied tenure at Harvard, where, after she defined Substance P's structure, she discovered that the peptide's activities went beyond those we knew about ... (Pert 1999, 67)

The first peptide to be synthetically replicated was oxytocin. Oxytocin is released from the pituitary gland during childbirth and binds to receptors in the uterus where it causes the contractions that expel the baby. It was later learned that oxytocin is not only released during labor, but that it is also responsible for the uterine contractions of the female orgasm. It also binds to receptors in the brain, producing thinking changes that we refer to as maternal behavior. Oxytocin is an eight-amino-acid peptide. It is the active ingredient of the Pituitary gland.

The synthetic creation of peptides includes experimental substitution of one or more of the amino acids in the chain, which can make a drug that is more potent, longer-lasting, and more resistant to decay than the body's own substance. And this, of course, suggests a sort of breakfast of champions for the cosmic lunch bunch.

As time went on in the mad rush to discover all the peptides and what they might do, it was thought that they were all produced in the brain, and sent out to do their jobs all over the body, as in the instance of localized pain relief on-site, so to speak. It was not until later that it was discovered each and every peptide can actually be made all over the body.

Although the structure of peptides is simple, their effects are complex. This is why they are subcategorized as hormones, neurotransmitters, neuromodulators, growth factors, gut peptides, interleukins, cytokines, chemikines, and growth-inhibiting factors. But, in the end, they are all doing a single thing – *conveying information* to the body cells. They are a cell phone system composed of protein, or *prime* substances. Light, if you will.

Peptide receptors were once thought to be confined to the hypothalamus. The discoveries and mapping experiments of Dr. Pert demonstrated that they exist also in the cortex, the part of the brain where higher functions are controlled, and in the limbic system, or emotional brain.

In gathering data to show the map of the opiate receptors, it was discovered that they exist in the lowliest of creatures, right up the evolutionary ladder. This suggested that this molecule had been conserved over time, through eons of evolution. As it turned out, the opiate receptors are most concentrated in the limbic system, or the classical emotional circuit. The opiate receptor has a lot to do with the organism's pleasure and pain continuum, which programs the body for survival.

Back in the 1950s, behavioral psychologists had discovered that by electrically stimulating certain centers of the brains of rats, the creatures would behave in ways that indicated they were in pain. They also found that other points in the brain processed pleasure, and if the rat was wired to be able to self stimulate this pleasure area, it would do so for hours until collapsing from exhaustion.

There is an area in the brain called the *periaqueductal gray*, located at the juncture of the third and fourth ventricle in the midbrain. It is a nodal point where many nerves converge for information processing. Although it was not considered in classical terms a part of the limbic system, it has neuronal pathways that hook it into the limbic system. This is an area where opiate receptors are highly concentrated – it is also the area of the brain where pain thresholds are set.

If you're squeamish, you're welcome to skip the next few paragraphs and pick up where I mention *Expression of the Emotions in Man and Animals.*

As the research progressed, it was realized that for a drug addict the first intravenous injection of heroin hits the brain like a sexual orgasm. From this observation, it was thought that the pleasure experienced during orgasm was accompanied by a surge of endorphins into the bloodstream. Experiments were undertaken to measure the levels of endorphins in the blood relating to different behaviors.

Hamsters were used for one study because they are very predictable in sexual terms. As Dr. Pert baldly phrases it:

... [T]wo minutes of licking this or that, three minutes of humping, etc., and the act was complete. The males ... ejaculate about twenty-three times per cycle. (Pert 1999, 103)

The animals were injected with a radioactive opiate before copulation, and then, at various points in the cycle, decapitated. The brains were removed and autoradiography was used to see where the endorphins were released during orgasm, and in what quantity. It was found that blood endorphin levels increased by about 200 percent from the beginning to the end of the sex act.

Well, I was pretty green to learn how science discovers things in this particular instance. So, let us hope that if any good comes from this horrible work, that it will in some way bless the sufferings of those poor hamsters. And, let us also keep in mind that similar experiments might be taking place on human beings.

Dr. Pert continued her experiments with the chemistry of emotions for many years. She developed a conceptual understanding based on her assessment that "these biochemicals are the physiological substrates of emotion, the molecular underpinnings of what we experience as feelings, sensation, thoughts, drives, perhaps even spirit or soul."

In *Expression of the Emotions in Man and Animals*, naturalist Charles Darwin wrote about the fact that people everywhere have common emotional facial expressions, some of which are also shared by animals. A wolf baring its fangs uses the same muscles of the face that a human does when angry or threatened. It seems that the same physiology of emotions has been preserved and used over and over again throughout eons of time and across species. On the basis of this observation, Darwin theorized that emotions must be a key to the survival of the fittest.

There is clear scientific experimental evidence that the facial expressions for anger, fear, sadness, enjoyment, and disgust are identical whether an Eskimo or an Italian is being studied. Facial expressions that register other emotions such as surprise, contempt, and guilt are likely also pancultural. This suggests that emotions have inborn genetic mechanisms for their expression.

There are other distinctions made in these studies relating to distinguishing between emotion, mood, and temperament. Emotion is the most transient; moods can last for hours or days; and temperament is that which lasts for life. Temperament has been shown, experimentally, to be genetically based, and it is likely that the parameters for mood and emotion are similarly based in our genes.

When talking about emotions in this way, it has to be understood that it includes all the familiar human experiences of anger, fear, sadness, joy, contentment, courage; as well as the sensations of pleasure and pain, and the drive states such as hunger and thirst. All of these are measurable in chemical terms.

However, Dr. Pert, as I have already noted, goes even further and refers to more intangible states, or subjective experiences, such as spiritual inspiration, awe, bliss and other states of consciousness. I think she has failed to make the distinction between chemicals that produce states and *states that produce chemicals.*

Getting back to our opiate receptors and the limbic system: it has been shown that core limbic brain structures such as the amygdala, hippocampus, and limbic cortex, believed to be involved in emotional behavior, contain 85 to 95 percent of the various neuropeptide receptors. Wilder Penfield, working in the 1920s, experimented during open-brain surgeries undertaken to control severe epilepsy. He found that when he electrically stimulated the limbic cortex over the amygdala (the two almond-shaped structures on either side of the forebrain, about an inch or so into your brain from your earlobes), he could elicit a whole gamut of emotional displays. His patients gave powerful reactions of grief, anger, joy and more as they relived old memories. Their bodies would shake with rage or laughter, they would weep copious tears, and their blood pressure and temperature would fluctuate appropriately in accordance with whatever was being experienced.

NIMH researcher Paul MacLean popularized the idea that the limbic system was the seat of the emotions. His triune brain theory held that there are three layers to the human brain, as we have already discussed in psychological terms of imprinting. MacLean proposed that these three layers represent different stages of humanity's evolution. The brain stem, or first circuit, is called the reptilian brain (isn't that interesting?). This is the seat of autonomic functions, including the fight or flight response. It is here that safety of the organism is monitored and, if certain threats are perceived, it will trigger an automatic cascade of responses designed to preserve life of the organism.

The limbic system, or second circuit, encircles the top of the brain stem and is, as we have already discussed, the seat of the emotions. The cerebral cortex, or third circuit, the forebrain, is the seat of reason. But it can also manifest emotions!

This leads us to the fact that opiate receptors are also very dense in the frontal lobes of the cerebral cortex of the human brain, and this part of the brain shares many connections with the amygdala, one of the limbic structures, or part of the seat of emotions.

The frontal cortex, theoretically the most newly evolved, the most human, of the brain structures must forge pathways between itself and the rest of the brain to enable humans to learn to control their emotions and act unselfishly. Although the capacity to learn this is present to some extent in even the simplest of creatures, willpower is the uniquely human element. And, it is thought that it resides in the frontal cortex.

Psychologist and philosopher William James theorized that emotions originate in the body and are then perceived in the head, where we invent a story to explain them. Writing in 1884, he concluded that the source of emotions is purely visceral, originating in the body and is not cognitive, and that there is very likely no brain center for emotions. He thought that we perceive events and have bodily feelings, and after the perception, which jogs our memories and imagination, we label our physical sensations as one or the other emotion. He believed that there is simply perception and bodily response based on memory of other events that relate to the present experience. He thought that their immediate sensory and motor reactions that occur in response to the perception, such as a pounding heart, a tight stomach, tension and perspiration, *are* emotions.

Physiologist Walter Cannon posited that they originated in the head and trickle down to the body. Writing in *Wisdom of the Body*, he explained the workings of the sympathetic autonomic nervous system. A single nerve called the vagus (wandering) nerve exits the back of the brain through a hole in the bottom of the skull called the foramen magnum. There, it splits to run down the bundles of nerve cells, or ganglia, along either side of the spinal cord to send branches to many organs, including the pupils of the eye, the salivary glands, the heart, the bronchi of the lungs, the stomach, the intestines, the bladder, the sex organs, and the adrenal glands.

When Cannon stimulated the vagus through electrodes implanted in the hypothalamus in the bottom of the brain just above the pituitary gland, he demonstrated physiological changes in all these organs consistent with what would be needed by the body in an emergency. Cannon was able to measure how much time it took from the moment the hypothalamus got the jolt to the moment the bodily changes in blood flow, digestion, and heartbeat began to occur as a result. The conclusion was that these changes were too slow to be the cause of emotions rather than the effect. Not only that, but animals whose vagus nerve had been cut, and presumable were incapable of sympathetic visceral bodily changes, still seemed to behave just as emotionally when placed in a threatening situation.

It took over a hundred years to realize that both James and Cannon were correct.

Biofeedback is demonstrative of this fact because it is a technique that can enable a person to gain conscious control over physiological processes previously thought to be autonomic and not susceptible to volitional modification.

Elmer Green, a pioneer of biofeedback stated, "Every change in the physiological state is accompanied by an appropriate change in the mental emotional state, conscious or unconscious, and conversely, every change in the mental emotional state, conscious or unconscious, is accompanied by an appropriate change in the physiological state" (Pert 1999, 137).

And it is in this idea that we find a key. If it is true that our physiological state can be manipulated, causing a change in our mental and emotional state, then what we must do is learn to control the emotional and physiological state by conscious will.

There is a tiny cluster of cell bodies in the hindbrain called the *locus coeruleus*. It projects its norepinephrine-containing nerve endings into the forebrain, and it seems that all the norepinephrine in the forebrain comes from this one source. It was discovered that the pleasure center – the area that, when electrically stimulated, will cause rats and humans to ignore the need for food and sleep in a frenzy of pleasure – is contained within this *locus coeruleus*.

It seems that, unbeknownst to the earlier researchers, the electrical stimulus for pleasure had worked by causing the release of norepinephrine from the nerve endings along the pathway. Amphetamines and cocaine also work by amplifying this same pleasure pathway by blocking the re-uptake of the body's own norepinephrine, and thereby increasing the ligand binding to the norepinephrine receptors.

The problem with this idea was that, if peptides and their receptors were only communicating across synapses, they should be only very tiny distances apart. But, the evidence indicated that many of the receptors responding to this were located too far away to be part of specific synaptic gaps. The conclusion was that the greatest source of control of information in the brain – that which determines its state – is the specificity of the receptors and their ability to bind with only one kind of ligand.

In other words, it seems that less than two percent of neuronal communication actually occurs at the synapse. It was seen that the way in which peptides circulate through the body, finding their targets all over the place, makes the brain's communication system itself more like an endocrine system. As Dr. Pert baldly puts it, the brain is like a bag of hormones!

Yeah. A lunch bag!

And what is being communicated by these peptides is crucial to everything in the body. For example, receptors for sex hormones were identified as the means by which, if testosterone or estrogen is released into the fetus during pregnancy, determines the neuronal connections in the brain and permanently affects the sexual identity of the child. Females fetuses exposed to testosterone like steroids aberrantly produced by their pregnant mothers adrenal gland are more likely to become tomboys. Conversely, excessive estrogen can orient a male fetus to more feminine pursuits in later life.

One very interesting discovery made by Rita Valentino of the University of Pennsylvania showed that the nucleus of Barrington in the hindbrain, formerly believed to control just the emptying of the bladder, has axons continuing the neuropeptide CRF that extend through the vagus nerve all the way to the most distant part of the large intestine, the anus. It has been proven that the sensation of colonic distention, or the feeling of needing to empty the bowels, as well as genital arousal is carried back to the nucleus of Barrington. From that point, there is a short neuronal pathway that connects to the *locus coeruleus*, the norepinephrine source of the pleasure pathway, which is also loaded with opiate receptors. Once again, Dr. Pert says plainly:

The pleasure pathway hooks up to the control area of these bathroom functions, which is located in the front of the brain. Goodness, is it any wonder ... that toilet training is loaded with emotional stuff! Or that people get into some unusual sexual practices involving bathroom behaviors! ...

If we accept the idea that peptides and other informational substances are the bio-chemicals of emotions, their distribution in the body's nerves has all kinds of signifi-cance ... the body is the unconscious mind! Repressed traumas caused by overwhelming emotion can be stored in a body part, thereafter affecting our ability to feel that part or even move it. The new work suggests there are almost infinite path-ways for the conscious mind to access – and modify – the unconscious mind and the body ... (Pert 1999, 141)

As I have already mentioned, it has also been discovered that other areas of the body have high concentrations of almost every neuropeptide receptor known to exist. These areas include the dorsal horn, or back side of the spinal cord in a pattern analogous to the chakras. In fact, in virtually every location where information from any of the five senses enters the nervous system, there are high concentra-tions of neuropeptide receptors. They are called nodal points. The already men-tioned nucleus of Barrington is a nodal point and, depending on what neuropeptide is occupying its receptors, feelings related to sexual arousal or bathroom functions can be switched or modified, made unconscious, or made a priority. Thus, emo-tions and bodily sensations are intricately intertwined in such a way that each can alter the other – usually at the level of unconsciousness. It can also emerge to con-sciousness spontaneously, or be deliberately brought to consciousness.

All sensory data coming into the body goes through a filtering process that may or may not reach the frontal lobes. It is in the frontal lobes that the sensory input enters our consciousness. The efficiency of the filtering process, which chooses what stimuli we pay attention to at any given moment, is determined by the quan-tity and quality of the receptors at these nodal points. The quantity and quality of these receptors is determined by many things, one of the most important being your experiences.

In other words, biochemical changes wrought at the receptor level is the molec-ular basis of memory. When a receptor is flooded with a ligand, it changes the cell membrane in such a way that the probability of an electrical impulse traveling across the membrane where the receptor resides is facilitated or inhibited, thereaf-ter affecting the choice of neuronal circuitry that will be used. This principle is important not only for understanding how memories are stored in the brain, but that *they are also stored in a psychosomatic network extending into the body itself.* It is also the underlying principle of imprinting. Just like a printed circuit is embedded in a computer chip, so are our brains *and* bodies programmed by chemistry and elec-tricity. The decision about what becomes a thought, rising to consciousness, and what remains an automatic circuit pattern, is buried in the body and mediated by the receptors. And memories are stored with their respective emotional content. The emotion can bring up the memory, and conversely a single cue element of the memory can bring on the emotion – even if the memory itself never becomes conscious.

What this means, in the clearest of terms, is this: many memory processes are emotion-driven and unconscious; but they can sometimes be made conscious.

Donald Overton of Temple University documented a widespread phenomenon in animals which was later shown to be equally true in human beings: a rat that learns a maze or receives a shock while under the influence of a drug – which you now know is merely a synthetic ligand – will remember how to solve the maze or avoid the shock most efficiently if it is re-tested under the influence of the same drug. Dr. Pert elaborates:

> When we consider emotions as chemical ligands – that is to say, peptides – we can better understand the phenomenon known as *dissociated states of learning*, or *state-dependent recall.* Just as a drug facilitates recall of an earlier learning experience under the influence of that same drug for the rat, so the emotion-carrying peptide ligand facilitates memory in human beings. The emotion is the equivalent of the drug, both being ligands that bind to receptors in the body. ...
>
> ... Clearly, just as drugs can affect what we remember, neuropeptides can act as internal ligands to shape our memories as we are forming them, and put us back in the same frame of mind when we need to retrieve them. This is learning.
>
> ... Emotional states or moods are produced by the various neuropeptide ligands, and what we experience as an emotion or a feeling is also a mechanism for activating a particular neuronal circuit – simultaneously throughout the brain and body – which generates a behavior involving the whole creature ... (Pert 1999, 145)

What this translates into is that you will automatically run the maze when the emotion-ligand is present. Or, if you find yourself in the maze, and the chemical was one produced by your own body when you first learned the maze, you will produce the same chemicals again – repeatedly.

What this also means in the plainest of terms is that you can feel love when the right ligand bonds to the right receptor stimulated by whatever you are programmed to be stimulated by; you will feel it in all the areas where these receptors are clustered; and you will be certain that it is a positive experience because it feels really good. It doesn't matter if the ligand is being stimulated by a logically consistent experience or by an illogically inculcated program. And until the element of knowledge and logical analysis are brought into the picture, it's anybody's best guess where the feelings come from.

And, that is all fine and good if it is a positive experience. But statistics of our world in practically every arena of life clearly demonstrate that it is very likely that most of humanity do not experience real love when their love ligands are binding. Just take a look at divorce, child abuse, and neglect statistics to get an idea about how terribly wrong we human beings can be about our assessments. And, if we are really paying attention we will take a long hard look at our own lives and experiences and try to determine what our personal track records are. If they aren't good; if we spend more time being unhappy than happy; if we keep making the same open-hearted mistakes over and over again, we need to take a good look at how our programs are being activated and used to keep us in the lunchbox of the Matrix.

More frightening than that is the fact that higher-level negative beings can most definitely control our emotions by controlling our chemistry, as described. This means they can cause us to feel love or hate or aversion or attraction based on their agenda, not our own.

Going back to the filtering of reality, it seems that most of our body-mind attention shifts are directed subconsciously by our ligands and receptors. They direct our attention by their activities and we are not consciously involved in deciding what gets processed, remembered, or learned. But we do have the possibility of bringing some of it to awareness with the help of various types of intentional training. But, of course, no one undertakes intentional training until the system is so bogged down and there is so much suffering that a cure is sought. And for the most part the cures are sought in pharmacology, which merely exacerbates the problems. As the prodigal son sought to glue himself to a citizen of the far country, we seek our cures in religions of all kinds, including the religion of the American Medical Association. This amounts to being sent to feed and live and eat with the pigs. And only when we have suffered that condition a sufficient period of time will we come to ourselves.

Clearly, based on research, we can see that repressed emotions are stored in the body via the circuit creation effected by the release of neuropeptide ligands. It is also proposed that when the soul finally seats in the body, the soul's wounds or scars will energetically affect the body, producing any number of neuropeptide stimulating frequencies that then lay circuits of their own that cannot be related to present life experiences. Hypnosis, yogic practices, deep tissue bodywork, can all be methods used to heal or change the circuits without the conscious mind ever figuring out what is going on. The drawback to this is that, not knowing what is going on prevents the conscious mind from avoiding recurrence. My *Éiriú Eolas* program avoids these drawbacks by healing these circuits while simultaneously working to utilize the conscious mind.

Emotions constantly regulate what we experience as reality. The research suggests that the nervous system scans the outer world for material that it is *prepared to find by virtue of is already laid circuits*, its internal patterns of past experience including early imprinting in infancy. The *superior colliculus* in the midbrain, another nodal point, controls the muscles that direct the eyeball, and *controls which images are permitted to fall on the retina*. This means that an emotional center of the brain literally controls what we *see*.

For example, when the tall European ships first approached the early Native Americans, it was such an "impossible" vision in their reality that their highly filtered perceptions couldn't register what was happening, and they literally failed to "see" the ships. Similarly, the cuckolded husband may fail to see what everyone else sees because his emotional belief in his wife's faithfulness is so strong that his eyeballs are directed to look away from the incriminating behavior obvious to everyone else. (Pert 1999, 148)

I have recently witnessed a great deal of this activity in various people reading *The Wave* who simply read what they are programmed to read, and *not* what is really being said. One of the chief clues of STS control is that a person twists what they read. In the past, before I understood the nature of fourth-density control, when I witnessed this phenomenon I would think that the person was deliberately twisting my words. Now, I realize clearly that it is not deliberate. They have not yet come to themselves and overcome the Predator's mind and admitted the possibility that their very thoughts may be manipulated or controlled. Until they do, they are not ready to admit they "have sinned against heaven". Because Heaven is the essence of the Creator within, and sinning against it is to allow it to be used as a transducer for food for the STS lunch bunch.

The fact is, we read and understand what we are programmed to *believe*, regardless of what we are actually reading. Like the alcoholic who finally admits he *is* an alcoholic, we must admit that we are an addict to our emotional beliefs.

Now, what we have been talking about in terms of these chemical systems of the body is plainly and simply information transmission systems. Information can be unconscious, occurring below the level of awareness. We see this happening all the time in the autonomic nervous system.

The mind is not material, yet it has an interface system with the body, and this is the neurochemical network. The mind of the body is the Predator's mind, connected to strings like a marionette, with the strings in the hands of the fourth-density puppet masters – the Control System.

For the Darwinists, the body is nothing but energy and matter with hardwired reflexes caused by electrical stimulation; it operates in a more or less mechanical, reactive fashion with little option for change. Intelligence is merely the byproduct of the survival of the fittest genes. The concept of the body as an unintelligent bundle of cells run on electricity as the pinnacle of mindless evolution is a product of an ultimately godless, mechanical universe peopled by clock-like organisms.

Unfortunately, this happens to be the way it is for most human beings. They are computers running programs controlled by someone or something other than themselves. We can no longer think of emotions as necessarily of the soul. While it is likely that the consciousness *can* enter into the emotional process, for most people this never happens. Their emotions are simply cellular signals involved in the process of translating information into physical reality – generally an unpleasant one which can include all kinds of illnesses, aches, pains and transpersonal suffering.

Neuropeptides and their receptors are in constant communication with the immune system and there are many studies that show a powerful link between emotions and illness, even to a specificity of emotion-disease link. Immune cells constantly squirt out peptides that either increase or decrease the buildup of plaque in coronary blood vessels. Viruses use the same receptors as neuropeptides to enter a cell. Depending on how much of the natural peptide for a particular receptor is available to bind, the virus that fits that receptor will have more or less difficulty getting into the cell. This clearly indicates that the state of our emotions even plays a part in whether or not we contract a viral infection.

I'm sure that most readers have heard of some of the amazing feats of yogis of the East who have achieved control over not only their conscious minds, but also over what are considered to be solely autonomic systems of the body. Various disciplines are used, and we have already talked about the way of the Yogi, the Fakir and the Monk, so we know the basic principles involved. And, we are going to take this principle and apply it in a new way here. Taking just one example of what yogis and fakirs can do, i.e. consciously control pain, let's look at what might be happening.

As mentioned above, there is an area in the brain called the *periaqueductal gray*, located around the aqueduct between the third and fourth ventricles of the midbrain. It is filled with opiate receptors, making it a control area for pain perception. It is also loaded with receptors for virtually all the neuropeptides that have been studied.

What seems to happen when yogis and fakirs learn to control their perception of pain is that they are able to gain access to this area of the brain with conscious intent and to reset the pain threshold. That is to say: reframed by conscious expectations and subconscious beliefs, pain can be abolished by being interpreted as either a neutral experience or even pleasant.

And this is our Ace in the hole. We can make ourselves unavailable as food; we can change our systemic responses so that the Matrix unplugs us and dumps us out of the system just like Neo was unceremoniously plucked from his pod when he "woke up."

But, more importantly: we can train ourselves to *not blink*. With knowledge and awareness of what *is*, and what might be, we can never be confronted with a situation, either in the body or out, that will cause us to fall into a negative state.

It seems from all the studies that are done that an elevated mood – one of happy expectation of the possibility of adventure – is the greatest protection against illness. Perhaps it is also the one that makes one inedible to the Matrix?

In 1990, scientist Howard Hall demonstrated that the immune system could be controlled. He instructed his subjects in cyber-physiologic strategies. The word cyber comes from the Greek *kybernetes* (kubernetes), which means *to steer* or the *navigator*. It is interesting that one of the names for the goddess Isis is "the navigator." And the process of unveiling Isis is that of acquiring knowledge.

In the 1940s, psychologist and psychoanalyst Wilhelm Reich proposed that cancer is a result of the failure to express emotions, especially sexual emotions. Reich was not only ridiculed by the scientific community, he was persecuted in the most reprehensible way. One of the most shameful acts of the United States government was when they called for all copies of Reich's life's work to be rounded up by the FDA and incinerated. An official book burning in the land of the free! I rather suspect that Reich was onto something.

Another study showed that cancer patients who failed to release their anger had slower recovery rates. Another trait common to cancer victims was self-denial; this amounts to unawareness of their own, basic, emotional needs. It seems that emotions that are generated or suppressed due to lack of knowledge can be deadly. Since emotional expression is always tied to a specific flow of peptides in the body, the constant generation and suppression of emotions results in massive disturbances of the psychosomatic network. Many psychologists have said that depression is really suppressed anger or even anger redirected against the self.

Identifying, releasing and expressing emotion that has been suppressed is a significant step in the direction of taking charge of your ship and learning to navigate it. But at the same time it is essential to learn to transform emotions.

In the East, part of the training of many paths of yogic wisdom includes meditating in graveyards. Now, a graveyard in the East is quite different from a graveyard in the West. In the East, it is the custom to expose the bodies to the elements so that they will be devoured by birds and other predators. To meditate in such a place is to be confronted by physical horrors that Westerners may find difficult to contemplate. At the same time, there is the superstitious fear of specters and demons that the meditator must deal with. In Tantra yoga, one practice is to make love in a graveyard.

In both cases, the object is to train the consciousness to achieve higher states of mind in the face of the cold, hard facts of life in the material world; to gain mastery over the physical, programmed emotions; to become the navigator.

It is in this sense that the Cassiopaeans teach us that knowledge protects. To have a full field of awareness is to be in control of your ship no matter what may erupt into your life. Information is the bridge between consciousness and matter and without this bridge, matter and its programs – the Predator's mind – will dominate. The body-mind of the Predator is like the whirlpool of Charybdis and the temptation of the Sirens of ancient myth put together. Liky Ulysses, we must lash ourselves to the mast of our ship, stuff the ears of our rowers with wax, and call upon knowledge (nymphs) to help guide us through the dangers.

Information transcends time and space. It is, as Gregory Bateson has said, "the difference that makes a difference." Consciousness exists prior to the physical realm which is, literally, *an out-picturing of consciousness.* Denying the realities of the real world – denying the reality of the naturalness of the existence of darkness, is the same as being manipulated to have negative emotions while, at the same time being taught to suppress them. It will still exist and it will back up in your system and become the chief part of your reality because, like blocked emotions, it cannot be released so that positive emotions can take its place.

Now please note: I am not saying that we are to have, express, or embrace negative emotions; just as I have never said, nor have the Cassiopaeans ever said that we are to "embrace the darkness." Those who want to assure themselves of this fact need to go back and reread "Stripped to the Bone" in *Wave 3* while making sure that their manipulated emotional beliefs are set aside. That whole chapter is about the fact that we must choose an orientation that includes seeing the darkness and giving it the free will right to exist, since it is the free will choice of darkness to be darkness. However, to graduate to STO 4D, one must increase their STO polarization by choosing to divest themselves of darkness, even while allowing others the choice to embrace it.

And, in the same way, we must find appropriate ways to divest ourselves of the manipulated negative emotions that are backed up in our systems, as in practicing *Éiriú Eolas*, and learn how to use our reason and will to make sure that we only have positive emotions.

With an increase of information, the navigator steers the ship by constantly adjusting the tiller in response to the information. Constant feedback is required for the navigator to do the job and that is why knowledge must be combined with self-monitoring so as to have a more intelligent grasp of what is happening in your physical system and in its relation to the reality that you are experiencing. The faster and tighter the feedback loop, the more intelligence is available to your system. The body itself is a metaphor of your unconscious state. As more of it becomes conscious, there are fewer and fewer unexpected elements cropping up in your life. The body is a battlefield for the wargames of the mind. And these games are, very likely, planned and executed from higher densities. As above, so below. To think otherwise is to suffer the stress of separation from our source, to experience lack of unity. And what is it that flows between us all, linking and communicating, coordinating and integrating all of the cosmos?

Knowledge.

Just as neuropeptides flow among the cells of the body, causing all the receptors to vibrate in response to information, so does knowledge act on our consciousness the way the strings of a resting violin will vibrate when another violin is played. Knowledge produces resonance among different people who are unique, but unified in their diversity. With knowledge we can truly feel what others feel – not just assume that they feel what we feel. The oneness of life is based on the simple fact that with knowledge, we are all vibrating together.

Knowledge protects.

And now, let's learn about the strategy of some of these wargames.

CHAPTER 70
YOU TAKE THE HIGH ROAD
AND I'LL TAKE THE LOW ROAD
AND I'LL BE IN SCOTLAND AFORE YE!

Addiction.

I have made the statement that we are made addicts inside our own skins. And I am fairly certain that most people reading that remark are quite certain they are not! Especially if they are careful of their diet and habits of mental and physical hygiene.

But, I say again: we are made addicts inside our own skins. And what's more, we are addicted to our emotions. Curiously, the ones who resist that idea most strenuously are very much like an alcoholic who vigorously and vehemently declares that they are *not* an alcoholic.

Alcohol.

It's everywhere. Tens of millions of human beings experience the consequences of alcohol addiction, from decreased job performance to liver damage to spouse and child abuse, to total breakdown of social concepts and constraints ending in the proverbial skid-row bum looking every day for his MD 20–20 – or even a can of Sterno. And that is just alcohol. We aren't even going to list the statistics for other drugs as it would be tedious and pointless. You get the idea.

Alcohol and other drugs have the ability to do what they do in our systems because they are fixed. They are synthetic ligands, they bind to our receptors and in various ways produce their effects. It is the nature of these specific effects that we now want to examine.

When an ovulating female boar is exposed to a pheromone from a male boar's saliva, the scent travels along the olfactory nerve directly into the amygdala, stimulating the release of neurotransmitters, the result is that she becomes immediately and completely paralyzed in a spread–legged mating posture. Naturally, this fact has led to the marketing of a number of pheromone based men's colognes designed to produce the same effect in the human female. (Nice try, guys.)

If you give rats in a cage access to food and cocaine, the rats will consume the cocaine and ignore the food. And they will end up starving themselves to death, despite the limitless supply of available food. And of course that makes us think of the alcoholic who has gin for breakfast, bourbon for lunch, and brandy for dinner – ending up in the hospital with a severe case of malnutrition.

Caffeine is the most frequently used drug of all. In his *Coffee Cantata* of 1732, J.S. Bach wrote: "Ah! How sweet coffee tastes! Lovelier than a thousand kisses, sweeter far than muscatel wine!" A couple of centuries later, Isak Dinesen wrote: "Coffee … is to the body what the word of the Lord is to the soul."

Caffeine has a strong effect on nearly every animal species. Rats being taught to navigate through mazes learn their lessons faster after being given coffee. Not only that, but they remember better. Competitive cyclists have discovered that they can pedal twenty per cent longer if they drink caffeine an hour before racing. Some of them even go to the extreme of using caffeine suppositories before racing – sort of a time release kick in the behind!

Following ingestion of caffeine, even sperm get a kick. They swim faster and wiggle more vigorously increasing their ability to hit the spot.

What we want to know here is, how does caffeine work?

As our neurons process information, they produce cellular waste including a buildup of molecules of adenosine. Adenosine is a ligand that binds with the adenosine receptor, sending a message deep into the cell that it is time to sleep. As the production of adenosine continues throughout the day, as a byproduct of cerebral activity, more and more adenosine is produced, binding with more and more receptors, sending more and more sleep messages into more cells. And little by little our brain cells become more and more sluggish until we simply must go to sleep. We literally cannot remain conscious. We yawn, our eyes may water and try to close and we just want to curl up and let the lights go out.

So, we have a cup of espresso. The caffeine molecule just happens to be the right shape for the adenosine receptor. It hops on and binds, thereby blocking the real adenosine that sends the sleep message. Apparently, caffeine sends a different message, or at least prevents the sleep message from being sent. It interrupts the sleep signal.

This is just a small example of how dramatically chemicals can affect the brain.

We have already mentioned the rats who were implanted with electrodes for self–stimulation and would push the button until they were exhausted. Well, there were additional experiments done along this line. It seems that if the electric reward is doled out *only when the rats learn a new trick* – such as navigating a maze. The little critters would go to work like crazy to get the job done so that they could get their buzz. As long as the rewards keep coming, the rats will keep working, even mastering incredibly complex and seemingly impossible mazes that humans would find nearly impossible.

But it's not the learning they love. We already know that, given the opportunity, they will forget everything – food, mates, friends, whatever – to push that button until they collapse in mindless ecstasy.

Now, in the human being, as in other creatures, the sensation that is experienced as orgasm is the same release of chemicals that stimulate the same part of the brain that makes the rats so happy. Some scientists refer to this in technical jargon as the "do it again" center. (Cf. Burnham and Phelan.) When this center is stimulated, whatever activity is associated with it will be sought again and again.

We have, it seems, a lot of "do it again" chemicals with a lot of "do it again" receptor sites all over our bodies. Certain foods in different people act in this way. Some people feel euphoria when they achieve victory over a rival in some sort of competition. Aside from the most obvious example of sex, these are examples of other things that can cause the secretion of these "do it again" chemicals.

By having such a pleasure system in our bodies, we have a built in reward system by which we can be manipulated to pursue any number of activities that *may or may not be good for us*; mostly based on – you guessed it – early imprinting. And, we are generally unaware of it; we simply engage in certain behaviors because it feels good and we want to do it again. We were rewarded for them as infants and small children, and we constantly seek that programmed behavior in order to receive the reward. Never mind that our early programming may have been for behaviors that completely block the true expression of our essence, or that they are based on fairy tales or unrealistic perceptions of life.

Now, drugs short circuit these centers. The ways that drugs work are interesting, but in our context here we just want to look at them as a sort of path to understanding the body's own chemicals. When we take certain drugs, our brain acts as if the natural neurotransmitter was flooding the system. The brain thinks we have done something really great such as finding food or warmth while, in reality, we may be hunkered down in a flophouse with a hypodermic of heroin in our arm. Our pleasure centers know only that they are bathed in chemical bliss. Never mind that the first time we tried it, we were disgusted and repelled by the setting, the process, all the external elements. Once we have received that reward, we are convinced that this nasty setting, this ignominious behavior that is clearly damaging to the self, is okay and desirable for the reward we are going to get.

Now, let's take a look at this in a practical way. Psychologist Barbara De Angelis writes in her book *Are You the One for Me?*:

> Falling in love is a magical and powerful experience. Each kiss, each conversation, each moment in the beginning seems so right, so perfect. But soon attraction and infatuation become a "relationship," and we are brought down to earth with the challenging realities of sharing our life with another human being. And as those first enchanted weeks turn into months, one day we find ourselves asking: "Is this person right for me?"

… Since my first serious relationship at seventeen, and, until recently, I fell in love without giving serious consideration to whether the person was right for me, let alone whether they loved me enough. Someone showed up, and if he had something lovable about him, I would start a relationship. I'd convince myself he was "the one," only to find out that we were incompatible and watch the relationship fail. …

After too many heartbreaks, I was forced to face the sad truth: in spite of my experience, education, and my intense desire to be happy, I continually chose partners who were not right for me. I was falling in love with the wrong people for the wrong reasons. (De Angelis 1992, 3, 4)

Have you ever thought or said the following about one of your relationships?

"How could I have been so blind? Why didn't I see what he/she was really like?"

"I felt so sure that, this time, it would work. Where did I go wrong?"

"He seemed so wonderful when we first met. I can't figure out why he changed into someone I can't stand."

"All the signs were there from the beginning that she didn't feel the way I did. I guess I just ignored them and convinced myself things would get better."

"We loved each other, but we couldn't agree on anything, and all we did was argue."

"I was so sure he was different from the other men I'd been with. It took me almost two years to find out that I'd picked the same type of guy all over again! How could I have wasted so much time?"

"I remember feeling really in love with her at the time, but the truth is, I never told anyone we were together because I was embarrassed to admit I was even involved with a woman like that."

"Everything about him seemed so perfect; I kept telling myself that I should be happy with him, but there just wasn't any chemistry." (De Angelis 1992, 5)

Such situations arise because of the fairy tales we are taught as children. The examples of lying to ourselves about our true feelings, which are set because we are told and shown that rewards only come when we suppress our true feelings and follow the rules. Dr. De Angelis continues:

Ask most people why they fell in love with their partners, past or present, and you'll probably hear answers like this:

"I met Kathy at the gym where I work out. Something about the way she got so into that aerobics class and gave it so much energy really appealed to me."

All Kathy's boyfriend knows about her is that she has a lot of physical energy. [He is programmed by his particular socio–cultural system to believe that physical energy is very good and will be rewarded. Thus, somebody who has a lot of physical energy is "lovable." He may also have had very positive experiences with someone in his childhood who had a lot of physical energy, and who regularly made him feel loved.]

"Donna was a bridesmaid at my cousin's wedding. She looked so beautiful in this pink strapless dress – I knew on the spot I was going to fall in love with her."

All Donna's boyfriend knows about her is that she looked good in pink chiffon. [We might think that the color pink has powerful associations in his amygdala.]

"Jo Anne and I knew each other since we were kids. Everyone always said we'd probably get married when we grew up, and I guess I never even questioned it – it seemed like the right thing to do."

Jo Anne's husband has been so influenced by what his friends and family think that he doesn't even know why he loves her. [We might think that "obedience to the family" has received some very positive reinforcement in his life. Conversely, thinking for himself may have received a great deal of negative reinforcement.]

"Alex and I were assigned to work together on a project in our office. I think it was watching him problem-solve – he is so creative – that attracted me to him."

Alex's girlfriend is enthralled with his business skills but has no idea what his emotional skills are. [Creativity in solving problems may have been well rewarded in her home environment as a child. She may also have been exposed to highly creative "problem solvers" as male role models, receiving regular rewards from them. Thus, she associates these skills with love.]

"I've always been a sucker for music, so when I heard Frank play the guitar at a friend's house, I knew he was the one for me."

Frank's partner has fallen under a musical spell – she knows nothing about him except for the romantic personality she assumes all guitar players have. [And why does she assume this? Because it is programmed into her amygdala.]

"This sounds terrible, but I always had this fantasy of a tall, dark-haired man with a mustache. Dennis looked exactly like that, and nothing else really mattered."

Dennis's girlfriend likes the way he looks – she is attracted to a fantasy, but doesn't know anything about the person underneath. [And where did she get the fantasy? A program.]

None of these people thought they were making the wrong decision. They all sincerely believed that they were making intelligent, sensible choices in their partners. But the frightening truth is that many of them will discover in a month, or six months, or six years that they are in a relationship with the wrong person.

Most people put more time and effort into deciding what kind of car or video player to buy than they do into deciding whom to have a relationship with. (De Angelis 1992, 7, 8)

As De Angelis writes, "Love myths are beliefs many of us have about love and romance that actually prevent us from making intelligent love choices. ... Consciously and unconsciously, we base our decisions in relationships on these love myths." (p. 12) For example:

If I love my partner enough, it won't matter that:
He drinks
Our sex life isn't great
She criticizes me all the time
We fight constantly over how to raise the children
He is a strict Catholic and I am Jewish
I'm not really sexually attracted to her
He doesn't have a job and hasn't worked in two years
She has a terrible temper and blows up all the time

She constantly flirts with other women
I don't get along with her children
He has a hard time telling me how he feel
His family doesn't accept me
I want children and he doesn't
She still hasn't gotten over her ex–boyfriend (p. 14)

One way to tell if your relationships are simply running the program is to examine how you prove to yourself that you are really in love. Do you dwell on the intense connection of chemistry in the beginning, trying always to recapture this, and fail to examine the rest of the relationship?

Have you ever convinced yourself that you love your partner to justify continuing to have sex with them, even though the fire has gone out long ago? Conversely, have you ever been in a relationship where the only place you got along together was in bed?

When we believe the love myths, we inevitably become involved with people we are not really compatible with. We feel constantly empty and none of our needs are fulfilled. And at the same time, even if we are trying to fulfill their needs, we know it's an effort to get them to fulfill our needs, and the relationship has nowhere to go but down.

And then we are faced with the next love myth problem: we stay in the relationship longer than we should and have trouble letting go of a partner who, in moments of cold clarity, we realize are *not* right for us. We do this because we are taught to. We see the examples set for us as children; we are rewarded for not being a quitter, and are inculcated in the belief that a promise is a promise, and keeping promises, at whatever cost to us, is rewarded, while breaking them will result in dire consequences. The family pressures of our social and cultural beliefs strongly come into play here, and we are convinced that we must always sacrifice our wants and needs for those of others. We must suffer to be good, and to be rewarded. We live our lives like Dicken's *Oliver*, saying: "I want more." And we want more because we are starved and drained, and manipulated to suffer so as to be food for the upper echelons of the Control System: fourth-density STS.

Now, let's look at a real life situation that plays out the drama exactly as the theorists have predicted. Some time ago I received correspondence from a reader who wrote to me describing her years of suffering; her dreadful childhood, her marital unhappiness, suicidal feelings, and on and on. She described her father as "a highly intelligent and spectacularly manipulative individual, endowed with psychic energies and a very heavy 'presence'," and her mother as "beautiful, clever, unhappy, terrorized by my father – as was I – and learned to like alcohol."

She described her first marriage, children and divorce, increasing health problems and finally meeting her present husband who "was the first person I knew who was willing to accept me and my children. I was not 'in love' with him, though I found him attractive. I thought love would come later. ... Later we had two children of our own."

The next remark is particularly telling considering the description of her father as "highly intelligent and spectacularly manipulative individual, endowed with psychic energies and a very heavy 'presence' ... " She wrote:

> My husband also has strong intuitive and psychic abilities ... my husband and I bickered almost from the start, and it only grew worse. Not a day has gone by in over 30 years of marriage that we have not been at each other's throats, or without raised voices. Our life together has been chaotic, moving constantly, no coherent thread to my life, though it doesn't seem to affect him much. He loves to travel, and I did too at first. Now I am numb. Our misadventures along the way would make a saga. I have always turned them into comedies, but underneath there is a great waste of a life. My life.

But notice: even though she describes her husband as psychic, reflecting the programmed imprint of the father, and clearly she is looking for a father because she was not in love, but she married him because he accepted her and her children, she does not ascribe to her husband the same heaviness of the father, nor the spectacular ability to manipulate. She made a conscious effort to not marry the father. And yet, she did. Not only that, she had become her mother. No, she was not terrorized by her husband, not in the overt way her father terrorized, but the result was exactly the same. You could even say that it was a form of unconscious manipulation through poverty, as is clear in the following remark:

> And strangely he once said he wondered if I brought him my "bad luck," for our life together has been an unending series of bad choices, bad decisions, financial catastrophes. Even our friends over the years have shaken their heads in mystification.

Apparently, this husband is a far better manipulator than her father was – mainly because he seems to be not even conscious that he is manipulating. One of the clearest clues to being manipulated is feeling guilty.

> I am consumed by guilt, which has been **my overriding emotion for all the years of our marriage**. Guilt over what I can't imagine. The failure to make another happy? But why can't he see I am dying by inches? ... I have not accomplished what I need to in this life, and I never will as things are. ... Why had I always put off my own path and tried to please everybody else and live up to their own agendas?

So, even though we read in these words the fact that this woman clearly has all the answers to her problems right there in her own psyche, she cannot see them. The soul inside her is dying to live. But her programs are too strong. The belief in the love myths is dominating, and the clear and present danger of the predator is not even suspected.

> I have lost all interest in anything except the natural world I see on my daily walks. I must have wept gallons of tears in the past several months. Anything will trigger me off. I look at a cloud and start weeping. Yet my husband notices nothing. Nothing at all, save for the fact I am a little ... undemonstrative. I long for solitude, for inner freedom, for tranquility. **The thought of saying this to my husband is terrifying.** ... Every day I fade a little more.

Why is it terrifying to tell her husband what she is feeling? Remember, she has married someone who is not terrifying, someone she can fight with and talk back to … not someone like her father who terrorized her mother. Yet, she is no less terrorized!

> Two of my children – who love their father, by the way – agree with my assessment of him as an overbearing human "steamroller."

But, even with the agreement of her children, it seems this is a burden to be borne because of love. Nevertheless, it is a certainty that this spectacularly manipulative husband of hers senses that he is losing his grip on her, and the manipulation takes a new turn: health. You can't abandon a sick man, for sure, or society and everyone else will punish you and reject you and you definitely won't get your emotional fix by being a good girl.

> Last fall my husband was diagnosed with Hodgkins' Lymphoma. He almost died. He was away in the hospital for three months and I was here alone. For the first time in 30+ years I felt lighthearted, as if a weight were lifted off me. I was totally happy. I knew I could never tell him so. My mind became sharp again and I actually gained weight (I had grown gaunt). Now he is back and ending his chemotherapy. And I have become deeply depressed, talk myself out of it for several days, then once more think of death – and hope my body will respond to my wish.

And here we have the greatest clue of all as to the machinations of a typical feeder line of fourth-density STS: it must be in proximity to work. With the absence of the husband, everything changed. And, of course, it was an absence that was not due to her actions – at least not apparent to her, though it is exactly as likely that he is suffering inside as much as she is, with less ability to articulate it. Her proximity to him stimulates the chemicals of suffering in him that makes him a good meal; and conversely, his proximity to her stimulates the release of the chemicals that make her a good meal. It's a two-way street. But, of course, this period of respite helped her to come to a realization:

> I know I must leave him, though it will hurt him terribly. He has always loved me, and never understood why I am not more demonstrative. I have tried, but my heart is no-where.

And the problem here is the fact that, just as she is living in a love myth, so is he. Her myth says that he will suffer terribly if she leaves; and his myth says that he will suffer terribly if she leaves. Problem is, they are both myths. She ended her letter with:

> If the Cs can shed any light on this issue, or point out for me what I do not see clearly, it might save my life – if not in the physical sense, certainly in the greater sense. … I leave it up to you.

Well, as the reader has probably already figured out, it didn't take the Cassiopaeans or even a rocket scientist to figure this one out. I did think about one woman who advised me against my own divorce by telling me, "the devil you know is better than the devil you don't know." The idea was, that if I divorced, I might make the same mistake again, and be in an even worse situation. But, my response to that was that the devil I knew was well enough known that I didn't need to learn anymore about him to know that being alone was a better option.

I was, of course, hesitant to give advice. That's always a dangerous path to tread, even if the person really seems to be asking. More often than not, they are looking for something that will bring on a shakedown in their lives, which they can then blame on you. Nevertheless, it seemed pretty desperate and heartfelt a plea, and I responded:

> I saw your situation completely when you first wrote to me. It was very much my own with slight variations, and yours has lasted longer.
>
> What is the difference?
>
> Everything you have said, I could have said myself in one way or another. The same descriptions of the husband, the same descriptions of the relationships etc. What is the difference?
>
> I started to *read* the clues. And you have the same clues I had. I noticed that my health improved and my mind was clear when my ex was absent. I noticed that fortunes improved when and *only* when I was in charge of what happened. I noticed that he was also declining in health and that was a clue that I was as bad for him as he was for me. And by these small, subtle clues put alongside all the lessons I was being led through by the Cs and my life, I made a decision that went against everything that had ever been taught to me by my religion, my culture, my philosophy and so forth.
>
> I knew that there was no way to do it easy and that a clean, complete break was the only answer for both of us and that can't be done in the slow and gradual way. I knew that he would want an explanation, and the one I saw that would make the break the cleanest and fastest was to tell him that I never cared for him, that I made a big mistake, and everybody was suffering from my mistake, including him. And it was all my fault. And I let him lambaste me and say all the terrible things he wanted to say, and said, "Yes, you are right – I'm a lousy person." And I held my ground no matter how painful it was.
>
> So, that is what is different. I stopped living in the illusion that I could make anything better or different than it was. What is more, I chose to *see* it as it was, coldly, clearly, without emotion. Then, I *did* something about it. And the whole universe changed.
>
> That is the power of such as we are. If we only access it. It isn't easy. It flies in the face of all our human programming and all the emotional vectoring we live under. But the bottom line is: you cannot be unequally yoked. If you are, the effect is that of two mules harnessed ass to ass, pulling in opposite directions – spiritually, karmically, and even literally. Your life, your environment, your experiences reflect the state of your soul. Poverty, illness, instability, and so on. **All are reflections of what is being done to you spiritually *by your choices*. And your choices are being manipulated and influenced by early damage, which was done for the very purpose of [making you food.] That's the bottom line.**
>
> But again, what I am saying is something that has to be tested. There is no proof. I had no proof, just the small clues – all of which I was clever enough to explain away for many years; most of which explanations had to do with the idea that I could do more, I could try this; I could cut off another arm or open my figurative veins and give more of my blood to fix it, so to speak.

Well, I finally stopped making excuses. I stopped blaming myself for anything except that I had made the wrong choice and now I needed to make a different one – a *life* changing choice based on clues that were so subtle I couldn't even explain them to anyone.

Well, that isn't true. My friend Sandra gave me a gift. She told me that I must make a list of the clues. I must never forget them. When I felt weak, when I felt like I wanted to go back, when I started to forget why I was doing what I was doing, I should take out my list and remember all the horror, all the pain, all the suffering and that I should remind myself over and over again until it sank in that all of this was the biggest part of my marriage and my life. The little happiness or good time was few and far between and never sufficient to balance the negative.

So, I hope this helps. As the Cs once told us: if you have the courage of a lion, you don't have the fate of a mouse.

This poor woman truly made my heart bleed. And, it seemed that, perhaps, my words had helped her. She wrote back:

Thank you. I don't want the fate of the mouse. There is a lion somewhere in the back of the cave, it has been sleeping for many years.

The next day, she wrote again:

I woke up the lion this morning, and what you described is in full process. I don't need to give you a picture. Perhaps the difference is that we have been together 33 years, and there is a very strong bond between us. However it is like an umbilical cord that has to be cut for further growth to happen, and he cannot see it. For once I am being totally selfish, and my only pain is to see the pain he is undergoing. Thank you for giving me the impetus to go through with this.

Her description of her view of the process told me that she didn't really get it. She was still living in the myth. She was already excusing the difficulty of the situation by the length of time together. Then, she described the connection in nurturing terms as an umbilical cord, instead of what it was: a fourth-density STS feeding tube. And, finally, she described her actions as totally selfish, resulting in pain from seeing what he was going through. She just simply didn't realize that both of them were experiencing withdrawal, and that it was purely physical and based on associations in the amygdala. She didn't get that, in the deepest of terms, what she was doing was as much for him as it was for herself. He was as much an addict as she was.

Well, a couple of days went by and I was inclined to think that she was not going to make it, but I was leaving it open as a possibility. She finally wrote back:

For 36 hours I created hell for myself and everybody around me (my husband) and within telephone reach. By that time I was so exhausted I forgot the reason I wanted to leave and went to bed, as did my husband, and we both slept a long, long time. We have reached a new understanding and to my surprise he respects my courage and realizes he must take me more seriously than in the past. He is now being supportive of my goals, and the constant tension and resentment between us has dissolved.

This was not a surprise. And, it should not have been a surprise to her, either. I am sure that she went through a minor version of this scenario with every fight and argument they had over the years, all ending in agreement to continue the addiction. And, we also see an example of what I already described: an addiction to the whole reward system of fighting and making up. People are programmed to suffer because it feels so good when it's over. It is almost a deliberate creation of risk so that the rush of dopamine can come when the danger has passed.

Now, the most interesting thing is that it was clearly not apparent to this woman that her very life and relationships had also programmed her children to the same behavior, i.e. manipulation and addiction. The programs kicked in big time:

> The next day I called back my daughter who was sleeping off a drunk from not being able to bear the thought of her mom and dad separating. Then I called her brother who likewise had a bad hangover for the same reason, and was mighty relieved to hear I had changed my mind. Then I called my other son who was happy he didn't have to come pick me up with my considerable belongings. Then I emailed several friends to whom I had announced the sad news. By then I was tired again, but calm.

And here is the program:

> The point is that I discovered I am part of a family network, not just a solitary item responsible only to myself. I had never looked at it that way. Perhaps it's a combination of things: economic (I have literally no money of my own), the logistics of it all, and last but not least the fact that it tears me apart to give such pain to so many people. I seem to be divided into many selves all of which are a part of someone else. My strongest motive was perhaps the desire to find someone with whom I would feel more sexually/spiritually compatible. It is possible to achieve the former with my husband but not both together. ... Am I chickening out? ... Probably. But then is it all worth the upheaval? ... My husband now knows I am capable of what I never seriously threatened to do before, and he greatly respects my frankness. I was astonished at his reaction. I will tell you that he was my first husband/mate/whatever in my first life on this Earth, and we have been together for many, many lifetimes. I also know this is the last one, for we have taught each other all the lessons each needs to receive. I think my next life will be a more harmonious one, for in this one I have lived several lifetimes.

So, we see an enormous number of rationalizations coming together here. Will any of them change the situation? Not likely. For the moment, the control is in the hands of my correspondent; and perhaps this is what she was really looking for: a way to manipulate the situation herself. Perhaps this was a repeating dynamic on a lesser scale throughout their lives; I don't know.

And, in the end, it reminds me of certain remarks from the movie *The Matrix*:

> The Matrix is everywhere, it is all around us; even now in this very room. You can see it when you look out your window or when you turn on your television. You can feel it when you go to work; when you go to church; when you pay your taxes; it is the world that has been pulled over your eyes to blind you from the truth: that your are a slave. Like everyone else, you were born into bondage; born into a prison that you cannot smell or taste or touch; a prison for your mind.
>
> ... The Matrix is a system ... that system is our enemy.
>
> When you are inside [the Matrix] you look around; what do you see? Businessmen, teachers, lawyers, carpenters; the very minds of the people we are trying to save. But until we do, these people are still a part of that system and that makes them our enemy.

You have to understand: most of these people are not ready to be unplugged; and many of them are so inured, so hopelessly dependent on the system, that they will fight to protect it.

... We never free a mind once it's reached a certain age – it's dangerous – the mind has trouble letting go.

Now, even though the movie is an allegory that portrays the Matrix as a computer program, there are many things about this that can be highly instructive. For example, when Neo is being introduced to the Matrix, he touches a chair and asks, "This isn't real?" Morpheus replies:

What is real? How do you define real? If you are talking about what you can feel, what you can smell and taste and see; real is simply electrical signals interpreted by your brain. ... [the Matrix reality] is a neural interactive simulation ... a dream world created in order to change a human being into ...

And, I insert in place of the battery that Morpheus holds up, *food*.

Let me quote it one more time: the Matrix is *a neural interactive simulation.*

It is in this way that we are programmed to engage in damaging behavior via the Control System. If our chemicals are stimulated while we are being led down the primrose path in any of a number of situations, the brain will set a circuit to repeat this behavior in order to feel the pleasure chemicals released at the end of the behavior, regardless of the painful process by which the chemicals are ultimately obtained.

Now, let's go back to synthetic ligands: drugs, to see if we can glean any more clues.

When cocaine is snorted up the nose, it heads straight for the dopamine reuptake sites and blocks them. The feel good sensation is not, however, from the drug; but from the fact that dopamine is flooding your cells, binding with the dopamine receptors like crazy, unable to be reabsorbed. And the brain only knows one thing: this feels great! Crack cocaine reportedly produces a more intense sensation of pleasure than any natural act, including orgasm. And, take note that it is from the body's own chemical that this pleasure is experienced!

Morphine and heroin work in a slightly different way. They mimic endorphins, which trigger the release of dopamine. So, instead of the sensation occurring because the natural flow of dopamine is not reabsorbed, it occurs because there is too much dopamine to be absorbed.

But, there is something very curious about this: it seems that with repeated use of cocaine, heroin or morphine, the fake endorphin that binds with the opiate receptor and sends a signal into the cell body to release more dopamine, the body reacts by reducing the number of receptors. With fewer receptors, the effects of the drug – as well as the body's normal ability to bind dopamine that is naturally present – plummets. And, without the normal flow of dopamine into a normal number of receptors, the brain experiences withdrawal, which is interpreted quite literally as pain. It is the agony of a mind that can feel no pleasure at all. Clinicians describe it as:

> Abrupt discontinuation of cocaine, heroin or morphine leads to a state of dopamine depletion, which can cause the intense depression and agitation experienced during the crash phase as well as the subsequent anhedonia, dysphoria, lethargy, somnolence and apathy that can be present for six to eighteen weeks after discontinuation of cocaine. (Daly & Salloway 1994)

But, more serious than that is the fact that dopamine plays an important role in controlling movement, emotion and cognition. Dopamine dysfunction has been implicated in schizophrenia, mood disorders, attention-deficit disorder, Tourette's syndrome, substance dependency, tardive dyskinesia, Parkinson's disease and so on. Of course, the situation is a lot more complex because at least seven types of dopamine receptors have been identified.

The dopamine cells of the hypothalamus project to the anterior pituitary. In this area, dopamine acts directly to inhibit the release of prolactin. Prolactin possesses a myriad of effects with the most noticeable being lactation.

Now, going back to our programs and body chemicals, we begin to see how it is possible that anything which causes more dopamine to be released into the system will very likely manifest the same result as cocaine, heroin and morphine: we will go back to the behavior over and over again because the imprint of the way that pleasure is to be achieved has been set in the mind of the child.

Now, I have not been able to find any studies which suggest that the more dopamine secretion a person experiences from the body's own chemicals in the normal way, that the number of receptors diminishes. However, the very fact that the high of cocaine is the body's own chemical might suggest that this is so. This means that each time a person succeeds in some way in attaining that feel good moment – no matter how it is achieved – the more will be required to experience that same level of feeling again. This may be why love states will so rapidly diminish and turn into battles to produce threat of loss so that it can be averted and thereby produce the rush of dopamine. That is to say: the more that is experienced, the less it can be experienced; so it becomes a physiological and psychological carrot on a stick.

But, even in such situations, the point arrives when the body simply can no longer meet the demand and nothing works anymore. How soon this point is reached depends on many factors, and I am sure the reader can think of any number of situations of their acquaintance that will demonstrate the great variety of ways these scenarios can play out.

Another feel good body chemical is serotonin. The antidepressants, Prozac and Zoloft, block serotonin re-uptake sites causing the brain and body to be flooded with serotonin. People are happy because serotonin is lighting up the "do it again" center like a Hollywood Marquee.

In the early 1980s, clinical investigators discovered a link between serotonin and eating disorders. Richard and Judith Wurtman (Massachusetts Institute of Technology) had already implicated serotonin in eating disturbances. They theorized that dietary starch is converted to sugar, sugar stimulates the pancreas to release insulin, insulin raises brain levels of the amino acid tryptophan, tryptophan is a precursor of serotonin, and serotonin regulates mood, producing a sense of well-being. Therefore, obese people load up on carbohydrates to elevate mood.

According to the National Institue of Diabetes and Digestive and Kidney Diseases, 68% of adult Americans are overweight.[7] Those who are trying to lose weight have a good reason: obesity is severely stigmatized in our society. The health hazards of being moderately overweight are exaggerated (excess mortality is not seen until body weight is more than 40% above tabulated weights on life insurance tables), but it is a definite social no–no to be fat.

Anorexia nervosa and bulimia nervosa are psychiatric syndromes whose underlying pathology has been described as the relentless pursuit of thinness. The two diseases are separate entities, although there is considerable overlap; about 50% of anorectics binge and purge. Both diseases occur primarily in adolescence and young adulthood, they run a long and protracted course, and they interfere with normal development such as social maturation, separation from family of origin, and career decisions.

Anorexia has been described in psychiatric literature for more than a century, but bulimia has only been recognized as a clinical entity in the last 16 years. Patients are challenging and difficult to treat. Indeed, it seems that to be effective, any treatment must ultimately produce thinness. In other words, if a bulimic could achieve thinness without having to vomit, then that patient would be cured of bulimia. If an anorectic can get slim without having to starve, that patient could be cured of starvation.

The typical patient with anorexia nervosa or bulimia nervosa is female, young, single, and of middle-to-upper socioeconomic status and has previously shown a tendency to obesity. Depressive and obsessional symptoms are common, as are a strong family history of affective disorder. Depression is sometimes attributed to the starvation, which can produce the same psychological profile as that seen in mild to moderate major depression. However, true major depression (either before or after the emaciation) is far more prevalent in anorectic patients than in the general population. Although anorexia and bulimia are more often seen in females, both disorders also occur in males. Sharp et al. described the clinical features of 24 men with anorexia nervosa.

---

[7] Source: CDC/NCHS, Health, United States, 2008, Figure 7. Data from the National Health and Nutrition Examination Survey. (http://www.win.niddk.nih.gov/statistics/ index.htm#overweight)

Bingeing and vomiting were common (50%, the same as in females). Also remarkably common were depressed mood, early wakening, obsessional symptoms, and a family history of affective disorders and alcohol abuse. Age at onset (18.6 years) and at presentation (20.2 years) was older than in females. The men were mostly single and of higher socioeconomic status and had a premorbid tendency towards obesity. Laxative abuse was less frequent in males than has been reported in females, and excessive exercising was more frequent. (Sharp et al. 1994)

And, as it turns out, increasing the serotonin bath in the brain by administering serotonin reuptake inhibitors seems to help in controlling symptoms of bulimia. Increasing the serotonin in the brain also seems to produce improvement in depression, carbohydrate craving, and pathological eating habits. The only problem with this is that these reuptake inhibitors have been seriously implicated in both valvular heart problems and primary pulmonary hypertension.

Prozac is a serotonin reuptake inhibitor that produces many side effects, including: nausea, headache, nervousness, insomnia, drowsiness, diarrhea, weight loss, dizziness, and anxiety. It also causes a side effect that we need to think about for a moment after learning what we have about the reduction of dopamine receptors with repeated use of drugs. You see, one of the side effects of Prozac is an inability to have an orgasm.

The street drug "ecstasy" is the common name for MethyleneDioxyMethAmphetamine, or MDMA. Ecstasy is a central nervous system stimulant and it is thought to work by boosting the levels of serotonin and dopamine.

Immediate effects of ecstasy can include increased feelings of self confidence, well-being, and feeling close to others; a rise in blood pressure, body temperature and pulse rate, jaw clenching, teeth grinding, sweating, dehydration, nausea and anxiety. Higher doses of ecstasy can produce hallucinations, irrational behavior, vomiting and convulsions.

Now, since we already know that using such drugs reduces our dopamine and possibly our serotonin receptors, it's not surprising that ecstasy also produces tolerance.

Ecstasy is known as the love drug and commonly makes users feel warm and loving, even towards people they may not know well. Ecstasy can also heighten sexual desire and intensify the sexual experience, as well as decreasing inhibition. Lab results with animals have suggested possibilities of long-term brain damage arising from the reduction of serotonin and dopamine receptors and the ultimate failure of the brain to produce serotonin at all.

So, in a roundabout way, we have come to the fact that our addictions to our own chemicals may ultimately lead to permanent inability to feel any pleasure at all. And we all know that as we age our ability to be amused by simple things diminishes.

I am torn between being shocked and amused by the spate of recent commercials for sexual stimulants that promise to "revive the love nature." I think the funniest one is promoting a product called "Top Gun." But the problem it suggests is not very amusing. It seems that in our sexually permissive society, where for the past 20 or 30 years everyone has been encouraged to claim their natural right with more orgasms, better orgasms, extended, multiple and repeaters, and so on may be at the source of the present problem with achieving any orgasm at all for so many people.

The bottom line seems to be: if it feels good, you will want to do it again and again and more and better. And if you do you will be less and less able to do it at all; and in the end the imbalances will lead to more pain and suffering and feelings of inadequacy. And we know what all that is: lunch!

Now, nicotine is a most interesting drug. Nicotine mimics one of the body's most significant neurotransmitters, acetylcholine. This is the neurotransmitter most often associated with cognition in the cerebral cortex. Acetylcholine is the primary carrier of thought and memory in the brain. It is essential to have appropriate levels of acetylcholine to have new memories or recall old memories.

Now, let's go off to the side here for a moment. I cruised the net for sources on acetylcholine and the results were positively amazing, as you will see from the following excerpts:

> Acetyl–L–Carnitine (ALC) is the acetyl ester of carnitine, the carrier of fatty acids across Mitochondrial membranes. Like carnitine, ALC is naturally produced in the body and found in small amounts in some foods. … Research in recent years has hoisted ALC from its somewhat mundane role in energy production to nutritional cognitive enhancer and neuroprotective agent extraordinaire. Indeed, taken in its entirety, ALC has become one of the premiere "anti-aging" compounds under scientific investigation, especially in relation to brain and nervous system deterioration.
>
> ALC is found in various concentrations in the brain, and its levels are significantly reduced with aging. In numerous studies in animal models, ALC administration has been shown to have the remarkable ability of improving not only cognitive changes, but also morphological (structural) and neurochemical changes. … ALC has varied effects on cholinergic activity, *including promoting the release and synthesis of acetylcholine.* Additionally, ALC promotes high affinity uptake of choline, which declines significantly with age. While these cholinergic effects were first described almost a quarter of a century ago, it now appears that this is only the tip of the ALC iceberg. (Gissen 1995)

It turns out that Alzheimer's, a veritable epidemic in our country, is directly related to low levels of acetylcholine. In Alzheimer's disease, the neurons that make acetylcholine degenerate, resulting in memory deficits. In some Alzheimer's patients it can be a 90 per cent reduction! But, does anyone suggest smoking and exercising the brain as a possible cure? Nope.

Another interesting little snippet found in a doctoral dissertation by Galen Knight says:

> Thyrotropin is the single most important modulator of thyroid function. However, several of its effects are mimicked by neurotransmitters, acetylcholine and catecholamines ... [8]

Which suggests to us that low thyroid function can be partly ameliorated by nicotine as the Cassiopaeans have already stated in so many words.

The next excerpt is the most interesting. It is a from a Bioelectromagnetics Research Laboratory paper, first presented at a workshop to discuss possible biological and health effects of Radio Frequency Electromagnetic waves. The workshop was held by the Department of Bioengineering at the University of Washington, Seattle. The paper was later presented to "Mobile Phones and Health, Symposium," October 25–28, 1998, University of Vienna, Austria. What they are talking about here is the effects of cell phone towers and the use of cell phones and pagers, etc:

> We carried out a series of experiments to investigate the effect of RFR exposure on neurotransmitters in the brain of the rat. The main neurotransmitter we investigated was acetylcholine, a ubiquitous chemical in the brain involved in numerous physiological and behavioral functions.
>
> We found that exposure to RFR for 45 min decreased the activity of acetylcholine in various regions of the brain of the rat, particularly in the frontal cortex and hippocampus. Further study showed that the response depends on the duration of exposure. Shorter exposure time (20 min) actually increased, rather than decreasing the activity. Different brain areas have different sensitivities to RFR with respect to cholinergic responses [Lai et al., 1987b, 1988b, 1989a,b].
>
> In addition, repeated exposure can lead to some rather long lasting changes in the system: the number of acetylcholine receptors increase or decrease after repeated exposure to RFR to 45 min and 20 min sessions, respectively [Lai et al., 1989a].
>
> Changes in acetylcholine receptors are generally considered to be a compensatory response to repeated disturbance of acetylcholine activity in the brain. Such changes alter the response characteristic of the nervous system. Other studies have shown that endogenous opioids are also involved in the effect of RFR on acetylcholine [Lai et al., 1986b, 1991, 1992b, 1996.]
>
> Since acetylcholine in the frontal cortex and hippocampus is involved in learning and memory functions, we carried out experiments to study whether exposure to RFR affects these behavioral functions in the rat. Two types of memory functions: spatial "working" and "reference" memories were investigated.
>
> Acetylcholine in the brain, especially in the hippocampus, is known to play an important role in these behavioral functions. In the first experiment, "working" memory (short-term memory) was studied using the radial arm maze. This test is very easy to understand. Just imagine you are shopping in a grocery store with a list of items to

---

[8] http://www.highfiber.com/%7Egalenvtp/disrtatn.htm

buy in your mind. After picking up the items, at the check out stand, you find that there is one chicken at the top and another one at the bottom of your shopping cart. You had forgotten that you had already picked up a chicken at the beginning of your shopping spree and picked up another one later. This is a failure in short-term memory and is actually very common in daily life and generally not considered as being pathological. A distraction or a lapse in attention can affect short-term memory.

This analogy is similar to the task in the radial arm maze experiment. The maze consists of a circular center hub with arms radiating out like the spokes of a wheel. Rats are allowed to pick up food pellets at the end of each arm of the maze. There are 12 arms in our maze, and each rat in each testing session is allowed to make 12 arm entries. *Re-entering an arm is considered to be a memory deficit. The results of our experiment showed that after exposure to RFR, rats made significantly more arm re-entries than unexposed rats.* [Lai et al., 1994.]

This is like finding two chickens, three boxes of table salt, and two bags of potatoes in your shopping cart.

In another experiment, we studied the effect of RFR exposure on reference memory (long-term memory) [Wang and Lai, submitted for publication]. Performance in a water maze was investigated. In this test, a rat is required to locate a submerged platform in a circular water pool. It is released into the pool, and the time taken for it to land on the platform is recorded. Rats were trained in several sessions to learn the location of the platform. The learning rate of RFR-exposed rats was slower, but, after several learning trials, they finally caught up with the control (unexposed) rats. However, the story did not end here. After the rats had learned to locate the platform, in a last session, the platform was removed and rats were released one at a time into the pool. We observed that unexposed rats, after being released into the pool, would swim around circling the area where the platform was once located, whereas RFR-exposed rats showed more random swimming patterns.

To understand this, let us consider another analogy. If I am going to sail from the west coast of the United States to Australia, I can learn to read a map and use instruments to locate my position, in latitude and longitude, etc. However, there is an apparently easier way: just keep sailing southwest. But, imagine, if I sailed and missed Australia. In the first case, if I had sailed using maps and instruments, I would keep on sailing in the area that I thought where Australia would be located hoping that I would see land. On the other hand, if I sailed by the strategy of keeping going southwest, and missed Australia, I would not know what to do. Very soon, I would find myself circumnavigating the globe.

Thus, it seems that *unexposed rats learned to locate the platform using cues in the environment* (like using a map from memory), whereas RFR-exposed rats used a different strategy (perhaps, something called 'praxis learning', i.e., learning of a certain sequence of movements in the environment to reach a certain location. It is less flexible and does not involve cholinergic systems in the brain).

Thus, RFR exposure can completely alter the behavioral strategy of an animal in finding its way in the environment.

… What is significant is that the effects persist for sometime after RFR exposure. If I am reading a book and receive a call from a mobile phone, it probably will not matter if I cannot remember what I had just read. However, the consequence would be much serious, if I am an airplane technician responsible for putting screws and nuts on airplane parts. A phone call in the middle of my work can make me forget and miss several screws. Another adverse scenario of short-term memory deficit is that a person may overdose himself on medication because he has forgotten that he has already taken the medicine.

Lastly, I like to briefly describe the experiments we carried out to investigate the effects of RFR on DNA in brain cells of the rat. We [Lai and Singh 1995, 1996; Lai et al., 1997] reported *an increase in DNA single and double strand breaks, two forms of DNA damage, in brain cells of rats after exposure to RFR*. DNA damages in cells could have an important implication on health because *they are cumulative*. Normally, DNA is capable of repairing itself efficiently. Through a homeostatic mechanism, cells maintain a delicate balance between spontaneous and induced DNA damage. DNA damage accumulates if such a balance is altered. Most cells have considerable ability to repair DNA strand breaks; for example, some cells can repair as many as 200,000 breaks in one hour. However, *nerve cells have a low capability for DNA repair and DNA breaks could accumulate. Thus, the effect of RFR on DNA could conceivably be more significant on nerve cells than on other cell types of the body.*

Cumulative damages in DNA may in turn affect cell functions. DNA damage that accumulates in cells over a period of time may be the cause of slow onset diseases, such as cancer. ... Cumulative damage in DNA in cells also has been shown during aging. Particularly, cumulative DNA damage in nerve cells of the brain has been associated with neurodegenerative diseases, such as Alzheimer's, Huntington's, and Parkinson's diseases.

Since nerve cells do not divide and are not likely to become cancerous, more likely consequences of DNA damage in nerve cells are changes in functions and cell death, which could either lead to or accelerate the development of neurodegenerative diseases. *Double strand breaks, if not properly repaired, are known to lead to cell death. Indeed, we have observed an increase in apoptosis (a form of cell death) in cells exposed to RFR* (unpublished results).

However, another type of brain cells, the glial cells, can become cancerous, resulting from DNA damage. This type of response, i.e., *genotoxicity at low and medium cumulative doses and cell death at higher doses*, would lead to an inverted-U response function in cancer development and may explain recent reports of increase [Repacholi et al., 1997], decrease [Adey et al., 1996], and no significant effect [Adey et al., 1997] on cancer rate of animals exposed to RFR.

Understandably, it is very difficult to define and judge what constitute low, medium, and high cumulative doses of RFR exposure, since the conditions of exposure are so variable and complex in real life situations.

Interestingly, RFR-induced increases in single and double strand DNA breaks in rat brain cells can be blocked by treating the rats with melatonin ... [Lai and Singh, 1997]. Since it is a potent, free radical scavenger, this data suggest that free radicals may play a role in the genetic effect of RFR. [Lai and Singh, 1998].[9]

---

[9] http://www.tassie.net.au/emfacts/henrylai.html

Well, isn't that just fine and dandy!

What did the Cassiopaeans have to say about the use of cell phones and cell–phone towers?

August 15, 1998

Q: (L) Can you give me an approximate number of aliens currently interacting with, or on, or under our planet as a whole?

A: "Aliens?" What constitutes such?

Q: (L) Okay. Well then, non-human beings. Extra-terrestrials, ultra-terrestrials, and so forth.

A: These bases have naturalized the inhabitants. Anomalies occur as much because of where the bases are chosen to be located as any other factor. Magnetic faults and their inherent portals, you know!

Q: (L) This [source on the Internet] thinks that there is a rather limited number of aliens, and that people ought to get together and resist this threat because our numbers are greater. Is that, in fact, correct?

A: Not point. The question of the hour is: what is the motive? Build a house step by step, and when it is finished, you can move into the neighborhood and out of the motel.

Q: (L) Oh jeez. So, these are a bunch of aliens hanging out in motels waiting for their house to be built. That does not sound good.

A: Many of you have recently become "bedazzled" by the "information superhighway," and its accompanying computer hardware. Gee, we wonder why?

Q: (L) Well, you told us to network. We have been networking like crazy, digging up information, reading and comparing. Yes, there is a ton of garbage out there, but if we don't ask, how will we know?

A: Point was: who is manipulating thee? Not so much you specifically, but the others? So many kids and kids-at-heart are thunderstruck by techno-sensory toys. Those cellular phones, those pagers and the Christmas toy computers … they are like, so cool!

Q: (L) So what are you implying about these techno toys?

A: Ponder.

Q: (L) Give me a clue.

A: Fuzzy jello-brained kids.

Q: (L) Are you saying that pagers and cell phones, and techno toys that kids get for Christmas can have effects on them that turn their brains to jello?

A: In a figurative sense. All this technology represents a Brave New World. Like Huxley said: Woe is to those who have been led to eat their brains for lunch.

Q: (L) My kids have pagers. Are pagers, in particular …

A: What do you think comprises the signal content?

Q: (L) I don't know. What does comprise the signal content?

A: Microwaves.

Q: (L) What do these microwaves do to the individual?

A: Contour brain cell structure.

Q: (L) Do they emit a signal continuously, or only when they are being used?

A: Wave cycle low to high.

Q: (L) Well, that's not good. How close does the pager have to be to you to have this effect?

A: Four meters. Cell phones too and television and computer screens can be transmitted through thusly.

Q: (L) When you say "contouring brain cell structure," what would be evidence or results of such effects?

A: Increasingly narrow outlooks and being unable to employ discriminatory thinking.

Q: (L) Confusion?

A: No. Just lack of depth and breadth to one's mental and psychic abilities.

Q: (A) Now, about pagers ... we were told that pagers emit some radiation, which can be detrimental up to a distance of four meters. As far as I understand a pager is a passive device, a receiver. It is not emitting anything. How can a pager be detrimental?

A: Microwave "bounce effect."

Q: (A) So, they bounce from the receiver ... I see.

A: Cell phones too.

Q: (L) Is there any kind of device that we can build or purchase that can emit a blocking signal?

A: Knowledge protects.

And it is here and now that we are learning how true that statement is in just about every sense of the word! So, let's get on with it.

Work in the Laboratory of Neurochemistry at the Barrow Neurological Institute principally concerns molecules critically involved in such signaling called nicotinic acetylcholine receptors (nAChR). nAChR act throughout the brain and body as molecular switches to connect nerve cell circuits involved in essential functions ranging from vision and memory to the control of heart rate and muscle movement.

Defects in nAChR or their loss cause diseases such as myasthenia gravis and epilepsy and can contribute to Alzheimer's and Parkinson's diseases and schizophrenia.

nAChR also happen to be the principal targets of tobacco nicotine. ... Nicotine-like medicines show promise in the treatment of diseases such as attention deficit/hyperactivity disorder (ADHD) and Tourette's syndrome and in alleviation of anxiety, pain, and depression, suggesting involvement of nAChR in those disorders.

... We have shown that numbers and function of diverse nAChR subtypes can be influenced by many biologically active substances, ranging from steroids to local anesthetics, and by agents acting on the extracellular matrix, the cytoskeleton, on second messenger signaling, and at the nucleus. We also have shown that chronic *nicotine exposure induces numerical upregulation of many diverse nAChR subtypes via a post-transcriptional process that is dominated by effects on intracellular pools of receptors or their precursors.*

Some current studies are testing our hypothesis that chronic nicotine exposure, as occurs with habitual use of tobacco products, disables nAChR and the nerve cell circuits they subserve, thereby contributing to long-lasting changes in brain and body function. [Lukas, 1999.][10]

Now, notice in the above account how tricky they were when they said that "*nicotine exposure induces numerical upregulation of many diverse nAChR subtypes via a post-*

---

[10] http://www.thebni.com/learningcenter/research/neurobiology/nachr.asp

transcriptional process that is dominated by effects on intracellular pools of receptors or their precursors." That is jargon for "it increases the number of receptors" as well as the amount of acetylcholine. But, of course, the AMA wouldn't let them get away with any of their work if they weren't adding that they have a hypothesis that "habitual use of tobacco products ... disables acetylcholine." Never mind that in the beginning they are proposing it as a therapeutic drug for some of the very problems that have risen to almost epidemic numbers in the present time.

Let's say it again: research shows, however, that daily infusions of nicotine actually *increase* the number of acetylcholine receptors by up to 40%. Some researchers, such as the above, brush this finding off by saying "regardless, their function diminishes." But that is not empirically observed. Most people who smoke find a set point, and once they have reached this, it does not take more and more and more to satisfy it.

How does nicotine act?

There are two major types (or classes) of acetylcholine receptors in the body, and they are commonly named by the other drugs which bind to them: nicotine and muscarine. Muscarinic acetylcholine receptors (mAChRs) can bind muscarine as well as ACh, and they function to change the metabolism ...

Acetylcholine acts on nicotine acetylcholine receptors to open a channel in the cell's membrane. Opening such a channel allows certain types of ions (charged atoms) to flow into or out of the cell. ... When ions flow, there is an electrical current, and the same is true in the nervous system. The flowing of ions, or the passing of current, can cause other things to happen, usually those things involve the opening of other types of channels and the passing of information from one neuron to another.

Nicotinic AChRs are found throughout the body, but they are most concentrated in the nervous system (the brain, the spinal cord, and the rest of the nerve cells in the body) and on the muscles of the body (in vertebrates).

We say that nicotine acts like ACh at the receptors to activate them, and both substances are called agonists. The opposite type of drug, something that binds to the receptors and does not allow them to be activated is called an antagonist.

... When a substance comes into the body that can interfere with ACh binding to muscle nAChRs, that chemical can cause death in a relatively short time (because you use muscles to do things like breathe). A class of chemicals in snake and other poisonous venoms, neurotoxins, do exactly that. If you are bitten by a krait or a cobra, for example, and enough venom gets into the blood, there will be enough of their neurotoxin in your body to shut down the diaphragm muscle that expands your lungs. Without that muscle functioning, the person ceases to breathe and dies of asphyxiation.

One of the reasons we know so much about these receptors is precisely that – plants and people have used substances [acetylcholine antagonists] that cause paralysis and asphyxiation for a long time. Plants use them to prevent being eaten by herbivores. Animals use similar substances to paralyze their prey. At least one human neuromuscular disease is related to nAChRs, and that is myasthenia gravis ...

So, as you can see, nAChRs are important to life. … All known nicotinic receptors do share some common features. They are composed of *5 protein subunits* which assemble like barrel staves around a central pore. … When the ligand (ACh or nicotine) binds to the receptor, it causes the receptor complex to twist and open the pore in the center. [Pugh.][11]

Now, aside from noting that acetylcholine has our magic number 5, did you notice that it says, "animals use similar substances [acetylcholine antagonists] to paralyze their prey?" We have to wonder about the oft-reported conditions of paralysis associated with alien interactions. Keep acetylcholine in mind because we will be coming back to it repeatedly!

Now, let's go back to alcohol. Alcohol is a great pretender and can fool at least four types of receptors. It *blocks the acetylcholine receptors*. However, unlike nicotine, which also binds to the acetylcholine receptors, alcohol doesn't do anything useful while it is there. It simply sits there and blocks the ability to think. It also acts like cocaine in that it blocks the dopamine reuptake, flooding the brain with "feeling good." Alcohol stimulates the release of endorphins, thus resembling morphine and heroin to a greatly lessened extent, and it modifies and increases the efficiency of the serotonin receptors.

All of that in one brew. It almost makes you want to go and have a few beers!

And, if you could just have a few once in awhile, or a glass of wine with dinner or a single cocktail in the evening, it would not be as damaging. But for some people, it doesn't work that way with alcohol.

Generally mammals – from monkeys to dogs and cats – avoid alcohol. If you give them a choice, they will drink water instead. In some human beings, there is a genetic variation that results in decreased desire for alcohol. Scientists, however, have managed to breed rats with a taste for liquor. Rats that like to drink also, interestingly, produce abnormally low amounts of serotonin. And, recent research has indicated that human beings who are alcoholic have fewer dopamine receptors genetically. A large percentage of smokers also have an unusual copy of a gene called D2, which causes their bodies to make about a third fewer dopamine receptors. They get their buzz from acetylcholine.

Just saying no to drugs clearly is not going to work, considering our understanding of how they operate in our bodies. And, more importantly, we have to think about the fact that these drugs only work because they imitate natural substances that produce the same states of mind. That emotions or feelings can be so easily imitated chemically should give us pause when we say "I feel it". Do you really feel it? Or is the feeling being stimulated in you by some signal from your environment. And what kind of signal, how it was programmed, and where it might come from are open to all possibilities.

---

[11] http://www.geocities.com/CapeCanaveral/2257/nicaction.html

Our inability to control our emotions is as difficult as saying no to drugs. And it lies not in personality defects, but in the sheer strength of the physiology – the Predator's mind. The golfer, John Daly, was willing to pay three million dollars for a drink. A crack addict who had been arrested 31 times, who had been subjected to repeated fines and imprisonment, said, "Once that compulsion is there, it doesn't matter what the penalty or threat is."

Subtle differences in the way our brain is wired make us more or less susceptible to chemical manipulation. Most of us don't go to the extremes of paying three million dollars for a drink, nor are we willing to risk prison for drugs, but our inner cravings for the fix of emotions leave us helplessly at their mercy.

Because our internal chemicals are used to stimulate the genetic pleasure pathway, the battle we fight is within. When our neurons experience the euphoria of a dopamine bath, our brain is in heaven. Never mind that whatever it is we are doing will lead to disaster or, at the very least, another day of heartbreak and misery in a miserable relationship; or a faith that takes our money, gives us promises, and leaves us unable to cope with real life, we come back for more.

How can we stop the behaviors that provide our brain's highest reward?

Neuroscientist, Dr. Joseph LeDoux, professor of Science at New York University Center for Neuroscience, has examined the way the brain shapes our experiences and our memories. His studies have unraveled the workings of emotions in general. He discovered that many neural pathways bypass the higher thinking parts of the brain.

The brain mechanisms that generate a given mental state, or what we choose, for the sake of convenience to call emotion, also give rise to certain measurable physiological states, such as pulse rates or brain waves, as well as observable behaviors such as running away or smiling. Feelings, by contrast, are a conscious, subjective labeling of the individual's state. One person may say, "I feel excited," and another may say, "I feel afraid," and *both will exhibit the same physiological symptoms and characteristic brain waves.* So, trying to work backward is problematical. Dr. LeDoux writes:

> … [F]ear is pervasive. … fear is a good emotion to study [because] it's at the root of many psychiatric problems. The so-called anxiety disorders – panic attacks, obsessive-compulsive disorder, post-traumatic stress disorder – make up about half of all the psychiatric conditions that are treated every year, not including substance-abuse problems. …
>
> … [T]he brain system that generates fear behavior evolved to help animals stay alive and has been preserved for millions of years, across a variety of species. The way that we act when we're afraid – the way the body responds – is very similar to the way that other animals act when they're afraid, even though we aren't reacting to the same things. A rat would never be sent into a panic attack by the news that the stock market had crashed, and a human is not, ordinarily, afraid of a cat. But the way our body

responds to the news of a stock market crash is very similar to the way the rat's body responds when it encounters a cat. This is critically important, because it means that we can study the behavior of other animals, and the processes in their brains, to learn how the human fear system works.

... [We study fear with behavior tools] techniques and methods for studying such specific behavior ... and we also need good neuroscience tools, method that allow us to study what is going on in the brain when the animal is behaving in a fearful way.

One important behavior tool is known as classical fear conditioning, which is a version of what Pavlov described as the conditioned reflex. The process of classical conditioning involves pairing, or associating, an innocuous stimulus – a sound or a flash of light, something that is essentially meaningless in itself – with something that is meaningful to the animal. In the case of Pavlov's dogs, the meaningful stimulus was food; the meaningless stimulus was the bell. Food is not a useful stimulus if we're interested in studying fear, however. So, using laboratory rats as subjects, we might pair a sound with, for instance, a mild foot shock. (We keep the shock as weak as possible to allow the experiments to be performed, and we administer it as infrequently as is feasible.) (LeDoux 1999, 126–127)

I don't know about the reader, but I don't believe this last remark for one minute. Not after reading about Candace Pert decapitating orgasmic guinea pigs. But, even if we are repelled by what they are doing, we need to realize that this is the knowledge that the other side has and *uses*; and the only way we are going to deal with our situation on this planet is to learn what they know. Meanwhile, back to Dr. LeDoux:

On the basis of these kinds of pairings, the sound becomes something that the rat learns is associated with danger. Thus when the rat hears the sound, it reacts immediately: It freezes in anticipation of danger. This is a conditioned reflex, as is Pavlov's dogs' salivating at the sound of the bell, in anticipation of food.

An animal in the wild usually doesn't have the luxury of trial and error in learning what's dangerous; it doesn't get to practice until it gets things right. If it's lucky enough to escape once, it had better remember the sight of the predator, the smell of the predator, the sound of the predator, and so forth. In the laboratory, we need to apply the shock with the sound only once if it is sufficiently aversive.

When something like this occurs – the sound that's been paired with the shock – it activates a variety of responses that are identical to those that would occur in a real-life situation. Television tapes of the bombing during the 1996 Olympic Games in Atlanta, for example, reveal that when the bomb went off the first thing that happened was that everyone flinched; this was the startle reflex. But then the next thing they did was freeze: they just hunkered down and held still for about two seconds. That's evolution buying us a little time ... predators respond to movement ... so we freeze when we're in a dangerous situation, because our old evolutionary fear system detects danger and responds to it in an automatic way.

... In a situation of danger, a variety of physiological responses occur. Blood is redistributed to the body parts that are most in need (the muscles). This results in changes in blood pressure and heart rate. In addition, the hypothalamic-pituitary-adrenal, or HPA, axis is activated, releasing stress hormones. In addition, the brain activates the release of natural opiate peptides, morphine-like substances that block the sensation of pain. Called hypoalgesia, this reaction is an evolutionary carryover that allows a wounded animal to keep going. It's often seen in wartime, where wounded soldiers don't react to their injuries until they're off the battlefield. All of these things happen in the rat when it perceives a natural threat such as cat, or when it hears the sound that's been paired with the shock. And all of these fear responses are easily measured.

In addition to behavioral tools, we also need the tools of neuro-science to understand how the brain's fear system works. ... One is called a brain lesion, a small hole made in brain tissue to interrupt the flow of information between neurons. (pp. 127–129)

Well, we knew it was coming. He went from "mild shocks" to poking holes in rats' brains. Next he is going to be decapitating them ...

By blocking the flow of information in a given pathway with a lesion, we can determine whether that pathway is involved in the behavior we're studying. That is, lesions in some areas will have no effect on the behavior, and lesions in other areas will interfere with the behavior, thus implicating that area. People with strokes or tumors have natural lesions, which typically are not very precisely localized. (p. 129)

And we are sure there are some folks who are certainly studying humans with precisely localized lesions – to use the jargon. Knowledge protects!

Considerable research has produced precise maps of the brain of the rat, and of many other animals as well. (p. 129)

No doubt. And I expect that some of those animals stand on two feet.

As a result, we can go into a specific region of the rat brain on the basis of three co-ordinates – left/right, up/down, and front/back – and make a lesion by releasing a small amount of current or injecting a chemical.

The brain maps are also useful when we want to measure the electrical activity of a particular region. Because communication between neurons is based on electrical activity, we can insert electrodes attached to amplifiers to record responses in a given area of the brain. ... If neuron A activates neuron B, neuron B will fire ... which tells us that neuron B is part of the brain circuitry involved in the behavior we're studying.

Finally, we can trace actual connections in the brain – determining whether area X sends its axons to Area Y or to Area Z – by tracking chemical activity. ... We inject a tracer substance into Area X ... The tracer is taken up by the neurons in the area injected, then hitches a ride on molecules that are being shipped down the axon. We can then stain or dye the brain to see where the substance appears next; the region will stain brightly enough so that we can see it under the microscope. This tells us which areas Area X talks to.

Once we have conditioned the animal to respond to a sound – or that the sound produces freezing behavior, changes in blood pressure, heart rate, and so forth – the next step is to trace how the sound, coming into the ear, reaches the parts of the brain that produce these responses in the body. The strategy is to make a lesion in a certain part of the brain to determine whether damage to that area interferes with the fear conditioning. If it does, we then inject the tracer substance there to see which areas that part of the brain communicates with. Then we systematically make lesions in each of those downstream areas to see which one interferes with the fear conditioning, inject tracer substance at that point, look to see where it goes, and so on. We can then record electrical activity to see how cells in the area respond. In this way, we can walk our way, point by point, through whatever pathway of the brain we want to study.

... Years of research by many workers have given us extensive knowledge of the neural pathways involved in processing acoustic information, which is an excellent starting point for examining the neurological foundations of fear. The natural flow of auditory information – the way you hear music, speech, or anything else – is that the sound comes into the ear, enters the brain, goes up to a region called the auditory midbrain, then to the auditory thalamus, and ultimately to the auditory cortex. Thus, in the auditory pathway, as in other sensory systems, *the cortex is the highest level of processing.*

... Does the sound have to go all the way to the auditory cortex in order for the rat to learn that the sound paired with the shock is dangerous? When we made lesions in the auditory cortex, we found that the animal could still make the associations between the sound and the shock, and would still react with fear ... since information from all our senses is processed in the cortex ... the fact that the cortex didn't seem to be necessary was both intriguing and mystifying. We wanted to understand how something as important as the emotion of fear could be mediated by the brain if it wasn't going into the cortex, where all the higher processes occur. So we next made lesions in the auditory thalamus, and then in the auditory midbrain. ... What we found was that lesions in either of these subcortical areas completely eliminated the rat's susceptibility to fear conditioning. If the lesions were made in an unconditioned rat, the animal could not learn to make the association between sound and shock, and if the lesions were made on a rat that had already been conditioned to fear the sound, it would no longer react to the sound.

But if the stimulus didn't have to reach the cortex, where was it going from the thalamus? Some other area or areas of the brain must receive information from the thalamus and establish memories about experiences that stimulate a fear response. To find out, we made a tracer injection in the auditory thalamus and found that some cells in this structure projected axons into the amygdala. This is key, because the amygdala has for many years been known to be important in emotional responses. So it appeared that information went to the amygdala from the thalamus without going to the neocortex.

We then did experiments with rats that had amygdala lesions ... we found that the amygdala lesion prevented conditioning from taking place. ...

So the amygdala is critical to this pathway. It receives information about the outside world directly from the thalamus, and immediately sets in motion a variety of bodily responses. We call this thalamo-amygdala pathway the low road because it's not taking advantage of all the higher-level information processing that occurs in the neocortex, which also communicates with the amygdala.

... say that a hiker is walking through the woods and sees something on the ground. The image gets to the thalamus, which sends a very crude template to the amygdala; the amygdala, in turn, activates the heart rate, gets the muscles tense and ready to go. At the same time, the stimulus is making its way through the cortex, which is slowly building up a complete representation of – a snake. Now, the thalamus doesn't know if it's a snake or just a stick that looks like a snake, but as far as the amygdala is concerned in this situation you're better off treating the stick as a snake than you are treating a snake as a stick. The subcortical brain is over generalizing for the opportunity to stay alive in the presence of the snake. By getting the amygdala going instantly, it buys you time. If the object turns out to be a stick instead of a snake, nothing's lost; you can turn the fight-or-flight system off. But if it turns out to be a snake, you're ahead of the game: you've activated the amygdala, and your body is ready to respond effectively.

The low road, or the thalamo-amygdala pathway, is a quick and dirty system. Because it doesn't involve the cortex at all, it allows us to act first and think later. Or, rather, it lets evolution do the thinking for us, at least at the beginning, buying us time.

The cortex – the high road – also processes the stimulus, but it takes a little longer. You need the cortex for high-level perception in order to distinguish one kind of music from another ... or to distinguish between two speech sounds. But you don't need the cortex to carry out some of the emotional learning involved in the fear system. Thus we can have emotional reactions to something without knowing what we're responding to – even as we start responding to it. In other words, we're dealing with the unconscious processing of emotion. This is a neurological demonstration of at least part of what Freud was trying to get at when he talked about the unconscious emotions.

... what we're saying is that unconscious emotions are probably the rule rather than the exception.

We all know that there are many times in normal, day-to-day experience when we don't understand where our emotions are coming from – why we feel happy, sad, afraid. For example, let's say you're in a restaurant having a meal with a friend and you have a terrible argument at the table, which happens to be covered with a red and white checkered tablecloth. The next day you're walking down the street and you have this gut feeling that the person walking toward you is someone you don't like. You've never seen the person before, but you know you don't like him. We often hear about gut feelings and people say, "You have to trust your gut." But maybe in this case the reason you feel you don't like this person is simply that he's wearing a red and white checkered tie. This visual input is going in through your low road, activating your amygdala and causing you to have an unpleasant reaction to the person. You might attribute your reaction to the way this person looks or walks or acts, but in fact it's just the low road ... the unconscious activation of the amygdala.

Some of the time ... these low road reactions are useful. Certainly that was the evolutionary goal: to protect us from danger. But these can also be harmful, or at least counterproductive. As in the case of the red and white checkered tie/tablecloth, an unconscious response may not be revealing some sort of inner truth but may instead be doing nothing more than reviving past emotional learning. "Listening to your gut" … might simply mean you are responding to past learning.

… Other areas of the brain provide input to the amygdala as well. Information about what we might call sensory objects – visual objects such as apples, or complex sounds like music or speech – come from the sensory cortex.

Other parts of the cortex are involved in higher cognition. For example, a cortical area called the hippocampus is involved in such higher order aspects of cognition as long-term memory and the processing of the context of events, that kind of information that allows us to say where and when something happened, along with other elements of the scene, such as whether it was raining. If you damage or remove the hippocampus in rats, for instance, the animals are no longer able to recognize a familiar place; they are unable to distinguish whether the test chamber they're in is the one where they've been conditioned to mild foot shocks. As a result, they express fear responses in all similar chambers.

Let's say, for example, that you regard all snakes as dangerous, but you know that you needn't fear a snake in the zoo as much as you might a snake that you happened upon in the woods. Ordinarily, your hippocampus and cortex would recognize the context (are you in the woods or at the zoo?), and you would react appropriately to the sight of a snake. But if you had a hippocampal lesion, you might have trouble suppressing a strong fear reaction even at the zoo.

…

Another important player in the fear response is the prefrontal cortex. In rat studies, as well as in human experiments, when you give the sound over and over again, without the unpleasant event occurring, it eventually loses its ability to elicit the emotional fear reactions. This process is called extinction. But if the medial part of the prefrontal cortex is damaged, emotional memory is difficult to extinguish. So, for example, a rat that has a lesion in the prefrontal cortex tends to continue to respond to the sound as if it were still associated with the unpleasant event; the learned response is resistant to extinction

However, it's important to know that even without damage to the prefrontal cortex, fear memories are hard to extinguish completely. Many studies show, for example, that weeks after a rat has ceased to react to a sound that had been paired with a shock, it might suddenly react fearfully to the sound again. Or if the animal goes back into the chamber where it had the conditioning experience, the fear behavior can be reactivated. Stress can reactivate extinguished fears in humans as well. A patient with a phobia can be treated, apparently successfully; then something happens – say the patient's mother dies – and the phobia comes back.

What certain types of therapy can do – and what the extinction process does – is train the prefrontal cortex to inhibit the output of the amygdala. This training doesn't eliminate the unconscious fear; it simply holds it in check.

Therapists find this both depressing and informative; they now understand that fear memories can't be completely eliminated, but at least they know what battle they're up against. …

… I don't know of any animal that can't be conditioned … and in any animal that has an amygdala, that structure seems to be involved in fear conditioning. The fear system, therefore, is probably a very basic, fundamental learning mechanism that's built into the brain.

In this sense then, we're emotional lizards. We're running around with an amygdala that's designed to detect danger and respond to it. This system is very efficient, and it hasn't changed much in terms of how it works. What has changed, of course, are the kinds of things that will turn it on, the things that humans have learned [taught and conditioned] to respond to that have the same effect on us that seeing a cat has on a rat.

… the hippocampus is involved in the system whose job is to create the memories we mean when we say, "I remember." You remember your first day at school, your vacation last year, Sunday dinner last week, and so on. These are your memories and they involve the hippocampus. (pp. 129–140)

LeDoux then gives an example. Suppose you're driving down the road and you are involved in an accident. The horn gets stuck and is blasting while you are suffering pain and thinking that you might die. Sometime later, a horn sounds and stimulates you to remember the accident. The whole scene of where you were and the series of events parade through your mind as a series of facts. It happened. But these facts are cold and hold no emotion. This is a memory about an emotional experience, but it is not the emotion.

However, it is very unlikely that this will happen in this way because the sound of the horn will also go through the amygdala which will, at the same time that you are remembering from the hippocampus, cause the autonomic system to crank into action; your muscles will tense up and you may re-experience the whole gamut of "fight or flight" right there and then.

The important thing to understand is that these two memory systems are separate, even if they generally operate in tandem.

Patients in whome the hippocampal system is damaged have poor conscious memory. [There is a] famous case of a woman who had severe amnesia. Each day when her doctor walked into her room, he would have to reintroduce himself because the woman never remembered having seen him the day before. In fact, if he left the room for even just a few minutes, she wouldn't remember him when he returned. One day the doctor walked in and extended his hand to shake hers. But this time he held a pin in the palm of his hand. When their hands met, hers was pricked and she withdrew it immediately. The doctor left the room, and when he came back a few minutes later … she wouldn't shake hands with him. She had no conscious memory of being pricked by the doctor, but … her amygdala remembered [to] protect herself.

By contrast, patients whos hippocampus is intact but who have amygdala damage are unable to do this kind of pinprick learning, this kind of fear conditioning. They know all the details – that the doctor was in the room, that they were pricked – but they don't withdraw their hand when the doctor tries to shake. … the amygdala and the hippocampus systems mediate different kinds of memory. Normally, they work together so that emotional memories ... and memories of emotion ... are fused in our conscious experience so immediately and so tightly that we cannot dissect them by introspection. ...

A traumatic [or stressful] situation ... has separate consequences for these two memory systems. When ... stress hormones [are released] into the body, the hormones (especially cortisol) tend to inhibit the hippocampus, but they excite the amygdala. In other words, the amygdala will have no trouble forming an emotional, unconscious memories of the event – and, in fact, will form even stronger memories because of the stress hormones. But these same hormones can interfere with ... and prevent formation of a conscious memory of the event. (pp. 140–142)

This has a strong bearing on our early childhood programming. It is thought that the hippocampus is not fully formed and functional in early childhood, and, as a result, we are unable to develop long-term, conscious memories before that time.

Yet, the amygdala is fully formed and functioning. And it is for this reason that abused children form very strong emotional memories that cause them to react strongly to many things, while having no access at all to any conscious understanding of why they feel as they do. Unconscious emotional memories affect us all our lives, powerfully, and it is extremely difficult to work through them without conscious recall. The mere sight of anything that is associated with an early traumatic or stressful event can activate the emotional response, whether it is of a positive or negative nature.

More than this, these unconscious memories can generalize as we have already described in an earlier section.

Now, all animals have the fear-learning mechanism that enables them to survive. They can detect danger and respond to it appropriately. However, they do not have fearful feelings, they way we do when our basic "fear program" is activated in a braing which also has self-consciousness. Here, a new phenomenon occurs: subjective feelings.

Feelings of fear ... are what happen in consciousness when the activity generated by the subcortical neural system involved in detecting danger is perceived ... by certain systems in the cortex, especially the working memory system ...

A conscious feeling of fearfulness is not necessary to trigger an emotional fear response. The low road can take care of this just fine. That is, we can produce responses to danger without being consciously afraid, as when we jump back up onto the curb to avoid being hit by a car. In a situation like that, as people so often say, we don't "have time to be afraid." ... At other times we will first have some kind of response in our body and only later be able to name what the feeling was: anxious, sad or angry. In many cases, though, even if we can say that we feel anxious, we don't know what generated those feelings. Indeed, we see this again and again in the various disorders of the fear system, such as panic attacks and phobias. ...

Why is it so difficult to eliminate such fears? Once the amygdala is turned on, it can influence information processing in the cortex from the earliest stages onward, but only the later stages of cortical processing affect the amygdala. In other words, even though communication goes two ways, it's not equally effective in both directions. In general, the projections from the amygdala to the cortex are much stronger than vice versa. If we think of the routes from the amygdala to the cortex as superhighways, then those from the cortex to the amygdala are narrow back roads. Once the emotions are activated, they can influence the entire working of the cortex, whereas the cortex is very inefficient at controlling the amygdala. So, using thinking to overcome emotion is like using a back road or side street from the cortex, while the amygdala is bombarding the cortex with input via the superhighways. (LeDoux 1999, 144–145)

But thinking with the cortex, it turns out, is basically a way to rewire your brain. It is like working on the back roads to develop them into the commanding interstate system of the brain they were meant to be. Research shows that changes in the brain are the result of learning experiences, and it seems that learning – acquiring knowledge – is the path of rewiring the synaptic connections in the brain.

The key to this is the fact that learning, hard thinking and pondering, requires that certain brain chemicals – usually acetylcholine – be squirted out at just the right place and in the right quantities. It is becoming clear that the molecules of memory are blind to the kind of memory – whether it is conscious or unconscious – that is occurring. What determines the quality of different kinds of memories is not the molecules that do the storing but the systems in which those molecules act. If they act in the hippocampus, the memories that get recorded are factual and accessible to our consciousness. If the chemicals are acting in the amygdala, they are emotional and mostly inaccessible to conscious awareness.

So, even if we don't know what has triggered a given emotional response until after the fact, we do have an awareness that we are feeling a certain way. This awareness is called our "working memory."

Working memory, or awareness, involves the frontal lobes of the brain just above and behind the eyebrows. This is what we use when we want to remember a new phone number just long enough to dial it, or to remember what we went to the kitchen for long enough to get it. It is also the place where many different kinds of information are held simultaneously while we are comparing one thing to another. We can have all kinds of things going on there at once. We can look at something and hold this image in working memory along with the memory of something we have pulled from long-term memory that we wish to compare it to. Sounds, smells, and even the ongoing physiological input from our system. And while we do this, we are considering: does it make us feel peaceful, happy, sad, afraid?

All of these elements come together simultaneously. However, this working memory can only do one thing at a time, even if that one task is multi-factored. A classic example is when you try to remember a new phone number and someone asks you a question before you get to dial it. The number flies out the window as you answer the question and you have to go back and look it up again.

It seems that this "working memory" or awareness is – if not consciousness itself – at least a window to it. It is in working memory that conscious feelings occur. In working memory, three things come together to create conscious feeling: present stimuli, activation of the amygdala in some way and activation of conscious memory in the hippocampus.

Present stimuli might include standing inside a church. This would arouse the amygdala so that the unconscious memories of the many experienced in church – the flooding of the receptors with neurochemicals; and this would activate conscious memory of the last time you were in church, or several memorable times will pass through the mind. When all these things come together in working memory, with the body now activated with chemistry and past history, this is perceived as "feeling."

The same thing can occur in any kind of encounter as we have already described. Something that is present now will turn on the chemicals, which will arouse conscious memories that are related to those chemicals, and then the present moment will be interpreted in those same terms.

Since what we are looking at here is the fact that unconscious, chemical imprints have a much greater ability to influence thinking than vice versa, we realize that we are face to face with an age-old debate between reason and emotion, logic and passion, knowledge and faith.

When you are aroused emotionally, whether by fear or pleasure or sexual attraction, it is a cold hard fact that emotion dominates thinking.

Philosophers going all the way back to Plato have endlessly analyzed this fundamental schism. The body fills us with passions and desires and fears and fancies and foolishness and fairy tales made up to justify these chemical reactions. Plato opined that the true philosopher was one who could master his emotions by the use of reason. Socrates said, "Know thyself," by which he meant that we had to understand our emotions in order to be able to control them.

The vast majority of philosophers and philosophical writers throughout man's recorded history have believed that in order to be truly human – as opposed to just an animal – we must activate reason. Descartes didn't say, "I feel, therefore I am." Thinking seems to be the distinctly human thing that humans do which separates them from animals. But, as Theodore Dreiser said, "Our civilization is still in the middle stage, scarcely beast in that it is no longer guided by instinct, scarcely human in that it is not yet wholly guided by reason."

The prime example of this is, of course, *Star Trek*'s Dr. Spock. Captain Ahab, the hero of Melville's *Moby Dick* was just the opposite. Melville wrote: "Ahab never thinks, he just feels, feels, feels." Perhaps the mindless pursuit of a white whale is a good metaphor for the result of living by emotion.

However, I am not advocating domination of cognition; merely balance. There is, at present, such an imbalance between the amygdala's input to the cortex and the very sparse control of the cortex over the amygdala. Even though thoughts can readily trigger emotions by activating the amygdala, it is very difficult to will-fully turn off emotions.

As it happens, the cortical connections to the amygdala are actually far greater in primates than in other animals. It seems that more balanced cortical pathways are the evolutionary trend. It is my opinion that we will develop them or perish. A more harmonious integration of emotion and thinking would allow us to both know our true feelings, and why we have them, and to be able to use them more effectively.

The key is in learning. Knowledge protects. And if you haven't already begun to put the pieces of the puzzle together with the advantages of expanding and working the frontal cortex, perhaps what we are going to look at next will finally make the whole thing clear.

Let's take a walk into the back roads of the frontal cortex.

CHAPTER 71
IF I SPEAK IN THE TONGUES
OF MEN AND ANGELS

OR, JAGUARS: THE NONLINEAR DYNAMICS OF LOVE
AND COMPLEX SYSTEMS

Nobel Laureate Murray Gell-Mann writes in *The Quark and the Jaguar*:

I have never really seen a jaguar in the wild. In the course of many long walks through the forests of tropical America and many boat trips on Central and South American rivers, I never experienced that heart-stopping moment when the powerful spotted cat comes into full view. Several friends have told me, though, that meeting a jaguar can change one's way of looking at the world.

... [Arthur Sze writes] "The world of the quark has everything to do with a jaguar circling in the night." ...

The jaguar stands for the complexity of the world around us, especially as manifested in *complex adaptive systems*. ... *the quark and the* jaguar seem to me to convey perfectly the two aspects of nature that I call the simple and the complex: on the one hand, the underlying physical laws of matter and the Universe and, on the other, the rich fabric of the world that we perceive directly and of which we are a part. ... the jaguar is ... a possible metaphor for the elusive complex adaptive system, which continues to avoid a clear analytical gaze, though its pungent scent can be smelled in the bush. (Gell-Mann 1994, 3, 11)

In the last few chapters, we have met the Jaguar. We have described a reality out of your worst nightmare. Some of you have been able to actually see the Jaguar, and some of you have smelled its pungent scent, and some of you have covered your eyes and held your nose and have fled in terror to the safety of more congenial belief systems. These latter have concluded that the Cassiopaeans are presenting "just another of those the-world-is-damned and only a few are gonna be saved" rants. In regard to this, let me quote British novelist Donald James (aka Dresden James), who wrote:

A truth's initial commotion is directly proportional to how deeply the lie was believed. It wasn't the world being round that agitated people, but that the world wasn't flat. When a well-packaged web of lies has been sold gradually to the masses over generations, the truth will seem utterly preposterous and its speaker a raving lunatic.

In either case, whether you have seen or smelt the jaguar, or have denied its existence, holding the perfumed handkerchief of well-packaged lies to your nose, I think it is time to talk a few minutes about current realities. On July 16 1994, the information about the "project to create a new race" was given with a completion date of 13 years in the future. That would put it right around the year 2007. We should either be running for cover, or on our knees praying, right? Nice linear thought pattern.

Well, 2007 has come and gone. Around the time of editing this volume for print, we had a session that was relevant to his topic:

July 22, 2010

A: Remember we once told you that people would unite against the "invasion" at the time just before the earth changes?

Q: (L) Well, yeah. We were talking about the Nephalim and their stun guns and that sort of thing. But it looks like psychopaths are the new Nephalim, and they're already using stun guns - tasers. And then we asked if they were going to try to stage a fake alien invasion. All of this disclosure business is trying to point people in the direction of alien invasions, trying to get them prepared for some kind of fake alien invasion. Then you said yes, but a real invasion might take place first or earth changes would happen. Now, it's just been pressing on my mind, becoming more and more clear, that we don't need an alien invasion with psychopaths ruling this world as their transdimensional agents. And it has occurred to me that when you said that way back when, that basically the invasion has already occurred! It's here, now. It's psychopaths in power!

Everybody is looking and waiting for some kind of aliens; well, aliens are a supernatural phenomenon. Yeah, there is a certain physicality to it, but it strikes me that that physicality doesn't have ... what do I want to say? Endurance? It doesn't "vibrate" right in our reality. It can come and go, but it doesn't stay here. So they need agents. They've always needed agents. They've always needed human-looking beings to control, to manipulate, or to even "download into" in a funny sort of way, like a possession or an activation. It's like they're sitting at some control console in some hyperdimensional place controlling their agents the way we control remote control toys.

So anyhow, this is what I've been thinking. Everybody's waiting for something to happen, like disclosure, or after disclosure. But it's already happened. It's here NOW! Any so-called "disclosure" will be a fraud unless they come out and say that it is a supernatural or hyper-dimensional phenomenon, which they are NOT going to say because that completely counters their entire world view that worships the physical universe. That's where the whole Darwinism, material science, exclusion of scientific study of the paranormal, and so forth, comes from. That sort of thing can NEVER be studied honestly because it would destroy their reality construct.

(Perceval) That's a great screen.

(L) Yeah, they're trying to prepare people for physical, material aliens – "Disclosure" - because they're going to TRY to pull the alien invasion trick or the "alien god" trick and they'll say, "Worship the alien god! Join behind us! We're his high priests!" But it's not going to work.

(Perceval) It's almost like that's been held in reserve if it's necessary. They've prepped people with the idea of aliens.

(L) It's like this gigantic counterintelligence program. And the main thing that I've seen them working to counter is the idea, the concept, the understanding that this phenomenon is a supernatural one. To make that clear, what we have always called supernatural, which is not necessarily "supernatural", is really just hyperdimensional. We've been aware of these things – this other reality – for millennia. They come and go. It's like the finger in Flatland. We're Flatland! Am I on to something with this?

A: About as accurate as you can get without making direct predictions.

Q: (L) Who was it, this scientist guy… Was it Werner von Braun who said they were going to create this illusion about an alien invasion, and that it was all a big lie and a big fraud? And the real reason he said it was that he knew that it was a paranormal or a hyperdimensional phenomenon. Is that what he meant?

A: Yes.

Q: (L) Because that fits. We've already been invaded. It's already a done deal. (Perceval) An invasion of psychopaths. (L) Yeah.

(Ailén) It's a perfect excuse for not taking responsibility as human beings. They can blame it on aliens, and say, "We're all equal, we're all victims! We didn't know!"

The question has been asked: if the Cassiopaeans are the nice guys who serve self by serving others, as they claim, why in the world would they tell us about a reality that is so horrible? Is it their objective to create such a reality by planting it in our minds and convincing us it is real and that we have no hope? Doesn't making people afraid provide a wonderful feast of fear for those nasty old fourth-density STS controllers? Isn't that just what they want? And, if so, then the Cassiopaeans must be one of "them" in disguise, providing themselves with a feast of fear!

At the same time, when the Cassiopaeans suggest that the many sources of information or systems of belief that make you feel safe, saved, warm and fuzzy, could really be setting you up for a fall, aren't they driving us away from the *real* sources of peace and harmony in which we must have faith in the face of any other evidence?

Well, let me ask you a question: would you go hiking in the wilderness without proper clothing and equipment? If somebody told you about all the dreadful things that can happen on a hike in the woods, would it stop you from the hike? Would you be so terrorized by the prospect of encountering a bear or a snake or a jaguar that you would stay home? Or would you equip yourself properly, with both knowledge and tools, and go enjoy your hike in safety?

Well, this analogy goes only so far because, as it happens, we are already in the middle of the wilderness and there are a lot of teachers around who are repeatedly telling us, "There's nothing out there that can harm you! If you aren't afraid, no grizzly bears or snakes will appear! And, even if they do, if you don't feel fear, they won't bother you."

Well, on the occasions when just such a philosophy might seem to have worked, the survivor of the encounter is firmly convinced that it was just this quality of "see no evil, hear no evil, speak no evil" that preserved them. The only problem is, we have no way of knowing if the grizzly bear, the snake, or the jaguar declined to attack them simply because they weren't hungry at the moment, or they were distracted by other, more tasty prey. And a more compelling question is this: did they act in a manner so as to convince the person that their belief system worked, so that they would return and proclaim the gospel of faith and ignorance, thereby assuring their continued concealment? And, naturally, those who practice this philosophy and do not survive, we never hear about. Freud wrote that religion was "a system of wishful illusions together with a disavowal of reality, such as we find ... nowhere else ... but in a state of blissful hallucinatory confusion."

And, of course, the Cassiopaeans have identified the essence of Service to Self as "wishful thinking."

Now, let me propose another interpretation of what the Cassiopaeans have told us. One that is actually contained within their words for those who have eyes to see and ears to hear. Could it just be possible that they are, as they have said, probable future selves whose reality as sixth-density beings is increased in direct proportion to our level of knowledge, and subsequent *application*? In other words, are we not dealing with probable futures, and the only way of determining which future we experience is to choose based on accurate knowledge of the present?

Suppose that the information the Cassiopaeans disseminate is true and we ignore it, are we then possibly subject to the very reality they tell us about? Conversely, if we accept it as true, or possibly true, and then *act* based on this information, are we not then capable changing the reality? That is, assuming that the reality is a result of mass mind non-awareness, and that a critical mass of awareness can be achieved?

In short, does it not seem reasonable that our probable future selves – given increasing probability by the awakening of a few people – are capable of interacting in our reality to help us only because some of us accept the role of being contact points to receive and disseminate the information necessary to wake people up in order to *change* the future?

Ouspensky, quoting Gurdjieff, writes:

Furthermore no one can escape from prison without the help of those who have escaped before. Only they can say in what way escape is possible or can send tools, files, or whatever may be necessary. But one prisoner alone cannot find these people or get into touch with them. An organization is necessary, nothing can be achieved without an organization. (Ouspensky 1949)

Remember the most important principles the Cassiopaeans have given us: free will, and knowledge protects. These two concepts are inseparable. The more knowledge you have, the more awareness you have; and the more awareness you have, the more free will you have. And the only way to understand the advanced information from the Cassiopaeans that evolved as we interacted with them is to understand nonlinear dynamics and complex systems.

On this issue, my husband Ark speculates: one day we will have a smart gadget that will allow us to measure the "level of awareness". Then the term "the more awareness you have" will have a technical meaning, like blood pressure, cholesterol level or, less precisely, IQ quotient.

First of all, it is important to note that the law of free will contains within it the explicit condition of non-linearity. And for those who wish to take issue with my remarks here, claiming that the Cassiopaeans have said that we are controlled by fourth-density STS, and therefore this implies that there is no free will, keep in mind that we have as much free will in relation to fourth density as second-density creatures have in relation to us. The more awareness a second-density creature obtains about a third-density person, the more likely it is to avoid being captured and eaten. So, let's not slip into tetraphyloctomy on that point. (A term coined by Umberto Eco in *Foucault's Pendulum*; means "the art of splitting a hair four ways".)

Implicit in non-linearity is the fact that the future is, as the Cassiopaeans have said a thousand times, *open*. Not only is it open, it is multiple in probability. In their own words, there is an uncountable infinity of quasi-quantum propensities.

Even if they often oppose one another, belief in reductionism and mechanism go hand in hand with religious faith. God or Darwin are in heaven and all is right with the world. Phenomena are orderly and everything can be explained with some sort of cause and effect scheme represented by differential equations. Either God started things at some point in space-time, to follow a single linear path, at which point He will bring it to an end, saving some people and not others, according to survival of the fittest in terms of who has obeyed his commands; or everything began with the Big Bang and has followed the linear path of evolutionary survival of the fittest in terms of natural selection. Same song, different verse.

Newton introduced us to these ideas through his famous laws of motion which relate the rates of change of momentum to various forces. Very quickly science, and religion, came to rely on linear differential equations. Phenomena such as the flight of a baseball or the end of the world (which necessitates the damning of certain souls on a particular trajectory, and the saving of others) could be described by differential equations. You throw the ball a certain way with a certain force, and there are certain conditions, and it will land at a specified place. If you have faith in a certain system, and hold firm to that faith, or conversely, deny that faith, you will end up in heaven or hell; or you will die in a pole shift, or be translated to the great new pie-in-the-sky. In such systems, small changes produce small effects and large effects are obtained by summing up many small changes.

This reductionist thinking held sway over nearly all the world until the 1970s when mathematical advances and the advent of the high-speed computer enabled scientists to probe the complex interior of nonlinear equations. (Note: the new trend started earlier, in 1950s in Los Alamos, with simulations of Fermi-Ulam-Pasta model on the then state-of-the-art computer Maniac 1.)

Nonlinear equations are math from the Twilight Zone where the normal mathematical landscape can suddenly become an alternate reality. In nonlinear equations, a small change in one variable can have a disproportionate impact on other variables. This can be catastrophic or serendipitous.

Now, the Cassiopaean material that explicates these things, that I am in the process of trying to present, will be offered in due time, and in context. But, in direct response to the many attempts to block this presentation, I am taking a shorter route here by explaining this in advance of presenting the material itself in a future volume.

It seems that it has not been without some sort of definite plan in the mind of the Cassiopaeans that before coming to the US, Arkadiusz Jadczyk was heading a division of nonlinear dynamics and complex systems. You may have deduced that there was an essential need for the participation of a physicist of exactly his background in this plan. It might even be further conjectured that he and I both were aware of this plan prior to incarnating and that our different pathways, brought together by the direct intervention of the Cassiopaeans, were necessary experiences set up by our future selves in order to prepare the ground, as it were, for the seeds that are now bearing fruit in this present series.

Getting back to nonlinear systems: nonlinear equations can be used to model the way an earthquake erupts when two tectonic plates shove against one another, building up irregular pressure along a fault line. The equation can show how for decades this jagged pressure mounts as the subsurface topography squeezes closer until in the very next millimeter of movement a critical value is encountered. At this value, the pressure pops suddenly and one plate slips, riding up on the other and everything shakes, rattles and rolls in the aftershocks of instabilities. Sure gives new meaning to the expression, "The straw that broke the camel's back."

Now, while scientists can model how such complex events manifest, they cannot predict exactly where or when the next quake will happen. This is because in the nonlinear world – which includes most of the real world – long term prediction is both practically and theoretically impossible. Nonlinearity dashes the reductionist dream of science, and an open future dashes the dream of the faithful in standard religions and philosophies based on prophecy and determinism.

By crunching different numbers in the nonlinear equations, systems theory scientists are able to model the effects of various policies and strategies on such things as the evolution of cities, the growth of a corporation, the firing of neurons, photon emissions, the economy, and so on. Using nonlinear models, it is even possible to locate potential critical pressure points in such systems. At these critical points, a small change can have a tremendous impact.

The teachings of the Cassiopaeans are based on a nonlinear, complex, self-referencing and self-organizing cosmos. That is to say, when they answer our questions at any given moment, the answers are correct for that moment in space-time, for that branch of the Universe in which the question is asked. However, that information, if it is utilized, changes the complex system via a process of back-propagation or feedback, and the Universe can branch and change in a non-linear way. That this has happened will become evident as I proceed with the narrative. And maybe it has happened more than once, depending on our actions, or feedback into the system. What kind of feedback, you ask?

Nonlinear equations include feedback that repeatedly multiplies by themselves. But, there are two types of feedback. An example of a simple feedback loop is the thermostat in your home. The room cools down below a certain temperature set on the thermostat. The thermostat responds by switching on the heat pump, which then heats up the room. As the room warms up to the set temperature, the thermostat signals the heat pump to shut down. The action of the thermostat affects the heat pump and the activity of the heat pump affects the thermostat. The thermostat and heat pump are bound in what is technically called a negative feedback loop.

Negative feedback loops have been in used since as early as 250 BCE, when they were used to regulate the height of water in water clocks. In the 1930s, feedback loops were used to model the relationship between predators and prey. In the 1950s, scientists (mainly in cybernetics and control theory) began to take conscious note of positive feedback loops.

The ear splitting screech you hear in a PA system is an example of positive feedback. (Yeah, I know, that sounds weird because there is nothing positive about those noises, for sure!) But what this means is that output from the PA amplifier is picked up by the microphone and looped back into the amplifier where it is then emitted by the speakers in greatly amplified volume. The chaotic sound is the result of the output of one stage of the process adding to the input in another stage of the process.

So, calling it positive just means it amplifies, just as negative feedback is a system of control. Think carefully about these two systems of feedback. These two types of feedback are everywhere in our world. And nonlinearity is everywhere a potential.

If you think about our reality in terms of feedback loops, you can see how it might be possible to control us by pumping a measured amount of heat or teachings into the system when it gets too cool; when people begin to get restless and ask questions. This has been the state for millennia. Each time human beings have begun to awaken, it could be likened to the room becoming too cool. The control system then adds some heat in the form of a new variation on the old teachings that serve to stabilize the system. As soon as enough heat has been added, the feeding shuts down. We will come back to some practical examples of negative feedback loops in terms of standard religions of the past, and the new religion of the "alien rapture theory" soon.

Positive feedback loops are a bit more problematical, and are the stuff of non-linear dynamics. The key to positive feedback in terms that we are concerned with relates directly to the teachings of the Cassiopaeans. Their communications could be likened to the output from an amplifier, "us in the future," which is picked up by the microphone, or "us in the past", which is then looped back into the ampli-fier – us in the past (the present, from our frame of reference) again is then emit-ted by the speakers in a greatly amplified volume – or nonlinear change of the reality. This point is made clear in the following:

> June 9, 1996
>
> Q: (L) al-'Arabî describes unified thought forms as being the "names of God." His explication seems to be so identical to things you tell us that I wonder …
>
> A: We are all the names of God. Remember, this is a conduit. This means that *both termination/origination points are of equal value, importance.* … Don't deify us. And, be sure all others with which you communicate understand this too!
>
> Q: (L) What quality in us, what thing, enabled us to make contact?
>
> A: You asked.
>
> Q: (L) A lot of people ask!
>
> A: No they don't, they command.
>
> Q: (L) Well, a lot of people do ask or beg or plead, but they get all discombobulated with the answers.
>
> A: No, they command. Think about it. You did not beg or plead … that is commanding.

And this is an important point. Until an individual realizes that having faith is a form of commanding, they have no hope of truly asking the Universe for answers. The fiction writer, Ann Rice, gave eloquent voice to this problem in *The Vampire Lestat*:

> Very few beings really seek knowledge in this world – few really ask. On the contrary, they try to wring from the unknown the answers they have already shaped in their own minds – justifications, confirmations, forms of consolation without which they can't go on. To really ask is to open the door to a whirlwind. The answer may annihi-late the question and the questioner. (Rice 1997, 332–333)

To emphasize the above point, let me say that the most formidable difficulty I have found in sharing the Cassiopaean information is the fact that many people are incapable of esoteric understanding. There are many who say that they would very much like to inquire into the nature of reality and *being*, but their curiosity is ephemeral – they are dilettantes who will only reach the portal of the outer circles of understanding. The fearful "Dweller on the Threshold," nowadays manifesting as Grays and Reptoids, will block their path and they will find themselves too attached to their linear modes of thinking to enter the temple, so to speak.

This idea goes against the democratic egalitarianism of popular spiritual thinking, but the fact is:

> To those people who simply pry into the occult from mere curiosity, we have nothing to say. They will obtain just as much as they deserve, and nothing more. "Ask and ye shall receive, seek and ye shall find, knock and it shall be opened unto you" is equally as true today, in relation to esoteric knowledge, as it was 2000 years ago. ... It invariably presupposes that the supplicator and the knocker are in real earnest, and that they seek only to satisfy the deep yearnings of the immortal soul. The doorkeeper, or guardian of the temple of truth is as mute as a granite rock to all others. They may supplicate, they may shout and bawl until they are hoarse, they may knock and buffet the door until they rouse a nation with their clamour, and if they approach in any other spirit than [earnest desire to satisfy the deep yearnings of the immortal soul], it is all to no purpose. We can never take the Kingdom of Heaven by storm.
>
> Those students who are unable to comprehend the sublime import of the mighty system of cycles and periods ... would preferably be occupied in eschewing occult studies for the adoption of others adapted to their sphere of thought. ... They must remain contented until the time arrives when conditions are evolved in the scale of the succeeding human races, conditions which will permit of the expansive budding and blossoming of their soul's now latent attributes.
>
> ... There is no such thing in the entire cosmos as equality. There is, instead a hierarchy, not as something tyrannical, and especially not based on birth, riches, or the power of the stronger, but as a "sacred authority" sanctioned by *the nature of things*. There is only one royalty, one aristocracy: that of intelligence. ... This alone can lead to cosmic equilibrium and happiness.
>
> ... There are also numerous students who, although being in a condition suitable for the perception of truth, and for the true significance of nature's grand mysteries, are yet totally unqualified for the perception of this knowledge, owing to their natural but terrible elemental affinity. The result of this fearful psychical condition is ... that the occult powers which they might develop, would be used for purposes of a purely selfish and worldly nature ...
>
> It is quite a minority of this class who can grasp any actual power, for upon the contrary they frequently become the very dupes and slaves of the powers they so ardently seek to control.
>
> To all such we fervently and solemnly say: abandon all thoughts of spirit-intercourse, flee from occultism, and spiritualism, as you would from a pestilence, and may the divine guardians of the human race preserve your souls from the bottomless abyss, upon the brink of which you may possibly have been unconsciously reposing. ("Axioms of the Hermetic Brotherhood of Luxor", quoted by Godwin et al. 1995)

The Cassiopaeans have said about this same matter:

November 16, 1994

Q: (L) Is there any kind of hierarchy to this thing? Do these beings come before some kind of grand council and make plans and discuss things, and make decisions and implement them?

A: No.

Q: (L) Well, how do things happen? Do things just sort of happen as a natural interaction of things and energies?

A: Yes.

Q: (L) If the Lizzies have been feeding off of us frequently and are planning to come and take over our planet, why, when they achieved their domination 300,000 years ago, did they not just move here and take up residence and be in charge?

A: No desire to inhabit same realm. ... You are 3rd level they are 4th level.

Q: (L) Why are they planning to now?

A: They want to rule you in 4th density.

Q: (L) If the mother planet that the human race was seeded on originally, is burned up, or turned into a cinder, I would like to know how it burned up.

A: Star expanded.

Q: (L) Well, if the star expanded, it must have expanded recently, is that correct?

A: Time does not measure that way in that realm.

Q: (L) What realm is that?

A: Time/space warp. [...]

Q: (L) So, the star expanded and the mother planet was turned into a cinder. If this was the case, it means that it must have turned into a cinder very close to the point, using time loosely, when human beings were created.

A: You can't even use it loosely. ... Okay. Now: "shocker" for you. It hasn't become a cinder yet.

Q: (L) Okay. What is it? You told us it was a cinder ... burned up ... what is the real story here?

A: It will be at the same "time" that you go to 4th density. The human race is currently being formed on D'Ahnkiar. ... That closes realm grand cycle.

Q: (L) Are you saying that there are human beings being created on that planet at this current time ...

A: Yes, you are. Your race is forming there. ... Realm crossing understand?

Q: (L) Are you saying that there are fourth-density bodies being formed there ...

A: No. 3rd.

Q: (L) There are third-density bodies ... are we going to leave the bodies we are in and go into other bodies?

A: You are drifting ... think carefully. Realm is derivative of reality. Cycle.

Q: (L) So the human race is being formed on this other planet at the present time ...

A: Yes.

Q: (L) And at the time of the realm border crossing, this other planet will then become cindered ... burned up ...

A: Yes.

Q: (L) Where will the human beings go that are being formed on that planet at the time of the realm border crossing?

A: Ancient Earth. … There is no time as you know it; its all just lessons for the collective consciousness.

Q: (L) So at the closing of this grand cycle everything will just start all over again?

A: Not exactly; you see, there is no start.

Q: (L) Are a lot of souls on the earth going to recycle into these new bodies coming onto the earth?

A: Yes.

Q: (L) As ancient mankind?

A: Yes.

Q: (L) And do the whole thing all over again?

A: Yes.

Q: (L) So, in other words, a lot of people are going back to square one?

A: Close.

Q: (L) Is this punishment?

A: *No. Nature.*

Q: (L) Are some of the souls, at that point, going to move into a higher density level?

A: Yes.

Q: (L) Could you give us a percentage on this?

A: No. Open at this point.

Q: (L) Now, getting back to the planet, if at some point in the cycle, bodies were generated on this planet and brought to earth, who brought them?

A: Realm crossing.

Q: (L) It was not a who, it was a what, is that correct?

A: All is who and what. … What is chosen? Only you can choose. The choice comes by nature and free will and looking and listening. *Where you are is not important. Who you are is and also what you see.*

So we begin to have an inkling that linear thinking must be tossed out the window and that we must turn to nature with all the powers of both our intellect and our intuition in order to weigh and measure the forces at work here, in which we figure as points of nonlinear confluence.

French mathematician Henri Poincare first blew the whistle on the closed system thinking of Newtonian mechanics. According to classical physics, Newtonian physics, a closed system is perfectly orderly and predictable. A pendulum in a vacuum, free of friction and air resistance, will conserve its energy. The pendulum will swing back and forth for all eternity. It will not be subject to the dissipation of entropy, which eats its way into systems by causing them to give up their energy to the surrounding environment. Planets, like pendulums, cannot be disturbed unless by outside chance, and they must be unvarying in their perambulations around the sun.

But Poincare asked a question about the stability of the solar system. Why he asked this question, we do not know, but he did. And the reaction to his question was the standard linear-faith brush-off, "Of course they are stable! They've been stable for a long time. Heck, we can predict eclipses years in advance!" It was a tenet of the scientific faith that knowing the law of force and mass of the bodies, any good scientist could predict the interactions with Newton's equations. The law of force, the inverse square of the law of gravitation, was all wrapped up in a nice, neat package.

But Poincare had been doing some math on the side, and he knew that there was a small difficulty here: for a system containing only two bodies, Newton's equations work. For an ideal two-body system, the orbits are stable. The problem arises when going from two to three bodies, such as including the Sun in the equations, Newton's equations actually become unsolvable. For formal mathematical reasons, the three-body equation cannot be worked out closer than an approximation.

Well, one would think that an approximation might be okay. We can live with that. It's nothing to keep one awake at night, right? Well, Poincare knew that the approximation method appeared to work for the first few bodies added, but when that number increased, if you add more and more bodies to the system, even including a few spare asteroids and their very minute perturbations of the system, over long periods of time, at some point the orbits shift and the solar system begins to break apart under its own internal forces.

Mathematically, this problem is nonlinear and nonintegrable. When you add a term to a two-body system it increases the nonlinear complexity, or feedback of the system. Poincare did this, and was satisfied that a three-body system remained pretty stable. Small perturbations, but so what? With just the Sun, the Earth and the Moon, we can sleep safely in our beds at night. Right?

Wrong. What happened next was a shock. Poincare discovered that with even the very smallest perturbation, some orbits behaved in an erratic, even chaotic way. His calculations showed that a minute gravitational pull from a third body might cause a planet to wobble and weave drunkenly in its orbit and even fly out of the solar system altogether!

One will be struck by the complexity of this figure which I do not even attempt to draw. Nothing more properly gives us an idea of complication of the problem of three bodies and, in general, of all the problems in dynamics where there is no uniform integral. (H. Poincare quoted by Schroeder 1991)

Poincare had discovered that chaos is the essence of the nonlinear system. He revealed that even a completely deterministic system like our solar system could do crazy things with the least provocation. *The smallest effects could be magnified through positive feedback and a simple system can explode into shocking complexity.*

This is quite a different matter from the negative feedback control mechanism that controls the temperature of our reality.

Now, let's go in a slightly different direction. For a long time, matter and motion were accepted as the basis of reality and, to a great extent, continue to be. The Big Bang or Cosmic Firecracker theory is explained in these terms. A primal atom (matter) of incredible density exploded into motion. Where the primal atom came from, how the space it exploded into came into being, and where the impetus for this event originated, are still on the drawing board. Nevertheless, from this purported event, our Universe and the life within it just sort of accidentally happened. Man is the amoral end of a deadly biological evolution. The mind and soul are inexplicable byproducts of the struggle for survival. The Bible says, "In the Beginning, God created the heaven and the earth." Neither the Bible nor science has much to say about what happened before the beginning. St. Augustine was once asked the question, "What was God doing before He created the world?" The Bishop's rejoinder: "Creating Hell for those who ask that question!" put a period to such inquiries. Few have asked since.

However, physics, the study of the deeper realities of existence, has failed to support the matter-motion theory. To the average person, a table, a chair, an orange, are real objects. They have dimension – three, to be exact – they are real. But are they? The physicist (and the knowledgeable layperson) knows that the object is composed of atoms. And there lies the rub! The dissected atom (quantum particles) often displays some very disturbing properties.

Physicist Nick Herbert writes in *Quantum Reality*:

> Despite modern attempts to split it into finer bits, using energies a hundred billion times greater than those that hold the atom together, the electron remains steadfastly elementary. An electron, so it seems, simply doesn't have any parts. (Herbert 1985, 58)

One experiment shows that electrons are particles. Another demonstrates wave properties. The bottom line seems to be that, having pursued reality to its farthest limits within human capability, man finds that his real world is made up of particle–waves, which do not exist except as a mathematical object. Danish physicist Niels Bohr even put forth the theory that *there is no deep reality*.

So, just what is this estate in which we find our existence? Does reality run out when it becomes invisible? Obviously not as we cannot see electricity and other forces in the Universe measurable only by their effect upon matter. Do these forces run out when they become undetectable by our senses or by our instruments? Do the things we detect with the subtle mechanisms of our mind and organs of sensation not exist simply because we cannot see or measure them? And, as Ark dared to ask in his 1994 paper, published in a peer reviewed physics journal, *Annalen der Physik,* (the same journal in which Einstein published his famous 1905 paper), "Who are 'we', anyway?"

This is the crisis in physics and the crisis in our world, for the prevailing cosmic view in the ivory towers of physics and cosmology eventually filters down and influences our domestic, social and political patterns.

But, if science has failed us, how much more so has religion?

Some religions say that the only meaning to life is in having faith that our suffering is creating a better future in the afterlife or in future lives. Other religions say that the meaning to life lies in working to dissolve the ego into nothingness. One philosophy states that the true purpose of life is to align our self-created realities so that they become as one in love and light, thereby we may achieve a unified race, which will survive beyond predicted cataclysms for a thousand years before things wind down a bit into the usual state of decay. Naturally this effect can only be initiated and maintained by a group effort to dominate the thinking of the world by bombing them all with positive thoughts. There are other ideas and combinations of ideas similar to these – all leading where?

"A religion contradicting science and a science contradicting religion are equally false."

Surely there must be some way to reconcile the two.

Are we, in fact, an accident of evolution in an accidental Universe, on a race to nowhere except oblivion? Or, worse still, are our very minds – our desire for knowledge – our enemies; damning us for our lack of belief? The choice seems to be between a sick joke and a mistake, neither of which is conducive to faith.

But, help is on the way. In 1966, theoretical physicist John Stewart Bell constructed a proof that has since become known as Bell's Theorem. (Reprinted in *Speakable and Unspeakable in Quantum Mechanics.*) This theorem tells us that, if quantum theory is correct, reality must be non-local. That is to say, *anything happening anywhere whatsoever in the Universe, can, instantaneously affect everything else everywhere else in the Universe.* He demonstrated that, if we take the lesson of the quantum theory seriously, an atom's measured attributes are determined not just by events happening at the actual site of being, but by all events occurring in the entire Universe simultaneously and instantly.

Notice the key word above – instantaneous. This means superluminal or faster than the speed of light. But, assuming that no signal can travel faster than the speed of light, this must mean that *there is no actual distance separating events.* Bell's theorem can be interpreted as demonstrating the idea that all that exists – past, present, and future – should be combined into a single entity whose farthest parts are joined in an immediate manner. In other words, the world we perceive – the stars and planets, the land and seas, the trees, animals, buildings, people – are all manifestations of a single unmitigated process.

January 11, 1995

Q: (B) What is the purpose of this contact?

A: To help you to learn, thus gain knowledge, thus gain protection, thus progress.

Q: (B) What do the Cassiopaeans gain from this contact?

A: By helping you, we are moving toward fulfilling of our destiny of union with you and all else, thus completing the grand cycle.

Q: (B) Is this the only probability open to you or is this the best probability open to you?

A: Both.

Q: (B) Are you a great distance from us in light years?

A: Distance is a 3rd density idea.

Q: (B) Light years is third-density?

A: Yes.

Q: (B) What do you mean by traveling on the wave?

A: Traveling on thoughts.

Q: (F) Our thoughts or your thoughts?

A: Not correct concept.

Q: (L) What is the correct concept?

A: All is just lessons.

Q: (L) Whose thoughts are they?

A: Thoughts unify all reality in existence and are all shared.

Q: (S) You travel on a wave of energy created by all thought forms?

A: Thought forms are all that exists!

But, we are three-dimensional, are we not? Aren't the table, the chair, the dog and the steak we had for dinner solid objects with length, depth, height and existence in time? What exactly are these objects we perceive as existing solidly in space for varying periods of time? What is the space we define as separating the objects? How are they connected in time? If physics seems to indicate to us that all is one, then what is it – what characteristic do we possess – that separates us from this deeper reality? And, what is the true nature of this reality?

Space, as we perceive it, has only three dimensions; length, width, and height. We define this condition as three independent directions – that is, each measurement lies at *right angles* to the others *simultaneously*. But, again, if we take quantum theory seriously, then our space is merely an aspect of another space, possibly of infinite number of dimensions.

If space is infinite, then it must possess an infinite number of lines perpendicular and not parallel to one another. Is infinity, then, a foolishness and does space necessarily have a limit? If it does have a limit, in what space does our space exist?

Now, if space does possess an infinite number of lines perpendicular to one another, then we must ask *why we can only perceive three.* If we exist in a condition of mind that perceives only three dimensions, this can mean that the properties of space are created – or differentiated – by certain attributes within us. For some reason or another, the whole is inaccessible to us. The Cassiopaeans have said this is a choice that followed a "desire based imbalance," and that the desire was to accelerate our unification with the all.

For a very long time, materialist science has recognized the existence of two important concepts, matter and motion. Matter is that which moves and motion is changes in matter. However, Bell's theorem seems to show us that "all" simply is. Therefore, the changes must originate within ourselves.

There are no comparisons we can carry over from our real world into the world of quantum mechanics, so we must just plunge in and tell it like it is. The central mystery is described in what is called the Double-slit Experiment,[12] which goes something like this:

Imagine a barrier of some sort, such as a concrete wall, with two tiny holes in it. They can be elongated or round. On the one side of the wall is a screen with sensitive detectors on it that are sensitive to whatever we are going to send through the holes. On the other side of the holes is a device that shoots quantum things – photons of light, electrons, or whatever.

In our everyday world we can observe how waves diffract through a wall by working with a similar setup in a tank of water. A wave-making machine sends waves toward the concrete wall. The waves pass through the two holes and set up two identical little wave patterns on the other side. The intensity of each individual wave pattern, taken alone with one or other of the holes closed off, is expressed as H^2, or height (amplitude) squared. But, with both holes open, there is a very large peak intensity exactly in line with the two holes, which can be expressed as $I=(H+J)^2$. This means that the sum of the two wave intensities is not H^2+J^2. At the points where the two daughter wave patterns touch each other, they set up an interference pattern. So, the extra term added into the equation is the contribution due to interference and accounts for all the energy whether negative or positive. For a water tank the amplitudes are real numbers, for quantum waves" they are complex numbers, and what is squared is the magnitude, thus interference patterns are somewhat different in the two cases, but the idea is the same. So much for waves.

Now, if we take solid things, such as bullets being fired from a machine gun[13] at the concrete walls, we would not find the interference term. We would find a lot of bullets close to one spot (some can ricochet from the interior of the hole) on the other side of each hole. Period.

Now, what do you think is going to happen when we shoot quantum things through the holes? It is natural to believe that each individual electron or photon must go through one hole or the other, like bullets, particularly since we have slowed down our quantum gun to shoot one electron at a time. Guess again.

When we block off one hole or the other, we get the usual pattern for single-hole experiments – that is, a whole bunch of electrons hit the same spot. But, when we open up both holes, we do not get the pattern we would get for bullets. We get the wave diffraction pattern. And, if we do the experiment a thousand times with only one electron released in each experiment, adding them all together we still get the wave diffraction pattern. A single electron or photon, on its way to

---

[12] http://nobelprize.org/nobel_prizes/physics/articles/ekspong/
[13] http://www.physics2000.com/PDF%27s/Quantum.pdf

the wall, *knows* whether or not the other hole is open and that it must obey the statistical laws.[14]

When we try to observe which of the holes the electron goes through, we always see the electron at one hole or the other, never both at once. And, *if we continue to watch*, the pattern built up on our detector is exactly that as for the bullets. So, we can only conclude that *the electron knows not only which hole is open, it knows if we are watching it.*[15]

When we try to observe the electron, it collapses into a particle, but when we are not looking, it seems that it goes through both holes. It is as though *the world keeps all its options open until the very last instant of observation*. So, from an array of ghost – or potential – electrons, our observation crystallizes one and collapses the wave.

So what are we seeing and experiencing with our five senses? Could it be that each moment of reality is like a slice of the "all", similar to a slide on a carousel slide projector?

When we look at the table, the chair, the salad and the dog, they seem to be solid and stable – but the physicist can assure us that they are a dance of atoms ever moving into and out of being – the atoms making up the table a minute from now being perhaps an entirely different group from the atomic constitution a moment before.

So, we might say that reality is a continuous flow or invisible something passing momentarily into a focused object, much like a light shining through a slide creates an image upon a screen. What is the screen? you ask. We will come to that when we discuss the nature of matter itself. But for now, let us say that the slide is our mind and the source of light is our consciousness. But the ultimate source of this consciousness is problematical, as will be seen in the following excerpt from the Cassiopaean transcripts:

June 17, 1995

Q: (L) I would like to ask a little bit about synchronicity. I would like to know what is the source of synchronous events. Is it a multiple source or is it something that comes out of the percipient's own mind or ... (J) Is it random?

A: It involves aspects in every imaginable state of reality merging together in what could best be described, if seen visually, as a massive mosaic in perfect balance. But, that is not adequate to a response for your question, however, hopefully, maybe you can contemplate the visual image presented and help yourself to learn a more complete answer.

---

[14] Ark's note: Physicist Alfred Landé came with another idea: that it is the wall rather than the electron that knows whether one or two holes are open, and scatters the electrons according to this knowledge. Both interpretations are possible, the effect and the algebra of interference patterns remains the same.

[15] Ark's note: this process of diffraction pattern formation by shooting of single electrons, their path being watched or not, can be modeled by a nonlinear quantum dynamics. Simultaneous observation of several non-commessurable physical characteristics, like, for instance, position *and* velocity vectors, can lead to chaotic and fractal patterns.

Q: (T) Several sessions back when we were discussing perpendicular realities you were talking about something that happened to me and that I had to look back over my life and analyze my relationships with other people from a certain point up until now and you said that this was a perpendicular reality. What is the definition of a perpendicular reality?

A: The perpendicular reality primarily, though not exclusively, refers to one's life path and how one's life path fits together in the cycle or in a wheel when connected with those of a similar life path. And, oddly enough, relates very closely to the previous question involving synchronicity. If you can picture an inlaid wheel formed by a circle within a circle, and adjoining partitions in a perfect balance, that would be the best representation of perpendicular reality for it does not completely involve one individual's experience, but rather a group of individual's experience for the progression of a greater purpose, if you understand what we mean. This is what we mean when we say: perpendicular reality. Picture again, a circle within a circle adjoined by equally spaced partitions in a perfect cycle. That is perpendicular reality.

Q: (T) You had us draw this symbol and put seven spokes or partitions between the two circles.

A: Correct.

Q: (T) Is seven the optimal number?

A: Seven is always the optimal number. There are seven levels of density. This reflects through all phases of reality.

Q: (T) You also said that each of us in this group came from a different perpendicular reality.

A: That is correct.

Q: (T) Is it at this point where we merge our different perpendicular realities in order to learn from each other's experiences?

A: That could be described as correct.

Q: (L) It was said at the time that the inner circle was the connection with this reality and that the outer circle and connecting segments were where the perpendicular reality is "joined with the Wave." Is it implied in that statement that the forming of this conduit through these perpendicular realities is instrumental in bringing forth this wave, bringing forth this change, this dimensional shift, or density shift, and is that something that is being done in other places?

A: We wish to congratulate you for asking six questions in one.

Q: (T) One more question and you would have a perfect perpendicular question! Mirth! (L) Are we connected in some way with the Wave, individually and as a group?

A: Well, of course. Everything is connected to the Wave.

Q: (L) Are we, by connecting into this wheel, so to speak, activating the wave in some way?

A: We are not clear about your interesting interpretation there, but it is true that you have an interactive relationship with the Wave. As stated before, you are in an interactive relationship with the Wave in a sense, in that the Wave is a part of your reality, always has been and always will be. And, of course, it does involve your progress through the grand cycle. And the perpendicular reality, again is, of course, an advancement from the core outward which is yet another reflection of all reality and all that exists. Now, we wish to return to the visual representation as mentioned previously. If you notice the core circle connects with all seven sections to the outer circle. Now, picture that outer circle as being an ever expanding circle, and each one of the seven segments as being an ever expanding line. Of course, now, this will expand outward in a circular or cyclical pattern. Please picture visually an expanding outer circle and a non-expanding inner circle. Contemplate that and then please give us your feelings as to what that represents.

Q: (L) Does it represent an expansion of our knowledge and consciousness?

A: That's part of it.

Q: (L) Does it represent also expanding influence of what and who we are on the reality which is around us?

A: That is correct.

Q: (L) Does it also represent a more ...

A: Oop! We detected a slippage of your visual representation! Contemplate, if you will, the ever-expanding outer circle and the non-expanding inner circle, and, of course, the seven partitions also moving outwardly. What type of shape does that form in your mind's eye?

Q: (L) A wheel?

A: Is that all?

Q: (T) A pie?

A: Keep going.

Q: (L) An eye.

A: Now we are starting to turn it into a sphere! Why would it turn into a sphere?

Q: (L) How can it turn into a sphere?

A: How can it not!

Q: (SV) It is going in *all* directions; it's not just flat ...

A: Is a straight line a straight line or a ... ?

Q: (L) Oh, you're not talking about a circle?

A: We are talking about a circle. What becomes of a circle if you expand it outward forever?

Q: (T) The outer circle is used to encompass more and more.

A: And what shape does it begin to take on? I want you to look at this outer circle expanding outward!

Q: (J) Are we to assume that the seven spokes remain the same size in relation to the circle?

A: Well, answer that question for yourself.

Q: (L) Okay, we are looking at it as a plane representation. As a flat surface.

A: Well, what happens to a flat surface if you extend it outward forever?

Q: (L) Well, we don't know. That, that ... (SV) It keeps on going.

A: It keeps on going?

Q: (L) Yeah, bigger and flatter!

A: It does? What happens to a line if you extend it forever and ever?

Q: (L) It keeps on going.

A: It does?

Q: (L) Um hmmm!

A: Where does it go to?

Q: (SV) Forever. (J) Back to itself. (L) We don't know that.

A: Oh, someone said "back to itself."

Q: (J) Like a snake taking hold of its own tail.

A: Why don't we know that?

Q: (L) Because we don't. It is conjectured that space is curved …

A: "Because we don't know." Now, why don't we know?

Q: (L) Because we haven't been there.

A: Had Columbus been outside of Italy and Spain?

Q: (L) Okay, we are going to assume that if it keeps on expanding it will eventually come back to itself …

A: No, no, no wait! We asked a question!

Q: (L) Well, of course Columbus had an idea that there was something but he hadn't been there, no. But he went and checked it out.

A: Did he have just and idea?

Q: (L) Well, pretty much, I guess.

A: Hmmm. That's not the way we remember it. The way we remember it is that he had instinct and imagination and when he married his instinct with imagination, it became reality. And, when it became reality, he had created a reality which he was fully confident would be manifest in the physical third density reality. It wasn't that he was confident. He knew it to be so. He didn't stop himself by adding prejudice to the equation which is what you are doing when you say: "Well, we don't know what happens because we have never been there!" Think logically, please. We have told you so many times that everything is a grand cycle. If it's a grand cycle, we have told you about circles within circles. We have told you about cycles. We have told you about short wave cycles and long wave cycles. Now, after all this information that you have asked of us, which we have more than happily given to you, would you expect that a straight line would just go out forever and ever and ever as a straight line? How could it possibly do that? What happens, if you draw on you third density earth a straight line to the East or to the West or to the North or to the South?

Q: (J) It comes all the way back to itself.

A: Right …

Q: (L) Okay, so we're living in a big globe!

A: Are we?

Q: (L) Well, that is what it sounds like, a big circle?

A: Oh, my, my, my. You need more study and learning, my dear. Need more study. Even your Albert Einstein had a theory about what happened.

Q: (L) Yes, but that was just a theory.

A: Oh, well we guess then it must be dropped. We'll never know. It's just a theory. Well, we'll just forget about it.

Q: (T) I'm still expanding the circle … (SV) Me too.

A: Very good, that was the idea. It keeps going and going and going.

Q: (L) Well, mine does too, but it hasn't come back and met anything. So, what's the point?

A: Does there need to be a point?

Q: (L) Of course!

A: Who says? We are trying to help you learn. When do you expect to shut down this process?

Q: (J) Never.(L) Gee, I hope never.

A: Then there never is a point!

Q: (J) Point taken! (L) There is no point. [Laughter.] Well, if you expand the circle outward and continue expanding it in all directions, it pulls the seven spokes with it which encompasses more and more space in a cross section, and then turn that circle, you have a sphere.

A: Precisely. But Laura says that means we are living in a big globe. And, maybe we are.

Q: (T) Well, it wouldn't be a big globe, so to speak, it would only be a big globe within the circle. If the circle continues to expand, it would just continue to go outward and outward and the globe would become bigger and bigger and bigger ... (L) You're making me nervous ... (T) But it goes outward forever ... cause there is no end to going out ...

A: There isn't?

Q: (SV) Nope.

A: Well, then maybe there's no beginning. If there's no end and no beginning, then what do you have?

Q: (J) The here and now.

A: The here and now which is also the future and the past. Everything that was, is and will be, all at once. This is why only a very few of your third density persons have been able to understand space travel, because even though traveling into space in your third density is every bit as third density as lying on your bed at night in your comfortable home, the time reference is taken away. Something that you hold very close to your bosom as if it were your mother. And, it is the biggest illusion that you have. We have repeatedly told you over and over that there is no time, and yet, of course, you have been so brainwashed into this concept that you cannot get rid of it no matter what you do, now can you? Imagine going out into space. You'd be lost when confronted with reality that everything is completely all at one? Would you not? Picture yourself floating around in space!

Q: (T) Does the sphere keep expanding ... as the circle expands and you turn the circle 180, you get a sphere. As the sphere continues to expand it, you take a point on the outer edge of the sphere in order to take the sphere about itself, you get a donut, an ever expanding inner tube. If you take that and twist it, you get an even larger inner tube. It just continues to expand and encompasses more space ...

A: And now, *when you merge densities, or traverse densities, what you have is the merging of physical reality and ethereal reality, which involves thought form versus physicality.* When you can merge those perfectly, what you realize then, is that the reason there is no beginning and no end is merely because there is no need for you to contemplate a beginning or an end after you have completed your development. When you are at union with the One at seventh density, that is when you have accomplished this and then there is no longer any need for difference between physical and ethereal forms.

Q: (L) On the subject of time as we discussed the other day: we talked about the fact that at the constant of light there is no time, there is no matter, there is no gravity, but that any unit, infinitesimally small to the downward side of the constant of light, suddenly there is gravity and suddenly there is matter. And we asked what is it that congeals this matter out of the energy of light, so to speak, and I believe that the answer we received was that it was consciousness from seventh level. From our perspective, would it be possible to achieve this constant and move through to the other side of it, or at least stay fixed with it, without dematerializing? Is the speed of light interconnected with the state of no time and no gravity?

A: No in an absolute sense, in a third density sense.

Q: (L) Okay, if you are in fourth density, for example, does everything move at the speed of light and is that why there is no time there and no gravity?

A: No. That is an incorrect concept ...

Q: (T) There is no speed of light, light is everywhere.

A: Precisely. There is no speed of light in fourth density because there is no need for any "speed." Speed, itself, is a third density concept. You remember, all there is is lessons. That's it! There's nothing else. It is all for your perception. For our perception. For all consciousness. That's all there is.

Q: (L) Well, I am still trying to get a handle on what it is, what is the source of this gravity, this state of time because they seem to be so intimately connected.

A: Let us ask you a question now: do you remember going to school?

Q: (L) Yes.

A: What did you do in third grade?

Q: (L) A lot of things. I learned cursive writing. I learned to multiply and divide.

A: Do you remember what you did in first grade?

Q: (L) Yes.

A: Please name one.

Q: (L) Learned to count in several ways. Learned to read and write.

A: Okay. When you were in the process of learning to multiply and divide, did you drop your pen or pencil and steadfastly return in your mind to first grade and try and figure out why you had to learn the alphabet?

Q: (L) No.

A: Why not?

Q: (L) Because I already knew it.

A: You already knew it. In other words, you did not need to learn the alphabet because you already knew it. Correct?

Q: (L) Yes.

A: Are you going to need to learn about the speed of light when there is no longer a speed of light?

Q: (L) Well, that is what I am trying to do. Once you learn it, maybe you are not subject to its lessons anymore. I mean, you get concepts presented, you absorb them, practice them, they become part of you and then you go to the next thing.

A: Yes, but you are asking about the speed of light as relates to fourth density and above density levels and we are telling you that there is no speed of light there because there is no need for that, because once you reach fourth density level, you have learned the lessons of third density level.

Q: (L) Well, if a person on third density gets into some kind of vehicle and achieves light speed, does that automatically translate them into fourth density?

A: Could you please point out one of these vehicles?

Q: (L) Well, we don't have any ... yet.

A: Do you expect to have any before you go to fourth density?

Q: (L) No.

A: Then the lesson is learned, yes?

Q: (L) Sort of.

A: If you trust in what we are saying, which is in response to what you are asking, then the lesson is learned. Now, contemplate, because all there is is lessons.

Q: (L) Well, you talk about time being an illusion, time being something we hold dear to us like a mother, and that sort of thing, and I would be perfectly happy to let go of time ...

A: You do! Let go!

Q: (L) Well, it is one thing to want to do it in your mind and another thing altogether to do it in your system, your internal operating system.

A: Your internal operating system?

Q: (T) Is that DOS or WARM?

A: Could you please explain what an internal operating system is?

Q: (L) I guess it is the subconscious mind.

A: It is?

Q: (L) Maybe.

A: My, my.

Q: (T) The subconscious mind has no idea of time.

(J) Time is an artificial constraint ... (L) For example: a person can have a belief about prosperity in their conscious mind and can talk about it and say affirmations and all kinds of positive things for themselves, and yet, for some reason that individual continually lives on the edge of poverty because something keeps happening that they keep screwing up to keep themselves at the level of poverty. And, when you start digging around in their subconscious mind you find out that somewhere there is the belief in poverty or there is a past life connection where they feel they need or deserve to be poor, so, their internal operating system takes precedence over their conscious beliefs and thoughts. That is what I am talking about here.

A: Yes, but what is your point?

Q: (L) The point is that you may say that you would like to get rid of time and you may understand it conceptually, but something internal keeps you tied to it. How do you get rid of that internal connection?

A: Something internal keeps you tied to it?

Q: (J) Like circadian rhythms, it's physical.

A: We feel you are missing the point.

Q: (L) Well, maybe I am.

A: You see, we speak to all of you when we say this. It's now time for you, as individuals, to try to move away, as much as possible, not to force yourselves, of course, but to try and move away at your own pace as much as possible, from the constraints of third density. You have all learned lessons to the level where you are more than ready to begin to prepare for fourth density. Third density involves a level of physicality and restriction and restraint and all of the things that go along with those, that you no longer need. So, therefore, even though we understand that at times it may feel comfortable to cling to this, there is time for you, and there is that word again, it is time for you to consider moving ahead and get ready for fourth density and not to be concerned with such things as time or how to free yourself from the illusion of time. That really is not important. That's like the third grade student delving into mathematics and stopping everything to go back and contemplate the ABCs and why it isn't CBA or BAC. There really is no point. It is what it is. They are what they are.

Q: (L) That is what I want to know, what is it?

A: Why do you need to know this?

Q: (L) Because I am curious. What is time?

A: We have already told you that it is a nonexistent, artificial creation of illusion for the point of learning at the level where you are at or were, and once you have left that level, you no longer need it.

Q: (T) Maybe one of the lessons is to learn not to worry about time. Once you learn that time is not real ... (SV) Tell that to your boss!

A: If something is not real, is there any concern in worrying about what it is? Imagine a conversation between two people: Billy and Gene. Billy says to Gene, "There is no such thing as time." Gene says, "Oh, really? But I want to know what it is.' Billy says, "But I just told you there is no such thing. Time does not exist. It is not real in any form, in any frame of reference, in any form of reality, any level of density. It simply does not exist." And, Gene says: "Oh, that's interesting. Now, again, what is this time?"

Q: (L) Point taken. (T) Do you wear a watch? (L) No. (SV) I have to because of my schedule. (T) But, you wear the watch because other people believe in time? (SV) Yes. (T) And that is out of courtesy for their belief, not your belief.

A: That is precisely correct. While you are still in this third density it is still necessary for you to conform, to a certain extent, to the ways of others who are more comfortable within the realm of third density. But, as we have stated previously, perhaps it is "time" for you to begin preparing for fourth density and not concern yourself any more than is absolutely necessary with all the where's and why's and what for's of third density reality. This truly is behind you, now, and we know that because we can see from all levels six through one and back again in full cycle.

Q: (L) Going along with that statement, not too long ago I asked a question about the purpose of this group and the answer was that if we knew, or, more specifically if I knew, I would become "unglued." Was that meant literally?

A: Oh, yes certainly. Every single bone in your body is going to unglue itself from every other.

Q: (L) Well, since you are saying that it is time for us to begin preparing for fourth density, maybe it is time to deal with that question?

A: Well, perhaps you are trying to steer us, now. This is amusing because, of course, you sought our help, now we guess you are going to put us in your place and vice versa. But, actually, in a way, that is what is already happening, because, again, we must remind, that we are you in the future and we have already experienced all that you are experiencing. And, of course, we are experiencing as it is always being experienced. But, it is important to note that you have been making progress despite our occasional chidings, and we are very proud of the progress you have been making. Also, we want to remind you again not to worry about the extent of the progress or the direction it is taking. Just let it happen. All knowledge that it is absolutely necessary for you to gain to sustain this progress will be gained at the appropriate point in ... [chorus] *time*. Therefore, not to worry as it will all fall into place, as we have told you. Now, we do not feel that you are ready, as yet, to know what your ultimate purpose is, nor is it necessary for you to know, and it certainly would not be helpful in any way, so we ask again that you please not worry about that because when the "time" comes for you to know, you will.

Q: (SV) I want to ask one question: If there is no time, there is no past and no future; there are no past lives and no future lives, there is no such thing as reincarnation, then how can you be us ...

A: Yes, there is reincarnation. You are getting ahead of yourself there. We never said there is no reincarnation.

Q: (SV) But, if there is no time? (J) It is our perception of it. (L) It is all happening simultaneously. We are having all of these lifetimes at once. (SV) Is there a way that we can connect ourselves with all our other selves?

A: Picture it this way: we will access some of your memory banks and give you another reference which, interestingly enough, fits very closely with the perpendicular reality wheel that we described earlier. You know what a slide projector looks like? To give you some feeling of what this expanded nature of reality really is, picture yourself watching a big slide presentation with a big slide wheel on the projector. At any given point along the way you are watching one particular slide. But, all the rest of the slides are present on the wheel, are they not? And, of course, this fits in with the perpendicular reality, which fits in with the circles within circles and cycles within cycles, which also fits in the Grand Cycle, which also fits in with what we have told you before: All there is is lessons. That's all there is, and we ask that you enjoy them as you are watching the slide presentation ...

Q: (J) In that analogy, the light that shines through the slide, as it projects it upon the screen, is our perception.

A: And, if you look back at the center of the projector, you see the origin and essence of all creation itself, which, is level seven where you are in union with the One.

If the origin of the light of consciousness is at seventh density, and it projects through consciousness units, or individual perception, we come to the idea that archetypal images may be extremely important. Archetypes are the patterns of human, societal, and national interactions as conceived, and created by beings of higher densities. And, it may be that these archetypal images are viewed or perceived by those who we have come to know as prophets.

In more recent times I discovered a curious reference to the above remark by the Cassiopaeans about becoming unglued. Author Ira Friedlander writes in *The Whirling Dervishes*:

Everything in the world is invisible except that which we make semi-visible. By the introduction of awareness, all things can become visible. The aim of the dervish is to open the eyes of the heart and see infinity in eternity. His goal is to loosen himself from the earth's glue which binds him and become one with God, to become a channel for His Light. (Friedlander 1975)

It must be noted that in Sufi terms, the eyes of the heart do not refer to emotion or love in any sense that Western minds have tended to interpret it. In fact, the term *heart* in Eastern mysticism refers more to the consciousness of the soul – awareness – than to the many corruptions of this term that pass in New Age teachings as "the way of the heart." Mystic, revolutionary writer and Sufism teacher, Mansur al Hallaj, has said: "When truth has overwhelmed a human heart, it empties it of all that is not truth. When God loves a being, He kills everything that is not Him."

And that brings us back to the remark of the Cassiopaeans:

A: The perpendicular reality primarily, though not exclusively, refers to one's life path and *how one's life path fits together in the cycle or in a wheel when connected with those of a similar life path*. And, oddly enough, relates very closely to the previous question involving synchronicity. If you can picture an inlaid wheel formed by a circle within a circle, and adjoining partitions in a perfect balance, that would be the best representation of perpendicular reality for *it does not completely involve one individual's experience, but rather a group of individual's experience for the progression of a greater purpose*. [Columbus] had instinct and imagination and when he married his instinct with imagination, it became reality. And, when it became reality, he had created a reality which he was fully confident would be manifest in the physical third density reality. It wasn't that he was confident. He knew it to be so. He didn't stop himself by adding prejudice to the equation which is what you are doing when you say, "Well, we don't know what happens because we have never been there!" ... The core circle connects with all seven sections to the outer circle. Now, picture that outer circle as being an ever expanding circle ...
Q: (L) Does it represent an expansion of our knowledge and consciousness?
A: That's part of it.
Q: (L) Does it represent also expanding influence of what and who we are on the reality which is around us?
A: That is correct.

And here the question must be asked: why have we created a world in which material extinction is a real possibility? Where has the human race gone wrong? Are we truly on the edge of an abyss, losing our balance, preparing to fall into a hole so deep and dark that we shall never come out of it?

What is this mysterious gap between intent/desire and physical manifestation? What darkness exists in our subconscious minds that has created a world so hostile and uncaring? What power separates us from knowledge of our inner creative selves and leaves us exposed to suffering and pain?

For, no matter how one defines reality – as a self-created manifestation, or as an accomplished fact thrust upon us – the reality of suffering must be seen as a consequence of this separation. And, if the world of matter is created and maintained by us, what are we doing about it that is new and different?

For millennia we have worked with the idea that pain and suffering is a consequence of willful disobedience. If this is so, then man's being is a blight on the cosmos, and this is certainly the core belief system that is inherent in all philosophies and teachings that promote faith in this or that savior or mode of salvation. And we have to note, because our lives may depend on it, that it simply hasn't worked.

If we accept that, for whatever reason, some aspect of creation has manifested the limited three dimensions in which our consciousnesses find themselves, how would we describe this condition and its potential for change?

We usually consider the past as no longer existing. The future does not exist either and the present refers to the momentary transition of nonexistence into nonexistence. How absurd that seems, but trying to understand it in linear terms, that's what you end up with.

Physicist John Archibald Wheeler, who takes the lesson of quantum physics seriously, writes:

> The point is that the Universe is a grand synthesis, putting itself together all the time as a whole. Its history is not a history as we usually conceive history. It is not one thing happening after another. It is a totality in which what happens "now" gives reality to what happened "then," perhaps *even determines* what happened then. (Wheeler 2000, 338)

But, if it is true that only *now* exists, then the problem is our concept of time. We regard time as linear, long or short, an endless line, a progression from past into future. But this creates an insurmountable problem. On a line, *now* is a mathematical point of infinitesimal smallness – it has no dimension. By scientific logic, it does not exist!

Russian philosopher P.D. Ouspensky, in his *Tertium Organum*, illustrates this for us using the example of a snail on a journey:

> We know nothing about its inner life, but we may be sure that its perception is very different from ours. In all probability a snail's sensations of its surroundings are very vague. It probably feels warmth, cold, light, darkness, hunger, and instinctively (i.e. incited by pleasure/pain guidance) it crawls toward the uneaten edge of the leaf it sits on, and draws away from a dead leaf. Its movements are governed by pleasure/pain. It always advances toward the one and retreats from the other. It always moves on one line, from the unpleasant towards the pleasant. And, in all probability it senses and knows nothing except this line. This line constitutes the whole of its world. All the sensations entering from the outside are sensed by the snail on this line of motion. And, these come to it out of time – from potentiality they become actuality. For a snail, the whole of our Universe exists in the future and the past, i.e., in time. (Ouspensky 1920)

The snail is probably not self-aware – that is, aware that it is surging across so vast a landscape, all of which exists simultaneously, of which the snail could be aware if it were possible to expand its awareness through some process of meta-morphosis and lift it high above the garden to expand its scope. But, it only per-ceives the various phenomena – the leaf, the grass, the twig, the sand, the walkway – at the moment it interacts with them. They are events of long or short duration, past and future, which "come to pass" as the snail inches along.

In the same manner do we experience our world, our five sense organs are merely feelers by means of which we touch and interpret the world through the mathematical constructs of our brains and in the limited terms of three-dimensional consciousness. Scientific gadgetry only lengthens our feelers a bit.

Imagine a consciousness not limited by the conditions of sense perception. Such a consciousness can rise above the plane on which we move; it can see far beyond the bounds of the circle illumined by our ordinary consciousness; it can see that not only does the line along which we move exist, but also all the other lines perpendicular to it which we cross (in our series of nows). Rising above the plane, this consciousness will be able to see the plane, make sure that it actually is a plane and not only a line, then it will be able to see the past and the future living side by side and existing simultaneously.

> The past and future cannot be nonexistent. They must exist together somewhere, on-ly we do not see them. ... We must admit that the past, the present and the future do not differ from one another in any way, that the only thing that exists is the Eternal Now of Indian philosophy. (Ouspensky 1920)

The Alpha and Omega. But we do not see this – at least very few of us do – and then we only see imperfectly, "through a glass darkly." We are snails crossing the landscape of the Universe, aware only momentarily of the earth, the leaf, the flow-er, or the raindrop before us. At any given moment we are only aware of a small fragment of the Universe and we continue to deny the existence of everything else – namely the *coexistent past and future* and the possibility of perceiving it. The Cassi-opaeans refer to it as a state in which a person merges densities, or traverses densi-ties. It is the merging of physical reality and ethereal reality, which involves thought form versus physicality. In other words, superluminal communication with the self in the future.

January 14, 1995
Q: (L) You have told us in the past that you are us in the future and that you are [traveling on the Wave], moving this way to merge with us.
A: Yes.
Q: (L) As we measure time, how far in the future are you us?
A: Indeterminate as you measure time.
Q: (L) Does this mean that at the point in time when the Wave arrives on the earth in

this upcoming event that you have given us the information to plot the ETA, is that the time at which you will merge with us and become us in the future?

A: No, that is not the correct concept.

Q: (L) You have said that when the Wave arrives that you will merge with us. Is this the same thing that you are talking about when you say that you are us in the future?

A: No. You are again slipping into trying to apply 3rd density logic to higher levels of density reality. We are trying to help everyone to advance.

Q: (L) So, we are not talking about the same event …

A: What is "future," anyway?

Q: (L) The future is simultaneous events, just different locales in space/time, just a different focus of consciousness, is that correct?

A: Yes, so if that is true, why try to apply linear thinking here, you see, we are merging with you right now!

Q: (T) So, what you are trying to say is that when the Wave comes it is going to take us to fourth density, if we are ready, but we are not actually going to merge with you in sixth density at that point, but we may experience a merge at that point because all points of focus merge during transition from one density to another?

A: Partly correct, partly way off.

Q: (J) What part is right and what part is wrong?

(T) The Wave is going to take those of us who are, at that point ready, to move us into fourth density, is this part correct?

A: Open.

Q: (T) Which part of it is open?

A: You are a 4th density candidate.

Q: (T) So, we are fourth density candidates but that doesn't necessarily mean that we will make it into fourth density, true?

A: Partly.

Q: (T) As fourth density candidates, anyone that is, when the Wave comes, if they have reached the correct frequency vibration, and have raised themselves up to the point that the Wave will take them, they will, at that point, move into fourth density, true?

A: Close enough.

Q: (T) Now, when those who move into fourth density make the move, will they experience a completeness or merge with all other densities of their being, at that point, even if it is for a short time?

A: For one immeasurably small instant, this is what is meant by "illumination"!

Q: (T) But, for that small instant, because there really is no time, maybe an instant or an aeon, depending on how any individual might measure it, we might experience oneness with ourselves?

A: It may seem to last "forever."

Q: (L) Is this what is known as the "rapture?"

A: Some have attempted to explain instinctive thought patterns this way.

There are two main theories of the future – that of a predestined future and that of a free future. The theory of predestination asserts that every future event is the result of past events and if we know all the past then we could know all the future. The idea of a free future is based on quantum probabilities. The future is either only partially determined or undetermined because of the varied interactions possible at any given point.

This idea of free will says that quite deliberate volitional acts may bring about a subsequent change in events. Those who support predestination say that so-called voluntary actions are actually the results of incompletely understood causes that have made them imperative acts. In short, nothing is accidental. On the one hand we have the cold predestination – come what may, nothing can be changed – and on the other hand we have a reality of which is only a point on some sort of needle we call the present, surrounded on all sides by the gulf of nonexistence: a world that is born and that dies every moment.

Ouspensky unifies these views:

> At every given moment all the future of the world is predestined and existing, but *it is predestined conditionally*, i.e., there must be one or another future in accordance with the direction of events of the given moment, *if no new factor comes in*. And a new factor can come in only from the side of consciousness and the will resulting from it. (Ouspensky 1920)

In other words, the snail can choose to change his direction by overcoming his instinctive urge for pleasure and avoidance of pain. But this can only come about by *becoming aware* of the probable course he is on. If his natural tendencies are leading him to an abyss that will plunge him into a blazing inferno below, then it would behoove him to learn exactly what it is he must do to avoid it.

> In the past, what is behind us lies not only in what was, but also in what could have been. In the same way, in the future lies not only what will be but also what may be. (Ouspensky 1920)

All exists simultaneously – it is only we who, singly and collectively, can change the focus of our consciousness. And we can only make this change if we have objective awareness of the true state of our reality.

Now we must ask the question: Why can we not perceive reality as it is? Why can we not enlarge our perception – why are we chained in this painful existence we call reality? *Can our consciousness get beyond the conditions of three dimensions without fundamental alterations in material existence?* How long can we sustain it there? In order to live in that state of expanded consciousness is it necessary for the fundamental nature of our individual reality to change dramatically? I believe it is.

Quantum theory may demonstrate that all that exists, past, present, and future, is combined into a single entity whose farthest parts are joined in an immediate manner. No field mechanism is required for this oneness. Perhaps this entity carries the Wave. But, as the Cassiopaeans have pointed out:

DEBUGGING THE UNIVERSE

December 10, 1994

A: The Wave is transport mode.

Q: (L) Is that transport mode for many beings?

A: Yes. *Wave is "crowded."*

Q: (L) Are you coming to invade us?

A: No, merge.

Q: (L) Are others coming with the intention of invading us?

A: Yes.

Q: (T) So, everybody out in the whole Universe who want a piece of the earth action are on this wave?

A: At realm border crossing. … Huge wave of UFO activity. All manner and origins. Just you wait, it will give you chills and that feeling in the pit of your stomach. Many aliens will appear and we will be visible too. Think of it as a convention. All must awaken to this. It is happening right now. The whole populace will play individual roles according to their individual frequencies. This is only the beginning …

Q: (L) How do you relate to the Pleiadians?

A: Pleiadians are communicating with many others; we are bursting upon the scene with you, but we are essentially the same, just *at slightly different focus points on the realm border.*

Q: (L) Well, why is all this activity happening now?

A: The grand cycle is about to close presenting a unique opportunity.

Q: (L) Does this mean that this is a unique opportunity to change the future?

A: Future, past and present.

Q: (L) Well, that sort of makes me think that if things are not changed somewhat at this point on the grand cycle that things could get really direfully screwed up, is that correct?

A: But they won't. You have not grasped concept.

Q: (L) Yeah I have, I got you, I understand. It's just part of the cycle. It's all a cycle. I mean their being here is part of us being here …

A: You do??? [giant question mark inscribed on board]

Q: (L) Do what?

A: You said you understood concept. Really? Learn.

Q: (V) I am just concerned about the previously mentioned "convention" …

A: Convention is because of realm border crossing.

Q: (L) And why is there a convention attending this realm border crossing? I mean, is it just a "really big shew"?

A: *It is an opportunity.*

Q: (V) As in the windows are all opening at one time so that all these beings can get in at one time?

A: *As in an opportunity to affect whole Universe.* Picture cosmic playing of "Pomp and Circumstance" AKA *"Hope and Glory."*

Q: (L) So, do realm borders have something to do with location?

A: Realm borders ride waves.

Q: (L) And where do these waves come from?

A: They constantly cycle.

Q: (L) Does it have something to do with the movement of the planet Earth into it or does it move onto us?

A: Either or.

Q: (F) Does this convention or convergence have something to do with the fact that there are living beings on the earth?

A: Yes. And because you are at critical juncture in development.

Q: (L) Are the sixth density Orions, also known as Transient Passengers, are they the same TPs that have been referred to as the ones who genetically engineered us or put us here?

A: Close. They are Wave riders.

Q: (L) Are those groups that ride the Wave, is riding the wave part of the definition of Transient Passengers?

A: Yes.

Q: (L) Do they like to ride this Wave?

A: Is it "fun" for you to live on Earth?

Q: (L) Well, I like living on Earth a great deal, but I don't like pain and suffering, and I don't like man's inhumanity to man and I don't like to see other people suffer.

A: Do you live on Earth for amusement?

Q: (L) I would like to live on Earth for amusement but I haven't had a whole heck of a lot of laughs since I have been here this time. I would like to have a life on the planet where things were pleasant ...

A: You misunderstood.

Q: (L) I see what you are saying. That's where they live because that's where they live.

A: Yes.

What is of particular interest in the above discussion of the Wave is the fact that different sources of information apparently come from different focus points on the Wave. Putting that together with the idea of perpendicular realities, or the connection of certain human beings with the Wave in an interactive way, or merging, as well as the idea of archetypes as slides through which the consciousness of 7th density projects itself into consciousness units, we come to the idea the Cassiopaeans mentioned above, which is that "the whole populace will play individual roles according to their individual frequencies." This must mean that each individual is a manifestation of the frequency with which they connect to the Wave.

The study of wave motion is a precise science and all waves follow the same fundamental rules, which are clearly demonstrable both practically and mathematically. One of these rules states that *a wave takes its character from what is doing the waving.* Also, waves go through exactly determined cycles, which have phases that can be known or estimated. Since this is the case, what we perceive as reality is nothing more than the myriad oscillations of the primeval waveform, or 7th density. It is implied in physics that a wave usually have a waver, so we may assume that our reality has a waver also.

We must perceive that man is an oscillation of the absolute and, as such, has the potential of being augmented by other waveform expressions of energy and thus expanding, so to speak, his own awareness. Just as certain mechanical aids can augment the perception of certain ranges of light such as infrared, ultraviolet, x-rays, and radio waves, so might personal energies be synchronized by psychic means, or even, at the very deepest level, move into phase with the primal wave itself.

This is what I believe happens during mystical states of being which bring about enlightenment or during which information is received from Higher Sources. This brings us to ask the question: Who or what is doing the waving?

The descriptions of the greater reality beyond time and space are, of necessity, beyond words. In many instances, the individual receiving such information indicates the impossibility of explaining what they have experienced. So, I think we can assume that the finite nature of our physical brains is self-limiting in a certain sense. But they can certainly do much, much more than what we consider to be normal.

The brain is an instrument devised to focus reality in mathematical constructs – interpreting waveforms as material objects. The abilities of certain individuals to achieve such higher states of consciousness in the realms of physiological science is being documented by fantastic examples every day. We should understand that these abilities might extend even into the realms of perceiving the motions of the vast primal wave in other ways. These individuals might be able to perceive the effects of other waveforms and, depending upon the amplitudes and energies, predict the outcomes of certain motions, even, perhaps, in very precise terms based upon the direction which consciousness is taking.

The new research in physics sounds provocatively like ancient mystical teachings, yet I believe that the true nature of the reality behind our world is beyond quantum mechanics and field theory. We may find that much truth was known by the peoples of the past and that they did, in fact, express deep, mysterious, realities in their poetic and obscure messages. Mystics and seers perceive quantum-like states, which are demonstrably difficult to translate into language. Additionally, with the passage of time and changes in word usage, we find a very great barrier to understanding.

There are numerous instances in literature and history when individuals have claimed to achieve just such an elevation of consciousness – at least for periods of time. There is much information pertaining to how this state may be achieved, which involves great self-discipline and extended preparation, but under certain circumstances may occur spontaneously.

The experience of viewing simultaneous, cause/effect reality may be extremely difficult to maintain when one is constantly being bombarded by three-dimensional interpretation and the difficulty of translating this into linguistic expressions may be even more difficult.

Imagine the difficulty of explaining to a snail the expanse of an acre of ground! Mystics and Seers have attempted to do just that for millennia with the result that the vast majority of humankind have absolutely and totally misunderstood these concepts. And, there is no worse lie than a truth misunderstood by those who hear it. The greatest lies are the dark and evil systems of religion created by those who do not understand. (Of course, that is not to say that a religion based on Truth could not be created by those who *do* understand, as seems to have been the case in the religion of Paleolithic civilzations.)

Until quite recent times, science has lumped all psychic or mystical states under the heading of pathological or unhealthy conditions of the mind. Many scientists still hold this opinion. There are conditions of pseudo-mystical perversion, purely psychopathic states and conscious deceit that are often manifested in churches and cults around the globe and have been so for centuries.

How do you separate the true from the false?

If a mystical state can be defined as cognition under conditions of expanded consciousness, what may the results be? William James, in *Varieties of Religious Experience* gives a checklist:

1. Mystical states give knowledge, which nothing else can give
2. Mystical states give knowledge of the real world with all its attributes
3. The mystical states of men belonging to different ages and different peoples show astonishing similarity and at times complete identity
4. The results of mystical experience are totally illogical from our ordinary point of view.

I would like to pose another question: maybe we ought to look at our reality here on this Earth in a different fashion? In the human being, the pre-birth life of the fetus is as different from the afterbirth life of the human as life, perhaps, is from death. Does death mean annihilation? Surely not since we know that our material world comes into being from that which can be neither seen nor measured. And, if the real deeper reality of the world passes into three dimensions as a phase, might we not assume that the reality, itself, could do the same? That is, if our observation of the life of an individual human is a microcosm, perhaps the material world is a gestational state – a preparation for an existence of an entirely different order in quantum terms. Preparation for a fundamental transformation of matter itself?

Although there is a great movement toward transcendentalism, this movement cannot transform due to the fact that the fundamental forces of the world are antithetical to this physical reality. While we all might like to think we can transform our world by thinking positively, we must remember that there is a great deal of scientific evidence that transformations of the planet have repeatedly been cataclysmic. A philosophy that ignores this fact is courting disaster.

It may be that their focus upon a New Age quite literally contributes energy to the dissolution of the current age *in a manner that follows scientific principles*. To think that the transition will occur by thought alone ignores certain very important scientific factors. We are looking to find the threads of identity – the points of agreement in science, philosophy and religion.

Matter, as we experience it, seems to be opposed to spirit, otherwise we would easily be able to manifest and ascertain our spiritual natures from our present state of existence. Research will show that this is possible, but only on a very limited level, to very few people who work very hard and devote their lives to this pursuit (or experience severe trauma).

Therefore, in order to manifest the prophesied or projected *unity* of spirit and matter, either the spiritual estate must become grosser and more material, or the material estate must become finer and less dense and material. And, *in order for either of these events to occur, macrocosmic quantum changes must occur according to the observable processes of microcosmic quantum mechanics.*

In any event, it is my thought that the idea of the end of the world is essentially correct from many points of view – but the result is as unknown to us as adult life is to an unborn child. The obvious thing to conclude is that the fundamental three-dimensional nature of the Universe is that which must be altered in order for any of the prognosticated eschatological scenarios to manifest.

But, the understanding of this concept, if it is true, reveals a cataclysmic holocaust so soul-chilling that the psyche reels into mindless denial. Prophetic truth, revealed when the time for fulfillment draws near, gives birth to visions of primeval destruction beyond the most gripping and searing nightmare; concepts that make the obscenity of nuclear war seem like child's play.

But, maybe not. Maybe it depends on which archetype on the Wave the mind of humanity aligns with?

The Cassiopaeans are asking us to look at the concepts of doomsday – admittedly a violent and horrendous prospect – in an entirely new light. The end may indeed be the end; the end of the world as we know it. And I mean that in a very basic sense.

But, more than that, they are asking us to understand that it is not just the end of a civilization – though it will be that, too. It is not just the beginning of the New Age – it will be that, also. But we are looking at a possibility that we may manifest the end of matter as we presently know it, and the quantum alteration of the Universe according to observable scientific principles, which will enable the earth, life and the cosmos to manifest in a new way: restoration of perfection and the Edenic state – the harmony of spirit and matter. The end that is the beginning.

Palle Yourgrau writes in Gödel Meets Einstein: Time Travel in the Gödel Universe:

Adopting ... an ontological ... point of view, we pose the question: where do we come from? (And where are we going?) That babies come from the womb is a familiar biological fact concerning our early *bodies*, but it is of no help with the present question. I thus lay down my ... alarming proposition: We don't really know *where* we (as babies) came from. ... [Gödel wrote] "the idea that the world and everything in it has meaning and reason, and in particular a good and indubitable meaning ... it follows immediately that our worldly existence, since it has in itself at most a very dubious meaning, can only be means to the end of another existence. ... Since we came into existence one day in this world *without knowing how-so and whence*, the same can happen again in the same way in another world." ...

Birth and death, then, are changes (with respect to existence) ... living ... is a process that takes place in time, and ... birth obviously precedes death. And that is, of course, why we naturally *fear death* but *not* our *prenatal nonexistence* ...

... Gödel ... views our embodied existence, in this world, as at best a confused and cloudy preparation for something more meaningful – in our postnatal nonexistence (i.e., nonexistence after death in this world). "Without a next life," he writes, "the potential of each person and the preparations of this life make no sense for what would be the point of bringing forth an essence (the human being) that has so wide a range of possible (individual) developments ... but is never allowed to realize one thousandth of them? ... Mind, in its use, is not static but constantly developing ... there is no reason why the number of mind's states should not converge to infinity in the course of its development. ... The greater part of learning will take place in the next world, and we could very well be born into the next world with latent memories of our experiences in this world." (Yourgrau 1999, 188–192)

Now, let's look at this idea of nonlinear dynamics in terms of specific human beings enacting an archetype, and their thoughts and actions in this world. The following excerpt is from Ark's journals. It was written at a turning point in his life, shortly after he had spent some time in Florence. A few years earlier he had nearly died of pneumonia while in Göttingen, during which time he experienced a vision, and The Call to Adventure. When he began to return to health, he knew that he must begin to wake up, though he was not sure what this call meant for him to do. It was written in Bielefeld, Sunday, May 25, 1988:

Determination is needed. Thinking in terms of weeks and months instead of years. What is needed is setting a goal and striving to achieve it. Because as it is, I am in no way different from other people. I am drifting the same way they are drifting. My only chance is to find a *different way*.

Thus, I want to change my priorities. I want to change my way of living. To change to what?

I have ideal conditions. It could not be better. I am, in principle, absolutely free. So what?

I see no other way than setting and realizing goals. Setting and realizing goals. Setting and realizing. Setting and realizing.

Otherwise, there is drifting. "Life is real only when *I am*." If I am living consciously, then I know that *I am*.

If we set goals and are not conscious, if we are not attentive, if we are not wise – then we are drifting. And, sooner or later there is a reversal in direction. I want to avoid this. But first, I need to understand what is:

Drifting.

Days and years are passing. I am drifting. Again I am drifting. I am thinking back. What was good and what was bad? It was good when I knew where I was going. When from my depths I designed a goal and when I was striving to get it. What is my goal today? Where do I go? Where do I want to get to? Have I reconciled myself with life? Has a crystallization occurred? Am I satisfied with it? What is my way?

I have ideal – best of the best – conditions to answer this question. What do I choose? And then, how do I want to realize this choice?

I am drifting. Again I am drifting because first, I was supposed to understand "drifting."

No, it is better without planning. It is better if it will be based on free association until the subject is exhausted.

Bielefeld, West Germany. Europe. Earth. Solar System. The Galaxy. The Universe. That's me in this perspective. The New Age is coming. Do I need a greater scale of things? No, this is enough. So, here I am, on the planet Earth, in the Solar System. I know nothing of other living beings in the Universe. The purpose of my existence: unknown. So, a hypothesis is necessary. A working hypothesis to be falsified or confirmed. A kind of a compass. An axiom, a postulate to be verified by developing a system based on this postulate and by checking if it is useful, if it leads somewhere and does not drift in a circle.

And it seems that the only reasonable hypothesis is one that comes from the unknown system taught by Gurdjieff. This system tells us that the world has a certain purpose. It tells us that not everything works well. It tells us that there are certain bugs in the construction. It is quite possible that using the meta-language, one can prove that any program on that scale must have bugs. So, *the Universe is a program*, a program that has bugs, but which has *the in-built capacity for self-improving*.

There are, consequently, certain units that are brought to existence with this specific purpose: to self-evolve to a degree high enough to be able to discover the methods of debugging. These repairs can only be done on a local scale, therefore local units are created. Of course, there are ways to act non-locally, but for that, one has to have some knowledge of the operating system. Thus, this is the allegory.

I am such a unit. I am alive, and I am endowed with some inputs and outputs and peripherals; with some modems for communication. The computer allegory. So, potentially, I have everything necessary for self-development. Of course, during my life certain things went wrong, therefore certain connections are wrong, certain others are even deadly wrong. But these defects can and must be circumvented by closing certain channels and by opening of others. Anyway, I can only do what I can do – no more.

This is a general perspective. From this general perspective, my aim is to save the Universe. Or, rather: to help save the Universe. And this I have to do, whatever the future might be. Independently of the fact that there *may* be an immortal soul that can be developed by conscious effort and intellectual suffering, I have no other choice but to help to *debug the Universe*.

"In the beginning was the Word ... " Only today do I understand this message. This means we are entering into an important era. In a sense into a final era: when to decide to be of or not of the Universe. This is the general perspective.

Now my role in this opus: I am a worker; I have a mission that is to be fulfilled. I have been sent here; sent into this time, this place, in this and not in some other form. The first thing to do is to *find and read the designated task*. But there is more. There are, namely, *information channels with which I can communicate with those that sent me here and that are controlling the mission*. Because the higher intelligence must have some control, but it cannot do the work which only I can do. So, there are certain information channels.

Of course, I am not able to make free use of them. I cannot use them until there is a guarantee that using of these channels will not bring harm.

Summary:

Universe is a Computer Program

Self organizing, Self evolving Units, some of these are

Debugging Local Units on a

Mission. There is a

Higher Intelligence and

Communication Channels.

Of course, all this process is based on the law of big numbers. That is: not everything can be programmed. Statistical fluctuations must be allowed. Otherwise nothing will evolve by itself. Otherwise there will be no self-evolution!

It follows thus that probabilistics, that stochastics, that elements of uncertainty, elements of choice, are at the base of the construction of the Universe. This is interesting and I want to work on this. This is very important.

I want to return to this point later on. But now, I want to proceed further: What is my aim, what is my goal, what is my task? What kind of work am I to perform? What kind of work do I want to perform?

The Universe may be a deterministic automaton, nevertheless, with such a complex action that there is no other method of predicting than running the Universe to see what will happen. In this sense, therefore, we must be satisfied with a statistical description when we want to foresee the future. Let us say that this is a rough picture. But then, where is free will? The ability to choose? For precognition? Something is therefore lacking in this picture.

Workings of the Universe.

The problem of determinism and indeterminism. The problem of free will and the problem of chance. All this relates to the problem of time and to the problem of other dimensions. Therefore I must not discuss these things on too simple a level. So, we have the following circle of problems:

Time – Causality – Determinism – Chance – Phase – Other Dimensions – Quantum and Classical – Complementarity – Information – Organization.

What is important here is that these are general laws – these are objective. There are statistical laws that are valid on average, and there are laws that concern each individual case. But these laws leave a certain rather big freedom. Within this freedom there is what *is* and within this freedom we are given [a] free hand. Thus, not everything is determined and *predictions for the future have the form:* **if** *this,* **then** *this;* **if not,** *then that.*

I am living in the world based on technology. I am using this technology. We have computers. We know something about computer programs. Only now we understand what it means, "In the beginning was the Word." Therefore we should not alienate ourselves from this technology. Our cognizance goes through technology – which does not exclude the fact that for some so-called "chosen" people, there are other possibilities of gaining knowledge. These are possibilities which are not, however, saving *all* of humanity.

Thus, I am aware of the fact that I am not developing for myself. I am not working for salvation or immortality. I am sent here with a *mission* and my task is to add to the saving of the Universe. I can do it by helping humanity. But in order to do it, I need *knowledge*, I need to be able to *discern*. So, the goal appears:

To discover the workings of the Universe, to learn about human beings, about myself.

To learn to help the Universe means to help the Creator. To be of some help to the Creator of *everything*. Everything-that-*is* is a great thing. So, this is my ultimate goal. The goal from which all other goals stem.

Now, come back to the beginning. If this is my goal, then there should be no time for drifting, no place for pleasures. Somebody told me that I need to rest, but I do not need to rest when there is work to be done. At each moment I can choose. At these moments I have to be careful not to let things just go *their* way.

So, the ultimate goal is clear. Now must come realization. It is clear, psychologically, that the goal is difficult. And there are all kinds of obstacles, there are phantoms that can delude ... all of mythology is *full* of temptation stories!

The goal is high and right and good, but for some reason, it cannot be obtained by just anybody who can *see* it. There is some sort of filter in action, there is a selection criteria. The goal can be reached only by some chosen ones, some who can pass a test, who can oppose temptations, who can prove to have enough strength, who can show that the Gods have them under their care. Otherwise, I will perish. (Arkadiusz Jadczyk, Research Journals, 1988)

I have tried to reproduce the actual setup of this journal entry above because it is important. What this tells us is that, as early as 1988, Ark was "in contact" with the Cassiopaeans. While I was living in the woods, meditating in my garden and wrestling with God about my own purpose, or trying to read impossible physics texts, he was already formulating ideas that have a powerful bearing on the present subject; debugging the Universe; local "debugging units" that produce nonlinear changes. And it is in these present pages that the dynamics of debugging are being presented. For every mind that is unplugged and debugged, the potential effects on the Universe are literally staggering.

Now, notice very carefully the following remark: *predictions for the future have the form: if this, then this; if not, then that.* If the situation, as it is, is not known, no one will take any action and the predictions for the future will be set. However, if there is a change, perhaps even so small a change as just what we are doing here in sharing this information, it can change everything in a nonlinear way. And it is this that the Cassiopaeans have endeavored to teach us. Yes, they will answer our questions objectively and clinically as to the state of the Universe in which we live at the moment the question is asked. And then they will tell us that we have free will if we have knowledge. And then, when we ask them what we ought to do, if anything, they say, "You will do what you will do."

You will do what you will do.

Physicist Julian Barbour writes in *The End of Time*:

Anyone committed to science has difficulty with free will. In *The Selfish Gene,* (2nd edition, pp. 270–71), Dawkins asks, "What on earth do you think you are, if not a robot, albeit a very complicated one?" From personal introspection, I do not believe that my conscious self exercises free will. Certainly I ponder difficult decisions at length, but the decision itself invariably comes into consciousness from a different, unconscious realm. Brain research confirms that what we think are spontaneous decisions, acts of free will, are prepared in the unconscious mind before we become aware of them.

However, the many-instants interpretation puts an intriguingly different slant on causality, suggesting that it operates in nothing like the way we normally belief it to. In both classical physics and Everett's original scheme, what happens now is the consequence of the past. But with many instants, each Now "competes" with all other Nows in a timeless beauty contest to win the highest probability. The ability of each Now to "resonate" with the other Nows is what counts. Its chance to exist is determined by what it is in itself. The structure of things is the determining power in a timeless world.

The same applies to us, for our conscious instants are embedded in the Nows. The probability of us experiencing ourselves doing something is just the sum of the probabilities for all the different Nows in which that experience is embedded. Everything we experience is brought into existence by being what it is. Our very nature determines whether we shall or shall not be. ... *We are because of what we are.* Our existence is determined by the way we relate to (or resonate with) everything else that can be. ... One day the theory of evolution will be subsumed in a greater scheme, just as Newtonian mechanics was subsumed in relativity without in any way ceasing to be great and valid science. ... I do not think that we are robots or that anything happens by chance. *That view arises because we do not have a large enough perspective on things. We are the answers to the question of what can be maximally sensitive to the totality of what is possible.* (Barbour 1999, 324–325)

What are *you* going to do?

CHAPTER 72
THE NONLINEAR DYNAMICS OF LOVE
AND COMPLEX SYSTEMS:
DEBUGGING THE UNIVERSE

Now, I would like to make some other comments before we move on. I would like to talk a little bit about "love."

Many readers seem to have grossly misunderstood the Cassiopaean remarks about love, mainly because they don't play the game of exciting your "feel good" brain chemicals with their words. They have said, "real love is not strictly hormonal". I subsequently remarked:

September 2, 1995

Q: (L) There are many teachings that are promulgated that love is the key, the answer. They say that illumination and knowledge and whatnot can all be achieved through love.

A: The problem is not the term "love," the problem is the interpretation of the term. Those on third density have a tendency to confuse the issue horribly. After all, they confuse many things as love. When the actual definition of love as you know it is not correct either. It is not necessarily a feeling that one has that can also be interpreted as an emotion, but rather, as we have told you before, the essence of light which is knowledge is love, and this has been corrupted when it is said that love leads to illumination. Love is Light is Knowledge. Love makes no sense when common definitions are used as they are in your environment. To love you must know. And to know is to have light. And to have light is to love. And to have knowledge is to love.

Now, please stop and ponder these words carefully.

When the Cassiopaeans use the term *knowledge*, they are using it in the deepest sense of the word. To have facts, to be able to remember things, or to relate things to one another, or to creatively utilize what one remembers or relates, has absolutely nothing to do with knowledge in the Cassiopaean sense of the word. They have asked us to consider this word carefully, asking:

October 22, 1994

A: Where is there any limitation in the concept behind the word "knowledge"? Being that there is no limitation, what is the value of that word? Infinite. Can you conceive of how that one concept, that one meaning frees you from all limitation? Use your sixth sense to conceive of how the word, the term, the meaning of knowledge can provide you with all that you could possibly ever need. If you think carefully you will begin to see glimpses of how this is true in its greatest possible form.

... Can you think of how it would be that simply with one term, this one word can carry so much meaning? We sense that you are not completely aware. You can have glimpses of illumination and illumination comes from knowledge. If you strive perpetually to gain and gather knowledge, you provide yourself with protection from every possible negative occurrence that could ever happen. Do you know why this is? The more knowledge you have, the more awareness you have as to how to protect yourself. Eventually this awareness becomes so powerful and so all encompassing that you do not even have to perform tasks or rituals, if you prefer, to protect yourself. The protection simply comes naturally with the awareness.

... Knowledge has all substance. It goes to the core of all existence. ... It includes adding everything to one's being *that is desirable.* And also, when you keep invoking the light, as you do, truly understand that the *light is knowledge.* That is *the knowledge which is at the core of all existence.* And being at the core of all existence it provides protection from every form of negativity in existence. Light is everything and everything is knowledge and knowledge is everything. ... If you simply have faith [in the concept of seeking knowledge], no knowledge that you could possibly acquire could possibly be false because there is no such thing.

That is, *knowledge,* by the Cassiopaean definition, is not false. Facts that later prove to be false, were never knowledge to begin with, even if they were erroneously counted as "knowledge."

Anyone or anything that tries to give you false knowledge, false information, will fail. The very material substance that the knowledge takes on, since it is at the root of all existence, will protect you from absorption of false information, which is not knowledge.

This suggests that each level of knowledge that we acquire prepares us for the next level, and the next, and so on. Those who seek to know things that they have no preparation to receive are subject to obfuscation. There is no need to fear the absorption of false information *when you are simply openly seeking to acquire knowledge.*

This last remark is crucial: "when you are simply openly seeking to acquire knowledge." I know that everyone who is seeking thinks that they are open, but if you carefully examine your thoughts, you will discover that you have a lot of beliefs and assumptions that you expect your seeking to confirm. The following comments elaborate on this:

October 22, 1994

A: And knowledge forms the protection – all the protection you could ever need. ... [People who claim to be receiving knowledge by faith who later find that they have received false information] ... are not really gathering knowledge. These people are stuck at some point in their pathway to progress and they are undergoing a hidden manifestation of what is referred to in your terms as obsession. Obsession is not knowledge, obsession is stagnation. So, when one becomes obsessed, one actually closes off the absorption and the growth and the progress of soul development which comes with the gaining of true knowledge. For when one becomes obsessed one deteriorates the protection therefore one is open to problems, to tragedies, to all sorts of difficulties. Therefore one experiences same.

Taking this *key* literally, if a person has problems or feels attacked or is suffering in any way, they have only to search their own mind to discover that they are holding on to a belief or an assumption that is an obsession. I have found this to be true in my own life, as well as the lives of others. If there are problems, illness, difficulties of all kinds, then one is obsessed in some way with a false belief. No exceptions.

The third density application of knowledge is, of course, awareness. And the Cassiopaeans have commented on this as well:

September 2, 1995

As we have told you, there are seven levels of density which involves, among other things, not only state of being physically, spiritually and etherically, and materially, but also, more importantly, *state of awareness*. You see, state of awareness is the key element to all existence in creation. You have undoubtedly remembered that we have told you that this is, after all, a grand illusion, have you not? So, therefore, if it is a grand illusion, what is more important, physical structure or state of awareness???

… Now, when we go from the measuring system, which of course has been nicely formulated so that you can understand it, of density levels one through seven, the key concept, of course, is state of awareness. All the way through. So, once you rise to a higher state of awareness, such things as physical limitation evaporate. And, when they evaporate, vast distances, as you perceive them, become nonexistent. So, *just because you are unable to see and understand has absolutely no bearing whatsoever on what is or is not possible*. Except within your own level of density. And this is what almost no one on your current level of density is able to understand. If you can understand it and convey it to them, you will be performing the greatest service that your kind has ever seen. Think about that for a moment. Let it seep into your consciousness. Analyze it. Dissect it. Look at it carefully and then put it back together again.

Q: (L) What is it that limits our awareness?

A: Your environment. And it is the environment that you have chosen. By your level of progress. And that is what limits everything. As you rise to higher levels of density, limitations are removed.

Q: (L) What creates this environment of limitation?

A: It is the grand illusion which is there for the purpose of learning.

Now, let's stop right here and consider this a moment. A recent post to one of our e-groups stated:

If you've been duped into believing that there is anything in life more important and powerful than love then you had best get back to basics. It is the fabric of everything

and it is never wrong. Granted, for many love is not really love but more about attachment and control, but if you go through this life without learning what love really
is and how to become an instrument for it to flow through then you have sold yourself
way short! ... Until you love yourself with every fiber of your being you will never be
able to love another and you will never be capable of serving anything or anyone but
your illusion of your self.

Know yourself ... Realize yourself! And then you will have something of value to offer. "Love is Light is Knowledge"? I suppose you could get away with saying it like
that but a much more accurate statement would be. From love comes light, comes
knowledge. See the difference?

This writer has just said that *learning* what love really is and *learning* how to become an instrument for love is the object of existence. He then follows with
"know yourself," (which you must do in order to love yourself), and that this
knowing of self is equal to *realizing* the self. And then he turns everything he has just
said completely around and says that you start with love in order to progress to
light, which leads to knowledge. I don't think he was even aware that his passion-
ate declaration about learning and knowing and realizing was exactly what the
Cassiopaeans said, as quoted below: "To love you must know. And to know is to
have light. And to have light is to love. And to have knowledge is to love."

He spent some time in commentary on the Cassiopaean remarks about sex,
without realizing that he was describing one part of the elephant. Just as the Cassiopaean comments on love have been twisted and misunderstood, so have the
remarks about sex. Suffice it to say that making love, as I have already intimated in
this series, is different from having sex. And just as a lot of people think they are
in love, or being loving when in fact they are not, a lot of people think they are
making love and they are not. As the writer above commented, this process the
Cassiopaeans advocate has to do with "learning what love really is and how to
become an instrument for it to flow through [you.]" And, he is absolutely correct
that you must "know yourself ... Realize yourself! And then you will have something of value to offer."

And that is what it's all about. As the Cassiopaeans have said:

September 2, 1995

Q: (L) And who put the illusion into place?

A: The Creator who is also the Created. Which is also you and us and all. As we have
told you, we are you and vice versa. And so is everything else.

Q: (L) Is the key that it is all illusion?

A: Basically, yes. As we have told you before, if you will be patient just a moment, the
universe is merely a school. And, a school is there for all to learn. That is why everything exists. There is no other reason. Now, if only you understood the true depth of
that statement, you would begin to start to see, and experience for yourself, all the
levels of density that it is possible to experience, all the dimensions that it is possible
to experience, all awareness. When an individual understands that statement to its
greatest possible depth, that individual becomes illumined. And, certainly you have

heard of that. And, for one moment, which lasts for all eternity, that individual knows absolutely everything that there is to know.

Q: (L) So, you are saying that the path to illumination is knowledge and not love?

A: That is correct.

Q: (L) Is it also correct that emotion can be used to mislead, that is emotions that are twisted and generated strictly from the flesh or false programming?

A: Emotion that limits is an impediment to progress. Emotion is also necessary to make progress in 3rd density. It is natural. *When you begin to separate limiting emotions based on assumptions from emotions that open one to unlimited possibilities, that means you are preparing for the next density.*

"You shall know the truth, and the truth shall set you free". It's a seemingly simple statement, but it's loaded with all sorts of explosive questions and ideas that have often led to, historically speaking, mayhem, murder and mass destruction. The problem seems to lie with differing definitions of what is or is not to be known, how to know it, and why.

The word *know* is derived from the Latin root *gnoscere*, which is "to know, have a clear perception or understanding of, be sure of or well informed about."

But *truth* is more difficult. It is actually derived from the same root as *tree*, and the problems immediately become apparent with this word. The first definition is "that which accords with reality or fact." But, it can also mean a "particular belief or teaching regarded by the speaker as the true one." And some trees are sturdier than others!

The problem with the first definition is related to our definitions of reality. And what is a fact? It seems that facts about our world change from one generation to the next. Many years ago it was a fact that it took weeks to cross the Atlantic by the fastest means; now it only takes hours. So it could be said that facts define our reality. But facts are not reality nor are they absolute. It seems that facts are based on knowledge, and knowledge seems to be predicated on what kinds of questions are being asked and how open the seeker is to receive answers.

Yet we come back to the statement, "You shall know the truth and the truth shall set you free." Those who think that truth is what is believed or taught by their particular religion or philosophy fail to note that the vast number of differing and often opposing beliefs suggest that either everybody is right, some are right, or there is something about this reality-making business we need to learn.

The Cassiopaeans have essentially said that there is no limit to knowledge, which suggests that all that can be conceived by the human mind, and even more, is not only possible, but probable. Nevertheless, we come back to that small problem that we are dealing with here: we happen to be on this planet, swinging through space like a seat on a Tilt-a-Whirl, perched upon the arm of the Milky Way galaxy, and whether we like it or not there are many of the people on said planet suffering mightily in ways too numerous to mention. I don't know about you, but that bugs me. And when something bugs me, my natural inclination is to find out what it is and why it is bugging me. And once I find out something about it, I *do* something. Can't help it, I'm a doer.

There are thousands upon thousands of people who advocate different views of what the answers to life's problems are. They operate much as the previously quoted writer who presents a logical series for the case, establishing knowledge as the basis of the answer, and then confounds his premise by reversing his conclusion based on an emotional belief rather than the highly developed cognition process of which he is obviously capable. This is why their answers do not seem to be leading to any active pursuit of specific measures that might serve to ameliorate the problem, much less lead to a universe changing solution. If they were clear and coherent in their own souls and minds, the result of this would be *action*. They would become doers, too.

Going back to complex systems, remember the idea that, by using nonlinear models, it is even possible to locate potential critical pressure points in such systems. At these critical points, which probably relate to what Gurdjieff called "semitones" or "stopinders" in *Law of Octaves*, a small change can have a tremendous impact.

It's now. It's here. It's happening.

Because it so happens that, at this particular point in history in this particular reality, there are these communicants from somewhere who call themselves the Cassiopaeans, who just happened to arrive on the scene after a lifetime of searching for the way back to God by yours truly.

And, as it happens, yours truly, like many others, possesses certain inner characteristics that include a powerful will and drive to serve others without violating their free will. She also speed reads, has a near photographic memory and picked up the skill of typing fairly rapidly along the way. Sounds pretty much like the ideal person for said beings to contact, right? If you want to get the message out, hook up with a walking-encyclopedia-workaholic-blabbermouth. And they did.

At the same time that this was happening, a world-class physicist of similar characteristics was searching the globe for the same answers in a different yet complementary mode. So, at this particular moment in history, scientist and walking-encyclopedia-workaholic-blabbermouth meet. They find extraordinary similarity of being, from their respective internal drives right down to skin tone and eye color. It is almost as if they are two halves of the same being.

Not only that, but she is quite taken with the idea of metamorphosis of Earth and he knows the intricacies of nonlinear dynamics and complex systems. She is looking for the *spiritual ark* and he is Ark. He is looking for the essence of existence, the *aether*, and she is L'aura, or *the air*. He's in Florence; she's in Florida. He's working on gravity waves; she's looking for explanations of gravity waves. He decides to create a webpage with an image of Magritte's *Le Chateau des Pyrenees*; and she is looking for secret masters in the Pyrenees, led on by a painting of *Arcadian Shepherds*, urged by said Cassiopaeans who tell her that her life will change suddenly and dramatically once she gets hooked up to the Internet. And his full name is Arkadiusz.

Can those guys get any funnier?

And what is even more important, both of these individuals are constitutionally incapable of taking anybody's word for anything. And if they don't like the way something is, they find out why, and then *do* something about it. In a nonlinear way.

And we come back to why the Cassiopaeans tell such awful things about our reality to us. Why would they teach us that there are horrors we don't even want to contemplate, existing not only in our world, but also at levels we can't even perceive? Never mind that they are probably true, they are scary! Why are they scaring us?

Remember the jaguar? When you encounter the jaguar, your life changes forever.

And remember the most important element: they are telling these things to people who are thinkers and, more importantly *doers*. Of all the many people on the planet with ideas about how to find the way out of the maze, many of them standing in criticism of what we are doing here, how many of them are *doing* anything about what they think will make a difference? How many of them are acting as local debugging units with knowledge of nonlinear dynamics and complex systems?

How many of them are spending ten or more hours a day gathering material and writing and producing something that might help, even if it may not be perfect or even the right answer? How many of them are working to produce a nonlinear change in this complex system of our individual and collective realities? We already know that the present reality isn't the one we want. We can already figure out, if we have one neuron in contact with another, that the old religions and philosophical systems don't work because they have been tried with little or no success for thousands of years. How many of these obsessed critics are building up out of a sense of hope and – dare I say it – even faith in themselves?

I would like to see every single individual who spends a single moment of time and energy attacking what we are doing here, take that exact amount of time each day and create your own website where you can give your information away too. Please put your money where your mouth is, and spend $10,000 a year on books and journals, computers and Internet access, as we do, so as to be informed about the things that may actually help others. And then, inform them! But don't try to violate my free will to do it the way I see fit. You have your faith, now show me your work.

So we find ourselves at that point on the jagged edge of the two crustal plates where there is a moment of critical energy influx, and we know that there is going to be an explosion. And the results are unpredictable.

Now, let's go back to this idea that seeking knowledge is the seeking of truth.

We do have a small key to this problem: the idea of being free. If it is truth, it will set one free.

But, what is it to be free? This word is derived from the Indo-European base *prie*, which means "to be fond of, to hold dear." It is related to the Sanskrit *priya*, or *desired*. It is from the same root that we get *friend*.

So, we might think that to be free means that we are full of friendliness and loving kindness and holding all we behold and experience as dear. To be free means that no power can take these feelings from us, that we have reached a level of knowing that is open and accepting of all we know. And that by knowing, we are capable of loving without conditions.

The idea of *friend* being related to freedom and knowledge is found in many ancient teachings. Sufi masters are called the "Friends of God." So we might think that to be free is to be a friend of God. But, the most important thing about a friend is that it is someone you know by virtue of being open to and accepting of without limitations. So, we have come around in a circle. And we might say that the thing that we need to know in order to be free is God.

The apostle, Paul wrote, "For that which is known about God is evident ... his nature and attributes ... have been made clearly discernible in and through the things that have been made ..." (Romans 1:19–20).

Which clearly indicates that study of the world and all within it is a pathway to God available to all. This is also a precise statement that all that exists is God, and therefore *worth knowing and being open to without conditions*. Paul further comments on those who substitute beliefs, "vain imaginings, foolish reasoning and stupid speculations," for true knowledge of God that can be obtained through study and observation of creation. He remarks that such people do not "see fit to consider Him *worth the knowing*." And we find ourselves facing the idea that refusing to learn, refusing to gather knowledge, to learn, to grow, is equivalent to refusing God! Paul remarks, "in posing as judge and passing sentence on another you condemn yourself." And what is it to judge and pass sentence? To limit one's openness to knowledge, to ask questions with pre-formed opinions, assumptions and answers.

These seed ideas are more clearly explicated in the Sufi teachings of Ibn al-'Arabî. There we find exactly what Paul has said in the first chapter of Romans, which can be reduced to the idea that everything that exists, by the fact of existing, manifests something of the divine presence, which by definition embraces all that exists. Therefore, God can be found everywhere, in everything, and all knowledge is knowledge of God.

Understanding the principles of creation tell us that the dynamic activity "to know" is expressed in creation by *the desire of God to know Himself through creation*. As the Sufis say, God was alone and desired a friend to love and be loved by. And from this desire, Creation came into being. Therefore, any limitation or assumption we make about the cosmos and all within it is a limitation placed upon God.

In the Sufi texts, *finding* is identical to consciousness and self-awareness, or with knowledge. Knowledge is a great bounty to be gathered, but it is obvious that everyone cannot have it equally. This is clearly described in the Parable of the Talents. In this story, Jesus describes knowledge as "riches" given to three servants. Two of the servants utilize their talents, or riches, to obtain even more. In fact, the exact description is that they invest, or take a risk by giving up what they have been given to multiply it. And the servant who clings desperately to his little bit of knowledge or riches, burying it in the ground from fear that his master is hard and demanding, loses even the little that he has. He closed his mind to more knowledge. He assumed that what he had was sufficient and stopped seeking. *He denied himself by denying knowledge.*

It may seem unfair, but the point is obvious that letting go of fear and wanting more knowledge to the extent of taking risks and working to get it, even if one must temporarily give up one level to gain another, is the key to being a friend of God. God wants Friends, not groveling, fearful slaves. And how can God have friends with whom he can communicate if they have no knowledge?

According to Ibn al-'Arabî's revelation, God says, "I was a Hidden Treasure, and I Loved to be known …" Which tells us that the love of God is love for the sake of knowledge. To know and be known. True love is love with knowledge. Without knowledge love loses its direction. It becomes diversified, split, a wasteland, like water losing itself in the desert. The love of the Sufi is directed toward God. And this is only possible with knowledge of Him.

So, we might think that one of the objectives of obtaining knowledge is to know how to be a friend of God. And here is where so many stumble and fall into assumptions. Every attribute or quality that we find in the cosmos must be an attribute or quality of God. The Sufis call this the "Names of God." And God has many names. Each name denotes a pair of opposites. God the Merciful can be known through Forgiveness and God the Wrathful is known through Vengeance. And these are just two examples. The variety of relationships that can be discerned in God is the reason, the primary cause, of the multiplicity of relationships in the cosmos. *All things* are manifestations and effects of the divine names or attributes in myriad combinations. God has many faces, not all of them pleasant to behold.

All beings are, in one way or another, seeking God. And the manner in which we seek determines the type of friendship we have. *God is a friend to us in the same way we are a friend to the cosmos.* The importance of this statement cannot be overestimated. It is only through knowledge of the meanings behind our experiences and the material world that we can truly discern and divide the essential attributes of any given manifestation so that we can exercise our free will in the direction of those who are known as the "Beautiful Faces of God." These are the archetypes, or points of focus on the Wave.

How does one obtain truth? How does one cast off the illusions? How does one differentiate between knowledge of light and knowledge that leads to darkness?

This comes from a combination of factors. The first is gaining and gathering knowledge of every form and sort. All sciences and arts are of value in increasing knowledge if they are approached with the intention of preparing a vessel for divine knowledge. For, in truth, all knowledge is divine. The more knowledge you have of the matters of your world, the greater the vessel you have prepared for receiving divine knowledge.

The word that is a stumbling block in many ways for many people comes in here: *faith*. But is faith, after all, so difficult? It is, in a pure sense, *feeling secure in your knowledge by virtue of experience and testing.*

But, how can you experience and test faith if you have no knowledge with which to experience and test faith? If your faith is small, you must establish it through knowledge. If you were given proof and the proof gave you faith, then everyone would have faith and then the virtue of faith, which is the building and brightening of the light within through knowledge combined with faith would have no value in moving you further along the upward path. Faith is self-evident knowledge of the inner light. It is light that grows within through effort to know truth and God by acquiring knowledge.

And it all begins by asking without belief, yet with absolute openness to receive an answer. Because, in the end, this openness of seeking without assumption or pre-formed answers is the essence of faith.

And, it seems that the asking or not asking of these questions establishes the difference between consciousness and unconsciousness. Of course, there are those who claim to ask, but really do not; they already have their answer formed by a belief system that has taken up residence in their minds. But those who ask, who *really* ask, are faced with moment-by-moment decisions, choices they must make to navigate the labyrinth, hoping that those choices will take them either to the center or the exit, depending upon their direction. Thus, if one asks with a completely open mind and heart, each moment they are open is a moment that they are conscious. Those who do not ask are unconscious; they exist in a state of fear.

Therefore, a practical plan, a mode of perception is needed by which we can understand the answers to our questions; each of us, individually, without giving our power away to some other external, dominating religion or philosophy. We need to learn to interact directly with the cosmos in a personal way. Because it is only in direct interaction with this creative force of existence that we truly are our authentic selves. When we are navigating the maze under our own power, by our own choices, we are experiencing true freedom of *being*. We are able to see that one way does not achieve our destination, and *we are free to turn around and try another.*

We are not forced to march in place, against a brick wall, not knowing that we are getting nowhere because we have allowed ourselves to be blindfolded by faith in some external source of power, be it material or philosophical or religious. We are free to *be*.

How?

We come back to learning. We are here to learn. If just finding the exact shade and tone of love would do it, there really wouldn't be any point in being here. But, as our correspondent above pointed out, we are here to learn how to love. The only difference is, instead of putting the cart before the horse, leading to failure and frustration in the student, the Cassiopaeans have undertaken to teach us the basics that seem to be sorely lacking in most of the teachings promulgated down through the millennia, perhaps by design. How can we learn the calculus of love, if we cannot do the arithmetic of awareness?

Naturalist and author Diane Ackerman writes:

> When I set a glass prism on a windowsill and allow the sun to flood through it, a spectrum of colors dances on the floor. What we call "white" is a rainbow of colored rays packed into a small space. The prism sets them free. Love is the white light of emotion. It includes many feelings which, out of laziness and confusion, we crowd into one simple word. ... Everyone admits that love is wonderful and necessary, yet no one can agree on what it is. ...
>
> *Love.* What a small word we use for an idea so immense and powerful it has altered the flow of history, calmed monsters, kindled works of art, cheered the forlorn, turned tough guys to mush, consoled the enslaved, driven strong women mad, glorified the humble, fueled national scandals, bankrupted robber barons, and made mincemeat of kings. ... the Sanskrit *lubhyati* ("he desires") [is the root of our word love]. ... Love is an ancient delirium, a desire older than civilization, with taproots stretching deep into dark and mysterious days.
>
> We use the word *love* in such a sloppy way that it can mean almost nothing or absolutely everything. ... It is a universally understood motive for crime. "Ah, he was in love," we sigh, "well, that explains it." In fact, in some European and South American countries, even murder is forgivable if it was "a crime of passion." Love, like truth, is the unassailable defense. (Ackerman 1994, xvii, xviii)

What can we say about this thing we call love which has so many effects in our lives, but which we still group together under the same term? One of the most famous writings on the subject of love, is that of the apostle Paul in the thirteenth chapter of his letter to the Corinthians:

> If I speak in the tongues of men and of angels, but have not love, I am only a noisy gong or a clanging cymbal.
>
> And if I have prophetic powers – that is, the gift of interpreting the divine will and purpose; and understand all the secret truths and mysteries and possess all knowledge, and if I have faith so that I can remove mountains, but have not love I am nothing – a useless nobody.

Even if I dole out all that I have to give food to the poor, and if I surrender my body to be burned, but have not love, I gain nothing.

Love endures long and is patient and kind; love never is envious nor boils over with jealousy; is not boastful or vainglorious, does not display itself haughtily.

It is not conceited – arrogant and inflated with pride; it is not rude, and does not act unbecomingly. Love does not insist on its own rights or its own way, for it is not self-seeking; it is not touchy or fretful or resentful; it takes no account of the evil done to it – pays no attention to a suffered wrong.

It does not rejoice at injustice and unrighteousness, but rejoices when right and truth prevail.

Love bears up under anything and everything that comes, is ever ready to believe the best of every person, its hopes are fadeless under all circumstance and it endures everything without weakening.

Love never fails – never fades out or becomes obsolete or comes to an end. As for prophecy, it will be fulfilled and pass away; as for tongues, they will be destroyed and cease; as for knowledge, it will be superseded by truth.

For our knowledge is fragmentary and our prophecy is fragmentary.

But when the complete and perfect comes, the incomplete and imperfect will vanish away – become antiquated, void and superseded.

When I was a child, I talked like a child, I thought like a child, I reasoned like a child; now that I have become a man, I am done with childish ways and have put them aside.

For now we are looking in a mirror that gives only a dim reflection of reality as in a riddle or an enigma, but then, when perfection comes, we shall see in reality and face to face! Now I know in part; but then I shall know and understand fully and clearly, even in the same manner as I have been fully and clearly known and understood by God.

And so, faith, hope, love abide; these three, but the greatest of these is love. (1 Corinthians 13:1–13)

As I said, Paul's discourse on love is one of the most famous and most quoted passages in the literature of love, and it is also one of the most poorly understood!

Why is this so? In the *King James Version*, the word that is translated above as "love" is given in Elizabethan English as "charity." So, it was "Faith, Hope and Charity" for hundreds of years. Generations of Christians engaged in acts of charity, believing this to be what was required of them. And this conceptualization of love as charity became inculcated into our consciousness. Why the translators chose charity, over some other available term, I don't know. But, the root of the word charity is the Indo-European base *karo*, which means, "to like, desire." It later became the Gothic term *hors*, which meant an adulterer.

Anyway, charity was used to express the Greek word *agape*, which actually means "love feast." It was described as "a meal that early Christians ate together." There have been many glosses and later interpretations of this love feast, none of which adequately explain exactly what Paul is talking about here. Clearly he had some idea about something extraordinary that is veiled from us.

So, we can right away get rid of the idea that this essay on love had anything to do with what has been made of it. But still, the standards of love in our society are, essentially, based on this chapter in the New Testament. Take note of this portion in particular: "Even if I dole out all that I have to give food to the poor, and if I surrender my body to be burned, *but have not love*, I gain nothing."

Clearly love is something other than giving to the poor, whether they are poor in fact, or just spirit. There has sure been a lot of giving to the poor and "surrendering of the body to be burned" in the course of Christian history, and most of it done to manipulate and control.

August 28, 1999
Q: For example: there are some people who like to suffer, because they believe that the flesh is sinful. That is a big thing that the Lizzies have instituted. For centuries they have wanted people to suffer, and they have made this big deal about sex and anything that might be considered pleasant or desirable should be denied, and that a person should suffer, and revel in their suffering. And, actually, making a person …
A: If one seeks to suffer, they do so in expectation of future reward. They desire to possess something in the end.

And, of course, in regard to:

Love endures long and is patient and kind; love never is envious nor boils over with jealousy; is not boastful or vainglorious, does not display itself haughtily.

It is not conceited – arrogant and inflated with pride; it is not rude, and does not act unbecomingly. Love does not insist on its own rights or its own way, for it is not self-seeking; it is not touchy or fretful or resentful; it takes no account of the evil done to it – pays no attention to a suffered wrong.

There is sure a lot of behavior modification by those who think that cultivating an external demeanor of humility, patience, kindness, self-sacrifice and so on will get them to heaven. And again we find, "If one seeks to suffer, they do so in expectation of future reward. They desire to possess something in the end."

Unconditional love. This is touted by religions and philosophies of all kinds, and most especially in the present time by New Age purveyors of wisdom. It is supposed to be the panacea, the solution to all our problems – if we can only love unconditionally, all barriers in our lives will fall aside and we will climb unhindered to the mountaintop of cosmic consciousness!

Paul's remarks above indicate that all of the qualities we usually associate with unconditional love, such as giving to the poor, surrendering our bodies to be burned, being humble, selfless and so on are nothing without this love he is talking about. So, clearly, those things that we define as love are *not* love, according to Paul's definition.

We can make the assertion that he considers doing it on the outside without the true feeling inside to be the problem; but I don't think it is that simple or that this was what he meant. And we find the answer in the aforementioned remark:

Love never fails – never fades out or becomes obsolete or comes to an end. As for prophecy, it will be fulfilled and pass away; as for tongues, they will be destroyed and cease; *as for knowledge, it will be superseded by truth.*

Here, Paul has said love never fades out or comes to an end. And then he lists those things that *do* come to an end, and follows this with the remark that *knowledge will be superseded by truth.* In other words, *love and truth are the same thing.*

But isn't knowledge truth? It depends on your definition of the word. Paul says:

For our knowledge is fragmentary and our prophecy is fragmentary. But when the complete and perfect comes, the incomplete and imperfect will vanish away - become antiquated, void and superseded.

Many people interpret this passage to mean that when Jesus comes, the incomplete and imperfect will vanish away. But, in the preceding paragraphs Paul has already told us what is coming: truth. Fragmentary knowledge and fragmentary prophecy will be superseded by truth. So, Paul is talking about completion and perfection of knowledge and prophecy. It should also be noted that the manner in which he uses the term prophecy, indicates a knowledge of the divine will and purpose, so that it is really only another level or type of knowledge. In short, what Paul seems to be describing is the fourth-density state of existence. He says:

For now we are looking in a mirror that gives only a dim reflection of reality as in a riddle or an enigma, but then, when perfection comes, we shall see in reality and face to face! Now I know in part; but then *I shall know and understand fully and clearly, even in the same manner as I have been fully and clearly known and understood by God.*

First he says that our knowledge of our reality is fragmentary – a dim reflection in a mirror, a riddle, an enigma; and that "when perfection comes," that is, truth as he has defined above, then and only then can we see "in reality and face to face!" He further amplifies this by saying, "Now I know in part; but then I shall know and understand fully and clearly … as I have been fully and clearly known and understood by God."

So we can see that what Paul is striving to convey to us is that *love and truth are the same things, intertwined, inseparable.* And this is the definition of knowledge as the Cassiopaeans have explained it: "To love you must know. And to know is to have light [i.e. truth]. And to have light is to love. And to have knowledge is to love." I was a hidden treasure and I loved to be known, so I created man in order that I may be known.

Philosopher P.D. Ouspensky wrote:

There is no side of life which does not reveal to us an infinity of the new and the un-expected if we approach it with the knowledge that it is not exhausted by its visible side, that behind this visible side there lies a whole world of the invisible, a whole world of new and incomprehensible forces and relations. *The knowledge of the existence of the invisible world is the first key to it.* (Ouspensky 1922)

In certain aspects of our lives we come into a more direct contact with this in-visible nature of God than in others. Love and death are two of these.

In Hindu mythology, love and death are the two faces of the One. Shiva, the god of the reproductive forces in nature is also the god of violent death, murder and destruction. His wife is Parvati, the goddess of beauty, love and happiness, while also being Kali, the goddess of evil, misfortune, sickness and death. Togeth-er, Shiva and Parvati/Kali are gods of wisdom, knowledge, good and evil.

"Love and Death move through this world of ours like things apart - underrunning it truly, and everywhere present, yet seeming to belong to some other mode of existence."
—Carpenter, *The Drama of Love and Death*, 1912

There have always been those who claim to know or teach philosophies of death – that we die once and are either saved or damned, that we die and are rein-carnated, or that we die and become nothing. In fact, it could be said that all reli-gions are just ways of teaching about death.

The problem is love. It is usually accepted by us that love is a given; it is already understood and known. The different systems of religion and philosophy are pret-ty much the same in their teachings about love. Yet, the fact remains that love is as great a mystery as death!

As Diane Ackerman says:

There are countless studies on war, hate, crime, prejudice, and so on. Social scientists prefer to study negative behaviors and emotions. Perhaps they don't feel as comfort-able studying love per se. I add that 'per se' because they are studying love – often they're studying what happens when love is deficient, thwarted, warped, or absent. (Ackerman 1994, xxii)

But, is that really the case? P. D. Ouspensky writes:

In reality *love is a cosmic phenomenon,* in which people ... are merely accidental; a cosmic phenomenon as little concerned with either the lives or the souls of men as the sun is concerned in shining so that, by its light, men may go about their trivial affairs and use it for their own ends. If men could understand this, be it only with one part of their consciousness, a new world would open up before them and it would become very strange for them to look at life from all the usual angles. They would understand then that *love is something quite different, and of a different order from the small events of earthly life.*

Perhaps it is a world of special spirits which at times take possession of men, sub-jugating them, making tools of them for the accomplishment of their own incompre-hensible aims. ... Perhaps it is the alchemical work of the Great Master, in which the souls and bodies of men play the part of the elements out of which is evolved the philosopher's stone or the elixir of life, or some special electricity, necessary to someone for some mysterious purpose.

… Men strive to subjugate love to themselves, to force it to serve their aims, both spiritual and material. But love cannot be subjugated to anything and it wreaks merciless vengeance on the puny mortals who strive to subjugate God to serve their own ends.

… Mistaken about the origin of love, men are mistaken about its result. … The propagation of species. But this objective result, which may or may not happen, is in any case only the result of the external, objective side of love, or the material fact of impregnation.

… But if we regard love from this standpoint, we shall have to admit that there is *more of this force than is necessary,* infinitely more! In reality, for the purposes of the propagation of species only a small fraction of one per cent of this force of love inherent in humanity is utilized.

Where then, does the main part of the force go?

Let us take an ordinary candle. It should give light. But *it gives much more heat than light.* Light is the direct function of the candle, heat is the indirect function, but there is more heat than light. *In order to give light, the candle must burn.* Burning is the necessary condition for obtaining light from a candle; burning cannot be done away with. But this same burning produces heat. It seems, at the first glance, that the heat produced by a candle is wasted unproductively and is, at times, even superfluous, unpleasant and hindering: if a room is lit by candles, it becomes too hot. But the fact of the matter is that light is obtained from a candle only owing to its burning – the evolution of heat and the incandescence of the gases evolved.

The same applies to love. We say that only an insignificant part of the energy of love goes to create progeny; the greater part seems to be spent by fathers and mothers on their personal emotions.

In springtime, with the first awakening of the emotions of love, birds begin to sing and to build nests. Naturally, a materialist will say that the singing is to attract the females or the males and so on. But even a materialist will not be able to deny that there is much more of this singing than is necessary for the propagation of the species. For the materialist, the singing is only accidental, only a byproduct. But, in reality, *the singing may be the main function of the given species,* the meaning of its existence, the purpose which nature had in view in creating this species. And this singing is needed not to attract the females, but for some general harmony of nature we only sometimes vaguely feel.

Thus, we see that what appears to be a collateral function of love, from the point of view of the individual, may serve as a principal function of the species.

Love has evoked a thirst for activity. Instinct governs this thirst for activity … *at the first awakening of love – work starts.*

We see the same thing in men. Love is a creative force. And the creative force of love manifests itself not in one but in many varied directions. Perhaps it is precisely by this force of love, Eros, that mankind is incited to fulfill its main function: *all the creative activity of mankind is the outcome of love.*

If creation, *the birth of ideas,* is *the light which comes from love,* then this light comes from *a great flame.* In this everlasting flame, in which all mankind and the whole of the world are burning, all the forces of the human spirit and genius are developed and refined; and perhaps it is precisely from this flame, or with the help of it, that a new force will spring into being which will lead those who follow it away from the shackles of matter.

I have dwelt so long on the question of the understanding of love because it is of the most vital importance; for the majority of people approaching the threshold of the mystery, it is precisely from this side that much becomes opened or closed and because for many precisely this question constitutes the greatest obstacle.

The most important thing in love is that which is not, which is completely nonexistent from an ordinary, everyday, materialistic point of view. In this sensing of that which is not, in the contact thus reached with the world of the miraculous, i.e. the truly real, lies the principal meaning of love in human life.

... All life by all its facts, events and accidents, agitations and attractions always leads us to the *knowledge of something.* The strongest emotion in man is a yearning for the unknown. Even in love, the strongest attraction to which everything else is sacrificed, is the attraction of the unknown, the *new* – curiosity.

... Man realizes his existence and the existence of the world of which he is a part. His relation to himself and to the world is called knowledge. *The broadening and deepening of the relation to oneself and the world is a broadening of knowledge.*

All the mental faculties of man, all the elements of his inner life – sensations, representations, concepts, ideas, judgments, conclusions, feelings, emotions, even creation – all these are the *instruments of knowledge* which we possess.

... Evolutionists will say that the struggle for existence and the selection of the fittest have created the mind and feeling of the modern man – that mind and feeling serve life, protect the species, and apart from this, can have no meaning.

The opposing argument is that, if intelligence exists, then nothing exists except for intelligence. The struggle for existence, and the survival of the fittest, if they in truth play such a role in the creation of life, are also not accidents, but products of an intelligence we do not know. And, like everything else, they serve *knowledge.*

But we do not, as a rule, see the presence of intelligence in the phenomena and laws of nature. This happens because we always study the parts and not the whole. By studying the little finger of a man, we cannot know the intelligence of the man. We always study the little finger of nature. If we realize this and understand that every life is the manifestation of a part of some whole, only then a possibility opens of knowing that whole.

Every separate human life is a moment of the life of the great being which lives in us. *The intelligences of these higher beings do not exist independently of the lower lives.* They are two sides of one and the same thing. Each single human mind, in some other section of the world may produce the illusion of many lives.

Life and mind seem to us different and separate from one another because we do not know how to look, how to see. And this in its turn is due to the fact that it is very hard for us to get out of the framework of our divisions. We see the life of a tree, this tree.

And if we are told that the life of the tree is a manifestation of some mind, we understand it to mean that the life of this tree is a manifestation of the mind of this tree.

This, of course, is an absurdity resulting from our three-dimensional thinking, the Euclidean mind. The life of this tree is a manifestation of the mind of the species or the variety, or perhaps, of the intelligence of the whole vegetable kingdom.

In the same way our individual lives are the manifestations of some great intelligence. Proof of this is found in the fact that our lives have no meaning whatsoever apart from the process of acquiring knowledge. And a thoughtful man ceases to feel painfully the absence of meaning in life only when he realizes this and begins to strive consciously in the direction he was unconsciously following before.

Moreover, *this acquisition of knowledge, which constitutes our function in the world*, is achieved not only by our intellect, but by our whole organism, all our body, all our life and the whole life of the human society, by its organizations, institutions, the whole culture and the whole civilization, by all we know in humankind and even more so by what we do not know. *And we get to know that which we deserve to know.*

If we say about the intellectual side of man that its purpose is the acquisition of knowledge, this will not evoke any doubt. All are agreed that man's intellect, with all its subordinate functions, exists for the purpose of acquiring knowledge, although very often the faculty of knowledge is regarded as subordinate. But as regards the emotions: joy, sorrow, anger, fear, love, hate, pride, compassion, jealousy, as regards the sense of beauty, aesthetic sense and artistic creation, as regards moral sense, as regards all religious emotions, faith, hope, veneration and so on, as regards all human activity, things are not so clear. *As a rule, we do not see that all emotions and all human activity serve knowledge.*

Usually the *emotional* is opposed to the *intellectual*: "heart" is opposed to "reason." Cold reason or intellect is placed on one side, and on the other side: feelings, emotions, artistic sense; then, again quite separately, moral sense, religious feeling, 'spirituality.'

The misunderstanding here lies in the interpretation of the words *intellect* and *emotion*.

Spirituality is not something opposed to "intellectuality" or "emotionality." It is only their higher flight. Reason has no bounds.

... In a man the growth of reason consists in the growth of the intellect and in the accompanying growth of higher emotions: aesthetic, religious, moral – which, as they grow, become more and more intellectualized; moreover, simultaneously with this the intellect becomes impregnated with emotionality and ceases to be "cold." Thus, *"spirituality" is the merging together of the intellect and the higher emotions; the emotions are spiritualized from the intellect.*

... Theoretically all emotions serve knowledge; all emotions arise as a consequence of the cognition of one or another thing. ... Undoubtedly there are relations which can be known only through fear. A man who has never experienced fear will never understand many things in life and in nature.

The sign of the growth of emotions is their liberation from the personal element and their transition to higher planes. The liberation from personal elements enhances the cognitive power of emotions, because the more personal elements there are in an emotion, the more capable it is of leading into delusion. A personal emotion is always biased, always unfair, if only for the reason that it opposes itself to everything else.

Thus the problem of right emotional knowledge is to feel in relation to people and the world from a point of view other than the personal. And the wider the circle for which a given person feels, the deeper the knowledge which his emotions give.

Christ driving the moneychangers out of the temple or expressing his opinion of the Pharisees was not at all meek or mild. And there are cases where meekness and mildness are not a virtue at all. Emotions of love, sympathy, pity are very easily transformed into sentimentality, into weakness. And in this form they naturally serve only absence of knowledge, i.e. matter.

There exists a division of emotions into *pure* and *impure*. We all know this, we all use these words, but we understand very little what this means.

Ordinary morality divides emotions, a priori, into pure and impure according to external traits. All carnal desires are relegated into the category of the impure. However, carnal desires are as pure as everything else in nature.

An impure emotion is exactly the same as a dirty glass, dirty water or an impure sound. An emotion which is not pure contains foreign matter or echoes of other emotions. It is mixed. A pure emotion gives a clear, pure image of the knowledge which it is intended to transmit.

If we discard the usual moral framework, we shall see that the matter is much more simple, that there are no emotions impure in their nature.

There may be pure sensuality, the sensuality of the "Song of Songs," which passes into the sensation of cosmic life and enables one to hear the beating pulse of nature. And there may be impure sensuality, mixed with other emotions, good or bad from the moral point of view, but equally making sensuality turbid. There is sensuality with anger that causes pain; there is sensuality with guilt that seeks pain.

There may be pure sympathy – and there may be sympathy mixed with calculation to receive something for one's sympathy. There may be pure desire to know, a thirst for knowledge for the sake of knowledge, and there may be a pursuit of knowledge led by considerations of profit and gain.

In their external manifestations pure and impure emotions may differ very little. Two men may play chess and be quite alike in their outward behaviour, but one may be driven by ambition, desire of victory, and he will be full of unpleasant feelings towards his opponent – apprehension, envy of a clever move, vexation, jealousy, animosity, or anticipation of his winnings; but another may simply try to solve the complicated mathematical problems before him, without giving a thought to his opponent.

Examples of such a division of outwardly similar emotions may be constantly seen in artistic, literary, scientific, social and even in spiritual and religious activities of men. In all domains, only complete victory over the self-element leads man to a right knowledge of the world and himself. All emotions coloured by the self-element are like concave, convex or distorting glasses which refract the rays incorrectly and so distort the image of the world.

Thus the problem of emotional knowledge consists in a corresponding preparation of the emotions which serve as instruments of knowledge.

"Become as little children … " and "Blessed are the pure in heart … " These words speak about the purification of emotions. It is impossible to know rightly through impure emotions. Therefore, in the interests of a right knowledge of the world and oneself, the work of purification and elevation of emotions should go on in man.

There are emotions through which we gain knowledge, and there are emotions by which we are led astray. (Ouspensky 1922)

All of these things discussed by Ouspensky are the very things we are trying to clarify in our study of the biophysical basis of emotions. Emotions that are programmed are impure, as he terms it. The self element is highly invested in these emotions, and they are for the most part the unconscious controllers of our behavior. What we are trying to do here is establish a basis for the overcoming of the Predator's controlling mind, and the experiential establishment of the higher emotions of the soul. As Ouspensky says above, "Spirituality is not something opposed to 'intellectuality' or 'emotionality.' It is only their higher flight. 'Spirituality' is the merging together of the intellect and the higher emotions; the emotions are spiritualized from the intellect."

Remember: *meeting a jaguar can change one's way of looking at the world.* And once we have met the jaguar, once we have understood that we "will do what we will do," let's remember the words from Ark's journals:

So, let's state the hypothesis. The only reasonable hypothesis that I can state is that one which comes from the unknown system taught by Gurdjieff. This system tells us that the world has a certain purpose. It tells us that not everything works well. It tells us that there are certain bugs in the construction.

It is quite possible that using the meta-language one can prove that any program on that scale must have bugs. So, *the Universe is a program*, a program which has bugs, but which has *the built-in capacity for self-improving.*

There are, therefore, certain units that are brought to existence with this specific purpose: to self-evolve to a degree high enough to be able to find out the methods of debugging.

So what do we do now? We debug the Universe, of course. Starting with our minds.

BIBLIOGRAPHY

Barbour, Julian. *The End of Time: The Next Revolution in Physics.* New York: Oxford University Press, 1999.

Bauval, Robert & Adrian Gilbert. *The Orion Mystery: Unlocking the Secrets of the Pyramids.* New York: Three Rivers Press, 1994.

Bramley, William. *The Gods of Eden.* New York: Avon Books, 1990.

Breault, Marc, and King, Martin. *Inside the Cult: A Member's Chilling, Exclusive Account of Madness and Depravity in David Koresh's Compound.* New York: Signet, 1993.

Campbell, Joseph. *The Hero With a Thousand Faces.* Novaro, CA: New World Library, 2008 [1949].

Castaneda, Carlos. *The Active Side of Infinity.* New York: HarperPerennial, 2000 [1998].

Conlan, Roberta & J. Allan Hobson. *States of Mind: New Discoveries About How Our Brains Make Us Who We Are.* New York: John Wiley & Sons, Inc., 1999.

Daly, Jeffrey & Stephen Salloway. "Dopamine Receptors in the Human Brain." *Psychiatric Times* 11 (1994), 27–32.

De Angelis, Barbara. *Are You the One for Me?: Knowing Who's Right and Avoiding Who's Wrong.* New York: Dell Publishing, 1992.

Eliade, Mircea. *The Myth of the Eternal Return.* Princeton, NJ: Princeton University Press, 2005 [1949/1954].

Gissen, A. S. "Acetyl-L-Carnitine: The King of Carnitines." *VRP's Nutritional News,* March 1995.

Hyman, Steven. "Susceptibility and "Second Hits"," in Conlan & Hobson, *States of Mind, New Discoveries About How Our Brains Make Us Who We Are* (New York: John Wiley & Sons, Inc., 1999), 9–28.

Gell-Mann, Murray. *The Quark and the Jaguar: Adventures in the Simple and the Complex.* New York: Henry Holt and Co., 1994.

Gettings, Fred. *The Secret Zodiac: The Hidden Art in Mediaeval Astrology.* Penguin: 1990.

Godwin, Joscelyn. *Arktos: The Polar Myth in Science, Symbolism, and Nazi Survival.* Adventures Unlimited Press, 1996.

Godwin, Joscelyn, Christian Chanel, and John P. Deveney. *The Hermetic Brotherhood of Luxor: Initiatic and Historical Documents of an Order of Practical Occultism.* York Beach, ME: Samuel Weiser, Inc., 1995.

Hamilton, Edith. *Mythology.* Little, Brown and Co., 1998 [1942].

Hedsel, Mark. *The Zelator: A Modern Initiate Explores the Ancient Mysteries.* York Beach, ME: Samuel Weiser, Inc., 2000 [1998].

Herbert, Nick. *Quantum Reality: Beyond the New Physics.* New York: Anchor Books, 1987 [1985].

James, William. *The Varieties of Religious Experience: A Study in Human Nature.* New York: Penguin, 1985 [1902].

LeDoux, Joseph. "Of Learning, Memory and Genetic Switches," in Conlan & Hobson, *States of Mind, New Discoveries About How Our Brains Make Us Who We Are* (New York: John Wiley & Sons, Inc., 1999), 123–150.

Milton, Richard. *Shattering the Myths of Darwinism.* Park Street Press, 2000 [1997].

Ouspensky, P. D. *In Search of the Miraculous.* Orlando, FL: Harcourt, Inc., 2001 [1949].

BIBLIOGRAPHY

Ouspensky, P. D. *Tertium Organum: The Third Canon of Thought – A Key to the Enigmas of the World.* Vintage, 1970 [1920].

Pearce, Joseph Chilton. *The Crack Cosmic in the Cosmic Egg: Challenging Constructs of Mind and Reality.* New York: Pocket Books, 1976 [1973].

Pert, Candace B. *Molecules of Emotion: The Science Behind Mind-Body Medicine.* New York: Touchstone, 1999 [1997].

Rice, Anne. *The Vampire Lestat.* Ballantine, 1997.

Schroeder, Manfred. *Fractals, Chaos, Power Laws: Minutes from an Infinite Paradise.* Dover, 2009 [1991].

Sharp, Cliff W., *et al. International Journal of Eating Disorders* 15:2 (1994), 125–134.

Shreve, James. *The Neandertal Enigma: Solving the Mystery of Modern Human Origins.* HarperPerennial, 1996.

Strieber, Whitley. *Majestic.* Berkley, 1990.

Valerian, Valdamar. *The Matrix: Understanding Aspects of Covert Interaction with Alien Culture, Technology, and Planetary Power Structures.* Leading Edge Research Group, 1988.

_____. *Matrix II: The Abduction and Manipulation of Human Beings Using Advanced Technology.* Leading Edge Research Group, 1991.

_____. *Matrix III: The Psychosocial, Chemical, Biological, and Electronic Manipulation of Human Consciousness.* Leading Edge Research Group, 1992.

Van Buren, Elizabeth. *Refuge of the Apocalypse: Doorway into Other Dimensions.* C.W. Daniel Company, 1986.

Wheeler, John Archibald & Kenneth Ford. *Geons, Black Holes and Quantum Foam: A Life in Physics.* New York: W. W. Norton & Co., 1998.

Woodman, Marion. *Leaving my Father's House: A Journey to Conscious Femininity.* Boston, MA: Shambhala Publications, 1992.

Yourgrau, Palle. *Gödel Meets Einstein: Time Travel in the Gödel Universe.* Peru, IL: Open Court Publishing, 1999.

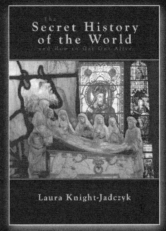